The author is to be congratulated for this important, well-written, and ground-breaking study of three prominent healers in Korean Christianity. The ministries of Ik-du Kim, Seong-bong Lee, and Yong-gi Cho spanned the twentieth century, and each brings a unique perspective. Such a comprehensive study that focuses on the theologies of these representative healers has not been done before in English. Dr Kim uses significant archival material, most of which is in the Korean language, to develop a Korean theology of healing that is accessible to the English-speaking public. This is essential reading for understanding the Korean healing movement.

Dr Allan H Anderson, University of Birmingham

The Korean Healing Movement *investigates three historic healing evangelists in Korea, representing different confessional traditions in various periods. Through this theological comparative study, Jun Kim constructs a Korean healing theology, taking both the socio-political context and the theological tradition of each Christian healer. This fine research will provide a model for other similar inquiries, particularly from the global South.*

Dr Wonsuk Ma, Executive Director of Center for Spirit-Empowered Research, Distinguished Professor of Global Christianity

Jun Kim maintains that the healing movement is a key component of Korean Christianity historically. The influences contextualizing the rise of this movement were not exclusively Christian, but Kim rightly notes its profound relevance for Christian theology. Using Ik-du Kim, Seong-bong Lee, and Yong-gi Cho as key interlocutors, Kim expertly discusses the various issues involved in constructing a holistic theology of healing. This is contextual theology at its absolute best, not only for Pentecostals, but for all those interested in the prominent themes emerging from Christianity outside the West.

Dr Frank D Macchia, Professor of Systematic Theology, Vanguard University

This is a well-researched book, supported by a wide bibliography. It is coherent, readable, interesting, clear, succinct and analytical. This is much more than a historical book, though the biographies of the people concerned are detailed and instructive, because they are set in their socio-political-economic and religio-cultural contexts which provide the opportunity to appreciate the impact they had and what influenced them. The section exploring a Korean healing theology explores key elements, supported by detailed research, which were evaluated judiciously. Not only is this book valuable and fascinating, it also provides a first-class template for similar examinations of key healers in other countries.

Dr Keith Warrington, Academic Dean, The New International University, Director of Word and Spirit, and Reader in Pentecostal Studies, Regents Theological College

REGNUM STUDIES IN MISSION

The Korean Healing Movement

Series Preface

Regnum Studies in Mission are born from the lived experience of Christians and Christian communities in mission, especially but not solely in the fast growing churches among the people of the developing world. These churches have more to tell than stories of growth. They are making significant impacts on their cultures in the cause of Christ They are producing 'cultural products' which express the reality of Christian faith, hope and love in their societies.

Regnum Studies in Mission are the fruit often of rigorous research to the highest international standards and always of authentic Christian engagement in the transformation of people and societies. These are for the world. The formation of Christian theology, missiology and practice in the twenty-first century will depend to a great extent on the active participation of growing churches contributing biblical and culturally appropriate expressions of Christian practice to inform World Christianity.

The Korean Healing Movement

Jun Kim

First published 2024 by Regnum Books International

Regnum is an imprint of the Oxford Centre for Mission Studies
St. Philip and St. James Church
Woodstock Road
Oxford OX2 6HR, UK
www.regnumbooks.net

British Library Cataloguing in Publication Data
A catalogue record for this book is available from the British Library

ISBN: 979-8-8898-3891-3
eBook ISBN: 979-8-8898-3892-0

Cover artwork by Da-eun Kim

Typeset by Words by Design

Distributed by Fortress Press in the US, Canada, India, and Brazil

Acknowledgments

First and foremost, I offer my heartfelt gratitude to God for providing the wisdom and guidance that were essential in completing this journey.

To my loving wife Jane, you are the cornerstone of my life. Your unwavering support has been my strength, making this achievement not just mine, but ours.

To my cheerful daughters, each of you brings a unique light into my life. Your joy is my inspiration, and your love fuels my endeavours.

To my faithful parents, whose unconditional support and prayers have been my foundation. Your belief in me has empowered me to reach new heights.

A special acknowledgment to my mentors, Dr Allan Anderson, Dr Keith Warrington, Dr Myeongsu Park, Dr Wonsuk Ma, and Dr Julie Ma, whose intellectual and relational engagement have enriched this journey immeasurably.

A special thanks to my colleagues at APTS. Your camaraderie and encouragement have been invaluable. And to Geun-Cheol Lee, your unwavering friendship has been a beacon during this project.

I dedicate this book to all of you who have enriched my life in so many incredible ways. Thank you for being part of this significant chapter of my life.

Contents

Contents

List of Abbreviations

AAG	American Assemblies of God
AJPS	Asian Journal of Pentecostal Studies
BHS	Baptism of the Holy Spirit
HSM	Holy Spirit Movement
IMK	Independence Movement of Korea
ITI	International Theological Institute
JYT	Journal of Yongsan Theology
KAG	Korea Assemblies of God
KHM	Korean Healing Movement
KIATS	Korea Institute for Advanced Theological Studies
YFGC	Yoido Full Gospel Church

Introduction

The Pentecostal movement has been a subject of intense scrutiny for over a century, leading to a broad recognition of its multifaceted significance across social, missiological, political, historical, cultural, religious, spiritual, and statistical dimensions. This is evident from various perspectives that have characterised the movement as "a spiritual and political force,"[1] "the reshaping of religion in the twenty-first century,"[2] "cultural revolution,"[3] "a global culture,"[4] "the single-most-significant development in twentieth century Christianity,"[5] "a great renewal movement of the Spirit,"[6] and "one of the most extraordinary religious phenomena in the world of any time."[7] Despite the diverse viewpoints, the missiological value is widely acknowledged, given its recognition as one of the "fastest growing components of Christianity."[8]

While multiple factors may contribute to the remarkable growth of Pentecostalism, divine healing has garnered particular attention. In this regard, divine healing has been the subject of investigation in relation to its potential missional significance, with prevailing views positing the pivotal role of divine healing in fostering church growth.[9] Notably, Donald A. McGavran, a prominent

---

[1] J. Moltmann, and K.J. Kuschel (eds), *Pentecostal Movements: As An Ecumenical Challenge* (New York: Orbis, 1996): vii.

[2] H.G. Cox, *Fire from Heaven: The Rise of Pentecostal Spirituality and The Reshaping of Religion in the Twenty-First Century* (Boston, MA: Da Capo, 1995).

[3] D. Martin, *Pentecostalism: The World Their Parish* (Oxford: Blackwell, 2008): 1-23.

[4] K. Poewe, *Charismatic Christianity as a Global Culture* (Columbia, SC: University of South Carolina Press, 1994): xi-xii.

[5] R.G. Robins, "Pentecostal Movement," in D.G. Reid *et al.* (eds), *Dictionary of Christianity in America* (Downers Grove, IL: InterVarsity Press, 1990): 885.

[6] S.M. Burgess, and G.B. McGee (eds), *Dictionary of Pentecostal and Charismatic Movements* (Grand Rapids, MI: Zondervan, 1988): 1.

[7] A.H. Anderson, "Introduction: World Pentecostalism at a Crossroads," in A.H. Anderson and W.J. Hollenweger (eds), *Pentecostals after a Century: Global Perspectives on a Movement in Transition* (Sheffield: Sheffield Academic Press, 1999): 19.

[8] W.W. Menzies, and R.P, Menzies, *Spirit and Power: Foundations of Pentecostal Experience* (Grand Rapids, MI: Zondervan, 2000): 9; E.L. Hyatt, *2000 Years of Charismatic Christianity: A 21st Century Look at Church History from a Pentecostal/Charismatic Perspective* (Lake Mary, FL: Charisma House, 2002): 3; K. Warrington, *Pentecostal Theology: A Theology of Encounter* (Edinburgh: T & T Clark, 2008): 1.

[9] Some mega-churches are mentioned as concrete examples proving that divine healing has been the main reason for church growth, including "Christ for all Nations" in South Africa, "Evangelical Cathedral of Jotabeche" in Chile, "Carlos Annacondia's Evangelism" in Argentina, "Vineyard Christian Fellowship" in America, and "Yoido

church growth researcher, has sought to establish a connection between church growth and divine healing.[10] Such growth has been observed particularly in Asian regions.[11] The Korean Church is a great example as Myeong-su Park underscores the prevalence of pastors' home visitations prompted by the health concerns of their church members.[12] David Yong-gi Cho also attributes the phenomenal growth of his church, which is one of the world's largest churches, in part to his healing ministry.[13]

Divine healing has not only been a catalyst for church growth, but it has also been regarded as the defining characteristic of Pentecostalism.[14] Dayton goes so far as to argue that divine healing is "more characteristic" of Pentecostalism than even the "doctrine of the baptism of the Spirit."[15] Consequently, the examination of divine healing is a noteworthy avenue towards formulating a theological comprehension of Pentecostal beliefs.

This need for examination becomes even more imperative for advancing Pentecostal studies in Asia, where adherents are striving to establish their theological identities. According to Wonsuk Ma, Asian Pentecostals are experiencing an "identity crisis."[16] This crisis seems attributable, in part, to the uncritical transplantation of Western theology into Asian churches without adequate contextualisation. Notably, while 81% of the Pentecostal population is non-white,[17] most of the major studies on the movement have been produced by Western scholars. Consequently, applying these Western theologies to non-

---

Full Gospel Church" in Korea. See Seong-hoon Myeong, "Sinyuwa Gyohoeseongjang" [Divine Healing and Church Growth], *Ministry and Theology* [Mokhoewa Sinhak] (April 1993): 73-74.

[10] D.A. McGavran, *Understanding Church Growth* (Grand Rapids, MI: William B. Eerdmans, 1990): 133-34.

[11] W.W. Menzies, "Frontiers in Theology: Issues at the Close of the First Pentecostal Century," in Young-hoon Lee (ed), *The 18th Pentecostal World Conference Seoul: Asian Issues on Pentecost*alism (Seoul, Republic of Korea 21 September 1998): 25; V. Synan, "Roots of Yong-gi Cho's Theology of Healing," in Young San Theological Institute (ed), *Dr Younggi Cho's Ministry & Theology* I (Seoul: Hansei University Logos, 2008): 284.

[12] Myeong-su Park, *Hanguk Gyohoe Buheungundong Yeongu* [A Study on the Revival Movement in Korean Church] (Seoul: The Institute of the History of Christianity in Korea, 2003): 65.

[13] Paul Yong-gi Cho, *More Than Numbers* (Waco, TX: Word Books, 1984): 87.

[14] F.D. Macchia, "The Struggle for Global Witness: Shifting Paradigms in Pentecostal Theology," in M.W. Dempster, *et al*. (eds), *Globalization of Pentecostalism: A Religion made to Travel* (Oxford: Regnum, 1999): 23.

[15] D.W. Dayton, *Theological Roots of Pentecostalism* (Grand Rapids, MI: Baker Academic, 1987): 115.

[16] Wonsuk Ma, "Hollenweger's Pentecostalism: An Asian Reflection," in Young-hoon Lee (ed), *The 18th Pentecostal World Conference Seoul: Asian Issues on Pentecostalism* (Seoul, Republic of Korea 21 September 1998): 176.

[17] T.M. Johnson, and K.R. Ross (eds), *Atlas of Global Christianity* (Edinburgh: Edinburgh University Press, 2009): 103.

Western cultures, especially in Asian contexts, poses significant challenges. As a result, Asian Christians are grappling with the divergent demands of their diverse cultures and Western perspectives on theology.

The unique identity crisis experienced by indigenous Pentecostal groups in Asian regions represents a complex issue. Interestingly, approximately 79% of these groups have no traditional Pentecostal or Charismatic denominational affiliations,[18] which highlights the diversity of perspectives present within Asian Pentecostalism today. It is worth observing that divine healing, an attribute typically regarded as "an integral part"[19] of Pentecostal/Charismatic beliefs and practices, existed even before the arrival of the first denominational Pentecostal missionary to Korea in 1928. Because the Korean healing movement can be traced back to the indigenous religious practices and beliefs of the Korean people, rather than being a product of foreign influence, the term Pentecostalism may not be entirely appropriate in defining the entire spectrum of spirit-led movements that include divine healing in Korea. As a result, Young-hoon Lee proposes the use of the term Holy Spirit Movement (HSM henceforth).[20] By employing this terminology, he emphasises the importance of further examination and inquiry into the Spirit-led movements to achieve a deeper comprehension of how the Holy Spirit has guided the Korean Church.

---

[18] D.B. Barrett, G.T. Kurian, and T.M. Johnson (eds), *World Christian Encyclopedia: A Comparative Survey of Churches and Religions in the Modern World,* 2nd ed. (Oxford: Oxford University Press, 2001): 289.

[19] H.G. Cox, *Fire from Heaven,* 222.

[20] The utilisation of the term Holy Spirit Movement in lieu of Pentecostalism is an effort to forestall any potential misinterpretation on the part of the reader, whereby Pentecostals would be understood to denote exclusively those modern Christians who were influenced by the Azusa Street Revival movement, as articulated by the three waves theory. Notably, the overarching tenets of the "three waves" theory, which assert that the expansion of Pentecostalism transpired sequentially via Pentecostal, Charismatic, and "Neocharismatic" phases, have been disavowed by non-Western scholars due to the presence of indigenous Pentecostals whose origins were unaffected by Western Pentecostal groups. These points are corroborated by sources such as S.M. Burgess, and E.M. Maas (eds), *New International Dictionary of Pentecostal and Charismatic Movements* (Grand Rapids, MI: Zondervan, 2002): xvii; A.H. Anderson, *An Introduction to Pentecostalism: Global Charismatic Christianity* (Cambridge: Cambridge University Press, 2004). In light of these considerations, select Korean scholars, including Young-hoon Lee in his work *The Holy Spirit Movement in Korea: Its Historical and Theological Development*, have intentionally opted to adopt the alternative term "Holy Spirit Movement" as a means of distinguishing this movement from the Korean Pentecostal Movement that originated in 1928 with the arrival of Mary Rumsey in Korea. Given that the phrase "Pentecostal/Charismatic" tends to be imbued with denominational connotations, such as classical Pentecostals and Catholics, the term "the Holy Spirit Movement" is utilised to broaden its purview. Consequently, the term "Holy Spirit Movement" is employed herein in a comprehensive sense to denote all Christians who espouse spiritual gifts, supernatural miracles, signs, and wonders, irrespective of their affiliations.

Despite the pressing need for research endeavours, the significance of divine healing within the Korean Church has been conspicuously disregarded and relegated to the periphery until the rise of Pentecostal/Charismatic convictions gained greater prominence. Throughout history, many healing practitioners were unwelcome and even perceived as heterodox. This issue can be attributed, in part, to the fact that divine healing had not been an official position within the dominant Korean Church and was sometimes misappropriated by mystical and superstitious groups.[21] Additionally, the perceived similarities between Christian healing practices and shamanistic healing rituals further complicated matters, leading to confusion between the two. Consequently, exploring the healing movement in Korea necessitates two significant tasks.

The first task involves introducing the development of the Korean healing movement to modern Christians and recognising divine healing as an integral part of the Korean Church tradition. By acknowledging the historical roots of divine healing within Korean religious practices and beliefs, a contextualised understanding can be fostered, challenging the perception of divine healing as a foreign import.

The second task entails establishing a healing theology that has been formulated and developed by validated Korean healing practitioners. Such a theological framework would provide a safeguard for present-day healing practitioners while being sensitive to the cultural aspects of the practice. This endeavour recognises the need for a theological discourse that bridges the gap between the rich healing traditions present in Korea and the contemporary demands of the Korean Church.

In light of the aforementioned focus, the objective of this book is to formulate a conceptual framework for examining the theological development of the healing movement in Korea. This objective is pursued through an investigation of select historical figures who possess a certain level of representativeness within the Korean healing movement. To accomplish this objective, the book undertakes an in-depth examination of three Christian personalities: Ik-du Kim (1874–1950), Seong-bong Lee (1900–1965), and Yong-gi Cho (1936–2008).[22] The initial three chapters individually delve into the biographies, ministries, and healing theologies of these individuals, while the final chapter presents a systematic approach to discuss the theological essence of the Korean healing movement as established by these three figures.

---

[21] The Holy Spirit Movement that emerged in the aftermath of the Korean War in 1950 was erroneously perceived as having affinities with cultic organisations, such as those led by Tae-seon Park and Seon-myeong Moon. This perception ultimately prompted a negative response from the Korean church towards the Holy Spirit Movement, leading to its rejection of practices such as healing. Young-hoon Lee, "Hanguk Osunjeol *Undonggwa* Sinyu" [Korean Pentecostalism and Divine Healing] *Seonggyeol Gyohoewa Sinhak* 11 [The Holiness Church and Theology 11] (Spring 2004): 187.

[22] The selection of these three people is based on their influence upon the Korean Church, their denominational diversity, and their chronological representativeness.

By means of this comprehensive exploration, a profound understanding of divine healing within the Korean context can be fostered, which facilitates a theological comprehension that resonates with the distinctive identity and cultural nuances of Asian Pentecostals. Moreover, this work contributes to the development of a theology of the healing movement in Korea, serving as an experimental endeavour that may prove applicable to similar investigations into Pentecostal/Charismatic beliefs within other Asian regions.

1. Ik-du Kim

Life and Ministry

Before Conversion

Ik-du Kim, born in 1874 to Eung-seon Kim and Ik-seon Jeon, was raised in a well-to-do family in Anak, Hwanghae state. Kim's childhood was marked by ten years of studying *Yuseo*[1] and *Sanbeob*,[2] during which he exhibited traits such as "filial piety," "honesty," "heroism," and "compassion."[3] However, Kim's life took a drastic turn following his father's death when he was only twelve years old. Matters worsened when a friend cheated him of some money, and he failed the *Gwageo*[4] in 1890. These hardships proved too much for Kim to bear, and he eventually fell into alcohol, sensuality, and exhibited increasingly violent behaviours.[5]

Despite his tumultuous lifestyle, Kim expressed an interest in life's issues, questioning why people die and lamenting the short tenure of life on Earth. In his quest to deal with these matters, Kim participated in *Seondo*[6] and *Donghak*.[7] He practised *Byeokgok*, the first stage of *Seondo*,[8] but his need to earn a livelihood for his family prevented him from continuing the practice. Moreover, it was challenging for him to join *Donghak* continuously, as its members were mainly from humble backgrounds, while Kim came from a noble family. Ultimately, after experiencing both religions, Kim concluded that *Seondo* could not help him avoid death, and *Donghak* was a meeting for foolish people.[9]

---

[1] *Yuseo* refers to books that originated in China and were later introduced to Korea. Those books were used in Confucianism. See Seong-ho Lee (ed), *Kim Ik-Du Mogsa Seolgyo Mit Yakjeonjib* [The Sermons and Biography of Ik-du Kim] (Seoul: Hyemunsa, 1977): 130.

[2] *Sanbeob* means mathematics books, including numerical calculation with an abacus. Seong-ho Lee, *Kim Ik-Du Mogsa Seolgyo Mit Yakjeonjib,* 130.

[3] In-seo Kim, *Kim Ik-Du Moksa SoJeon*, 126.

[4] *Gwageo* was the highest-level state examination to recruit ranking officials during the Goryeo and Josen Dynasty. See Seong-ho Lee, *Kim Ik-Du Mogsa Seolgyo Mit Yakjeonjib*, 137.

[5] Yong-gyu Park, *Anak Sangol*, 30-32.

[6] *Seondo* is a religion that seeks to live eternal life without food by gradually reducing the amount of food while just eating pine needles, jujubes, and chestnut. See Seong-ho Lee (ed), *Kim Ik-Du Mogsa Seolgyo Mit Yakjeonjib,* 139.

[7] *Donghak* was established by Choe Jae-woo as the religion of the people. It was a mixture of different religions such as Cheondogyo, Confucianism, Buddhism, and Taoism. See Seong-ho Lee, *Kim Ik-Du Mogsa Seolgyo Mit Yakjeonjib*, 139.

[8] In-seo Kim, *Kim Ik-Du Moksa SoJeon*, 135.

[9] In-seo Kim, *Kim Ik-Du Moksa SoJeon*, 136.

Conversion

In the beginning, Kim held a negative view of Christianity, perceiving it as a Western religion that undermined loyalty to the king and to one's parents. Despite his initial unfavourable impression, at the age of twenty-seven, Kim found himself deeply moved by a Christian message on eternal life, delivered by Presbyterian missionary W.L. Swallen.[10] This encounter occurred during his first visit to the Geumsan Church in Anak, led by Tae-hwan Park in 1900.[11]

The message not only addressed Kim's primary concerns in life but also highlighted his sinful nature[12] – a unique notion that Kim could not find in other religions. After attending the service for the third time, Kim decided to fully commit to the church. Following his conversion, he sought prayer from a missionary and began reading the Bible,[13] even completing the New Testament one hundred times in anticipation of a sacred ceremony.[14] Kim sought purification through prayer, reading the Bible, and abstaining from sexual relations with his wife until his water baptism. A month later, Swallen baptised Kim with water, but the Sacrament was postponed, causing Kim to continue his pursuit of purity for an additional nineteen months (twenty months in total).[15]

Kim's conversion was reaffirmed through a spiritual experience. Although he had been deeply inspired by Christian beliefs, he found himself susceptible to worldly temptations. Three months after his conversion, Kim encountered old friends and indulged in alcohol, becoming so intoxicated that he visited a prostitute. Suddenly, he heard an inner voice exclaiming, "Alas, Ik-du Kim! You need to thoroughly believe in Jesus again."[16] Upon sobering up, he rushed to a mountain and tearfully repented his sins, beating the ground with his hands. After returning from the mountain and falling asleep, Kim dreamt of a large fire descending upon his chest, causing him to wake up screaming. He interpreted this experience as "the baptism of fire."[17] After that incident, Kim developed a strong aversion towards sin and became apprehensive of relapsing. This transformation was so profound that he frequently found himself weeping and murmuring to himself, which caused his mother to worry about him.[18]

---

[10] Swallen graduated from McCormick Theological Seminary and came to Korea as a North American Presbyterian missionary in 1892. He was visiting various regions where his churches were established. The Geumsan Church was also one of the churches overseen by Swallen. See Deok-ju Lee, *Hanguk Tochak Gyohoe Hyeongseongsa Yeongu* [A Study of the Historical Formation of Korean Indigenous Churches] (Seoul: Institute of the History of Christianity in Korea, 2000): 57-58.

[11] In-seo Kim, *Kim Ik-Du Moksa SoJeon*, 143.

[12] Yong-gyu Park, *Anak Sangol*, 43.

[13] Yong-gyu Park, *Anak Sangol*, 47.

[14] The sacred ceremony consisted of two elements: the communion and water-baptism.

[15] Yong-gyu Park, *Anak Sangol*, 56.

[16] In-seo Kim, *Kim Ik-Du Moksa SoJeon*, 150.

[17] In-seo Kim, *Kim Ik-Du Moksa SoJeon*, 151.

[18] Yong-gyu Park, *Anak Sangol*, 52.

Ministry

Ik-du Kim's ministry commenced when he was working as an elementary school teacher and evangelist in Jaeryeong at the age of twenty-nine.[19] Within a year, the church experienced steady growth, boasting about thirty female members, ten male members, and fifty children.[20] Although Kim's first healing event occurred during this period, it was not the primary factor contributing to the ministry's expansion. According to Yong-gyu Park, Kim's humble and passionate demeanour, coupled with his transformed life, fuelled the church's growth.[21] Recognising Kim's successful ministry in Jaeryeong, Swallen officially appointed him as a pastor's assistant and entrusted him with the Sincheon area in 1901.[22]

The new ministry in Sincheon was fraught with challenges. Despite Kim's eagerness to share the Word of God with people in marketplaces, he faced constant persecution in the form of stoning and dousing with water, as Christianity was initially unwelcome in Korean society.[23] After ten months of ministry, Kim reached his breaking point and retreated to a mountain to fast and pray for three believers.[24] This prayer was answered, resulting in a male merchant, a child, and a woman to convert to Christianity. By 1910, these three individuals formed the foundation of a congregation of three hundred believers in less than two years.[25] Kim was ordained and became the first senior pastor of the church in 1911. His ordination took place one year after graduating from Bible school, indicating that his theological education occurred simultaneously with his ministry for about four years from 1906. Despite his hectic schedule, the Sincheon Church, which began in a small house with thirty members, needed a new facility to accommodate three hundred people by 1910. The congregation continued to grow, necessitating additional renovations to accommodate the rapid expansion when the congregation numbered seven hundred.[26] By the time that Kim left the church in 1920, the congregation had grown to approximately eight hundred members.[27]

Kim's specialised ministry in revival meetings officially began after graduating from the Pyongyang Joson Jesus Presbyterian Seminary in 1910, although he had been previously involved in healing on a few occasions before that. The year 1911 marked a significant turning point for Kim's healing ministry, as he began to take his healing practices more seriously than ever

---

[19] Kim served the church as a non-licensed minister since he had not yet started his theological education.
[20] In-seo Kim, *Kim Ik-Du Moksa SoJeon*, 160.
[21] Yong-gyu Park, *Anak Sangol*, 58.
[22] In-seo Kim, *Kim Ik-Du Moksa SoJeon*, 161.
[23] In-seo Kim, *Kim Ik-Du Moksa SoJeon*, 164.
[24] In-seo Kim, *Kim Ik-Du Moksa SoJeon*, 164.
[25] Yong-gyu Park, *Anak Sangol*, 63.
[26] In-seo Kim, *Kim Ik-Du Moksa SoJeon*, 167.
[27] Yong-gyu Park, *Anak Sangol*, 90.

before, becoming assured of the words written in Mark 9:23: "Everything is possible for him who believes." In the same year, he co-pastored outside the South Gate area of Seoul with Jae-hyeong Lee. Kim resigned from his pastoral duties at the Sincheon Church in 1923.

Despite his involvement in healing ministries since 1911, it was in 1920 that Kim began leading numerous revival services nationwide, upon becoming the moderator of the Korean Presbyterian Church before the Church was split in the 1950s.[28] Kim's revival meetings drew large crowds: over three thousand people attended the Sariwon church in August 1920, and in October of the same year, approximately ten thousand people gathered at the Sungdong church for Kim's healing revival meetings.[29] It is unsurprising that an American missionary regarded Kim's revival meeting as the largest evangelistic event of his time.[30]

Park accurately observed that the revival services primarily comprised three components: Bible studies, evangelism, and prayer meetings.[31] This structure was also noted by a Christian newspaper, which reported:

> Ik-du Kim was invited to lead a series of revival meetings at a church in *Shincheon-li* of *Hamheung* province since December 24 last year. He led revival services during the day while Bible study was conducted at night and special prayer meetings were held in the early morning.[32]

This newspaper also noted the fact that about a thousand people stayed awake every night to pray, resulting in a significant revival for the church.[33] Kim's revival meetings were described as emotionally dynamic and spiritually vibrant, often characterised by terms such as "listening courteously," "emotional explosion," "shouting," "tears," and "physical vibration."[34]

Kim was open to modernisation, incorporating it into his ministry. He contributed to the abolition of the topknot,[35] an old custom for men in Korea.[36]

---

[28] Yong-gyu Park, *Anak Sangol*, 90.
[29] See *Gi-Dok-Shin-Bo* [Christian Newspaper], 1920, August 8; Taek-kwon Im, *Joseon Yesugyohoe Ijeogmyeongjeung* [A Testament of Miracles in the Joseon Jesus Church] (Seoul: Christian Literature Society of Korea, 1921): 106-8.
[30] H.A. Rhodes, *History of the Korea Mission Presbyterian Church U.S.A., vol. 1, 1884–1934*, (Seoul: Chosen Mission Presbyterian Church USA, 1934): 151.
[31] Yong-gyu Park, *Anak Sangol*, 100.
[32] "Hamheung Gyohoe Daebuheung" [The Great Revival at Hamheung Church], *Gi-Dok-Shin-Bo* [Christian Newspaper], 1921, January, 19.
[33] "Hamheung Gyohoe Daebuheung" [The Great Revival at Hamheung Church], *Gi-Dok-Shin-Bo* [Christian Newspaper], 1921, January, 19.
[34] Gyeong-bae Min, *Iljehaeui Hanguk Gidokgyo Minjog Sinang Udongsa* [The History of Korean Christian Beliefs under Japanese Colonisation] (Seoul: Christian Literature Society of Korea, 1991): 307.
[35] This refers to *Sangtu* meaning a knot of hair that married men of the Joseon Dynasty wore in Korea.
[36] Adult Korean men did not cut their hair since they believed their parents gave them their entire body, and thus keeping their body as it is was taught in Confucianism as a

He cut the hair of numerous men and encouraged them to lead civilised lives, believing that wearing topknots was a waste of time and energy.[37] Kim removed the curtain that divided church members by gender and introduced chairs for seating, replacing the traditional practice of sitting on the floor.[38] Kim's ministry led to the adoption of new customs in the Hwanghae region.[39] Many women, who had offered their *wolja*[40] in their churches, chose to adopt a new hairstyle called *jjokmeori*.[41]

Kim became the senior pastor of the Seoul Namdeamun Church in 1936 and of Seoul Sungdong Church in 1939. However, his ministry was impacted by the Japanese colonisation. After enduring fifteen days of torture by Japanese police in 1942 for resisting Shinto worship, Kim was forced to resign his ministry and live as an ordinary man in the orchard of Eunryul from 1942 to 1945.[42] Following Japan's withdrawal from Korea, Kim joined the Korean Christian Federation (KCF) in 1946[43] and was appointed as a general superintendent of the KCF in 1949.[44] Ultimately, Ik-du Kim was martyred after the morning service on the 14th October 1950, in Sincheon Seobu Church of the Hwanghae state by the bullets of the retreating North Korean People's Army.

---

primary way of doing their filial duty. See *Sangtu* [topknot], *Encyclopedia of Korean Folk Culture*, [Available at: https://folkency.nfm.go.kr/kr/topic/detail/7061], [Last accessed: 15th October 2023].

[37] Yong-gyu Park, *Anak Sangol*, 86.

[38] Gyeong-bae Min, *Iljehaeui Hanguk Gidokgyo Minjog Sinang Udongsa*, 305.

[39] The Hwanghae region was one of the states in the Middle West of the Korean Peninsula from 1417 to 1954. It was divided into northern and southern parts in 1954, and now belongs to North Korea.

[40] "A braided hair extension worn by women during the Joseon period." See The Society of the History of Christianity in Korea (ed), *Korean Christian Classics Series,* vol. 2. *Joseon Yesugyohoe Ijeok Myeongjeung: A Testament of Miracles in the Joseon Jesus* Church (Seoul: KIATS Press, 2008): 62.

[41] "Hair pulled back into a bun." Previously, this hairstyle was normally adopted only by prostitutes and elderly male servants. See The Society of the History of Christianity in Korea (ed), *Korean Christian Classics Series* 62.

[42] Seong-ho Lee, *Kim Ik-Du Mogsa Seolgyo Mit Yakjeonjib*, 177.

[43] Regarding Kim's joining the KCF, which was established for a political purpose to support the Communist regime, Yong-gyu Park seeks to further explain the background: every church in North Korea was forced to join the KCF during that time. Otherwise, the church would not be able to exist. In this context, Kim chose to continue his ministry for the people in North-Korea waiting for reunification. See Yong-gyu Park, *Anak Sangol*, 213-21.

[44] Yong-gyu Park, *Anak Sangol*, 213-21.

The Formation of the Healing Theology

Socio-Politico-Economic Contexts

Although Kim had already experienced healing in his early ministry, it was the healing of Su-jin Park at the Hyeonpung revival meeting in December 1919 that elevated his healing ministry to national prominence. Kim's healing ministry is typically considered to have officially begun just after the failure of the 1919 Independence Movement of Korea (IMK hereafter). This was a vastly different environment from that of the Pyeonyang revival in 1907. Despite the fact that the Japanese occupation began in 1910, the oppression of Korean Christians intensified because of their role in leading the Declaration of the IMK in 1919, with 17.6% of the participants (3,426 out of 19,525) being Christians.[45] Korean Presbyterian Christians experienced the arrest of 3,804 church members and 336 Christian leaders, along with the destruction of 12 churches and the killing of 47 Christians.[46] The Korean Methodists also reported that 50% of their pastors were arrested, leaving only 10 in total.[47] This period was described as a crisis for the Korean Church,[48] with "a sense of emptiness," "suffering," and "anxiety" pervading the community.[49] The failure of the IMK created an environment where Korean society and churches were getting more interested in religious and spiritual issues than in social and political[50] problems as people began to realise the difficulty of changing the political situation of Korea.

In the midst of this despair, Ik-du Kim's healing events emerged as a popular topic throughout Korea.[51] After studying Kim's healing ministry for two years, Taek-kwon Im argued that its success was linked to God's divine intervention, with Kim's healing being the revelation of God's special comfort and strength for the persecuted and marginalised people struggling with poverty, tribulation, and suffering caused by the failure of the IMK.[52] Seen as "a great light lighting a dark valley,"[53] Kim's healing ministry served not only as miraculous events in themselves but also as reminders of God's love and power for those living in one of the darkest periods of the Korean Church. Kim's healing movement helped people to be healed not only physically but also emotionally, providing hope for

---

[45] The Society of the History of Christianity in Korea, *Hanguk Gidokgyoui Yeoksa* 2 [The History of Korean Christianity 2] (Seoul: Christian Literature Press, 2012): 43.
[46] The Society of the History of Christianity in Korea, *Hanguk Gidokgyoui Yeoksa* 2, 42.
[47] The Society of the History of Christianity in Korea, *Hanguk Gidokgyoui Yeoksa* 2, 43.
[48] Seong-ho Lee (ed), *Kim Ik-Du Moksa Seolgyo Mit Yakjeonjib*, 123.
[49] Doek-ju Lee, *Saerosseun Hanguk Geuriseudoinui Gaejong Iyaki* [Revision of The Conversion Stories of Korean Christians] (Seoul: Institute of the History of Christianity in Korea, 2003): 424.
[50] Young-hoon Lee, "Hangug Osunjeol Undonggwa Sinyu," 185.
[51] Jae-hyeon Kim (ed), *Joseon Yesugyohoe Ijeok Myeongjeung* [A Testament of Miracles in the Joseon Jesus Church] (Seoul: KIATS Press, 2008): 132.
[52] Taek-kwon Im, *Joseon Yesugyohoe Ijeogmyeongjeung*, 3-4.
[53] Taek-kwon Im, *Joseon Yesugyohoe Ijeogmyeongjeung* [A Testament of Miracles in the Joseon Jesus Church], trans. D.J. Torrey (Seoul: KIATS Press. 2008): 58.

those who had lost faith since the loss of their country.[54] While it is uncertain to what extent the specific context of Korea influenced the formation of Kim's healing theology, the belief in healing as God's miracle was instrumental in helping Korean Christians recognise that God was with them in the midst of their sufferings.

Cultural-Religious Contexts

Confucianism, Buddhism, and Shamanism were the dominant religions in Korea until the arrival of Christianity.[55] According to Jones' observations, Koreans were socially Confucians, philosophically Buddhists, and religiously Shamanists.[56] In fact, Shamanism was deeply ingrained in the religiosity of most Koreans.[57] Shamanism had numerous deities, and many Koreans believed that good and evil gods resided in various physical entities such as rocks, trees, the ground, the sky, the sea, etc.[58] It was also commonly understood that diseases and hardships came from evil spirits as punishment,[59] while good fortune was given to devoted worshippers.[60] Consequently, converting Korean Shamanists to Christianity was challenging because of their gods, who were believed to dispense rewards and punishments. Ellen Strong testified to a story in which she helped a church member who was captured by great fear to burn her idols after becoming a Christian.[61] The fear that arose during the conversion process was something that foreign missionaries could not fully comprehend.[62] Demolishing idols was a necessary step in converting to Christianity, and many Korean Christians faced a challenging time battling the evil spirits they had worshipped for a long time.[63] At times, converting Christians had to confront spiritual problems. Jones reported to her mission organisation regarding a demon-possessed woman who was believed to have fallen ill because of her backsliding from her god called *sai-pyol-sang*.[64] Similarly, Gale explained how his church members, who believed that their house was infested with demons, changed after

---

[54] Jang-hyun Ryu, *Hangukui Seonglyeongundonggwa Yengseong*, 95.
[55] G.H. Jones, *The Korea Mission of the Methodist Episcopal Church* (NY: The Board of Foreign Missions of the Methodist Episcopal Church, 1910): 14.
[56] G.H. Jones, *The Korea Mission of the Methodist Episcopal Church*, 14.
[57] C.C. Vinton, "Obstacles to Missionary Success in Korea," *MRW* (December 1894): 841.
[58] R.E. Shearer, *Wildfire: Church Growth in Korea* (Grand Rapids, MI: William B. Eerdmans, 1966): 30.
[59] J.R. Moose, "What Do the Korean Worship?" *The Korea Mission Field* (May 1905): 88-90.
[60] D.L. Gifford, *Joseonui Pungsoggwa Seongyo* [The Tradition of Korea and Mission], trans., Sim H.N. (Seoul: Society of the History of Christianity in Korea, 1995), 74.
[61] D.L. Gifford, *Joseonui Pungsoggwa Seongyo*, 80.
[62] D.L. Gifford, *Joseonui Pungsoggwa Seongyo*, 80-81.
[63] D.L. Gifford, *Joseonui Pungsoggwa Seongyo*, 80.
[64] D.L. Gifford, *Joseonui Pungsoggwa Seongyo*, 78-80.

understanding that Jesus could cast out demons and that the Holy Spirit could protect them from evil spirits.[65]

Healing in the early Korean Churches was strongly associated with spiritual warfare.[66] Myeong-seob Heo argues that healing was generally dealt with by the early Korean Church in terms of spiritual warfare or power encounter, as it was one of the most indigenous features of the Korean Church.[67] Spiritual warfare took place when the gospel of Jesus was proclaimed, bringing people to God.[68] Although missionaries did not teach their believers how to cast out demons, as most of them were ignorant or even sceptical about it, there was a need to heal the sick in terms of casting out demons in the mission field of Korea, especially in its early period.[69] In this context, Kim's healing theology was also developed. Interestingly, Kim's own conversion was a power encounter between God and *Cheon-Ja-Dae-Gam*,[70] and most of his early healing was for those who were demon-possessed or believed to be sick because of evil spirits.[71] While most missionaries were hesitant to believe in spiritual entities in Korea like *Guisin*, which could be translated as an evil spirit in English,[72] Ik-du Kim's perspective on evil spirits could be developed into the concept of spiritual warfare in the

---

[65] J.S. Gale, *Korea In Transition* (New York: Eaton and Mains, 1909), 88-89.
[66] Spiritual warfare refers to "a New Testament theme expressed in images of combat and athletics to indicate the cosmic struggles of those in the Christian life against the powers of evil." See D.K. McKim, "Spiritual warfare," *Westminster Dictionary of Theological Terms* (Grand Rapids, MI: Zondervan, 1996): 268. And "Spiritual warfare is a multilevel conflict between good and evil initiated on the supernatural plane with the prehistoric rebellion of Lucifer and transferred onto the natural plane with the fall of man. Satan, man's adversary, continues to work to deceive and divert people from salvation in Jesus Christ, and to harass and hinder Christians through enticement to sin and exploitation of weaknesses" See T.B. White, *The Believer's Guide to Spiritual Warfare* (Ann Arbor, MI: Servant Publications, 1990): 23.
[67] Myeong-seob Heo, "Chogi Haguk Gyohoeui Sinyu Ihae" [Understanding Healing in the Early Korean Church], *Seonggyeol Gyohoewa Sinhak* 11 [The Holiness Church and Theology 11] (Spring 2004): 163; see also Myeong-su Park, 2003, 67.
[68] Myeong-seob Heo, "Chogi Haguk Gyohoeui Sinyu Ihae," 157.
[69] Myeong-seob Heo, "Chogi Haguk Gyohoeui Sinyu Ihae," 147.
[70] Cheon-Ja-Dae-GamIt is one of the demons that Korean people (including Kim's mother before her conversion) worshipped in their folk religion. For further information, see "Spiritual warfare" in section 2.4.1.5.
[71] See previous section dealing with spiritual warfare under important elements of healing process.
[72] At the beginning of Protestant missions in Korea, most missionaries were not in favour of divine healing and exorcism as they brought the gospel from the West. This resulted in the strict prohibition of spirit worship in terms of iconoclasm. However, their encounters with demon-possessed people in the mission field became an important motivation to gradually accept Christian exorcism. However, it is to be observed that only a few missionaries "adopted the Korean view of spirits and practiced Christian exorcist rituals" while resisting amending their official doctrine on cessationism in Korea. See Sung-deunk Oak, "Healing and Exorcism: Christian Encounters with Shamanism in Early Modern Korea," *Asian Ethnology* 69(1), (2010): 95-128.

Bible. This concept was adopted and applied to the religious context of Korea. Sometimes, exorcism was a way of healing illnesses caused by demons.

Another significant element that influenced the formation of Kim's healing theology was his monotheistic belief in the high god called *Haneul*. Kim ran to the mountains to cry out before this god whenever he had problems, even before he converted to Christianity.[73] It was a religious and traditional practice which centred on a "realistic being who plays a very important role in aspects of human life, like birth, death, marriage and disease."[74] Sung-wook Hong characterises the high god in its monotheistic belief system with three categories: 1) as "the supreme ruler, the creator, and sustainer of the universe," 2) as "the being who so loves humankind that he sends his son," and 3) as "the final judge and decision-maker over all human affairs, including life and death."[75]

Kim's healing theology aligns well with the concept of the high god. According to Ahn-sik Kim's observation on Ik-du Kim's preaching, Kim's belief in God's omniscience and omnipotence is rooted in the Creator who made this world and all humankind.[76] Presbyterian historian Gyeong-bae Min also notes Kim's emphasis on the God who created the world in his preaching.[77] This idea is observed fairly often in Kim's preaching. Kim said that "God is always in control of the birth and death of numerous people [...] Look at His power" and that God created everything and knows even what would happen ten thousand years from now.[78] Kim also believed that God is the sustainer of human life[79] and that "the heart beats seventy times per minute only by the power and grace of God."[80] For Kim, "God had created everything and everything that people have comes from God as a blessing" and "God healed the sick who were almost put to death and delivered people from their sins leading to death."[81] As Kim's perspective holds that everything is under the control of the Creator, including life and death, his healing theology, associated with the God who created the world and controls life and death, was prompted by the belief in the high god. In this regard, it is understandable that the roles of Jesus and the Holy Spirit were not as significant as that of God in Kim's understanding of healing, since his healing theology was strongly influenced by the concept of the supreme high god

---

[73] In-seo Kim, *Kim Ik-Du Moksa SoJeon*, 136.

[74] Sung-wook Hong, *Naming God in Korea: The Case of Protestant Christianity* (Oxford: Regnum, 2009): 55.

[75] Sung-wook Hong, *Naming God in Korea*, 71.

[76] Ahn-sik Kim, "Kim Ik-Du Moksaui Seolgyosayeogeh Daehan Bunseokgwa Pyeongga" [The Analysis and Evaluation of Ik-du Kim's Preaching Ministry] (Seoul: Presbyterian Seminary, Th. M.): 53.

[77] Gyeong-bae Min, *Iljehaeui Hanguk Gidokgyo Minjog Sinang Udongsa*, 311.

[78] Ik-du Kim, *Kim Ik-Du Moksa Seolgyo Mit Yakjeonjib* [Sermons and A Short Biography of Rev. Ik-du Kim], edited by Seong-ho Lee (Seoul: Hyemunsa, 1977): 2.

[79] Ik-du Kim, *Kim Ik-Du Moksa Seolgyo Mit Yakjeonjib*, 3.

[80] Ik-du Kim, *Kim Ik-Du Moksa Seolgyo Mit Yakjeonjib*, 3.

[81] Yong-gyu Park, *Anak Sangol*, 161.

Haneul. He believed that a miracle [as divine healing][82] is "the power of God" manifested in Jesus' name.[83] Kim considered the power of God as the ultimate source of healing.

Christian Context

Kim's healing theology needs to be understood as part of the ongoing spiritual movement stemming from the 1907 revival.[84] According to Kim, the most powerful means of transforming people's hearts is through the Holy Spirit, as he believed that "power is mounted up to the fullest extent when it comes from the almighty Holy Spirit [...] Therefore, believers are transformed by receiving the Holy Spirit."[85] Given that Kim was serving as a pastor at Shincheon Church and receiving theological training at a Presbyterian theological seminary in Pyeongyang, where the 1907 revival had recently taken place, it is plausible that he was influenced by the revival. This suggests that there was a theological connection between Kim's revival and the Pyeongyang revival in terms of pneumatology, with both revivals centring on the works of the Holy Spirit.

When the Pyeongyang revival emphasised the power of the Holy Spirit to transform people's hearts, Kim's understanding of the Holy Spirit also focused more on transformation than on physical healing.[86] In this specific environment, Kim was cautious not to connect his healing theology to the Holy Spirit, as his pneumatology was primarily grounded in the concepts of transformation and love.[87] One possible explanation for Kim's reluctance to delve into the relationship between healing and the Holy Spirit is his negative attitude towards those who viewed the Holy Spirit as a mystical means or power for performing miracles. In one of his sermons on "the Baptism of the Holy Spirit," Kim provided a concrete example of a misunderstanding of the Baptism of the Holy Spirit as a provider of mystical power. Specifically, he criticised a woman who claimed to be able to discern people's past experiences because of her baptism in the Holy Spirit. Kim criticised this woman by arguing that that is what even

---

[82] In the early Korean context, a divine healing was generally understood as a miracle performed by God. See the *Dong-A Daily News* (30th May 1920, No. 58), that recorded Kim's healing events with the title of "The Miracles of Pastor Kim: A Mute Speaks and a Cripple Walks." It is also interesting to notice that the committee, that was established to investigate the healings of Kim Ik-du, was called *Ijeok Myeongjeunghoe* meaning Miracle Witness Committee. Even Kim Ik-du frequently used the term "miracle" to describe any occasion on which the sick were healed through his prayers. In fact, "divine healing" and "miracle" were used interchangeably.

[83] Deok-ju Lee, *Saerosseun Hanguk Geuriseudoinui Gaejong Iyagi*, 426.

[84] Myeong-su Park, *Hanguk Gyohoe Buheungundong Yeongu*, 72.

[85] Ik-du Kim, "Discerning How to Receive the Holy Spirit," in Jae-hyun Kim (ed), *Kim Ik-du: The D.L. Moody of Korea*, trans., Woong G. Kim (Seoul: KIATS Press, 2008): 107.

[86] Myeong-su Park, *Hanguk Gyohoe Buheungundong Yeongu* [A Study on the Revival Movement in Korean Church]: 55-64.

[87] Kim believed that those who were baptised with the Holy Spirit should be transformed and filled with love.

fortune-tellers and shamans could do.[88] In his ministry, Kim endeavoured to remove mystical aspects from his understanding of the works of the Holy Spirit.[89] He warned those who prayed for the baptism of the Holy Spirit in order to acquire the power to heal, cautioning them that they might become insane or demon-possessed in the end.[90] In response to the belief in the mystical power of the Holy Spirit, Kim developed a perspective that focused more on transformation than on healing.

Since the inception of Protestant missions projects in Korea in 1884, missionaries have played a pivotal role in shaping the identity and theology of the early Korean Church.[91] Denominational statistics from 1909 reveal that the Presbyterian and Methodist churches held the most influential positions.[92] Notably, a significant number of Presbyterian missionaries graduated from Princeton Theological Seminary, McCormick Theological Seminary, Park College, and Union Presbyterian Seminary of Richmond.[93] Among these institutions, McCormick Theological Seminary had a considerable impact on the early Korean Church's theological perspectives, owing to the presence of its influential graduates in the mission field. Key figures such as S.A. Moffett and W.M. Baird, who were faculty members at the Presbyterian Theological Seminary, were among the many McCormick Theological Seminary graduates who exerted their influence on the early Korean Church.[94] In this regard, Lee contends that the theological perspectives of most Presbyterian missionaries were rooted in sixteenth-century Calvinism, seventeenth-century Puritanism, and a conservative theological tradition based on the Westminster Confession.[95] It is noteworthy that Ik-du Kim's theological background was also marked by "evangelical," "conservative," and Pietist influences,[96] which further contributed to a limited perspective on divine healing during the early stages of his ministry. Consequently, Kim's focus on pneumatology centred on the process of conversion and sanctification, with little attention paid to divine healing.

---

88 Ik-du Kim, "Seongsin Serye" [the BHS] *Hwalcheon* (July 1934): 18.

89 When Kim was involved in healing ministries, the Korean Church was under the influence of a mystic healing practitioner named Yong-do Lee in the 1930s. Lee's theology was criticised by a famous theologian of the Holiness Church, Myeong-jik Lee. See Myeng-jik Lee, "Seongsinui Yeoksawa Akyeongui Yeoksa" [The Works of the Holy Spirit and the Evil Spirit], *Living Water* (April 1933): 1-4.

90 Ik-du Kim, "Gidoui Jonggyo" [Religion of Prayer], in Seong-Ho Lee (ed), *Kim Ik-du Mogsa Seolgyo Mit Yakjeonjib* [The Sermons and Biography of Ik-Du Kim] (Seoul: Hyemunsa, 1977): 18.

91 Deok-ju Lee, *Hanguk Tochak Gyohoe Hyeongseongsa Yeongu*, 51.

92 Deok-ju Lee, *Hanguk Tochak Gyohoe Hyeongseongsa Yeongu*, 40.

93 Deok-ju Lee, *Hanguk Tochak Gyohoe Hyeongseongsa Yeongu*, 57.

94 Deok-ju Lee, *Hanguk Tochak Gyohoe Hyeongseongsa Yeongu*, 57.

95 See Deok-ju Lee, *Hanguk Tochak Gyohoe Hyeongseongsa Yeongu*, 60-61, and The Society of the History of Christianity in Korea, *Hanguk Gidokgyoui Yeoksa* 2, 285.

96 Gyeong-bae Min, *Hanguk Gidok Gyohoesa* [The History of Korean Christianity] (Seoul: Yense University Press, 1993): 311.

Furthermore, the missionaries' dissemination of a cessationist perspective contributed to a diffused understanding of the spiritual gift of healing in Kim's theology.

Personal Context

Although certain missionaries were associated with Kim, the most significant relationship for Kim was with W.L. Swallen. It was through Swallen's pulpit ministry that Kim underwent his conversion to Christianity and he subsequently embarked on his pastoral activities as Swallen's assistant during the early stages of his ministry. Following his conversion, Kim devoted himself to daily prayer and Bible reading, as instructed by Swallen.[97] A notable point of convergence between Swallen and Kim was their shared belief in the pivotal role of the Holy Spirit within their respective ministerial endeavours. Both individuals held the view that the work of the Holy Spirit was indispensable in the execution of their ministerial duties. Swallen specifically emphasised the critical role of the Holy Spirit in training indigenous ministers and ensuring that the initial ministers ordained into the Korean Church were individuals who had been "filled" by the Holy Spirit.[98]

Of particular importance is the characterisation of Kim's ministry as one that operated under the influence "of the Holy Spirit."[99] The focal point of their pneumatology primarily revolved around the soteriological concepts of regeneration and sanctification.[100] The understanding of "Holy Spirit-filled men" can be derived from Swallen's account of the Pyeongyang revival, wherein he states, "We have not dictated as to the manner of His appearance, but during all this time there has been much united as well as private individual prayer that He [the Holy Spirit] would come to believers in mighty power, transforming their lives and character."[101] It is crucial to note that the Holy Spirit was not perceived as a means for physical healing, but rather as an internal force responsible for the transformation of Christian character and life. Furthermore, it is imperative to acknowledge that this pneumatological emphasis on inner transformation was derived from the missionary tradition and, consequently, limited the systematic development of Kim's perspective on the Holy Spirit in relation to divine healing.

---

97 Yong-gyu Park, *Anak Sangol*, 52.

98 W.L. Swallen, "God's Work of Grace Continued in Pyeong Yang, Korea," *The Korea Mission Field* 3 (1907): 79-80.

99 Myeong-su Park, *Hanguk Gyohoe Buheungundong Yeongu*, 91.

100 However, it is important to recognise the uniqueness of Kim's pneumatology in terms of healing since his pneumatological perspective differentiates Kim from other Presbyterian missionaries and ministers. This is to be discussed in the section on the Baptism of the Holy Spirit.

101 W.L. Swallen, "God's Work of Grace Continued in Pyeong Yang, Korea," 77-78.

Healing Theology

Healing and Suffering

Kim's theology of healing conceptualises divine healing as a miraculous manifestation of God's power, serving as a catalyst for soul-winning and facilitating effective evangelism. This conviction is prominently evident in the early stages of Kim's healing ministry, wherein he perceived divine healing as tangible proof of the Bible's veracity for those who doubted its authenticity. Kim regarded divine healing as the most persuasive means of demonstrating the existence of God, positing that the certainty of God's existence crystallises when individuals witness the fulfilment of their prayers for healing. Consequently, Kim wielded divine healing as a potent instrument to evangelise non-believers.

Furthermore, Kim construed healing as an expression of God's power, enabling individuals to embrace a new life devoted to God. Hence, he frequently entreated, "Lord, please grant these feeble souls and impoverished individuals the opportunity to experience the power of the Lord, that they may surrender their lives and live righteously."[102] Therefore, it comes as no surprise that many recipients of healing through Kim's ministry subsequently resolved to live for God. For instance, a man who had been incapacitated for a decade declared his commitment to living for Jesus, attributing his newfound lease on life to Kim's prayer. Before fellow believers, the man testified, "Today, having been granted a second life, I shall live for Jesus, who bore the Cross."[103] Kim's healing ministry frequently inspired adherents to embrace God's will throughout their lifetimes.[104] From Kim's perspective, healing served not as the ultimate objective of his ministry, but rather as an efficacious means of guiding individuals toward a renewed life devoted to God.

Kim proffered a compelling approach to the subject of suffering, characterised by a stance of submission. According to Kim, "Suffering eludes our control. Consequently, we lament our existence beset by infirmities and mortality […] It clings to us like an ever-present shadow. However, it is only upon entering the kingdom of God that we bid farewell to affliction."[105] Kim maintained that suffering constituted an inevitable facet of human existence, even positing that it was bestowed upon those who had undergone baptism with the Holy Spirit.[106] Given that Kim often delineated the baptism of the Holy Spirit as a transformative experience involving repentance, it can be inferred that he perceived suffering as an integral component of the Christian life.

---

[102] Yong-gyu Park, *Anak Sangol*, 175.
[103] Yong-gyu Park, *Anak Sangol*, 179-80.
[104] Yong-gyu Park, *Anak Sangol*, 175.
[105] Ik-du Kim, "Hoegaehara Cheonguki Gaggaunira," 113.
[106] Ik-du Kim, "Urineun seongryeonui sere bata damyeongeul gamdanghayeoboja" [Let's cope with our mission by receiving the BHS], in Seong-Ho Lee (ed), *Kim Ik-du Mogsa Seolgyo Mit Yakjeonjib* [The Sermons and Biography of Ik-Du Kim] (Seoul: Hyemunsa, 1977): 62-63.

Conversely, Kim contended that suffering could also yield a positive impact by motivating individuals to seek discernment of God's will. When Kim's wife fell gravely ill for an extended period, he acknowledged his misjudgement in trivialising her symptoms and neglecting to ascertain God's will, contrary to his previous practice. Subsequently, their circumstances compelled Kim and his wife to embark upon a five-day period of fasting and prayer atop a mountain, which purportedly resulted in her gradual recovery.[107] Kim maintained that suffering provided believers with an opportunity to pursue comprehension of God's will, even while actively seeking divine healing.

Faith

According to Taek-kwon Im's two-year investigation into Kim's healing practices, the faith of Kim was deemed indispensable to his healing ministry. Im's book provides a concise overview of Kim's work and emphasises the significance of faith, asserting that miracles occurred throughout Korea, from Sincheon to the Yellow Sea, solely through faith.[108] Eun-seok Yun also concurs that faith played a crucial role in Kim's healing ministry,[109] referring to it as the "theology of faith."[110] Yun believes that human faith was always a prerequisite for Kim's healing performances, suggesting that faith was not optional but rather an imperative in Kim's healing theology.[111] Im's and Yun's observations appear reasonable as they align with Kim's emphasis on faith. In his preaching on the "religion of prayer," Kim himself asserted that prayers without faith were a primary cause of unanswered prayers.[112] To illustrate this belief, Kim recounted the story of a dying child who experienced healing shortly after receiving Kim's prayer of faith.[113] Kim's conviction in the necessity of faith for healing was exegetically based on his interpretation of Mark 11:23 and James 1:5-8, which he used to argue that God would unquestionably answer prayers offered in faith.[114]

However, Ik-du Kim initially did not possess the belief that healing could be manifested by individuals during his time. Instead, he held a cessationist view, which maintained that healing was only possible through apostles and prophets in the Bible.[115] Nevertheless, his perspective on healing started to shift after encountering significant events. In December 1908, Kim and Myeong-min Choe

---

[107] Yong-gyu Park, *Anak Sangol*, 75-77.

[108] Taek-kwon Im, *Joseon YesuGyohoe Ijeogmyeongjeung*, 1-5.

[109] Kim also emphasised the faith of the sick. More information is to be provided later in this section.

[110] Eun-seok Yun, "Kim Ik-Du Mogsaui Sinyu Buheung Undong Yeongu" [An Investigation on the Healing Movement of Ik-du Kim] (Seoul Theological Seminary, M.Th. Thesis, 2012): 98.

[111] Eun-seok Yun, "Kim Ik-Du Mogsaui Sinyu Buheung Undong Yeongu," 98.

[112] Ik-du Kim, "Gidoui Jonggyo," 16.

[113] Ik-du Kim, "Gidoui Jonggyo," 17.

[114] Ik-du Kim, "Gidoui Jonggyo," 16.

[115] Taek-kwon Im, *Joseon YesuGyohoe Ijeogmyeongjeung*, 1921, 1.

were requested to pray for Gwan-seon Park, a Christian woman who had endured severe pain for thirteen years due to boils. The pain had caused considerable weight loss, leaving only tendons and bones in her legs. Kim prayed for three days, relying on James 5:15, which states that "the prayer offered in faith will make the sick person well."[116] Eventually, God answered Kim's prayer, and Park experienced healing.[117] This event served as an early healing experience in Kim's ministry and was recorded as an example of a prayer of faith.[118] Park, who was healed of her disease, praised the mighty power of God and believed that anything was possible with it, affirming that "Whoever prays for healing with Ik-du Kim believes the mighty power of God."[119] However, at this point, there was no further discussion regarding the nature of the faith required in prayers for healing. Perhaps it was merely a simple belief in divine healing itself, as an undeveloped theology. Kim began to perceive the possibility of healing through the power of God.

Ik-du Kim encountered another significant moment that prompted him to contemplate healing through the prayer of faith. In October 1919, Kim engaged in a series of Bible studies with Pastor Seok-jong Jeong who had healing experiences. During their discussions on Mark 16:17-18, which states that "these signs will accompany those who believe," Kim realised that he had not earnestly prayed for divine healing. He comprehended that if God's power to heal great diseases was evident in believers in the Bible, there was no reason for God to withhold the same power to heal the sick in Kim's time.[120] This realisation formed the foundation of Kim's theology of faith for healing. He began to pray more fervently for the faith to heal and became firmly convinced that the mighty power of God remains unchanged, and healing miracles can still be manifested today.[121]

Kim's belief that the omnipotent God continues to heal the sick gradually evolved into one of the most crucial elements of his healing ministry. A month later, upon his return to Sincheon, one of Kim's church members, Gyeong-sun Ha, was afflicted with a severe disease that was causing her great pain. Kim prayed for her, laying his hands upon her, and she was healed. This healing event further solidified Kim's faith in divine healing.[122] He firmly believed that healing was not limited only to the early church but was still accessible to Christians in the present day. Kim's perspective on healing was straightforward: he believed that it could occur just as it did in the Bible.

---

[116] "Pyeongyang Gwandong," 218.

[117] "Pyeongyang Gwandong" [Gwandong province in Pyeongyang], *Yesugyo Sinbo* [Christian Messenger], 15th December 1908, 218.

[118] "Pyeongyang Gwandong," 218.

[119] "Pyeongyang Gwandong," 218.

[120] Taek-kwon Im, *Joseon YesuGyohoe Ijeogmyeongjeung*, 1921, 2-3.

[121] Taek-kwon Im, *Joseon YesuGyohoe Ijeogmyeongjeung*, 1921, 3.

[122] Myeong-su Park, *Hanguk Gyohoe Buheungundong Yeongu*, 73.

While Ik-du Kim's faith played a significant role in his healing practices, he also emphasised the faith of the sick individuals seeking healing. Healing through faith was not a unidirectional process but rather a mutually interactive one between the practitioner and the sick person.[123] According to Park's account, Kim's healing ministry was not solely his own but also that of the sick individuals, as Kim always encouraged them to pray for healing with strong faith.[124] Kim never claimed that everyone who received prayer would be healed,[125] but he urged them to exercise their faith by assuring them that "God would cure your diseases according to your faith."[126] This perspective is exemplified when Kim prayed for Je-seong Jo, a boy born with a swollen kidney, and expressed that "everything is possible with faith but nothing would happen without believing in God."[127] The same idea was observed when Young-su Kim requested Ik-du Kim's prayer for his son, whose hands and legs were shrunken and bent. Kim stated that the extent of healing would be determined by "how much you believed in God."[128] Thus, in Kim's healing theology, the faith of the sick individual was deemed as crucial as that of the healing practitioner.

Taek-kwon Im presented some of Ik-du Kim's healing sessions to support the notion that the faith of the sick played a significant role in experiencing divine healing through Kim's practices. Taek-seon Gang, a fifty-one-year-old woman, had been suffering from uterine cancer and haemorrhage for three years. After several prayers offered by Kim, the woman became filled with faith and declared, "Now I will be healed," and her faith was promptly followed by healing.[129] Although this woman had received Kim's prayers multiple times before, no change occurred until she held the words of assurance firmly in her mind. Similarly, In-hwa O, a fifty-five-year-old woman who had endured back pain for five years, had her back straightened immediately when Kim prayed for her. She firmly believed that if she received prayer once, she would be healed instantly, and her faith was rewarded. It is noteworthy that while most of Kim's healing cases required several prayer sessions over time, these women experienced instantaneous healings.[130] This further reinforces the belief that faith played a crucial role in Kim's healing theology and that the faith of the sick person was an essential component in the healing process.

On the basis of Taek-kwon Im's observations of Kim's healing ministry, it can be concluded that only those who possessed a sincere desire and unwavering faith, truly believing in their own healing, were the ones who received healing

---

[123] Myeong-su Park, *Hanguk Gyohoe Buheungundong Yeongu*, 81.
[124] Myeong-su Park, *Hanguk Gyohoe Buheungundong Yeongu*, 83.
[125] H.A. Rhodes, "Some Results of the Kim Ik Tu Revival Meeting in Seoul," 114.
[126] Yong-gyu Park, *Anak Sangol*, 84.
[127] Yong-gyu Park, *Anak Sangol*, 167.
[128] Yong-gyu Park, *Anak Sangol*, 172.
[129] Taek-kwon Im, *Joseon YesuGyohoe Ijeogmyeongjeung*, 1921, 34.
[130] Taek-kwon Im, *Joseon YesuGyohoe Ijeogmyeongjeung*, 1921, 29-30.

among the hundreds and even thousands of sick people.[131] In Kim's healing theology, the principle of Mark 11:23[132] was adopted to argue that an unbelieving heart leads to unanswered prayers.[133] It was believed that "Power [healing] is not manifested in a place of unbelief."[134] An example supporting this concept was the lack of healing at the revival meeting held at Nammunoe Church in Jeonju, where differing opinions and scepticism among the committee members hindered the manifestation of God's power.[135] In Kim's healing theology, the lack of healing was not attributed to God's inability but rather understood as a result of unbelief obstructing the healing process. The idea was that God did not heal because of an individual's rejection, as faith in healing was considered indispensable for the manifestation of divine healing power.

Prayer

Many perceive prayer as a pivotal factor in Kim's successful healing ministry. Taek-kwon Im attributed the healing of the sick to "prayer" and the "laying on of hands" by Kim.[136] An American missionary corroborated the notion that Kim's fervent prayer facilitated the miracles within his healing ministry.[137] Gyeong-bae Min described Kim's revival as a prayer-centred healing movement,[138] where Kim's ministry served as a manifestation of God's power through his prayer.[139] Similarly, Yong-gyu Lee regarded Ik-du Kim as a prayerful man, asserting that Kim healed numerous sick individuals after preparing himself through a life of prayer.[140] These arguments find support in Kim's own admission that "earnest prayer,"[141] characterised by a unified and pure-hearted approach, would lead to God's answers and the healing of many, as he preached in Luke 11:5-13.[142]

However, Cheol-woong Kim's claim that Ik-du Kim's prayer entails borrowing power from God to heal[143] seems to misinterpret Kim's perspective.

---

131 Taek-kwon Im, *Joseon YesuGyohoe Ijeogmyeongjeung*, 1921, 119.

132 NIV says "I tell you the truth, if anyone says to this mountain, 'Go, throw yourself into the sea,' and does not doubt in his heart but believes that what he says will happen, it will be done for him."

133 Ik-du Kim, "*Gidoui Jonggyo*", 16.

134 Taek-kwon Im, *Joseon YesuGyohoe Ijeogmyeongjeung*, 2008, 84.

135 Taek-kwon Im, *Joseon YesuGyohoe Ijeogmyeongjeung*, 2008, 84.

136 Taek-kwon Im, *Joseon YesuGyohoe Ijeogmyeongjeung*, 1921, 147.

137 J.S. Gale, "The Revival in Seoul", *Korea Mission Field* 1 (January 1921): 4-5.

138 Gyeong-bae Min, *Hanguk GidokGyohoesa*, 297.

139 Gyeong-bae Min, *Hanguk GidokGyohoesa*, 302.

140 Yong-gyu Lee, *Hanguk Gyohoewa Shinyu Undong*, 64.

141 J.S. Gale, "The Revival in Seoul," *Korea Mission Field* 1, (January 1921): 4-5.

142 Ik-du Kim, *Gidoui Jonggyo*, 9.

143 Cheol-woong Kim, "Kim Ik-du moksae daehan yeongu: saenge, sinyu buheungundong, sinhakeul jongsimeuro" [A Study of Rev. Ik-du Kim: with special reference to his life, healing movement, and theology] (ThM diss., the Presbyterian University and Theological Seminary, 2001), 112.

While acknowledging the crucial role of prayer in Kim's healing theology, this assertion erroneously suggests that prayer itself empowers individuals to wield God's healing abilities. According to Ik-du Kim, prayer served as a means of dependence on the divine Healer, rather than a method of acquiring or borrowing healing power. It is important to recognise that, in Kim's understanding, the necessity of prayer for healing was interconnected with other significant aspects such as faith and spiritual reliance on God, rather than being entrusted with the authority to heal. Kim contended that "those who believe [in God's power] will certainly pray, while others will not due to their unbelief."[144] In Kim's healing theology, faith acted as the catalyst for prayer, whereby prayer became an expression of faith in action. Kim did not argue that God's healing power could be imparted through prayer; instead, he affirmed that prayer served as a means of relying on God, deepening the relationship with Him,[145] and maintaining one's faith.[146] These perspectives illustrate that, in Kim's theology, prayer was not the sole agent responsible for healing, but rather a means by which individuals surrendered themselves to God and acknowledged their dependence on Him as the ultimate Healer.

The term "earnest prayer," frequently used to describe Kim's prayer for healing, stands out as a defining characteristic of Ik-du Kim's healing theology.[147] Kim regarded prayer as arduous, akin to Jesus' prayer in Gethsemane. He believed that prayer for healing was not a simple task but required special efforts. Particularly when individuals approached God with specific requests for healing, they sometimes needed to engage in fervent prayer, abstaining from food and sleep until their prayers were answered.[148] Hence, scholars often associated Kim's healing ministry with fasting prayer.[149] Kim himself preached that it was through his fasting and prayer that an eleven-year-old girl experienced healing from her illness.[150] Similarly, in the case of Su-jin Park's healing from a dropped lower jaw, healing occurred after Kim engaged in fasting and prayer.[151] Notably, in this instance, Ik-du Kim decided to fast after observing that Su-jin Park had not been healed despite his prayers offered over a two-day period. As evident in Kim's healing theology, unanswered prayers for healing led to increased intensity in earnest prayers, which included practices such as fasting.

---

[144] Ik-du Kim, *Gidoui Jonggyo*, 10.
[145] Ik-du Kim, *Gidoui Jonggyo*, 10.
[146] Ik-du Kim, "Cheotsarangeul Ilchimalja" [Do not Lose Your First Faith], 1939, Jae-Hyun Kim (ed), *Kim Ik-Du: The D.L. Moody of Korea*, trans. Woong G. Kim (Seoul: KIATS Press, 2008): 218.
[147] Ik-du Kim, "Chiljungui Jobeunmun," 108.
[148] Ik-du Kim, "Gidoui Jonggyo," 15.
[149] Young-hoon Lee, "Hanguk Osunjeol Undonggwa Sinyu," 186.
[150] Ik-du Kim, "Gidoui Jonggyo," 18.
[151] Taek-kwon Im, *Joseon YesuGyohoe Ijeogmyeongjeung*, 1921, 4-5.

Kim conducted many successful healing services especially while fasting. The revival meeting at Seungdong Church in December 1920 held remarkable significance in the history of the Korean Church due to the high number of attendees and spiritual experiences. American, British, and Canadian individuals present at the meeting reported that it resembled the second Pentecost descending upon Korea.[152] Many foreign missionaries and church leaders from various countries were deeply influenced by Kim's services. Notably, during this revival meeting, the renowned Korean Presbyterian theologian Jae-jun Kim[153] was greatly impacted by Ik-du Kim. Interestingly, Kim led the revival services while observing a ten-day fast. In this regard, Gyeong-bae Min argues that the power of healing emanated solely from Kim's earnest prayer.[154] Particular attention should be paid to the fact that he went to Sungdeok School and prayed there for five hours when he had free time between the revival services. Recalling this moment, Kim also emphasised the significance of fervent prayer.[155] Furthermore, a secular newspaper reported that Kim sacrificed sleep and nourishment to preach and pray during a revival meeting at Jangdaehyeon Church in Pyeonyang.[156] Such instances highlight the association of fasting with Kim's earnest prayer, emphasising the urgency he attributed to his prayer requests.

Kim's earnest prayer found expression in another form known as mountain prayer, which was closely associated with his healing ministries. Kim would regularly retreat to a mountain to engage in prayer, preparing himself for the revival meetings he would lead.[157] Observing this pattern, Myeong-su Park asserts that Ik-du Kim would immerse himself in prayer to prepare for revival meetings where numerous individuals experienced healing.[158] Additionally, when Kim's wife fell ill with a throat abscess, both Kim and his wife embarked on a five-day mountain prayer retreat, praying day and night while fasting. Gradually, her condition improved as a result of their prayer on the mountain.[159]

The value of mountain prayer for healing was acknowledged by those who attended Kim's revival meetings. Kim encouraged the sick to continue praying for healing even after the services had concluded. Numerous testimonies exist of sick individuals experiencing divine healing as a result of their earnest prayers,

---

152 Yong-gyu Park, *Anak Sangol*, 98.

153 Jae-jun Kim contributed to the establishment of Joseon Theological Seminary, which later became Hanshin University.

154 Gyeong-bae Min, *Iljehaui Hanguk Gidokgyo Minjog Sinang Udongsa*, 308.

155 Ik-du Kim, "Gidoui Jonggyo," 15.

156 "Janyeogyoyugeul Wuihayeo Osibgaeui Geumjihwan" [Fifty Pieces of Gold for Children's Education], *Dong-A-Il-Bo*, 3rd July 1920.

157 Yong-gyu Park, *Anak Sangol*, 95.

158 Myeong-su Park, *Hanguk Gyohoe Buheungundong Yeongu*, 80.

159 Yong-gyu Park, *Anak Sangol*, 75-77.

even after the official services had ended.[160] Following the Yeonbaek revival meetings, many people continued praying on Namsan Mountain, and numerous individuals were healed of various ailments during that time.[161] Kim's life and healing ministries reveal a consistent pattern of combining prayer with fasting and engaging in mountain prayer when a heightened intensity of prayer was required. This further exemplifies the centrality of Kim's earnest prayer, embodied in fasting and mountain prayers, to his healing theology.

Repentance

Since the inception of Protestant missions in Korea, repentance has assumed a prominent position as a distinctive characteristic within Korean churches. Missionary Jones bestowed significant attention upon the receptive disposition towards the "sense of guilt and repentance,"[162] designating it as one of the ten foundational theological pillars of the early Korean Church.[163] Kim's perspective on healing aligns with this established tradition of the Korean Church, whereby repentance constitutes a pivotal component of his healing theology. Park asserts that Kim's healing theology should be comprehended as an integral facet of an Evangelical theology of healing, emphasising the interrelationship between healing and repentance.[164] From Kim's standpoint, the supplication of the afflicted for healing is also contingent upon the acknowledgment of their transgressions and appropriate repentance. Preceding Kim's prayers for the sick, a simple inquiry was posed: "Do you believe in God and do you acknowledge your sins?"[165] This confessional process is recognised as a characteristic hallmark of Ik-du Kim's healing practice.

Another significant aspect of repentance for healing stems from the belief that one's plea for healing remains ineffective unless accompanied by the confession of sins. Kim substantiated this belief by referring to Isaiah 1:15 and 59:1-2, which respectively state, "even when you offer many prayers, I am not listening. Your hands are full of blood," and "your sins have hidden his face from you, so that he will not hear."[166] Within Kim's framework, repentance assumes a crucial

---

[160] Sin-geun Kim's palsy was cured (Taek-kwon Im, *Joseon Yesu Gyohoe Ijeogmyeongjeung*, 61); Yeon-ah Kim, who was not able to move her body at will, became well (Yong-gyu Park, *Anak Sangol*, 143-44); Ryeol-gak Kim was healed of serious headaches that had caused her limbs to become weak (Taek-kwon Im, *Joseon Yesu Gyohoe Ijeogmyeongjeung*, 32); Jeon-hwan An who lost his hearing received healing (Yong-gyu Park, *Anak Sangol*, 149); Nap-gyeol Gang's protrusion of her uterus disappeared (Taek-kwon Im, *Joseon Yesu Gyohoe Ijeogmyeongjeung*, 154); Jun-seung Cha who had contracted beriberi became whole (Taek-kwon Im, *Joseon Yesu Gyohoe Ijeogmyeongjeung*, 152-53).

[161] Taek-kwon Im, *Joseon Yesu Gyohoe Ijeogmyeongjeung*, 1921, 93.

[162] This was later associated with the notion of sin as one of the leading causes of sickness.

[163] G.H. Jones, "The Growth of the Church in the Mission Field," 416-21.

[164] Myeong-su Park, *Hanguk Gyohoe Buheungundong Yeongu*, 81.

[165] Yong-gyu Park, *Anak Sangol*, 173.

[166] Ik-du Kim, "Gidoui Jonggyo" [Religion of Prayer], 17.

role in facilitating the efficacy of prayers for healing. Consequently, it is unsurprising that Kim's revival gatherings were consistently permeated by the sounds of "penitent weeping,"[167] "earnest prayer," and individuals "beating their chests and weeping in repentance."[168]

Although Kim did not contend that illness invariably arises from sin, his healing theology encapsulated the belief that sickness often emanates from transgressions. A courtesan named Gyeong-ae Kim, who had endured a life-threatening condition caused by her inability to urinate for forty days, sought Ik-du Kim's intercession. In response, Ik-du Kim informed her that her sickness had arisen because of her sinful lifestyle, thus emphasising the necessity of repentance and faith in God as prerequisites for him to pray for her bodily healing.[169] Kim acknowledged that sin could engender illness, as evidenced by his admonition to the sick based on the message of John 5:10-16, "See, you are well again. Stop sinning or something worse may happen to you."[170]

To substantiate Kim's healing theology on repentance further, it is imperative to scrutinise Kim's definition of sin. Kim posited that "sin entails not only a failure to observe the Ten Commandments but also the absence of devoted loyalty or service to the Master our Lord."[171] Consequently, the cessation of prayer was regarded as a literal transgression within Kim's perspective.[172] Kim maintained exacting standards regarding a Christian's conduct in relation to sin. In regard to the fourth commandment, which Kim considered the most frequently violated, his concept of observing the Lord's Day extended beyond mere attendance at church services on Sundays. His perspective on sin manifests legalistic tendencies, delineating that Christians should refrain from work or from engaging in commercial transactions subsequent to Sunday services.[173] Moreover, the entire household ought to abstain from work and refrain from participating in family events such as birthdays, funerals, and weddings. Even the commemoration of Jesus' birth should not take place on Sundays.[174]

Kim's healing ministry witnessed instances of illness relapse associated with sins. For instance, Taek-sin Jeon, a thirty-three-year-old woman, experienced healing from her paraplegic condition but later suffered a recurrence. Kim attributed this relapse to her gradual spiritual decline and her failure to heed the admonitions of her pastor, who had reprimanded her for not attending church for

---

[167] Taek-kwon Im, *Joseon YesuGyohoe Ijeogmyeongjeung*, 46.
[168] Taek-kwon Im, *Joseon YesuGyohoe Ijeogmyeongjeung*, 70.
[169] Yong-gyu Park, *Anak Sangol*, 132.
[170] Myeong-su Park, *Hanguk Gyohoe Buheungundong Yeongu*, 84.
[171] Ik-du Kim, "The Servant of Christ," in Jae-hyun Kim (ed), *Kim Ik-du: The D.L. Moddy of Korea*, trans., Woong G. Kim (Seoul: KIATS Press, 2008): 122.
[172] Ik-du Kim, "Gidoui Jonggyo," 19.
[173] Ik-du Kim, "Juileul Georukhui Jikija" [Keep the Lord's Day Holy], in Seong-Ho Lee (ed), *Kim Ik-du Mogsa Seolgyo Mit Yakjeonjib* [The Sermons and Biography of Ik-Du Kim] (Seoul: Hyemunsa, 1977): 99-105.
[174] Ik-du Kim, "Juileul Georukgui Jikija," 103.

three consecutive weeks.[175] Similarly, another woman had witnessed her daughter's legs being healed during Kim's revival meeting, only to see a relapse occur. This prompted the mother to repent for her and her husband's negligence in not attending church for three weeks, as well as her husband's descent into heavy drinking and apostasy despite the previous miraculous healing of their daughter.[176] Additionally, a nineteen-year-old woman, who had experienced healing from paralysis affecting half her body, faced obstacles in attending church due to her parents' forceful obstruction. Several months later, this woman fell ill once again.[177] According to Kim's healing theology, repentance assumes a pivotal role as a conduit for divine healing, particularly for those who have not found their prayers for healing answered because of their sins and for those whose illnesses have been caused by their transgressions. Ik-du Kim's specific role in his healing ministry involved assisting the sick in recognising and repenting of their sins, thereby facilitating the effective fulfilment of their prayers for healing and the subsequent restoration of health in cases where illnesses had been induced by sin.

Physical Touch

Kim's early healing ministry was characterised by prayer with the laying on of hands. The official record for Kim's first use of this prayer was during the healing of Gyeong-sun Ha in November 1919.[178] However, prior to this occasion, Kim used different types of prayer. For instance, in Kim's first [or second][179] healing session, as described by In-seo Kim, he prayed for a ten-year-old girl, Su-eun Park, while holding her in his hands.[180] Kim also prayed for a crippled beggar, holding his hands, although the cripple was not healed.[181] Obviously, it was one of Kim's early healing practices because it happened when Kim first worked in Sincheon as a pastor's assistant. Even in 1908, Kim did not use the laying on of hands.[182] It was only after his ordination in 1911 that he began to use this practice, which is normally reserved as a special privilege for ordained ministers in the Korean Church.

During the early period of Kim's healing ministry, the laying on of hands was a necessary ceremony in the prayers for the sick. Whenever the sick sought

---

175 Taek-kwon Im, *Joseon YesuGyohoe Ijeogmyeongjeung*, 31.
176 Taek-kwon Im, *Joseon YesuGyohoe Ijeogmyeongjeung*, 137.
177 Taek-kwon Im, *Joseon YesuGyohoe Ijeogmyeongjeung*, 114.
178 Taek-kwon Im, *Joseon YesuGyohoe Ijeogmyeongjeung*, 2-3.
179 There are two healing occurrences witnessed as the first miracle of Kim by two different primary sources which were respectively written by Taek-kown Im and In-seo Kim. It is not clear which one happened first. Even then, there is a possibility that the two events refer to the same healing occasion.
180 In-seo Kim, *Kim Ik-Du Moksa SoJeon*, 165.
181 Yong-gyu Park, *Anak Sangol*, 74.
182 See Yesugyosinbo, 1908, December 15. It was recorded that Kim prayed earnestly with Choe Myeongmin who was another pastor's assistance. This record does not witness Kim's prayer with the laying on of hands.

Kim's prayers, he would pray for them with the laying on of hands.[183] As a result, Kim had to set aside special sessions every day for his healing ministry, spending two to three hours praying for about four to five hundred sick people with the laying on of hands.[184] Although physical touch was significant in the early period of Kim's ministry, its significance was not explained or hinted at by Kim.[185] It is worth noting that physical touch was not as significant in the later period of Kim's healing ministry as it was in the early period. As Kim's revival meetings grew in popularity, numerous sick people came to him for prayers, and he had to use even his free time to pray for the sick individually, causing him to adjust his healing practices.[186] Thus, Kim's healing practices were changed to accommodate the increasing number of sick people seeking his prayers:

> At the beginning, it was only after he had fasted three days for one sick person that the person would be made whole. Later, he would touch or strike[187] the body of a sick person, and those who believed would be healed. Now, even when he prayed with only his voice for many people at once, those who believed were healed. After this, at the Gyeongseong revival meetings, even those who merely looked upon the Reverend with earnest faith were healed, and some who were a thousand *li*[188] removed were healed through proxy prayer.[189]

During the later period of his healing ministry, Kim made changes to his prayer practices to accommodate the growing number of sick people seeking his help. He would ask sick people with similar symptoms to gather in different places during the last hour of each day's revival meeting, and then pray for them as a group. This change in prayer practice resulted in more people being healed than when Kim prayed individually with the laying on of hands, as reported by Taek-kwon Im.[190] It is not assumed that Kim's healing power was strengthened, but rather that the increased possibility of healing was due to his ability to pray for many more sick people at once by changing his prayer method. There is also a record of Kim praying for a sick person who had sent him a letter requesting prayer. Remarkably, when Kim prayed from a distance, the sick person was healed. This account further illustrates the potency of Kim's healing practices, even from a distance.[191]

---

183 Yong-gyu Park, *Anak Sangol*, 174.
184 Taek-kwon Im, *Joseon Yesu Gyohoe Ijeogmyeongjeung*, 29.
185 Taek-kwon Im, *Joseon Yesu Gyohoe Ijeogmyeongjeung*, 1921, 86
186 Taek-kwon Im, *Joseon Yesu Gyohoe Ijeogmyeongjeung*, 1921, 86.
187 It is very interesting that describing Kim's healing practices, Taek-kwon Im adopted the Korean word, *Anchal* which means striking the body of a sick person. It is also a unique style of Korean prayer. However, it is not clear whether it was meant to be *Anchal* or the laying on of hands.
188 *Li* is an old unit to measure distance. 1 *li* is about 420 meters.
189 Taek-kwon Im, *Joseon YesuGyohoe Ijeogmyeongjeung*, 2008, 78-79.
190 Taek-kwon Im, *Joseon Yesu Gyohoe Ijeogmyeongjeung*, 1921, 87.
191 Yong-gyu Park, *Anak Sangol*, 176.

Spiritual Warfare[192]

During the early spread of Christianity in Korea, its dissemination was often characterised as a form of spiritual warfare,[193] as noted by Baird, a member of the faculty at the Pyeongyang Theological Seminary.[194] He posited that exorcism was a significant aspect of the Korean Church's battle against certain elements of traditional Korean culture.[195] Notably, American missionary accounts describe Kim's healing revivals as marked by the Holy Spirit's power, evidenced by acts of healing, miracles, and exorcism.[196] Some scholars of church history have underscored the importance of Kim's healing practices as part of a broader "spiritual warfare," aimed at liberating those enslaved by demons and transforming them into children of God.[197] In Kim's healing theology, exorcism served as an introductory process for Korean Christians to experience God's power and presence. The process of Kim's conversion was a good example. When Kim was converted to Christianity, his mother dreamed a strange dream that *Cheojadaegam*, a spiritual being whom Kim's mother had worshipped and which was believed to rule the world as a Son of God, was shouting, "Ik-du Kim is trying to kill me with a club."[198] It was an event that made Kim and his family members realise that God's power is much stronger than that of the being they had previously worshipped.

Kim's approach to healing often involved exorcism as a means to deliver individuals from demon possession. The majority of Kim's early healing experiences were related to spiritual warfare, as illustrated by his first healing encounter, which was a battle against a demonic force. In another instance, Kim

---

192 Kim did not directly use this terminology since it is comparatively recent. As the research needs to demonstrate theological aspects of evil spirits and their roles in bringing sickness to people, this terminology is conventionally used. Especially, the term spiritual warfare is adopted from Dickason's definition: the battle in which we, as Christians, are engaged. Christians generally recognise three major enemies: the flesh, the world, and the devil (with his demonic armies). 1) The flesh: Our enemy the flesh is that evil spiritual capacity within each human… and "a part of a human person that is in rebellion toward God" (p. 59). 2) The world: "a spirit of the age that rejects the true God and sets up a counterfeit life and substitute religion with the creature at the centre […] and an ordered system of which Satan is the ruler […] It includes individuals and nations" (p. 62). 3) Satan and demons: fallen angels who promote rebellion against God among men (p. 27). See C.F. Dickason, *Demon Possession & the Christian: A New Perspective* (Wheaton, IL: Crossway, 1987): 27-62.

193 Myeong-seob Heo, "Chogi Hanguk Gyohoui Sinyu Ihae," 140.

194 Ik-du Kim studied at this school and his theology of healing was also influenced in some ways by his teachers in the school. This topic is to be discussed in a special section designed to understand the formation of Kim's healing theology.

195 R.H. Baird, "Wm. M. Baird of Korea: A Profile" (Oakland, 1968), 239, in M. Huntley, *To Start A Work: The Foundation of Protestant Mission in Korea, 1884-1919* (Seoul: Presbyterian Church of Korea, 1983), 376.

196 H.A. Rhodes, *History of the Korea Mission Presbyterian Church U.S.A.*, 289.

197 Myeong-su Park, *Hanguk Gyohoe Buheungundong Yeongu*, 84; Yong-gyu Lee, *Hanguk Gyohoewa Shinyu Undong*, 123.

198 In-seo Kim, *Kim Ik-Du Moksa SoJeon*, 144.

healed a church member who had collapsed after refusing to participate in a shamanic ritual,[199] an event that Myeong-su Park describes as "a battle against an evil spirit."[200] In-seo Kim likewise characterised Kim's ministry in Sincheon as "a holy fight,"[201] and an exorcism occurred there when Kim prayed for a demon-possessed woman. This was followed by another healing event of exorcism in Sincheon as Ik-du Kim was asked by Gi-hwa Lee to pray for his wife who was demon-possessed. Kim prayed for the woman earnestly for a week and she became well.

Another exorcism occurred when one woman brought her demon-possessed son to Ik-du Kim during a revival in Masan. Her son started speaking nonsense, smiling, weeping, cursing, and running away from people. This boy eventually became well after Kim prayed for him.[202] Regarding this specific healing occasion, Im wrote in his report that "although the son believed in the Lord, such symptoms appeared because he had harboured corrupt thoughts in his heart."[203] In this sense, Kim seems to support the idea that even Christians can be demon-possessed.

Medicine

The primary sources that discuss Ik-du Kim's attitude towards medicine are limited, and it remains unclear whether he was for or against it. At the outset of his ministry, Kim appeared to have no qualms about using medicine, as he sold Western medicine for six months while teaching at a public school in Anak.[204] When his wife developed painful boils in her throat, Kim initially brought her to a doctor and used medicine to treat her.[205] However, after her condition failed to improve, they decided to fast and pray on a mountain, and his wife gradually recovered.[206] This healing event may have reinforced Kim and his wife's reliance on God over medicine, but they did not reject medicine as useless or anti-Christian. Kim also preached that if a friend who could not afford to see a doctor was sick, they should be taken to a doctor, even if it meant borrowing money.[207] From this preaching, it could be extrapolated that Kim implied that sick people needed to see a doctor.

Taek-kwon Im gave a momentous statement as to the use of medicine as follows: "I do not mean you should not see a doctor, or not use medicine, but

---

[199] In-seo Kim, *Kim Ik-Du Moksa SoJeon*, 161.
[200] Myeong-su Park, *Hanguk Gyohoe Buheungundong Yeongu*, 72.
[201] According to In-seo Kim, the process of propagation of the gospel is like a holy fight for early Christians. See In-seo Kim, *Kim Ik-Du Moksa SoJeon*, 161-64.
[202] Yong-gyu Park, *Anak Sangol*, 141.
[203] Taek-kwon Im, *Joseon Yesu Gyohoe Ijeogmyeongjeung*, 2008, 49.
[204] In-seo Kim, *Kim Ik-Du Moksa SoJeon*, 160.
[205] Yong-gyu Park, *Anak Sangol*, 75-78.
[206] Yong-gyu Park, *Anak Sangol*, 78.
[207] Ik-du Kim, "Seolo Salanghala" [Love One Another], in Seong-ho Lee (ed), *Hanguk Sinang Jeojakjib* [Collected Writings of Korean Beliefs] (Seoul: Hyemunsa, 1977): 24.

you should not put more faith in it and give more honour to doctors and medicine than you do to God."[208] Although this is not a direct quotation from Ik-du Kim, it appears to be fair enough for Im to argue that on behalf of Kim considering Kim's attitude towards the benefits of modernisation. In fact, Kim was very receptive to the new developments although he was conservative when it came to religious belief.[209] This contention can be extracted from Kim's opinions about general science. He once concluded his sermon by expressing his own thoughts on the subject: "Do I refuse science as a whole? No, science is what we really need for our living in the world, but we need the Bible more than science."[210] It was Kim's argument that depending more on the benefits made by human skills than on God is problematic. Kim did not deny the benefits of medicine. However, Kim's healing theology concerning medicine was that the sick should rely on God first even when they also use medicine.

The Baptism of the Holy Spirit (BHS hereafter)[211]

When describing Kim's healing ministry, many scholars have appended the phrase "of the Holy Spirit" to acknowledge the power of the Holy Spirit. Park, for example, regards Kim's healing movement as "all part of the Holy Spirit movement."[212] This perception appears accurate when considering a report in a Christian newspaper on one of Kim's revival meetings: "A great work of the Holy Spirit was manifested that degenerated people repented, the arrogant became humble, lukewarm Christians were revived, and the sick were healed."[213]

Despite this understanding of the Holy Spirit's role in miraculous healing, the primary focus of Kim's pneumatology is soteriological. Kim viewed the BHS as a "special right of blessed grace given only to Christians"[214] and as a "prerequisite for Christian life" in the sense that those who have not been baptised with the Holy Spirit are not Christians in terms of regeneration.[215] Kim's initial perception of the BHS is not primarily as a source of spiritual empowerment, but as a means of inner transformation. This is evidenced by his

---

[208] Taek-kwon Im, *Joseon Yesu Gyohoe Ijeogmyeongjeung*, 2008, 121.
[209] Yong-gyu Park, *Anak Sangol*, 86.
[210] Ik-du Kim, "Samui Pilyowa Seonggyeong," 56.
[211] The primary aim of this section is to investigate the connection between divine healing and the theological traits of the BHS in Kim's healing theology in order to understand how the works of the Holy Spirit can lead to divine healing, particularly as a consequence of the BHS.
[212] Myeong-su Park, *Hanguk Gyohoe Buheungundong Yeongu*, 91.
[213] "Gyeongseong gyohoe hwaserye," *Gi-Dok-Shin-Bo* [Christian Newspaper], 1902, November, 3.
[214] Ik-du Kim, "Seongryeongui sere" [the BHS], in Seong-Ho Lee (ed), *Kim Ik-du Mogsa Seolgyo Mit Yakjeonjib* [The Sermons and Biography of Ik-Du Kim] (Seoul: Hyemunsa, 1977): 58.
[215] Ik-du Kim, "Seongryeongeul bateura" [Receive the BHS], in Seong-Ho Lee (ed), *Kim Ik-du Mogsa Seolgyo Mit Yakjeonjib* [The Sermons and Biography of Ik-Du Kim] (Seoul: Hyemunsa, 1977): 42.

delineation of the six consequences of the BHS, which include love, gentleness and humility, cleansing, the power of the Holy Spirit as an internal revolutionary force, passion and honesty, and sealing.[216] In particular, cleansing as a part of the BHS is central to Kim's pneumatology. He asserted that "Baptism [of the Holy Spirit] means cleansing,"[217] "to walk with God,"[218] and he firmly believed that "the repentance of sin does not occur without the inspiration of the Holy Spirit."[219] This idea is expressed in his statement:

> That power [to transform the heart of people] is mounted up to the fullest extent when it comes from the almighty Holy Spirit who is capable of greatly transforming human minds by His words [...] Therefore, believers are transformed by receiving the Holy Spirit.[220]

It is indisputable that, for Kim, the primary function of the Holy Spirit is regeneration. However, many still maintain that Kim's healing practices were strongly linked to the works of the Holy Spirit. What is the intrinsic connection between the BHS and healing in Kim's healing theology? In Kim's healing theology, healing is perceived as a power given through the Holy Spirit; this is a critical formula. Interestingly, in the early stages of Kim's ministry, he frequently sought to obtain a special power to heal the sick.[221] One day, while returning from his ministry, he encountered a beggar who was lame. In attempting to heal the man, Kim sought to discern whether God would bestow "a power to heal"[222] upon him. At that time, Kim's faith appeared to be put to the test, as he was not yet a firm believer in divine healing. Nonetheless, he came to the realisation that "If the power of the Lord to heal grave diseases is with the believers, for what reason would he not allow us the power to heal those who are deformed and disabled?"[223] Kim viewed divine healing as something that could be manifested as a given power.

This idea leads to another important observation of Kim's prayer for healing. Whenever Kim heard people testifying to miraculous works in his healing services, he prayed for "more power of the Holy Spirit."[224] What can commonly be observed in Kim's healing ministry is that healing was regarded as "the power

---

216 Ik-du Kim,"Seongryeongsereui yeoseokgaji hyeongtae" [Six types of the BHS], in Seong-Ho Lee (ed), *Kim Ik-du Mogsa Seolgyo Mit Yakjeonjib* [The Sermons and Biography of Ik-Du Kim] (Seoul: Hyemunsa, 1977): 58-63

217 Ik-du Kim, "Receive the Holy Spirit," in Jae-hyun Kim (ed), *Kim Ik-du: The D.L. Moody of Korea*, trans., Woong G. Kim (Seoul: KIATS Press, 2008): 91.

218 Ik-du Kim, "Receive the Holy Spirit," 95.

219 Ik-du Kim, "Discerning How to Receive the Holy Spirit," 112.

220 Ik-du Kim, "Discerning How to Receive the Holy Spirit," 107.

221 The gift of healing in 1 Corinthians 12:9 appears to be in line with Kim's early perspective on divine healing.

222 Yong-gyu Park, *Anak Sangol*, 74-75.

223 Taek-kwon Im, *Joseon Yesu Gyohoe Ijeogmyeongjeung*, 1921, 2-3

224 Yong-gyu Park, *Anak Sangol*, 88.

of the Holy Spirit," as reported in a newspaper.[225] While God is the ultimate source of divine healing, healing is imparted as a power through the Holy Spirit. Interestingly, this notion appears to contradict Kim's cautionary stance regarding people's inclination to seek the mystical power believed to be imparted through the Holy Spirit. It is worth noting, however, that Kim's understanding of the spiritual gift of healing is not that it is an imparted power permanently bestowed by God upon the healing practitioners to the extent that they can exercise the healing power at will, without God's consent. Kim expounded on the relationship between divine healing and the BHS in his sermon entitled "Discerning How to Receive the Holy Spirit," as follows:

> Even among the prophets of the ancient days some had such power but others did not […] Even in the New Testament era John did not have it, but Peter and Paul did. We receive the wonders and miracles only according to the Holy Spirit's permission.[226]

When miraculous healing is described as a special endowment, the Holy Spirit is still described as the important One who has the final authority for healing. It is important to recognise that Kim understood divine healing as God's power itself, whereas mystical healing practitioners sought a special dispensation of the power to heal.

Another significant point can be made in a more ethical than theological sense. Kim warned those who had a mystical belief by telling them "those who pray for the BHS to heal the sick and to be honoured for themselves end up being insane," and he continued to edify the people to pray for the BHS for others not for themselves.[227] In fact, it was Kim's main argument that praying for the BHS is not problematic, but praying for the sick to be honoured in place of God is wrong. Kim did not reject the idea that the Holy Spirit works in power, as argued in his claim that "the baptism of the Holy Spirit comes with passion, love, truth, joy and an indescribable power."[228] The attitude of the people to abuse the healing power for their glory, not to glorify God, is what Kim tried to correct.

In addition, Kim adopted the notion of the BHS in a functional way, believing that Christians could better serve God in terms of their calling. In his preaching on "Let's serve the Lord by receiving the baptism of the Holy Spirit,"[229] Kim emphasised that healing given through the BHS should be instrumental in serving God's kingdom. From Kim's perspective, the Holy Spirit is not merely

---

225 "Pyeongyang Gwandong" [Gwandong province in Pyeongyang], *Yesugyo Sinbo* [Christian Messenger], 15 December 1908, 218.
226 Ik-du Kim, "Juileul Georukhui Jikija" [Keep the Lord's Day Holy], in *Kim Ik-du*, edited by KIATS (Seoul: Hongseongsa, 2008): 116-17.
227 Ik-du Kim, "Seongryeongui sere," 62-63.
228 Ik-du Kim,"Seongsin Batneun Bunbyeol" [Discerning the BHS], in *Kim Ik-du*, edited by KIATS (Seoul: Hongseongsa, 2008): 98-100.
229 Ik-du Kim, "Seongryeongui sere," 62-63.

a power to heal, but a person whose permission is central to his healing practice and who empowers His people for ministry. Kim's contribution lies in his emphasis that the BHS is not a religious exercise to receive healing power, but rather results from a relationship with the Holy Spirit, who has the final approval. Therefore, in Kim's healing theology, the Holy Spirit works not only in transforming the hearts of people but also in approving healing and empowering Christians for their ministries.

Love and Compassion

As part of his healing theology, Kim emphasised that love is essential in the church and is the first indication of receiving the Holy Spirit.[230] He believed that a healing ministry should be motivated by love and compassion, which is evident in his preaching:

> When Jesus saw the piteous, he could not bear to see their pain, so he healed the sick and poor people. He saw the physically ill, the blind, the lame, the paraplegics, and all the people who were groaning in all kinds of pain. He began to feel their wretchedness and he loved them. Therefore, he healed their physical needs [...] The Lord cared for their physical bodies, and overflowing with love.[231]

Kim's understanding was that Jesus healed people not just because of his power, but because he saw them through the eyes of love and compassion. In fact, most of Kim's healing stories testify that he was filled with love and compassion for the sick. For instance, in the first miracle at Hyeonpung, Kim prayed for the healing of a man whose lower jaw dropped not because of the sick person's request but because of his feelings of pity and compassion for him.[232] Kim later used this healing as an example in his preaching and said, "My heart felt pity and compassion, and I prayed weeping without food or drink for a day. Ah! His lower jaw closed up."[233] Even in Kim's memory, it was his sincere prayer, filled with compassion, that led to the man's healing.

Furthermore, when Kim prayed for a woman to be healed, he prayed that God would revive her by reducing his own life.[234] After this woman received healing, Kim continued to care for her and her child by regularly supplying them with goat's milk from Jaeryeong, as the woman could not breastfeed her child.

---

230 Ik-du Kim, "Seoro Saranghara," 22.

231 Ik-du Kim, "Seoro Saranghara" [Love One Another], in The Korea Institute for Advanced Theological Studies (ed), *Kim Ik-Du: The D.L. Moody of Korea* trans. Woong G. Kim (Seoul: KIATS Press, 2008): 181.

232 Taek-kwon Im, *Joseon Yesugyohoe Ijeogmyeongjeung*, 1921, 4; Yong-gyu Park, *Anak Sangol*, 216.

233 Ik-du Kim, "Hananimi Gibbeohaneun Adeul Ddalidoeja" [Let Us Become Sons and Daughters with Whom God is Pleased], in The Korea Institute for Advanced Theological Studies (ed), *Kim Ik-Du: The D.L. Moody of Korea*, trans. Woong G. Kim (Seoul: KIATS Press, 2008): 209.

234 In-seo Kim, *Kim Ik-Du Moksa SoJeon*, 165.

Through Kim's loving care, a new church was established in that region.[235] Kim often prayed for his church members with tears of compassion. During a revival meeting, he was suddenly moved with compassion for one of his church members who had left her faith. Kim could not stop praying with tears for her, so he earnestly fasted and prayed for her.[236] Kim's love and compassion motivated his healing ministry and served as the means of divine healing to bring God's healing to the poor and sick people, irrespective of time and place.

Evaluation of the Contribution of Kim's Healing Ministry

Social Perspective

The impact of Kim's healing movement on society was evaluated differently as the socio-political contexts changed. Initially, Kim's healing ministry was a significant issue, not only in the Christian realm but also in Korean society, to the extent that there was a song with lyrics about Kim's healing ability, which children sang during playtime.[237] Kim's healing events were also reported many times in newspapers, reflecting the society's attitude towards them from various perspectives. In the beginning of his healing ministry, a Korean newspaper, *Dong-A-Il-Bo*, described Kim as "a sage of high repute"[238] and reported the news under the title, "The Miracles of Pastor Kim: a Mute speaks and a Cripple walks,"[239] giving him a good reputation. However, this positive attitude towards Kim did not last long. In 1926, the same newspaper denigrated Kim as "the Avatar of Superstition" and "a High Shaman."[240] Furthermore, a Japanese newspaper, *Maeilsinbo*,[241] criticised him, stating that Kim was taking advantage of superstitious curiosity to evangelise.[242] These evaluations do not provide a fair understanding of Kim's healing movement as they merely reflected the social atmosphere in which socialism, liberalism, and rationalism gradually exerted influence over the general society of Korea.[243] Both unbelievers and many Korean Christians of the mainstream Church, known as cessationists, found

---

[235] In-seo Kim, *Kim Ik-Du Moksa SoJeon*, 165-66.

[236] Ik-du Kim, "Seoro Saranghara," 1977, 26.

[237] Yong-gyu Park, *Anak Sangol*, 176.

[238] "Janyeo Gyoyugeul Uihayeo Osibgaeui Geumjihwan," [Fifty Pieces of Gold for Children's education], *Dong-A-Il-Bo*, no. 92, 3rd July 1920: 3.

[239] "Kim Mogsaui Ijeok" [The Miracles of Pastor Kim], *Dong-A-Il-Bo*, 30th May 1920, quoted in Taek-kwon Im, *Joseon Yesugyohoe Ijeogmyeongjeung*, 1921: 42-43.

[240] "Hyeondaeinui Sinangsaeanhwal" [Today's Christian Life], *Dong-A-Il-Bo,* 21st May 1926.

[241] Myeong-su Park argues that the nature of *Maeilsinbo* was anti-religion and anti-miracles. It looked down on people's religiosity and considered it for people of low intellect. See Park, 90.

[242] "Misinjeok Hogisimeul Iyonghaneun Jeondo" [Using Superstitious Curiosity for Evangelism], *Maeilsinbo* [Daily Newspaper], 28th October 1920, in Taek-kwon Im, *Joseon Yesugyohoe Ijeogmyeongjeung*, 124-26.

[243] Myeong-su Park, *Hanguk Gyohoe Buheungundong Yeongu*, 65.

Kim's healing ministry challenging to accept. The negative attitude towards Kim's healing in the late 1920s was particularly strong, influenced by the rise of Communists who considered Christianity a religious opium and persecuted Kim.[244] As a result of these cynical reactions, Kim restrained his healing performances for a while.[245]

Some scholars argue that Kim's ministry mainly focused on marginalised people from the lower classes, which is generally considered to be Kim's contribution.[246] However, I believe that a significant contribution of Kim was that numerous people from various social classes attended his revival meetings, providing a place of equal human rights. That is why one of the early missionaries, J.S. Gale, paid great attention to the fact that some intellectual people and important nobles[247] were attending Kim's healing revival meetings. In fact, Kim brought down social barriers between different groups of people. There was no dividing curtain between men and women in the church and, in Kim's revival meetings, all Christians sat together in the same place to pray and worship God.

From an alternative perspective, Kim's healing ministry served as a mechanism to transform feelings of despair and frustration into feelings of comfort and hope. Deok-ju Lee maintains that supernatural religious experiences were necessary for individuals to overcome the unfavourable realities of their circumstances.[248] This is substantiated by T. Stanley Saltau's observation that Kim frequently initiated his preaching by drawing attention to the biblical fact that despite severe persecution, the early Christian church was protected by God. Kim thus reassured the Korean Church that there was no need to worry as they faced similar challenges.[249] Furthermore, Gale's account attests to the fact that most people attended Kim's revival meetings in search of spiritual satisfaction.[250] Kim not only provided physical healing but also alleviated emotional wounds, highlighting the fact that his healing theology extended to all facets of human existence. Jae-hyeon Kim supports this by asserting that Ik-du Kim's revival meetings healed both the body and soul of the people.[251] Furthermore, Taek-kwon Im underscores the importance of Kim's healing ministry, particularly within the context of Japanese colonisation, where most Koreans were starving

---

[244] Myeong-su Park, *Hanguk Gyohoe Buheungundong Yeongu*, 92.

[245] In-seo Kim, *Hanguk Gidokgyohoeui Yeoksa* [The History of Korean Church] (Seoul: Jangrohoe Sinhak Deahaggyo Press, 1997): 425.

[246] Hyeon Choe, *Daebuheungsa Kim Ik-Du* [Great Revivalist Ik-du Kim] (Seoul: Jerusalem, 2000): 96-98.

[247] This evidence indicates that Kim's healing theology can be identified with the *Minjung* concept of Boo-woong Yoo.

[248] Deok-ju Lee, *Saerosseun Hanguk Geuriseudoinui Gaejong IYaki*, 427.

[249] T. Stanley Saltau, *Yin Yang: Korean Voices* (Wheaton, IL: Key Publishers, 1971): 27.

[250] J.S. Gale, "The Revival in Seoul," 5.

[251] Jae-hyeon Kim (ed), *Joseon Yesugyohoe Ijeok Myeongjeung*, 34.

and being persecuted after the failure of the 1919 Independence Movement. Im argues that it was God's design for suffering individuals to find solace and fortitude in their faith by experiencing the miraculous signs and wonders of God through Kim's healing ministry.[252] Kim's healing ministry provided hope and comfort not only to those belonging to lower social classes but also to Koreans across different social strata who were grappling with the effects of Japanese colonisation.

Moreover, it is worth noting that Kim's contributions extend beyond his healing ministry. For example, many women had abandoned the traditional hairstyles which supported the patriarchal and class-based social structure, opting to imitate the hairstyles of prostitutes and elderly male servants.[253] Kim's ministry played a pivotal role in fostering a paradigm shift, one that acknowledged human equality before God. Kim's establishment of the Gyeongsin school for enlightenment, which provided new education to Korean society, was instrumental in bringing about these changes and advancing civilisation.[254] Therefore, Kim's exceptional efforts to educate the population had a positive impact on the development of Korean society.

Nonetheless, there exists a negative aspect to Kim's healing ministry with regards to social participation. While Ik-du Kim supported the education of the uncivilised population, it is often believed that his healing practices caused the Korean Church to lose sight of socio-political affairs. Many Christians felt that they were limited in their ability to challenge the Japanese authorities, particularly after the failure of the 1919 IMK. Consequently, they avoided conflict and shifted their focus towards the afterlife from an eschatological standpoint.[255] Kim's healing ministry, in this regard, appeared to contribute to many Christians prioritising Christian activities such as evangelism over meeting social needs. However, it would be unfair to attribute the Korean Church's indifference towards social and political situations entirely to Kim's healing ministry. Rather, it was an inevitable outcome of the Japanese tyranny, and most

---

[252] Taek-kwon Im, *Joseon YesuGyohoe Ijeogmyeongjeung*, 3-4.

[253] Previously, most Korean women wore their hair in styles reflecting their social class. The material of their hair accessories and the size of the braided hair revealed their identity: the higher and more successful family they were from, the more splendid and the bigger hairstyle they had. Many women who attended Kim's revival meetings offered their hair accessories to God and chose to wear their hair in simpler styles than before.

[254] In-seo Kim, *Kim Ik-Du Moksa SoJeon*, 176.

[255] In Kim's perspective, the Kingdom of Heaven is the only way of escaping from worries and fear of illness and death on the earth because he believed that people could not avoid illness on the earth; it always follows people like a shadow. So, life is always filled with fear of death. Only when people go to heaven can they become free from illness. Therefore, people need to be eager to go to heaven. See Ik-du Kim, "Hoegaehara Cheonguki Gaggaunira" [Repent, for the kingdom of heaven is at hand], in Seong-Ho Lee (ed), *Kim Ik-du Mogsa Seolgyo Mit Yakjeonjib* [The Sermons and Biography of Ik-Du Kim], (Seoul: Hyemunsa, 1977): 113.

Korean Christians had already become apathetic towards social participation. Kim's healing ministry became popular among those who were *already* indifferent towards social engagement because of the challenging political climate with the growing Japanese tyranny caused by the failure of the IMK. It is therefore more accurate to assert that Kim's healing movement provided a new sense of comfort and hope to those who had lost faith in social activism, rather than it being the driving force behind their apathy. While it is reasonable to expect that Kim's healing ministry would encourage the suffering Korean Church to remain active in revolutionising society, it is unjust to misconstrue Kim's contribution as promoting indifference towards society.

Missional Perspective

Ik-du Kim's most significant contribution is evidenced in the growth of the Korean Church. The apotheosis of Kim commenced in 1920, coinciding with his appointment as the moderator of the General Assembly of the Presbyterian Church and his subsequent leadership of numerous revival meetings. The period under Kim's leadership witnessed a remarkable surge in growth, as evidenced by the following data:

Table 1: The Statistics of the Korean Presbyterian Church[256]

Years	**1919**	**1920**	**1921**	**1922**	**1923**
Number of Pastors	192	180 (-12)[257]	208 (+28)	246 (+38)	234 (-12)
Number of Believers	144,062	153,915 (9,853)	179,158 (25,243)	187,271 (8,113)	193,850 (6,579)
Number of Churches	3,640	3,659 (19)	3,969 (310)	4,248 (279)	4,503 (255)

Whilst the Korean Church had been experiencing steady growth since 1919, it was during the period spanning 1920 and 1921 that the increase in the number of believers surged to more than three times that of previous years. A substantial rise was also noted in the number of established churches by 1921.

However, establishing a direct causal relationship between Kim's appointment as the moderator and the denominational growth by 1921 necessitates further empirical evidence. To this end, it may be useful to consider the following data, which compares the growth of the Presbyterian Church under Kim's leadership with that of another influential denomination, the Korean Methodist Church.

[256] Gyeong-bae Min, *Iljehaui Hanguk Gidokgyo Minjog Sinang Udongsa*, 290.
[257] The numbers in parentheses represent the growth compared to the previous year.

Figure 1: The numbers of Presbyterians and the Methodists in Korea[258]

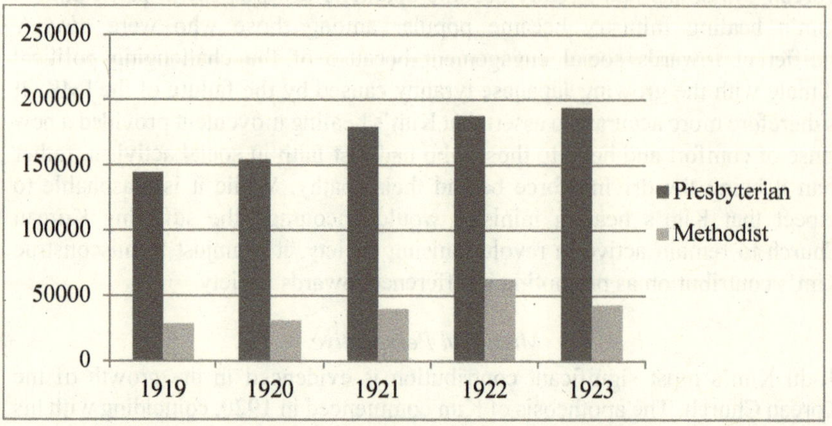

The chart presented above provides compelling evidence of the notable population growth experienced by the Presbyterian Church, particularly during the years 1920 to 1921. During this period, the Presbyterian Church saw a staggering increase of 25,243 new members, compared to only 8,817 for the Methodist Church. Scholars have attributed this substantial growth, in part, to Kim's healing ministry, which is regarded as one of the most influential catalysts for church growth in the early 1920s, particularly within the Presbyterian Church.[259] Missionary Rhodes bears witness to this phenomenon of revival, as follows:

> Nevertheless, the whole New Era Movement which began in our Korean Presbyterian Church more than a year before had not produced any appreciable results in and around Seoul until Rev. Mr Kim launched his meetings. From that time on the whole aspect of our evangelistic work has changed […] As a result of these meetings, the number of church members has continued to increase […] Many families with only one church-going member now joined the church all together, and there were many backsliders who received new strength. Church members were inspired to evangelise, and each Sunday they would go out in large groups to evangelise.[260]

Kim's healing meetings served not only as a place of healing for the sick but also as a source of motivation for more active evangelism. As a result of their

---

[258] The Korean Methodist Church, "Seongyochogi Mi,Namgamrihoe Joseonyeonhoe Gyosehyeonhwang (~1930)" [The total number of believers of the Korean Methodist Church in the beginning of its missions until 1930], [Available at: https://kmc.or.kr/head-quater-kmc/resources-history-of-kmc/historical-resources?uid=62239&mod=document&pageid=1], [Last accessed: 25th October 2023].

[259] Myeong-su Park, *Hanguk Gyohoe Buheungundong Yeongu*, 84-85.

[260] H.A. Rhodes, "Some Results of the Kim Ik Tu Revival Meeting in Seoul," 113-14.

participation in these meetings, individuals became "zealous Christians and faithful in attendance ever since," having received "a new baptism of grace in the Kim Ik Tu [Ik-du Kim] meetings."[261] Moreover, the healing received by many sick individuals at Kim's revival meetings led to group conversions.[262]

Kim's ministry had a profound impact not only on ordinary church members and new believers, but also on numerous pastors. As Im notes, one of the benefits of Kim's healing ministry was the development of a bolder faith among church workers.[263] Two hundred and fifty-eight people decided to become pastors because of the influence of Ik-du Kim's ministry.[264] Jae-jun Kim, who would later become an influential theologian, made his commitment to Christianity at Kim's revival meeting in 1920.[265] Additionally, Seong-bong Lee, one of the most representative Korean revivalists, was taught and influenced by Kim.[266] Other notable individuals, such as Jae-seon Jeon, a revivalist, and Gi-cheol Ju, a respected Korean pastor who died a martyr, were also ordained as pastors under Ik-du Kim's pastoral care.[267] It can be argued, therefore, that Kim's contributions to the Korean Church were made by kindling revival fires and empowering church workers, such as pastors and evangelists.

Theological Perspective

Ik-du Kim's theology of healing constituted a significant discovery, challenging the theological stance on divine healing held hitherto. The Presbyterian Church, for instance, had adopted an official position regarding divine healing, purporting that "In the present age, the authority to perform miracles is suspended."[268] This position explains why the Miracle Witness Committee felt compelled to investigate Kim's healing practices. Following the investigation, the committee submitted a proposal during the General Assembly of 1922, suggesting that the constitution be amended to acknowledge Kim's healing powers as genuine miracles akin to those witnessed in the Bible.[269] Although the proposal failed to garner enough support in 1923 with ten Presbyterians voting

---

[261] H.A. Rhodes, "Some Results of the Kim Ik Tu Revival Meeting in Seoul," 114.
[262] See Yong-gyu Park, *Anak Sangol*, 164 and Taek-kwon Im, *Joseon YesuGyohoe Ijeogmyeongjeung*, 1921, 71-72; 76; 163. One healing performance by Kim could bring scores of men and women into churches. According to Im, the number of those people who became Christians because of their witnessing the healing occasion of one sick person cannot be known.
[263] Taek-kwon Im, *Joseon Yesugyohoe Ijeogmyeongjeung*, 1921, 167.
[264] Yong-gyu Park, *Anak Sangol*, 105-106.
[265] Deok-ju Lee, *Saerosseun Hanguk Geuriseudoinui Gaejong Iyagi*, 425.
[266] Yong-gyu Park, *Anak Sangol*, 107.
[267] Sung-kuh Chung, "Reverend Ik-du Kim (1874-1950): The D.L. Moody of Korea," in The KIATS (ed), *Kim Ik-Du*, trans. Woong G. Kim (Seoul: KIATS Press, 2008): 17.
[268] The Presbyterian Constitution, Article One, Chapter Three.
[269] Deok-ju Lee, *Saerosseun Hanguk Geuriseudoinui Gaejong Iyagi*, 426.

against it and only six in favour,[270] it was a momentous occasion that reflected a change in the theological climate surrounding healing.[271] As Myeong-su Park points out, Kim's influence on the issue of divine healing was profound, making him a model for the healing movement in Korea.[272] According to a Presbyterian historian, "Kim had made the Korean Church realise that divine healing can take place not only in the Early Church of the Bible but also in the current days."[273]

This moment also marked a remarkable epoch for the Korean Church, as it sought to initiate theological discourse with the Western perspective[274] and develop an autochthonous theology of healing. Kim's theological contribution rests in the cornerstone he laid for an indigenous Korean HSM with respect to divine healing. In this regard, a Pentecostal theologian, Young-hoon Lee, rightly acknowledges the significance of Kim's healing ministry and identifies him as the pioneer of the healing movement and the most Pentecostal-like[275] spiritual leader in Korea.[276]

One negative evaluation of Ik-du Kim's healing practices was that "some missionaries and a few of the Korean leaders have wished that the evangelist would make less prominent this part of his programme."[277] Due to the indirect influence that Kim had on the proliferation of mystical healing practices, H.A. Rhodes, who gave a positive appraisal of Kim's healing ministry, expressed concern about church leaders, saying:

> Other Koreans, however, have attempted to imitate the evangelist [Ik-du Kim] in healings and the results have not always been beneficial. In one of my churches the leader has been useless and a great worry to us all ever since because he covets the power to heal and insists upon having special revelations.[278]

It is noteworthy that some church leaders were enamoured with the idea of possessing a special power to heal the sick, whereas Kim's healing theology was grounded in the prayer of faith. Although Kim consistently cautioned Christians not to pursue the Holy Spirit as a means of acquiring healing power, the fact that many people were healed during his revival meetings was a source of admiration

---

270 *Joseon Yesugyo Jangrohoe Je 13hoe Hoerok* [The Minutes of the 13th Korean Presbytery] (1924), 10-20.
271 See Taek-kwon Im, *Joseon Yesugyohoe Ijeogmyeongjeung*, 1921, 167. Kim's healing ministry brought a new custom in the region that when a family member was sick, the elders and pastors of the church were asked to lead worship and pray for the sick person.
272 Myeong-su Park, *Hanguk Gyohoe Buheungundong Yeongu*, 71.
273 Yong-gyu Park, *Haguk Gidok Gyohoesa 2: 1910-1960*, 284.
274 Yong-gyu Park, *Haguk Gidok Gyohoesa 2: 1910-1960*, 284.
275 Lee Young-hoon uses the term Pentecostal to refer to the groups originating from the Azusa Street revival movement in North America. From his perspective, Korean Pentecostalism began when the first Pentecostal missionary, Mary C. Rumsey, arrived in Korea in 1928. Young-hoon Lee, "Hanguk Osunjeol Undonggwa Sinyu," 173.
276 Young-hoon Lee, "Hanguk Osunjeol Undonggwa Sinyu," 185.
277 H.A. Rhodes, "Some Results of the Kim Ik Tu Revival Meeting in Seoul," 114.
278 H.A. Rhodes, "Some Results of the Kim Ik Tu Revival Meeting in Seoul," 114.

for some church leaders. Consequently, they became drawn to mystical religious experiences.

Conclusion

To summarise Chapter One, the findings regarding Ik-du Kim's healing movement were divided into three categories: the contexts of theological developments, the theological contents, and its evaluation. First, the chapter discussed the Japanese occupation as the most significant backdrop to Kim's healing ministry, where his perspectives on healing developed as a theology of hope and comfort for the suffering Korean Church. The failure of the IMK intensified the persecution of the Korean Church and provided a crucial foundation for Kim's active healing ministry nationwide. In the cultural-religious contexts, Shamanism and belief in the high God *Haneul* were instrumental in the processes of adoption and propagation of Christian divine healing. The healing theology focused on the power and love of God rather than the spiritual gift of healing. The prevalence of occultism, which equated the BHS with a mystic healing power, and the dominant perspective of cessationism caused the rejection of the spiritual gifts of healing and emphasised soteriological aspects such as regeneration and repentance.

According to Kim's theology of healing, the process of healing entails a mutual endeavour between the healing practitioner and the sick person, rather than a unidirectional path. Kim posited that faith plays an indispensable role in the healing process, with prayer serving as a potent conduit for seeking God's restorative power. Kim did not perceive prayer as a means of manipulating or coercing God into healing the sick. Rather, to foster a greater reliance on God, Kim's approach employed practices such as fasting, overnight vigils, and mountaintop supplication. Repentance was deemed essential not only for those who had fallen ill as a result of their sins, but also for those who interceded on behalf of the ailing. Despite these tenets, Kim's theology did not fully consider God's will as a determinant factor in every instance of healing. Kim's emphasis on human exertion for attaining divine healing appeared to overshadow the role of God's sovereignty in cases of affliction and illness.

In assessing Ik-du Kim's healing ministry, it becomes apparent that his viewpoint on healing evolved and took hold as a grassroots theology within the specific framework of suffering that resulted from Japanese colonisation, and the reluctance of the denomination to embrace healing in its theological paradigm. Kim's healing theology, which underscored the significance of repentance, spiritual warfare, love, and compassion, resonated with many individuals in Korea who were weighed down by deep-seated feelings of resentment and sadness. Therefore, Kim's healing movement served as a divine source of solace, attesting to the presence of God for those who were undergoing distress. The link between the prayer of faith, which expresses the conviction that God would unquestionably heal, and the reality of the deprivation experienced by the marginalised was instrumental in comprehending the efficacy of Kim's healing ministry. Furthermore, the cultural and religious backdrop of the belief system in spiritual entities provided a fertile ground for the development of the indigenous Pentecostal healing theology of Ik-du Kim. Nonetheless, it is imperative to acknowledge that the theology of suffering could scarcely coexist with the sanguine expectation of spiritual, emotional, and physical healing among those who sought relief.

2. Seong-bong Lee

Life and Ministry

Before the Conversion

Seong-bong Lee, frequently viewed as the Korean equivalent to D.L. Moody, was born in the humble village of Ganli, situated in Pyeonangnam-do,[1] as the eldest offspring of In-sil Lee and Jin-sil Kim on 4th July 1900. This was approximately seven months after the death of D.L. Moody.[2] His family origins, as he articulated in his autobiography, were neither of high social standing nor characterised by profound religious devotion, as he wrote, "My forefathers and parents originate from the lower stratum of society and are fettered by sins."[3] Amid the pervasive political and economic turbulence brought about by Japanese colonisation, a crisis that dramatically impacted the entirety of Korean society, Lee's family was no exception to the pervasive distress caused by severe impoverishment and deplorable living conditions. Lee vividly recollected the dire straits that his mother found herself in, compelling her to contemplate suicide by drinking lethal water on two separate occasions. Remarkably, she managed to survive both attempts, a miraculous outcome Lee ascribed to "God's providence."[4]

Nevertheless, a significant transformation took place within Lee's family following their adoption of the Christian faith. Lee's parents embraced Christianity when he was approximately five years old, leading to a life imbued with joy. Rain or shine, Lee and his family faithfully attended a Methodist church in Seogyori, Pyeongyang city, enduring a sixteen-kilometre journey every Sunday morning.[5] In terms of Lee's education, an opportunity for learning arose when his mother assumed a teaching position at a Christian school established by the Junghwa-eub Presbyterian Church six months after their conversion.[6] Under the strict guidance of his mother, who instilled in him Christian values and practices, Lee's spiritual journey started. At the age of five, he had already read the entire New Testament and, by six, was leading public prayers at his church.[7] Despite his young age, he believed that "Whatever we pray for, God

---

1 This state is now located in North Korea.

2 D.L. Moody died on the 22nd of December, 1899.

3 Seong-bong Lee, *Malo Mothamyeon Jukeumeuro* [If You Cannot Preach in Words, Preach by Death] (Seoul: Word of Life Books, 1993): 17.

4 Seong-bong Lee, *Malo Mothamyeon Jukeumeuro*, 17.

5 Seong-bong Lee, *Malo Mothamyeon Jukeumeuro*, 18.

6 Seong-bong Lee, *Malo Mothamyeon Jukeumeuro*, 18.

7 Seong-bong Lee, *Malo Mothamyeon Jukeumeuro*, 21.

will answer," and concurrently emphasised the profound importance of prayers steeped in sincere repentance.[8]

Even though Lee and his family had strong foundations of faith, Lee's own life remained beset by health problems and poverty. Because of his sickly appearance, exacerbated by his frailty and paragonimiasis[9], Lee earned the nickname *Ggaldagui* (*Ggalddgu*), meaning mayfly. Tragically, Lee's two brothers also succumbed to illnesses,[10] compounding the family's challenges. Health issues aside, economic hardships further burdened Lee and his family. Following his graduation from Gyeongsin Elementary School, Lee's impoverished background prevented him from pursuing further education. This dire circumstance drove him to contemplate suicide, fuelled by a sense of inferiority and disappointment.[11]

Lee's attempts to sustain himself by selling wood and fruits proved insufficient, often resulting in skipped meals. Consequently, Lee lost his way, adopting a pessimistic outlook on life. He later described his youthful days as a period of extreme decadence, characterised by bitterness towards the unjust world and denial of the existence of God, the Kingdom of Heaven, and Hell.[12] At the age of eighteen, he entered into a marriage of convenience with Eun-sil Lee, approved by his parents as an attempt to reintroduce him to his initial love for God and to redirect his life. Unfortunately, instead of leading him onto the right path, the situation worsened, ultimately leading to mistreatment of his wife and a continued dissolute existence.[13]

Conversion

Lee's journey of conversion was initiated by a disease he contracted on a Sunday while returning from a bar, having earned money from fruit sales. In a state of intoxication, he engaged in "various disgraceful and wicked acts on that night" and developed periostitis on his right thigh.[14] At the age of twenty, a doctor suggested amputating his leg as the symptoms worsened day by day, despite undergoing various medical treatments. This seemingly hopeless predicament, however, served as a catalyst for Lee's encounter with Jesus, as expressed by Lee himself: "Only God knew that a great transformation would take place on

---

[8] Seong-bong Lee, *Malo Mothamyeon Jukeumeuro*, 21-22.

[9] "Paragonimiasis, or lung fluke disease, is a foodborne trematode infection caused by a number of species of trematodes belonging to the genus Paragonimus." World Health Organization, [Available at: https://www.who.int/news-room/questions-and-answers/item/neglected-tropical-diseases-paragonimiasis], [Last accessed: 25th October 2023].

[10] Lee's first younger brother died when he was two years old while his second younger brother lived half of his life with a disease contracted at the age of six and died when he was thirty-three. Seong-bong Lee, *Malo Mothamyeon Jukeumeuro*, 20-23.

[11] Seong-bong Lee, *Malo Mothamyeon Jukeumeuro*, 24.

[12] Seong-bong Lee, *Malo Mothamyeon Jukeumeuro*, 26.

[13] Seong-bong Lee, *Malo Mothamyeon Jukeumeuro*, 29.

[14] Seong-bong Lee, *Malo Mothamyeon Jukeumeuro*, 30.

that day."[15] When his mother encouraged him to repent of his sins, believe in Jesus, and dedicate his entire life to the Lord, he sensed "the voice of the Holy Spirit inspiring his heart."[16]

Lee became aware of his transgressions and fervently beseeched God, declaring, "I will surrender my life to you and employ it as a testimony to your works if you grant me a second chance at life."[17] Lee believed that God answered his prayer, as he experienced a tranquil state of mind that enabled him to overcome his vices, all the while expressing gratitude and praising God despite enduring the three-year-long affliction.[18] Lee regarded this period as a profoundly transformative experience, a veritable "conversion," during which he gained a deeper understanding of God.[19]

Following his conversion, Lee dedicated his life to the study of the Bible. Subsequently, from 1925 to 1928, he enrolled in Gyeongseong[20] Bible School, which is presently known as Seoul Theological Seminary, under the auspices of the Oriental Missionary Society.[21] This period of theological education held great significance for Lee, akin to being "refined in a blazing furnace for three years," as he placed greater emphasis on his spiritual development rather than mere academic pursuits.[22]

Ministry

Pastoral Ministry (1925–1937)[23]

Lee embarked on his ministry while still attending Bible school, focusing primarily on evangelistic endeavours aimed at children. During this period, he received numerous invitations from various churches to lead revival services specifically tailored for children. As his ministry grew, its success was attributed to his prior experience as an elementary school teacher, as well as his spiritual gifts of singing and delivering narrative sermons.[24]

Following his graduation in 1928, Lee was imbued with an ardent sense of responsibility for evangelism, a calling that the Holiness Church recognised by

---

[15] Seong-bong Lee, *Malo Mothamyeon Jukeumeuro*, 29.
[16] Seong-bong Lee, *Malo Mothamyeon Jukeumeuro*, 32-33.
[17] Seong-bong Lee, *Malo Mothamyeon Jukeumeuro*, 33.
[18] Seong-bong Lee, *Malo Mothamyeon Jukeumeuro*, 34.
[19] Seong-bong Lee, *Sarangui Gangdan* [The Pulpit of Love] (Seoul: Word of Life Books, 1993): 201.
[20] The capital of South Korea, Seoul, used to be called Gyeongseong.
[21] The Oriental Missionary Society was founded by C.E. Cowman and E.A. Kilbolune to support the missions in the Far East, and it became the historical matrix of the Korean Holiness Church.
[22] Seong-bong Lee, *Malo Mothamyeon Jukeumeuro*, 38.
[23] Although it is normally believed that Lee's pastoral works officially started when he served Suwon Church after his graduation in 1928, Lee was already doing pastoral ministries in a vigorous way since his Bible school time. The year 1925 was considered, therefore, to be the starting point of Lee's pastoral engagement, not 1928.
[24] Seong-bong Lee, *Malo Mothamyeon Jukeumeuro*, 39.

assigning him the task of establishing a new congregation in the Suwon region. His first church was founded in a small rented house, and flourished because of an unwavering commitment to evangelistic endeavours and services, including in-person gatherings, public preaching in street settings, and pastoral visitations to the homes of potential congregants.[25] Lee further explained how the Suwon church could grow:

> Through God's blessings many people were sent to be saved and numerous signs and wonders took place. A lot of people returned to God, praising Him for His power and love because of the wonders that the sick were raised from the bed and the demon-possessed were set free.[26]

It was posited that divine healing served as a critical catalyst for the swift expansion of the church. Lee introduced a healing event that took place during this time. An elderly female shaman, who had been completely paralysed for seven months, experienced healing when Lee laid his hand upon her chest and prayed.[27] Subsequently, the shaman embraced Christianity, renouncing her former idols.

The healing event and the conversion of the shaman not only accelerated the church growth but also caused some ministerial crises and challenges. The sudden death of one of his female pastoral staff, occurring approximately a month after the Shaman's healing and conversion, led to the departure of many church members. This incident was perceived by some as divine retribution for intruding upon the shaman's temple, leading them to believe that the power of the shaman's god surpassed that of Jesus.[28]

Despite these critical challenges, the church continued to grow steadily, amassing around four hundred members, and eventually constructing a new brick building spanning one hundred thirty-nine square meters.[29] According to Lee, this time of his ministry centred on life-changing experiences as the spiritual transformation of sinners was viewed as another miracle when people repented of their sins, demolished idols, and discontinued their bad habits by the power of the Holy Spirit.[30]

Following his ministry in Suwon, Lee assumed pastoral responsibilities at another church in the Mokpo area from 1930 to 1936. When he arrived, the Mokpo Church had approximately fifty members, and under his leadership, the church commenced successful daily evangelistic work, resulting in notable growth.[31] Establishing a youth prayer team called *Cheong-Sin*, dedicated to early

---

[25] Seong-bong Lee, *Malo Mothamyeon Jukeumeuro*, 42
[26] Seong-bong Lee, *Malo Mothamyeon Jukeumeuro*, 42.
[27] Seong-bong Lee, *Malo Mothamyeon Jukeumeuro*, 44.
[28] See Seong-bong Lee, *Malo Mothamyeon Jukeumeuro*, 44-45.
[29] Seong-bong Lee, *Malo Mothamyeon Jukeumeuro*, 45.
[30] Seong-bong Lee, *Malo Mothamyeon Jukeumeuro*, 43.
[31] Seong-bong Lee, *Malo Mothamyeon Jukeumeuro*, 51.

morning prayer sessions on Yudal Mountain, Lee and his team were able to construct a new church building measuring approximately one hundred sixty-five square meters within a year.[32] Lee's ordination took place in 1932 and, over the course of his six-year ministry, he bore abundant pastoral fruit, including the establishment of seven district churches and the training of numerous future church leaders.[33]

The third church (1936–1937) started in Sineuju. Lee described his ministries for this church as the most "revived and enjoyable" works during his pastoral career for several reasons.[34] First, his efforts in evangelism, in collaboration with the leaders of his church, resulted in the successful conversion of numerous individuals. Secondly, the church experienced significant growth, boasting a membership of approximately one thousand individuals, with twenty-four district cell leaders and fifty church staff. Thirdly, Lee's church building was constructed to accommodate approximately one thousand people, establishing itself as the largest among the Holiness churches of that time. Fourthly, Lee played an instrumental role in the establishment of a Bible school, thereby imparting theological education to local pastors and fostering the planting of district churches. Lastly, Lee's prominence and influence were demonstrated through his invitations to lead various denominations' revival meetings in numerous cities. Particularly noteworthy was the revival meeting held in 1936 at the Gyeongchan Gate in Pyeonyang, which attracted thousands of attendees, marking a significant event in Lee's early revivalist career.[35]

REVIVAL MINISTRY UNDER JAPANESE COLONISATION (1937–1945)[36]

Lee's influence as a revivalist experienced a notable increase following his appointment as a circulating national revivalist in 1937. He embarked on a series of tours across various provinces, leading numerous revival services in churches of varying sizes. These revival meetings were characterised by multiple elements, including experiences of repentance, conversion, sanctification, divine healing, and material commitment. Lee's account of the revival meeting at Youngjong reveals a significant number of individuals who repented and underwent regeneration experiences. Out of two thousand attendees, approximately one hundred thirty people converted to Christianity, while substantial monetary offerings, including gold rings and watches, were donated for the construction of a new church building.[37] Regarding his theological

---

[32] Seong-bong Lee, *Malo Mothamyeon Jukeumeuro*, 51-52.

[33] Seong-bong Lee, *Malo Mothamyeon Jukeumeuro*, 55-56.

[34] Seong-bong Lee, *Malo Mothamyeon Jukeumeuro*, 58.

[35] Seong-bong Lee, *Malo Mothamyeon Jukeumeuro*, 58.

[36] This period exclusively pertains to the duration of Lee's revivalist ministries, occurring in conjunction with the imminent conclusion of the Japanese occupation. It encompasses a span of merely eight years, whereas Korea endured a total colonisation period of thirty-five years under Japanese rule, commencing in 1910 and concluding in 1945.

[37] Seong-bong Lee, *Malo Mothamyeon Jukeumeuro*, 69.

message, Lee placed great emphasis on divine healing as one of the four foundational pillars of his homiletics, alongside regeneration, sanctification, and the Second Coming of Jesus.[38] Notably, divine healing played a prominent role in defining Lee's revival ministry, as numerous sick individuals experienced healing through his ministry.[39]

As Lee's popularity grew, he began leading revival meetings, not only within the Holiness Church but also in other denominations, including Presbyterian and Methodist churches. This posed a predicament because of his unwillingness to comply with an order that restricted him to leading revival meetings within the Holiness Church exclusively,[40] leading Lee to take a leave of absence from his responsibilities within the Holiness Church in 1938. After approximately one year of leading revival meetings, Lee relocated to Japan in 1939 to pursue studies at *Ilbonsinhakgyo* (Japan Theological Seminary).[41] During this time, he remained engaged in various ministries, including: 1) leading revival meetings to spread the gospel among overseas Koreans and Japanese, 2) serving as a pastor at Dongkyeong (Tokyo) Holiness Church, and 3) producing a music album featuring his four songs as a means of evangelism.[42] Upon his return to Korea, Lee resumed his pastoral work with the endorsement and approval of the General Council of the Holiness Church in Manju (located in Northeast China and Inner Mongolia). Lee intentionally chose to conduct his ministry in this region to avoid the challenges posed by the growing persecution of the Korean Church under Japanese rule.[43] From 1941 to 1945, he pastored a church and engaged in evangelistic activities in Manju while continuing to conduct revival meetings in various locations. Despite his focus on the Manju area for revival meetings, he occasionally received invitations from churches in other areas that were subject to increasing Japanese control. This resulted in his imprisonment for one month in 1941 at the Sariweon police jail of Hwanghae state, where he endured daily torture.[44]

REVIVAL MINISTRY AFTER INDEPENDENCE (1945–1965)

The Korean Peninsula experienced a fleeting illumination of liberty subsequent to Japan's surrender at the conclusion of World War II, five years prior to the onset of the Korean War. Upon Korea's achieving independence from Japan on 15th August 1945, Lee returned to North Korea with the purpose of rejuvenating

---

[38] This theological foundation is also the main doctrine of the four-fold gospel of the Holiness Church.

[39] Some of Lee's healing ministries at his revival meetings were recorded in his autobiography, such as the healing of a demon-possessed woman, a woman who could not walk for ten years, and another woman suffering from scrofula. Seong-bong Lee, *Malo Mothamyeon Jukeumeuro*, 69-70.

[40] Seong-bong Lee, *Malo Mothamyeon Jukeumeuro*, 79.

[41] Myeong-su Park, *Hanguk Gyohoe Buheungundong Yeongu*, 171-72.

[42] Seong-bong Lee, *Malo Mothamyeon Jukeumeuro*, 80.

[43] Seong-bong Lee, *Malo Mothamyeon Jukeumeuro*, 82.

[44] Seong-bong Lee, *Malo Mothamyeon Jukeumeuro*, 92-94

the Holiness Church. Lee's ministry seemed to be going well, as he said that "all the oppressed souls under Japanese colonisation who were hungry and thirsty became full of joy and great revivals continued to break out."[45]

However, in the wake of these revivals, Lee made the decision to cross the 38th parallel,[46] which served as a demarcation line between the two Koreas, owing to the escalating oppression imposed by the Communists upon the Korean Church. In 1946, subsequent to his arrival in the southern region, his ministerial endeavours centred on the reconstruction of the Holiness Church. In the span of a year, Lee visited eighty-two churches, conducting three services daily for three to five days per church. It was reported that approximately ten thousand individuals attended his revival meetings during this period.[47]

Despite the eruption of the Korean War on 25th June 1950, resulting in extensive religious persecution, particularly targeting Christians, Lee's ministry persisted through the establishment of the Immanuel Prayer Centre and the Immanuel publishers. However, this commitment to his faith led to his subsequent imprisonment and torture in Mokpo by an advance party of the North Korean People's Army, which had seized the southern parts of South Korea in August 1950.[48] After the Korean Army recaptured Seoul on 28th September 1950, Lee initiated a significant ministry known as the Immanuel Commando, which he described as follows:

> Even though our small Holiness Church, which previously declined because of the negative effect[49] of the Japanese rule just before its disbandment, was about to barely grow, many churches were burnt and some leading pastors in the Holiness Church were killed or abducted during the Korean War. I could not turn a blind eye to the Church undergoing suffering again and again.[50]

Following the conclusion of the war, the primary objective of the Immanuel Commando, from 25th May 1954, to 27th April 1955, was to extensively visit rural villages and mountainous districts, aiming to "rebuild all the atrophied Holiness churches."[51] This ministry's theological foundation rested upon Lee's

---

[45] Seong-bong Lee, *Malo Mothamyeon Jukeumeuro*, 97.
[46] The 38th parallel was first made as the border between the North (occupied by the Soviet Union) and the South (occupied by the United States) in 1945 at the end of World War II.
[47] Seong-bong Lee, *Malo Mothamyeon Jukeumeuro*, 99.
[48] Seong-bong Lee, *Malo Mothamyeon Jukeumeuro*, 104-9.
[49] The Holiness Church was persecuted and forced by Japan to disperse because of their radical view of the Second Coming of Jesus which was believed to be against the Japanese Emperor worship. See Seong-deuk Oak, "The Disbandment of the Holiness Church on the 29th of December in 1943," [Available at: https://koreanchristianity.tistory.com/749], [Last accessed: 26th October 2023].
[50] Seong-bong Lee, *Malo Mothamyeon Jukeumeuro*, 112.
[51] Seong-bong Lee, *Malo Mothamyeon Jukeumeuro*, 112.

belief that "the Lord is the friend of the weak and the poor, and He wants His servants to be like Him as well."[52]

From 1955 until his passing in 1965, Lee dedicated his life to a range of revival ministries, including: 1) revival meetings for the Jubilee Celebration, taking place from 27th April 1955 to 18th March 1956, with a focus on establishing one thousand district churches in preparation for the Jubilee celebration within the Holiness Church.[53] 2) The Jubilee Evangelistic Team, operating for seven months from May to December in 1957, leading fifty revival meetings annually to support the Holiness Church[54] – this effort aimed to raise funds for assisting needy churches, establishing the Jubilee Commemoration Church in Munrae-dong, and supporting missionaries in Taiwan.[55] 3) He led seven revival meetings on Jeju Island. 4) He conducted an evangelism tour in the United States in 1959, with the purpose of repaying Korea's debt to American missionaries and expressing solidarity with Korean residents in the United States. A significant outcome of this ministry was the recruitment of numerous financial supporters for the Korean Church when Lee delivered a sermon as a Korean representative at the National Association of Evangelicals meeting.[56] 5) He embarked on a tour of revival meetings from 1961 to 1963, during which Lee led one daily revival service, visiting a total of four hundred and eighty churches.[57] 6) Lee's final sermon on 23rd July 1965 for the Holiness Church[58] at the Assembly was titled "Those who love the Lord" and took place just days before his passing on 2nd August 1965.[59]

The Formation of the Healing Theology

Socio-Politico-Economic Contexts

The distinctiveness of Lee's ministry of healing is underscored by his ministry's commitment to the Korean people amidst periods of profound suffering.[60] Lee's historical background is inextricably intertwined with some of the most poignant epochs of the Korean Church, including: 1) the era of Japanese occupation (1910–1945), 2) the Communist persecution (1945–1950), and 3) the Korean

[52] Seong-bong Lee, *Malo Mothamyeon Jukeumeuro*, 124.
[53] Seong-bong Lee, *Malo Mothamyeon Jukeumeuro*, 154.
[54] Seong-bong Lee, *Malo Mothamyeon Jukeumeuro*, 185.
[55] Seong-bong Lee, *Malo Mothamyeon Jukeumeuro*, 187.
[56] Seong-bong Lee, *Malo Mothamyeon Jukeumeuro*, 207.
[57] Seong-bong Lee, *Malo Mothamyeon Jukeumeuro*, 250.
[58] The Holiness Church was previously divided into two groups. Both groups joined the Assembly.
[59] Seong-bong Lee, *Malo Mothamyeon Jukeumeuro*, 250.
[60] Comparing the contexts of Kim and Cho, Lee is the only one whose ministry underwent the two most significant challenges from the Japanese occupation and the Korean War. Kim's ministry ended just four months after the breakout of the Korean War and Cho started his ministry after the Korean War.

War (1950–1953). This historical and societal context played a significant role in guiding Lee to shape his healing theology, centred around providing solace and inspiring hope among those who were emotionally distressed and socially marginalised.

During Lee's fervent pursuit of biblical studies (from his conversion in 1920 to his graduation from a Bible school in 1928), the Korean Church endured severe persecution under Japanese rule. This period was characterised by what was regarded as "the most frustrating crisis of disappointment" marked by a sense of "nihilism."[61] This sentiment emerged as a result of the failure of the March 1st Independence Demonstration in 1919, the widespread proliferation of Communism in the northern part of Korea during the independence movement, and the secularisation influenced by the West in the southern part of Korea after achieving independence.[62] Evidence of the impact on the Korean Church is reflected in a survey that reveals a significant decline in the population of the Presbyterian and Methodist Churches, from 179,544 to 22,409, with only 88 of the 2,177 churches surviving.[63] Considering the influence of Christians on the movement, it is not surprising that among those arrested for leading or participating in the Independence Movement, 244 individuals (approximately 50%) were Christians, while 125 (25.6%) were *Chondogyo*[64] followers, and 120 (24.5%) were Buddhists.[65]

When Lee commenced his revival ministries in 1938, the level of hardship experienced was not markedly different. The people endured oppressive circumstances characterised by forced *Shinto* shrine worship, compulsory conscription, Japanese military sexual slavery, compulsory labour, and the imposition of Japanese names, among other challenges. In this regard, Kang views Lee's ministry as the catalyst for bringing "joy," "peace," "courage," and

---

[61] Gyeong-bae Min, "Lee Seong-Bong Moksaui Buheungundong Jaejomyeong" [Re-examination of Seong-bong Lee's Revival Movement], edited by The Commemoration Committee of the 100th Anniversary of Lee Seong-Bong's Birth, *Lee Seong-Bong Moksaui Buheungundong Jomyeong* [The Examination of Seong-bong Lee's Revival Movement] (Seoul: Lifebook, 2000): 195.

[62] Gyeong-bae Min, "Lee Seong-Bong Moksaui Buheungundong Jaejomyeong," 195.

[63] The Society of the History of Christianity in Korea, *Hanguk Gidokgyoui Yeoksa* 2, 48.

[64] *Chondogyo* originated from *Donghak,* which was founded by Je-Woo Choe for equality for all. The spirit of *Donghak* was inherited by Byeong-Hui Son through Si-Hyeong Choe, and Son established *Cheondogyo* in 1905. It was the ideal of *Chondogyo* to situate heaven not in the afterlife but in this present life by establishing an egalitarian and ethical society. Encyclopedia of Korean Culture, "천도교" [*Cheondogyo*] [Available at: https://encykorea.aks.ac.kr/Contents/Item/E0055819], [Last accessed: 26th October 2023] and "동학" [*Donghak*] [Available at: https://encykorea.aks.ac.kr/Contents/SearchNavi?keyword=%EB%8F%99%ED%95%99%EC%9A%B4%EB%8F%99&ridx=1&tot=1411], [Last accessed: 26th October 2023].

[65] The Society of the History of Christianity in Korea, *Hanguk Gidokgyoui Yeoksa* 2, 48.

"hope" to the oppressed people.[66] Min similarly concurs that "Lee was sent by God as His ambassador to proclaim comfort and hope," enabling the Korean people to endure the pain of one of Korea's darkest periods.[67] This was evidenced in Lee's report on his revival meetings conducted immediately after Independence Day in 1945. He noted that "all the oppressed with hunger and thirst under Japanese rule were filled with joy, and wherever I went spiritual fire was kindled," resulting in the conversion of numerous individuals to Christianity.[68]

The Communist regime persisted in its persecution of the Korean Church, even post-Independence Day, particularly in the northern half of the country. This was primarily due to misconceptions surrounding the Korean Christian community, including the beliefs that: 1) they were subservient to imperialistic and capitalistic forces; 2) they undermined the spirit of independence by fostering complacency; and 3) they promulgated superstition and fallacy, despite the advancement of scientific thought.[69] Even amid the outbreak of the Korean War, when the Korean Peninsula teetered on the brink of Communist occupation in the South, Lee remained steadfast in his mission to instil hope and courage within the disheartened people. This determination was manifested in his composition of a poignant song entitled "Wait A Little More":

> 1. When the One admired by all nations will descend shaking heaven and earth, your wish will come true.
> 2. Do not be discouraged when your prayer seems not to be answered. Wait a little more since everything has its time.
> 3. Although you are tired body and soul and suffer defeat after defeat, Wait a little more while desiring God.
>
> (Chorus) Taking hold of faithful promise, wait a little more, wait a little more.[70]

This song represents a recurring message of hope and comfort from God to the suffering Korean people. It is undisputed that Lee played a pivotal role in the Korean context, as his healing ministry extended beyond traditional notions of revivalism, encompassing the imperative to provide solace and encouragement to the oppressed, enabling them to confront the reality of suffering and await God's salvation. Lee's healing ministry served as a powerful tool, not only in

---

[66] Geun-hwan Kang, "Lee Seong-Bong Moksaui Buheungsayeok" [The Revival Ministry of Seong-bong Lee], edited by The Commemoration Committee of the 100th Anniversary of Lee Seong-Bong's Birth, *Lee Seong-Bong Moksaui Buheungundong Jomyeong* [The Examination of Seong-bong Lee's Revival Movement] (Seoul: Lifebook, 2000): 138.

[67] Gyeong-bae Min, "Lee Seong-Bong Moksaui Buheungundong Jaejomyeong," 187.

[68] Seong-bong Lee, *Malo Mothamyeon Jukeumeuro*, 97.

[69] The Society of the History of Christianity in Korea, *Hanguk Gidokgyoui Yeoksa* 2, 57.

[70] Seong-bong Lee, *Malo Mothamyeon Jukeumeuro*, 109-10.

facilitating physical healing but also in instilling a profound awareness of God's unwavering faithfulness and love within individuals.

Lee's theology of healing was intricately intertwined with his hamartiology, particularly when the Korean Church experienced times of deep spiritual, emotional, and physical turmoil. It is worth noting that while Lee attributed the cause of illnesses to sin, he did not proclaim that every sickness was a direct consequence of sin. This theological framework was further developed and solidified within the historical Korean contexts of suffering. Lee depicted his understanding of God's punishment in the following excerpt:

> As God used the Babylonians to punish the Israelites when they committed sins, Korea has been beaten with the bat of the 36-year Japanese colonisation because of the sins committed by the *Choseon* Dynasty for five hundred years. We are being beaten with the bat of communists since we are not grateful to God for giving us the independence and have continued to live sinful lives.[71]

According to Lee's perspective, the trials and tribulations faced by Koreans were a result of their transgressions against God.[72] He believed that a sinful life could engender suffering as a form of divine punishment. In this sense, Lee urgently conveyed a message of repentance to the suffering Korean Church, urging individuals to seek God's forgiveness in order to put an end to the punishment. However, the strength of Lee's healing theology lay in its focal point, not solely on the punishment itself, but rather on God's unwavering faithfulness and love, which served to uplift and encourage the Korean Church to return to God.[73] This theological framework of divine healing developed in tandem with Lee's understanding of salvation. Thus, Lee's hamartiology and soteriology were closely interlinked within his healing theology.

Furthermore, Lee's theology of spiritual warfare took shape within the war-torn context of Korea. One of the remarkable aspects of Lee's revival ministry was his establishment of the Immanuel Commando, a unique ministry marked by its usage of military terminology, which was not previously employed by Lee until the Korean War. When embarking on the mission to reconstruct the war-ravaged Holiness Church, Lee described his new ministry background as "I am being taken as a captive of the Cross commando to serve the evangelistic teams battling in their own places […] First of all, I am going to Gangwon province where the unit on the frontline is more inactive than that in the rear area."[74] The utilisation of terms such as "commando," "captive," "battling," "frontline," and "rear area" featured prominently in his reports on these events. In his initial report on the Immanuel Commando, Lee portrayed the revival meeting using

---

[71] Seong-bong Lee, *Malo Mothamyeon Jukeumeuro*, 108.

[72] This is a stark contrast to later healing preachers like Cho, whose theology is deeply rooted in the notion of the Good Father.

[73] Seong-bong Lee, *Sarangui Gangdan*, 106.

[74] Seong-bong Lee, *Malo Mothamyeon Jukeumeuro*, 124.

various military metaphors, referring to the gathering as an "array," the lead pastor as a "veteran," the church members as "soldiers," and the spiritual renewal as "rearmament." He also perceived his revival ministry as a "hand-to-hand fight" against the "large force of Satan."[75] These observations highlight how the context of the war-torn Korean Church significantly influenced the development of Lee's theology of spiritual warfare.

Christian Context

Although it can be argued that Lee's theological development was significantly influenced by his denominational teaching, particularly with regards to the four-fold Gospel of Regeneration, Sanctification, Divine Healing, and the Second Coming of Jesus,[76] it is essential to consider his healing theology as a continuation of the legacy of the Korean Church, particularly in the areas of repentance and healing. Lee himself acknowledged that his experiences of regeneration and healing predated his involvement in the Holiness Church, stating, "I was first saved in a Presbyterian church, spent about ten years in a Methodist church, and moved to a Holiness church when I was 24 years old."[77] This shows that Lee underwent his regeneration in a Presbyterian church and experienced healing in a Methodist church, specifically for his periostitis which he had suffered since 1918.[78] Consequently, Lee's perspective on repentance and healing was initially shaped outside of the Holiness Church. Therefore, his theology should be understood within a broader arena, beyond his affiliation with the Holiness Church, even though the Holiness Church played a significant role in his theological orientation.

The proposition that repentance is an integral spiritual heritage of the Korean Church, a legacy that was passed down to Lee as an extension of the substantial revival movements in Korea commencing in 1903 and 1907, is highly compelling. Since the inception of the Korean Church, the concept of repentance has held a pivotal role. It is unsurprising, then, that repentance was a frequently preached message in Lee's sermons.[79] Lee conducted numerous revival meetings

---

[75] Seong-bong Lee, *Malo Mothamyeon Jukeumeuro*, 125.
[76] Gi-ho Seong, "Sajung Bokeumgwa Lee Seong-Bong Moksaui Buheungundong" [The Four-Fold Gospel and the Revival Movement of Seong-bong Lee's Revival Movement], edited by The Commemoration Committee of the 100th Anniversary of Lee Seong-Bong's Birth, *Lee Seong-Bong Moksaui Buheungundong Jomyeong* [The Examination of Seong-bong Lee's Revival Movement] (Seoul: Lifebook, 2000): 278.
[77] This later became one of his motivations to serve not only in the Holiness Church but also other denominational churches. See Seong-bong Lee, *Malo Mothamyeon Jukeumeuro*, 79.
[78] It was 1923 when Lee joined the Holiness Church.
[79] Dong-seon Lim, "Hanguk Gidokgyo Yeoksaae Yeongweonhi Bitnal Keun Byeol" [The Big Star that will always Shine in the History of the Korean Christianity], edited by The Commemoration Committee of the 100th Anniversary of Lee Seong-Bong's Birth, *Lee Seong-Bong Moksaui Buheungundong Jomyeong* [The Examination of Seong-bong Lee's Revival Movement] (Seoul: Lifebook, 2000): 76.

centred on the theology of repentance.[80] This crucial legacy of the Korean Church was characterised with a modifying word "thorough" as Lee admitted that his understanding of repentance was inadequate upon realising that "a thorough repentance should bear its fruits." Consequently, he sought to make amends for past wrongs, exemplified by his attempt to repay four times the cost of a rail ticket he had cheated on when he was 14 years old.[81] Others who attended his healing services similarly engaged in acts of restitution, such as an elder at a revival meeting in Andonghyeon who paid back what he had stolen from his nephew's house several decades ago.[82]

Thorough repentance, accompanied by practical indemnification, had been a tradition in the Korean Church since the Great Revival of 1907. A report by northern Presbyterian missionary William Blair on the outcome of the Spiritual Awakening in 1907 reveals that many individuals repented of their sins by making restitution for what they had stolen. Blair found it poignant when he witnessed members of his church returning what they had taken from the missionaries.[83] This type of thorough repentance, coupled with practical indemnification, characterised the Korean Church from its earliest days under the influence of the Revival movement, leaving a profound impact on Christian life. Lee was not an exception to this Christian tradition of thorough repentance.

Considering Lee's deep connection to the Holiness Church and its impact on his revival ministry, particularly in divine healing, it is undeniable that the Holiness Church played a significant role. As scholars have often observed, Lee's ministry was greatly influenced by the Holiness Church in terms of its motives, processes, methods, and character.[84] Lee himself openly attributes his successful ministries to his time at the Holiness Church Bible school, stating that "the 3-year training at the Bible school was a good preparation for my evangelistic life."[85] Lee firmly believed that he could witness divine healing by "receiving, relying on, experiencing, and preaching it [divine healing] as part of the four-fold Gospel of the Holiness Church."[86]

Another significant factor that influenced Lee's healing theology was the mystical context of the Korean Church. During the 1930s, when Lee emerged as a revivalist, the Korean Church was being swayed by the mysticism associated

---

[80] Gyeong-bae Min, "Lee Seong-Bong Moksaui Buheungundong Jaejomyeong," 213.
[81] Moreover, it is understandable that there were many similar results in Lee's revival meetings. Seong-bong Lee, *Malo Mothamyeon Jukeumeuro*, 38-39.
[82] Seong-bong Lee, *Immanuel Gangdan* [The Pulpit of Immanuel] (Seoul: Word of Life Books, 1993): 165.
[83] Yong-gyu Park, *Ibuleul Ggeuji Mara* [Do Not Quench This Fire] (Seoul: Seoul Cultural Publishers, 1968): 115.
[84] Geun-hwan Kang, "Lee Seong-Bong Moksaui Buheungsayeok," 137.
[85] Seong-bong Lee, *Malo Mothamyeon Jukeumeuro*, 41.
[86] Seong-bong Lee, *Malo Mothamyeon Jukeumeuro*, 100.

with Yong-do Lee, a movement that was not endorsed by the Holiness Church.[87] Myeong-jik Lee, a prominent theologian of the Holiness Church at the time, criticised Yong-do Lee's mysticism in an article titled "The Works of the Holy Spirit and of the Evil Spirit,"[88] published in the denominational magazine, *Hwalcheon*, in 1933. This created an environment where caution was necessary when it came to healing practitioners. It is evident that Lee's healing theology developed within this context while he was receiving theological education at his Bible school. He seemed to be aware of many mystical events, as expressed in his article for *Hwalcheon*:

> According to the Bible, divine healing is one of the Spiritual gifts. However, it has been reported many times in newspapers that someone prayed for the sick without knowing whether or not they are truly given the Spiritual gift of divine healing, and as a result caused big problems while behaving irrationally.[89]

Interestingly, despite being associated with numerous healing experiences in his revival meetings, Lee deliberately avoided making divine healing the central focus of his ministry. Instead, he cautioned that individuals who became Christians solely through miraculous experiences like healing could easily be tempted to embrace superstition and seek personal glory rather than acknowledging God.[90] Lee's belief was not merely theoretical; he had witnessed a female church member in Mokpo who strayed from the path of faith by succumbing to superstition and ultimately leaving the church.[91] Thus, Lee encouraged his audience to prioritise reading the Bible over seeking "signs and wonders."[92] In this specific context, he felt compelled to develop and present his perspective on divine healing in relation to the works of the Holy Spirit. He advised the Korean Church that "the baptism of the Holy Spirit is not about what can be seen in appearance, such as shaking of the body, seeing, smelling, or hearing something special."[93] Instead, he emphasised that the true transformation of the inner being is the fruit by which the genuine presence of the Holy Spirit

---

87 Myeong-su Park, "Lee Seong-Bong Moksaui Saengaewa Buheungundong" [Seong-bong Lee's Life and Revival Movement], edited by The Commemoration Committee of the 100th Anniversary of Lee Seong-Bong's Birth, *Lee Seong-Bong Moksaui Buheungundong Jomyeong* [The Examination of Seong-bong Lee's Revival Movement] (Seoul: Lifebook, 2000): 226.

88 Myeng-jik Lee, "Seongsinui Yeoksawa Akyeongui Yeoksa" [The Works of the Holy Spirit and the Evil Spirit], *Living Water* (April 1933): 1-4.

89 Seong-bong Lee, "Sowi Sinyu Godojareul Juuihal Il" [Be Careful with the so-called Healing Practitioners] *Living Water* (March 1938): 1.

90 Seong-bong Lee, "Bokheungsaeob Sunhoe Yakbo" [Report on Revival Ministry], *Hwal Cheon* (June 1939): 37.

91 Seong-bong Lee, *Malo Mothamyeon Jukeumeuro*, 50.

92 Seong-bong Lee, *Sarangui Gangdan*, 209-10.

93 Seong-bong Lee, *Sarangui Gangdan*, 48-49.

can be discerned.[94] This sheds light on why and how Lee's pneumatology needed to be developed from a soteriological perspective, without explicitly addressing the spiritual gift of healing.

Personal Context

The influence of Lee's parents on his life is an essential aspect that must be taken into account in any discussion of his biography. A significant transformation took place within Lee's family when they embraced Christianity, leading to a profound shift from a life of suffering to one filled with joy and a newfound devotion to God. The altered mindset of Lee's parents played a significant role in shaping his perspective on sin. Remarkably, Lee's initial observation of his parents' repentance became one of the fundamental theological pillars of his ministry. During a moment when his parents, accompanied by Lee, ascended a mountain to repent, he discerned a crucial truth: he had inherited a sinful nature from his parents.[95] This early recognition of human depravity from Lee's perspective engendered a conviction regarding the necessity of repentance, which naturally developed into the idea that illness stems from one's transgressions, thus making repentance the foremost priority.

Lee's personal life saw the development of a crucial concept: retributive justice. Drawing on his own experiences and the prevalent belief system in Korean society, Lee firmly believed in God's retributive justice as the cause behind most illnesses afflicting his family members. This theological orientation originated from his parents' acceptance of the deaths of Lee's two siblings as divine punishment, attributing the tragedy to their own sins.[96] Such notions became deeply ingrained in Lee's childhood, fostering the conviction that sins lead to illnesses as retribution. Conversations between Lee and his parents often revolved around this theological framework. When Lee strayed from his faith and doubted God, his mother consistently admonished him, warning that failure to repent when prompted by God would result in punishment.[97] These words foreshadowed the tragic consequences of Lee's wayward life, as he eventually fell gravely ill and experienced a sense of hopelessness while awaiting his impending demise. This message, conveyed by his mother, later became one of the central themes in Lee's revivalist ministry: "Repent! It is not true that sinners go to hell; rather, only those who do not repent face damnation."[98]

Within Korean society, there was a widespread belief that sickness was caused by spiritual entities and served as a form of "punishment."[99] Given the pervasive influence of the notion of retributive justice in Korean culture, Lee's

---

94 Seong-bong Lee, *Sarangui Gangdan*, 48-49.
95 Seong-bong Lee, *Malo Mothamyeon Jukeumeuro*, 17.
96 Seong-bong Lee, *Malo Mothamyeon Jukeumeuro*, 23.
97 Seong-bong Lee, *Malo Mothamyeon Jukeumeuro*, 28.
98 Seong-bong Lee, *Malo Mothamyeon Jukeumeuro*, 32-33.
99 Sung-deuk Oak, "Healing and Exorcism: Christian Encounters with Shamanism in early Modern Korea," *Asian Ethnology*, 69(1), (2010): 101.

perspective on retributive justice in the context of sickness as God's punishment naturally evolved.[100] This perspective found its roots in the broader concept of retributive justice,[101] which Lee theologised as God's justice. According to Lee, the presence of retributive justice manifesting in individuals, families, nations, and the world serves as evidence for the existence of God and underscores His just nature.[102] The surface resemblance between the justice of God and retributive justice represents part of this larger current in Lee's theological framework of God's punishment for which sicknesses can be instrumental. It becomes even more evident that the notion of retribution was highlighted in his sermons. He preached that "people must be recompensed for what they have done,"[103] and that "it is a natural principle that sin goes to the sinners, water flows through watercourses, we get out what we put in, and we get compensated for what we have done."[104] From the outset of his Christian life and ministry, Lee recognised the intrinsic connection between sickness and God's punishment.

The fervent devotion and zeal for God that Lee inherited from his mother formed the bedrock of his ministries. Reflecting on his childhood, Lee held deep admiration for his mother, who exhibited unwavering religious fervour immediately following her conversion. Describing her as possessing "zeal for the truth" and being "passionate in supplication," Lee quite often talked about this mother's enthusiasm for God while describing it as "the zeal for the truth," "in a passion of supplication that she wants to learn a hymn," "studying so hard," and "she became a teacher at a Christian school only six months after believing Jesus."[105] From these informative accounts, it becomes apparent that Lee extrapolated the valuable lesson of approaching life with earnestness and passion from his mother. It is evident that his mother's enthusiasm played a pivotal role in shaping Lee into the renowned revivalist he became, as her influence continuously encouraged and awakened his spiritual calling. Lee himself attested to the significant impact of his mother's devotion, stating, "I often find encouragement in memories of my mother […] Whenever I contemplate her

[100] It is notable that this theological notion was found before Lee's theological education. In this regard, cultural and religious factors seem to be more influential than Lee's theological training in forming retributive justice in Lee's healing theology.

[101] Retributive justice has been used to denote the idea of "what goes around comes around" in the sense that everything that occurs to us is the consequence of our own actions.

[102] Seong-bong Lee, *Sarangui Gangdan*, 195.

[103] Seong-bong Lee, "Myeongsimdo Ganghwa" [The Heart of Man], 1949, in *Cheolroyeokjeongganghwa, Myeongsimdoganghwa, Yonaseoganghwa*, edited by Seongbonghoe (Seoul: Lifebook, 1993): 259.

[104] Seong-bong Lee, "Yonaseoganghwa" [Jonah], 1957, in *Cheolroyeokjeongganghwa, Myeongsimdoganghwa, Yonaseoganghwa*, edited by Seongbonghoe (Seoul: Lifebook, 1993): 165.

[105] Sung-deuk Oak, "Healing and Exorcism," 18-20.

zeal, I am awakened."[106] Consequently, one cannot overlook the profound influence Lee's mother had on his upbringing, instilling in him Christian practices and values by frequently praying for him, teaching him the Korean language, encouraging his Bible reading to the extent that he completed the New Testament by the age of five, and guiding him in public prayer by the age of six.[107]

Another prominent figure in the establishment of Lee's healing theology is Ik-du Kim. The profound impact of Kim's influence on the evolution of Korean healing theology cannot be exaggerated, as exemplified by the inception of this research undertaking involving Ik-du Kim. The association between Kim and Lee exhibited remarkable strength, even during the formative years of Lee's life. The commencement of Lee's initial spiritual odyssey within the Presbyterian Church, where he spent his formative decade, is not a mere coincidence.[108] Lee's initial interaction with Kim occurred during Lee's attendance at Kim's Sincheon Presbyterian Church in Hwanghae state, as Lee's mother was invited by Kim to serve as a teacher at Gyeongsin Elementary School, an institution established by Kim's church. Lee remained under the tutelage of Kim until his family's departure from the Sincheon vicinity, transpiring when Lee reached the age of thirteen.[109] This encounter left a profound impression on the young Lee, as he revered Kim and was frequently inspired by his preaching, to the point of fostering an aspiration to become a revivalist like him in the future.[110] The influence of Kim persisted in Lee's life beyond his elementary school years, although Lee's autobiography does not provide detailed information regarding their relationship after 1913.

It is evident that Kim continued to wield influence even within the Holiness Church during the 1930s. Park's observations indicate that Kim's healing ministry found acceptance and garnered attention in the Holiness Church publication, *Hwalcheon*. Specifically, Kim's works such as "Heaven and Hell" in 1932, "The Baptism of the Holy Spirit" in 1934, and "The Demand of Life and the Bible" in 1937 were positively introduced in the magazine.[111] This suggests that Lee maintained a deep admiration for the esteemed revivalist Kim, particularly during periods when Kim focused primarily on pastoral endeavours, despite occasional involvement in revivalist ministries. This reverence for Kim as a revivalist is evident in Lee's testimony of his appointment as a national tour revivalist in 1937, 24 years after their last encounter. In a dream, Lee experienced a reconnection with his role model:

---

[106] Sung-deuk Oak, "Healing and Exorcism," 18-20, and Seong-bong Lee, *Immanuel Gangdan*, 102.
[107] Seong-bong Lee, *Malo Mothamyeon Jukeumeuro*, 21.
[108] Seong-bong Lee, *Malo Mothamyeon Jukeumeuro*, 79.
[109] Seong-bong Lee, *Malo Mothamyeon Jukeumeuro*, 23.
[110] Seong-bong Lee, *Malo Mothamyeon Jukeumeuro*, 24.
[111] Myeong-su Park, "Lee Seong-Bong Moksaui Saengaewa Buheungundong," 225.

> When I was attending the General Assembly, I was taking a nap in a small room on the fourth floor of the Bible school since I was so exhausted from praying all night and having meetings. Only half awake, I saw Pastor Kim coming to me and laying his hand in my right side to pray for me. As soon as his hot hands touched me, an explosion of fire took place in my body. It was so hot. I was taken by surprise while jumping off the bed, and realised that it was a dream [...] It was the baptism of the fire. On that night I was appointed as revival pastor.[112]

Lee correlated this encounter with his previous aspiration to emulate Kim as a renowned evangelist. This narrative demonstrates Lee's deep admiration for Kim, suggesting his desire to carry forward Kim's revivalist ministries. Remarkably, Kim was forcibly dismissed from his pastoral duties by Japanese authorities in 1942 because of his resistance against Shrine worship. It is noteworthy that this occurred just a few years after Lee embarked on his nationwide revival ministry. In this context, Hong argues that despite Lee's Holiness Church background, he inherited Kim's spiritual legacy as a revivalist.[113] Min advocates for the inclusion of the "structure" and "message" of Kim's revival meetings,[114] while Hong adds the element of "divine healing."[115]

While Ik-du Kim played a pivotal role in providing Lee with a practical model of revival ministry, Myeong-jik Lee's influence on Lee's healing theology surpassed that of Kim in terms of theological foundations. While Kim excelled as a nationwide revivalist, Myeong-jik Lee stood out as the most prominent scholar and revivalist within the Holiness Church. According to Noh, Myeong-jik Lee held the highest authority at the Gyeongseong Bible School, the denominational Bible school of the Korean Holiness Church, second only to foreign missionaries. By 1921, he became the driving force behind the Holiness Church's revival.[116] His influence extended to the denominational magazine, where he served as editor-in-chief in 1922, and to an administrative role on the board of directors for the Holiness Church in 1924.[117] Myeong-jik Lee had already established himself as a prominent figure when Seong-bong Lee entered the Bible school in 1925. Lee's admiration for Myeong-jik Lee as his teacher stemmed not only from his role and position but also from the profound impact of his lectures and sermons.[118] Lee's love and admiration for his teacher were

---

[112] Seong-bong Lee, *Malo Mothamyeon Jukeumeuro*, 62.
[113] Gyeong-bae Min, "Lee Seong-Bong Moksaui Buheungundong Jaejomyeong," 192.
[114] Gyeong-bae Min, "Lee Seong-Bong Moksaui Buheungundong Jaejomyeong," 189.
[115] Chi-mo Hong, "Lee Seong-Bong Moksaui Saengaewa Sinang Sasang" [Seong-bong Lee's Life and Religious Belief], edited by The Commemoration Committee of the 100th Anniversary of Lee Seong-Bong's Birth, *Lee Seong-Bong Moksaui Buheungundong Jomyeong* [The Examination of Seong-bong Lee's Revival Movement] (Seoul: Lifebook, 2000): 497.
[116] Jae-yang Noh, "A Study on Revival Movement by Rev. Sung Bong Lee" (Ph.D. diss., Hoseo Divinity School, 2004): 58.
[117] Jae-yang Noh, "A Study on Revival Movement by Rev. Sung Bong Lee," 58.
[118] Seong-bong Lee, *Malo Mothamyeon Jukeumeuro*, 38.

frequently observed by others. Kang, who later served as the general superintendent of the Holiness Church, witnessed that "Lee always trusted his teacher and listened to him."[119] If Lee's theological perspectives were shaped during his time at the Bible school, the influence of Myeong-jik Lee, both in terms of his position and the respect Lee held for him as his teacher, must be considered the most significant factor.

One shared aspect between Myeong-jik Lee and Seong-bong Lee was their emphasis on the four-fold Gospel centred on repentance. A report on Myeong-jik Lee's revival meeting vividly describes the atmosphere as follows:

> Because of the prominent works of the Holy Spirit, the general attendants were showed by grace when the thick cloud was opened and the rain of grace fell down. The place was filled with the feeling of effervescence through the repentance of sin offering, humble testimony and fierce repentance from all the audience together with male and female ministers.[120]

While this depiction possesses a more poetic quality than Seong-bong Lee's report, the salient point remains the same: it is the works of the Holy Spirit that prompt repentance among individuals, always accompanied by an indescribable sense of joy.[121] This recurring message within the Korean Church, particularly within the Holiness Church, was further developed in a more systematic manner following the revival movements of 1903 and 1907, specifically concerning the four-fold Gospel. In this context, the influence of Myeong-jik Lee appears to be twofold: repentance and healing. Repentance was a key factor in understanding the significant works of the Holy Spirit, while healing was regarded as a core message that the church should proclaim as part of the gospel. Especially noteworthy is Lee's understanding, learned from his time at the Bible school under Myeong-jik Lee, that thorough repentance is a prerequisite for divine healing.

Lastly, Lee's personal encounter with healing in the context of his illness played a crucial and formative role in the development of his theology on the subject of healing. Park asserts that Lee's extraordinary encounters with divine healing subsequently became the fundamental underpinnings of his healing

---

[119] Shin-chan Kang, "Naega Mannan Geoin Lee Seong-Bong Moksa" [Seong-bong Lee, The Giant that I have met], edited by The Commemoration Committee of the 100th Anniversary of Lee Seong-Bong's Birth, *Lee Seong-Bong Moksaui Buheungundong Jomyeong* [The Examination of Seong-bong Lee's Revival Movement] (Seoul: Lifebook, 2000): 17.

[120] Myeong-jik Lee, "*Gyeongnameseo Iljugan*" [A Week in Gyeongnam] *Living Water* (October 1924): 47.

[121] This echoes Kim's notion of repentance. Kim and Lee shared a basic pneumatological concept of regeneration, although Lee added one more aspect of sanctification to it.

ministries.[122] This line of argumentation holds persuasive merit, particularly when one acknowledges that Lee was not merely a healing practitioner who administered numerous healings to others, but rather a living testimony to the transformative power of divine healing in his own life. Lee exclusively relied on his personal instances of healing when composing one of the chapters of his autobiography titled "The Miracle of Divine Healing," choosing to highlight his own experience rather than recounting healing narratives pertaining to others. In this chapter, Lee meticulously expounded upon his personal encounter with healing, providing a comprehensive and detailed account of his own transformative experience:

> I was suffering from pulmonary distoma for a long time which caused me to be called Mayfly [since his appearance was awfully thin as if he may die soon]. I was so emaciated when I studied at my Bible school and when I pastored in Suwon. However, I was healed of diseases including peritonitis by praying day and night while recuperating for several months. I later became a fatty [*sic*] weighing about 82.5 kilograms.[123]

From the outset of his life and throughout his ministry, experiences of divine healing served as a powerful message deeply rooted in Lee's personal life.

These personal healing experiences provided tangible evidence for Lee's theological premise that sickness can be a consequence of sin. In his initial encounter with healing, he had to confess all his sins, such as breaking the Sabbath, indulging in excessive drinking, and engaging in various immoral actions. Interestingly, Lee's mother directly equated these actions with "breaking God's commandments" and believed that his sickness was a direct consequence.[124] A similar event occurred when Lee faced a life-threatening illness at the age of 28, when he chose to rely solely on repentance and divine healing, refusing medical treatment.[125] These personal experiences of sickness and healing served as powerful reminders of the teachings Lee had received at the Bible school, namely that sickness is the result of sin and originates from Satan.[126] Lee's personal encounters with divine healing from the earliest stages of his Christian life became the firm foundation for his healing theology, emphasising that repentance should be sought first when people fall ill.

---

[122] Myeong-su Park, "Lee Seong-bong Moksaui Saengaewa Buheungundong," 226.

[123] Seong-bong Lee, *Malo Mothamyeon Jukeumeuro*, 100.

[124] Interestingly, Lee's mother was more straightforward in rebuking Lee for his sins of "breaking God's commandment" and "disobeying his parents." See Seong-bong Lee, *Malo Mothamyeon Jukeumeuro*, 29-30.

[125] Seong-bong Lee, *Malo Mothamyeon Jukeumeuro*, 47.

[126] See Seong-bong Lee, *Buheungui Bigyeol* [The Secret of Revival] (Seoul: Word of Life Books, 1993): 49; Seong-bong Lee, *Sarangui Gangdan*, 151. However, Lee also presented other causes of sickness such as carelessness, overwork, immoderation, God's punishment, training for blessings, for God's glory. See Seong-bong Lee, *Buheungui Bigyeol*, 48.

Furthermore, Lee's theological understanding expanded the simplified sequence of "sin leads to sickness" to a more nuanced theology of suffering. Drawing from his personal healing experiences, he believed that sickness or suffering were not always evil. This perspective necessitates further exploration under the theological concept of providence. Lee regarded God's providence as one of the three most crucial elements, alongside the power and love of God, that characterised his entire life, as stated in his autobiography:

> I thank God that I have lived my whole life under the Lord's power, love, and providence since my birth to the Korean Peninsula. I am composing this book wishing that many people may realise the Lord's power, love and providence through this humble autobiography.[127]

For Lee, every experience he went through was considered part of God's providence. The first incident that showcased God's providence occurred when his sickness was not immediately healed after his conversion but persisted for another three years. During this time, Lee was arrested by Japanese authorities for his involvement in supporting the independence movement but was subsequently released on account of his illness.[128] Lee's theology of healing posited that everything that transpired, whether it brought joy or sadness, health or sickness, life or death,[129] was under God's providence. This understanding was firmly rooted in his belief that God is in control of all things. Lee's personal encounters with sickness became an opportunity for him to reaffirm his faith.[130] In other words, sickness was not seen solely as a punitive aspect of God's providence in Lee's theology but also as a starting point for new life in Jesus. This perspective led Lee to develop the argument that "one must undergo a dramatic experience of miraculous healing in order to be trained as an influential evangelist."[131] Having delved into the various aspects of Lee's perspective on God's providence, it becomes evident that everything can be employed according to God's will, even sickness. This practical theology formed the core of Lee's understanding, grounded in his own experiences of personal suffering.

---

127 Seong-bong Lee, *Malo Mothamyeon Jukeumeuro*, preface.
128 Seong-bong Lee, *Malo Mothamyeon Jukeumeuro*, 34-35.
129 Seong-bong Lee, *Malo Mothamyeon Jukeumeuro*, preface.
130 Myeong-su Park, "Lee Seong-Bong Moksaui Saengaewa Buheungundong," 219.
131 Seong-bong Lee, *Buheungui Bigyeol*, 164.

Healing Theology

Healing and Suffering

Lee's definition of divine healing entails God's intervention, described as both "supernatural" [132] and "direct," [133] to bring about healing in the sick. Consequently, divine healing is regarded as a "supernatural treatment" while medical treatment is considered a "natural one."[134] The central focus of divine healing revolves around "the power and promise of God to heal."[135] While Lee's theology does not deem reliance on medical treatment as sinful, it emphasises the importance of prioritising God's supernatural treatment over natural methods. [136] Remarkably, Lee's autobiography contains no record of his utilisation of medical treatment; instead, he consistently declined it and relied on persistent prayer for divine healing.[137]

Lee's theology attributes the purpose and motivation behind divine healing to the glorification of God. He sought to establish his healing theology on Psalm 50:15, which states, "And call upon Me in the day of trouble; I shall rescue you, and you will honour Me." Lee's principal argument asserts that "the motivation of divine healing must be for the glory of God."[138] This notion gave rise to two additional theological arguments: first, that divine healing serves as a powerful tool "to spread the gospel,"[139] and second, that those seeking healing must commit to "living the rest of their lives for God."[140] In Lee's healing theology, divine healing is not merely a miraculous experience; rather, it marks the commencement of a new life dedicated to God's Kingdom. For Lee, a life lived for God's glory entails complete dedication to an evangelistic ministry that expands God's Kingdom through signs and wonders, including divine healing. His belief that the "authority and power to heal the sick was given to the disciples in the Bible for the spread of the gospel"[141] led him to a life and ministry wholly devoted to healing endeavours, with the goal of bringing numerous individuals to God. In this regard, Kim believed that his healing ministry provided an opportunity to share the gospel with countless people.[142]

In Lee's theology, suffering occupies a unique place, as he posits sin as the primary cause of sickness. Sin is perceived as capable of "destroying not only souls and bodies but also individuals, families, societies, and countries."[143]

---

132 Seong-bong Lee, *Sarangui Gangdan*, 65.
133 Seong-bong Lee, *Buheungui Bigyeol*, 48
134 Seong-bong Lee, *Buheungui Bigyeol*, 47.
135 Seong-bong Lee, *Buheungui Bigyeol*, 47.
136 Seong-bong Lee, *Buheungui Bigyeol*, 47.
137 Seong-bong Lee, *Malo Mothamyeon Jukeumeuro*, 101.
138 Seong-bong Lee, *Buheungui Bigyeol*, 47.
139 Seong-bong Lee, *Sarangui Gangdan*, 65.
140 Seong-bong Lee, *Buheungui Bigyeol*, 50.
141 Seong-bong Lee, *Sarangui Gangdan*, 65.
142 Seong-bong Lee, *Malo Mothamyeon Jukeumeuro*, 86.
143 Seong-bong Lee, *Sarangui Gangdan*, 150-51.

Consequently, the world is a place replete with tears and suffering, serving as a temporary dwelling before the eternal one.[144] This is where the significance of Jesus' ministry emerges in Lee's view. While complete healing will ultimately be bestowed in the *parousia*, it is crucial to recognise that Jesus desired to heal the sick in the present world.

Lee considered sin as "a doorway to God's punishment."[145] However, the good news embedded within his healing theology is that God's punishment does not signify the end of the story. Sickness and suffering also serve as another beginning of "God's providence."[146] In this respect, Park evaluates Lee's preaching of repentance during his revival meetings as a message of God's blessings following repentance, leading to a "happy end."[147]

Indeed, Lee's healing theology also ascribes meaning to suffering or sickness as another opportunity to "hear the voice of God,"[148] to "be renewed,"[149] and to "be fully dependent on God."[150] One of his sermons affirms, "It is God's providence that those who trust themselves and their environment become solely dependent on God through the instrument of suffering, which aids in our purification. Therefore, believe that suffering is permitted by God."[151] The significant role played by Lee's experience of illness and healing is evident in his confession that, through the suffering caused by his illnesses, he underwent training and purification to become God's servant.[152] Consequently, suffering should not be understood as a permanent divine punishment, but as an act of discipline enacted with love and care. Lee regarded his illness as a divine action stemming from "the absolute love of God" in order to "re-create" him as a new person for God's purpose.[153]

This theology of suffering further develops the notion that when faced with suffering, one should not fear it but instead consider it a source of pure joy. Lee's teachings emphasise that "everything comes from God," and that suffering serves as a crucial test of faith, ultimately becoming the foundations for joy.[154] In other words, God employs sickness as part of His sovereign plan, and those who are sick can still find joy not necessarily because they believe they will be physically healed, but because they have faith that God is in control and that His will is always what is best for them. The theological core of suffering in Lee's beliefs is firmly rooted in God's providence and sovereignty.

---

[144] Seong-bong Lee, *Sarangui Gangdan*, 144.
[145] Seong-bong Lee, *Buheungui Bigyeol*, 51.
[146] Seong-bong Lee, *Buheungui Bigyeol*, 227.
[147] Myeong-su Park, "Lee Seong-Bong Moksaui Saengaewa Buheungundong," 223.
[148] Seong-bong Lee, *Buheungui Bigyeol*, 50.
[149] Seong-bong Lee, *Immanuel Gangdan*, 54.
[150] Seong-bong Lee, *Buheungui Bigyeol*, 227.
[151] Seong-bong Lee, *Buheungui Bigyeol*, 227.
[152] Seong-bong Lee, *Sarangui Gangdan*, 28-29.
[153] Seong-bong Lee, *Malo Mothamyeon Jukeumeuro*, 34-35.
[154] Seong-bong Lee, *Sarangui Gangdan*, 25-28.

Prayer

Prayer played a pivotal role in the transformation of Lee's life, propelling him to become a successful revivalist renowned for performing numerous miracles in his ministries. From an early age, Lee cultivated a prayerful life and held a steadfast faith in the efficacy of prayer, firmly believing that God would answer all sincere prayers.[155] Unsurprisingly, Lee is widely remembered and esteemed as a "man of prayer,"[156] with his ministries being characterised as thoroughly undergirded by prayer.[157] This association stems from Lee's healing theology, which positions prayer as a practical tool for accessing God's healing power. He presented his idea on the power of prayer in arguing that "if one prays in troubles, the suffering disappears and all the hard problems are solved [...] Through prayer, all diseases can be healed and the weak become strong."[158]

In discussing the significance of prayer for healing, he asserted that he could not only receive healing for his sickness but also heal the sick because God's healing power is what God's children can deliver to the sick through their prayers.[159] Lee was aware of the power of prayer for healing not in the sense that special healing power abides in prayer but in the sense that the healing power always comes from the almighty God through prayer. Thus, prayer is the conduit of God's healing power. In other words, prayer is instrumental in the process of bringing healing power from the divine Healer to the sick since, for Lee, the power of prayer is to be given as the special privilege of being a child of the omnipotent and omniscience God.[160] From Lee's perspective, the essence of prayer for healing lies not in human efforts, but in surrendering to God's divine authority.

Lee's comprehensive definition of prayer encompasses its manifold dimensions, viewing it as "God's will," "commandment," "life of believers," "sanctified life," "spiritual warfare against Satan," "action of faith towards God," as well as "an action of love towards people."[161] However, in a narrower sense, Lee defined prayer as "a great weapon[162] to overcome sufferings."[163] The importance of prayer in relation to suffering is illuminated by his succinct statement that prayer allows one to comprehend the significance of hardships, and even if they persist, prayer endows individuals with the strength to overcome

---

155 Seong-bong Lee, *Malo Mothamyeon Jukeumeuro*, 21.

156 Dong-seon Lim, "Hanguk Gidokgyo Yeoksaae Yeongweonhi Bitnal Keun Byeol," 76.

157 In-gyo Jeong, *Sindeok Gyohoe 70 Junyeon Haksul Nonmunjib*, 149-52.

158 Seong-bong Lee, *Sarangui Gangdan*, 30-31.

159 Seong-bong Lee, "Revival Tour," 38; Seong-bong Lee, *Malo Mothamyeon Jukeumeuro*, 101; 119-20.

160 Seong-bong Lee, *Sarangui Gangdan*, 201.

161 Seong-bong Lee, *Sarangui Gangdan*, 82-83.

162 This concept was further developed in his healing theology of spiritual warfare soon after the Korean War.

163 Seong-bong Lee, *Buheungui Bigyeol*, 227.

or endure them.[164] In the context of sickness, prayer serves not only to bring physical healing but also fosters a deeper understanding of, gratitude toward, and love for God.[165] Thus, Lee's healing theology of prayer extends beyond prayers for healing to encompass endurance in suffering and the expression of love for God.

As far as the form of prayer is concerned, earnest prayer is the number one principle. Lee always emphasised its value in teaching his congregation how to pray with some keywords such as "desperate attitude,"[166] "sincerity, earnest, and ardent heart."[167] Lee's message emphasised that the greater the troubles one faces, the more fervent their prayers should be.[168] He suggested that one should pray earnestly and wholeheartedly in order to make the prayer effective.[169] This is because of his belief that a prayer without eagerness will not be answered[170] and God will answer the prayers of those who are desperately seeking Him.[171]

To support this theological standpoint, Lee referred to two biblical passages: Luke 11:8 and Mark 2:1-12. Lee interpreted the story of requesting three loaves of bread in Luke 11:8 to underscore the necessity of persistent and importunate prayer.[172] Likewise, he highlighted the passion exhibited by the four men who carried their sick friend to Jesus by creating an opening in the roof in Mark 2, arguing that this fervent and persistent entreaty "moved the heart of the Lord."[173] Lee also drew support from other significant biblical references, such as 2 Chronicles 16:9, which emphasises God's strengthening of those fully committed to Him, and Psalm 119:131, which expresses the longing for God's commandments. Lee's primary contention was that lukewarm prayers would not receive answers,[174] whereas earnest prayers would ultimately unleash God's power upon the infirm.

This theological concept was not merely a theoretical construct Lee acquired through study, but rather a living testimony derived from personal experience. During a revival meeting in Haenam, Lee himself encountered appendicitis. Despite a doctor's warning of potential death or permanent disability, Lee chose

---

164 Seong-bong Lee, *Buheungui Bigyeol*, 227.
165 Seong-bong Lee, *Sarangui Gangdan*, 123.
166 Seong-bong Lee, *Buheungui Bigyeol*, 90.
167 Seong-bong Lee, *Buheungui Bigyeol*, 93.
168 Deuk-hyeon Kim, "Pyeongsindorosseo Naegabon Lee Seong-Bong Moksanim" [Rev. Seong-bong Lee whom I have met as a Layperson], edited by The Commemoration Committee of the 100th Anniversary of Lee Seong-Bong's Birth, *Lee Seong-Bong Moksaui Buheungundong Jomyeong* [The Examination of Seong-bong Lee's Revival Movement] (Seoul: Lifebook, 2000): 30.
169 Seong-bong Lee, *Buheungui Bigyeol*, 94.
170 Seong-bong Lee, *Sarangui Gangdan*, 87.
171 Seong-bong Lee, *Immanuel Gangdan*, 21.
172 Seong-bong Lee, *Sarangui Gangdan*, 88.
173 Seong-bong Lee, *Sarangui Gangdan*, 88.
174 Seong-bong Lee, *Sarangui Gangdan*, 87.

not to pursue medical treatment but instead fervently prayed for healing. Miraculously, his prayers were answered, and he experienced divine healing. Inspired by this profound encounter with God's healing power through earnest prayer, Lee composed a song titled "I am the Jehovah who heals You," which encapsulated his theological understanding of prayer for healing as follows:

> 1. Little boy! Little boy! Look at me with an easy mind/ Look at me in silence. I am your Lord.
> 2. Look at me although the pain of your sickness is severe/The sip of the bitter glass of the Cross! The Living Water!
> 3. My Lord! Let your will be done. I trust you/ I will bring you the glory to you whether in death or in life/ Look up to me with hope and be saved/ Call upon my name in trouble days and I will deliver you/ You will glorify me.
>
> (Chorus) Stand firm in your faith and look up to me with hope.[175]

Notably, the central focus of the song is not on the sick individual but on God, with only a few sentences containing the words of the sick person. Interestingly, the sick person does not explicitly request healing but rather submits to God's will. Nevertheless, it becomes evident that the underlying theme is God's call for the sick person to continuously fix their gaze upon the divine Healer as a source of hope. This foundation underlies Lee's healing theology, emphasising that divine healing primarily originates from God. However, the individual seeking healing is called to actively participate in the process through consistent and earnest prayer, fuelled by hope and trust. Hence, Lee posited that "the Lord reveals Himself and bestows grace upon those who ardently desire Him."[176] In other words, the defining characteristic of divine healing is grace, which cannot be earned through human merit but is conditioned by the willingness and earnest desire of the sick through prayer *in response to* the grace.

Lee's earnest prayer was expressed in various forms, such as prayer vigils, prayer and fasting, early morning prayer, and mountain prayer. When Lee faced uncertainty about his calling and his preparedness to commence ministry upon graduating from Bible school, his initial response was to engage in a fast accompanied by prayer. For Lee, fasting prayer served as a means of dependency on God, seeking "new power and wisdom" for his ministry.[177] It was frequently observed that whenever Lee perceived limitations in his ministry or sought God's divine enablement, he turned to prayer and fasting,[178] recognising prayer as a

---

[175] Seong-bong Lee, *Malo Mothamyeon Jukeumeuro*, 102.
[176] Seong-bong Lee, *Immanuel Gangdan*, 25.
[177] Seong-bong Lee, *Malo Mothamyeon Jukeumeuro*, 41.
[178] Lee asked God for power and wisdom for his new ministry after graduation (Seong-bong Lee, *Malo Mothamyeon Jukeumeuro*, 41) and he prepared himself in prayer and fasting for an important preaching ministry in the United States. See Seong-bong Lee, "*Miguk Sunwoe Jeondogi*" [Report on Revival Tour in the United States] *Living Waters* (October 1959): 28-29.

means to dismantle Satan's authority through the work of God.[179] Testifying to the power of prayer, Lee recounted instances of divine healing he experienced throughout his life, including the healing of pulmonary distomiasis during his childhood and the recovery from various ailments during his college and pastoral years in the Suwon area. In his autobiography, he attributed these healings to his tireless prayers day and night.[180] Furthermore, mountain prayer held significant importance in Lee's life and ministry. His earliest encounter with mountain prayer occurred in his childhood and it later became a weekly church event for his congregation, particularly when extraordinary intervention from God was sought.[181] Mountain prayer was employed when Lee's prayers necessitated intensified focus, enabling him to present his urgent and fervent petitions before God.

Another manifestation of earnest prayer in Lee's ministry was evident in the practice of dawn prayer, which took place during his revival meetings. It has been often reported by Lee himself and observed by others that many individuals experienced healing during dawn services. Interestingly, the term 새벽기도회 (*sae-byeok-gido-hoe*), which literally means dawn prayer meetings, is widely accepted in Korean culture. It is to be noted that the morning services underscored the primacy of prayer within such gatherings. They were dedicated sessions of fervent prayer. Not surprisingly, many healings took place during the dawn meetings, and the healings witnessed during these gatherings were attributed to Lee's prayers and the laying on of his hands upon the sick.

Regarding the practice of laying on of hands, there are differing interpretations among scholars. Noh argues that divine healing in Lee's ministry was not a direct result of his prayers accompanied by the laying on of hands. Instead, Noh attributes healing to the collective prayers of the sick individual and those joining together to pray for healing.[182] In contrast, Hong asserts that Lee indeed facilitated healing through prayer and the laying on of hands, drawing parallels between Lee's approach and Ik-du Kim's healing ministries.[183] Considering the available evidence, Hong's viewpoint appears more substantiated, given the firsthand witness accounts of Lee's healing ministry. Deuk-hyeon Kim, who attended Lee's revival meetings, testified that Lee deliberately chose the dawn prayer meeting as a context for the laying on of hands, engaging in prayer alongside lead pastors after emphasising repentance.[184] Despite numerous witnesses attesting to Lee's practice of laying on of hands, he

---

[179] Seong-bong Lee, *Malo Mothamyeon Jukeumeuro*, 41.
[180] Seong-bong Lee, *Malo Mothamyeon Jukeumeuro*, 100.
[181] Seong-bong Lee, *Malo Mothamyeon Jukeumeuro*, 17; 51-52.
[182] Jae-yang Noh, "A Study on Revival Movement by Rev. Sung Bong Lee," 101.
[183] See Chi-mo Hong, "Lee Seong-Bong Moksaui Saengaewa Sinang Sasang," and as a witness to Lee's prayer of laying on hands, also see Shin-chang Kang, "Naega Mannan Geoin Lee Seong-Bong Moksa," 16.
[184] Deuk-hyeon Kim, "Pyeongsindorosseo Naegabon Lee Seong-Bong Moksanim," 31.

did not provide an elaborate theological explanation for its necessity, apart from brief comments during his teachings on divine healing. Nonetheless, Lee positioned prayer with laying on of hands as the foremost element among nine identified components.[185]

However, it is noteworthy that Lee did not endorse the notion that prayer itself possessed the ability to generate divine power or exert control over God. In fact, he cautioned against viewing prayer as a means to pursue supernatural wonders, revelations, fasting, speaking in tongues, healing, or prophecy.[186] Lee expressed concerns that excessive attention and significance attributed to prayer itself could lead individuals astray, fostering heretical beliefs. When considering prayer as a vehicle for accessing God's healing power, it is crucial to acknowledge that Lee placed greater emphasis on self-reflection, life transformation, and discerning God's will amidst suffering, rather than focusing solely on the physical restoration of the sick body.

Faith

Within Lee's theological framework of healing, prayer assumes a profound significance; however, its efficacy is contingent upon the presence of faith. In signifying the value of faith embodied in prayer, Lee introduced a story at a church in Geumcheon:

> There was a lady who showed signs of mental disorder due to the distress rooted from her sins. It was a worry in the church for a while. She eventually received her spiritual and physical salvation after praying in faith, leading to giving great glory to God.[187]

In fact, it was not prayer alone by which the sick could be healed, but prayer accompanied by faith was pointed out as a condition of divine healing. This is because for Lee, "the prayer without faith cannot please God, and it is like trifling with God."[188] Moreover, it is important to know that although faith takes a significant position in Lee's healing theology, Lee considered it as one of the "conditions"[189] and "methods"[190] of divine healing, which means faith is not the only element leading to divine healing.

Regarding the nature of faith necessary for divine healing, Lee elucidated several aspects. First, he argued that divine healing transpires through "faith in the promise and power of God, and God's will to heal."[191] Although Lee

---

[185] Commandment, holding hands, rebuke, repentance, faith of the sick, faith of middle person, the power of the Holy Spirit given through the BHS, and spiritual gift. See Seong-bong Lee, *Buheungui Bigyeol,* 48.

[186] Seong-bong Lee, *Sarangui Gangdan*, 173.

[187] Seong-bong Lee, "Revival Tour" *Living Waters* (October 1938): 38.

[188] Seong-bong Lee, *Sarangui Gangdan*, 88.

[189] Seong-bong Lee, *Buheungui Bigyeol*, 47.

[190] Seong-bong Lee, *Buheungui Bigyeol*, 48.

[191] Seong-bong Lee, *Buheungui Bigyeol*, 47.

acknowledged that God does not heal all afflicted individuals, his healing theology emphasised the faith that God desires to heal, based on biblical passages depicting instances of divine healing and the promised restoration of such healing in the same manner.

Secondly, the benevolent nature of God, characterised by love, was frequently acknowledged as the source of granting requests.[192] Observations repeatedly indicated that those who witnessed divine healing returned to God while praising Him for "His power and love."[193] This faith in God's power and love serves as the fundamental bedrock of Lee's healing theology, as he also stated that "divine healing is bestowed upon those who believe and rely on power and love."[194] This supports the notion that, within Lee's healing theology, God exhibits sufficient power to heal the sick, and healing is generally perceived as God's will, stemming from His loving nature.

Lee further introduced another crucial conditional phrase in his healing theology of faith: "Jesus is the same yesterday, today, and forever."[195] The unchanging nature of Jesus, who exemplified great divine healing, forms the core of Lee's healing theology. In his sermons on "How to receive Healing," Lee emphasised the significance of faith by asserting, "Believe in divine healing. Let it be done as you believe. Jesus is unchangeable."[196] Two notable points here are "as you believe" and "Jesus is unchangeable." These indicate that healing is granted in response to the faith of the sick individual and that faith should be anchored in Jesus, who remains constant. Lee reiterated this sentiment in another sermon, stating, "Since Jesus Christ is the same yesterday, today, and forever, He still heals through His power and love."[197] Belief in the unchanging power and love of Jesus stands as one of the most pivotal pillars of Lee's healing theology with respect to faith.

Additionally, the sovereignty of God merits further examination, given that numerous stories within Lee's personal experiences of suffering and healing revolve around the will of God. Lee boldly asserted that "since life, death, happiness, and misery" are all within God's control, "everything comes from and goes to God."[198] This premise, testified in the preface of Lee's autobiography,[199] lays the foundation for his life. For instance, when Lee's mother's suicide attempt failed, he regarded it as "God's providence."[200] Similarly, when he suffered an injury on a Sunday morning, he questioned God in his prayer to understand the reason behind his affliction, firmly believing that "not even a

---

192 Seong-bong Lee, *Sarangui Gangdan*, 109.
193 Seong-bong Lee, *Malo Mothamyeon Jukeumeuro*, 42.
194 Seong-bong Lee, *Sarangui Gangdan*, 65.
195 Seong-bong Lee, *Sarangui Gangdan*, 65.
196 Seong-bong Lee, *Buheungui Bigyeol*, 50.
197 Seong-bong Lee, *Sarangui Gangdan*, 154-55.
198 Seong-bong Lee, *Malo Mothamyeon Jukeumeuro*, preface.
199 Seong-bong Lee, *Malo Mothamyeon Jukeumeuro*, preface.
200 Seong-bong Lee, *Malo Mothamyeon Jukeumeuro*, 18.

single hair can be harmed without God's permission."[201] In this regard, Lee's healing theology evolved from the notion of petitioning God for healing to comprehending the underlying causes of suffering. Lee's understanding of divine healing focused on discerning the reasons behind afflictions, rather than merely proclaiming God's healing promises or power. This emphasis on the sovereignty of God emerges as a key element in Lee's healing theology. This profound belief significantly influenced his life, prompting him to seek God's will above all else, even when he himself was in need of divine healing.

Furthermore, it is noteworthy that in the song composed by Lee concerning divine healing, only two verses out of eleven are the words of the little sick boy while the other nine verses are of the healing God: "My Lord! Let your will be done. I trust you/ I will bring the glory to you whether in death or in life."[202] The song transcends the matter of life and death, as it serves as a prayer for God's will rather than a plea for healing. This highlights Lee's unwavering faith that everything originates from God and returns to Him.[203] According to Lee, God's sovereignty reigns supreme in his healing theology. In one of his sermons, Lee quoted a believer's definition of faith, stating that "Faith is the eyes to see God, the ears to listen to God's voice, the hands to hold God, and the tongue to taste God."[204] This quotation harmonises well with Lee's theology, underscoring the idea that faith itself does not generate healing power but rather facilitates the sick individual's understanding of God's nature. Lee's position, in its basic thrust, is that it is not human faith demanding God to heal the sick but the will of God revealing God's divine plan to the sick.

Repentance

The concept of repentance within the context of the Korean Church, as a foundational principle bequeathed through the great revival movements dating back to 1903 and 1907, has been substantially framed and organised by Lee, particularly through the prism of divine healing. Lee propounds the view that initial recognition of personal sins is a prerequisite for those who seek healing from illness.[205] This assertion stems from his conviction that "sickness is a consequence of sin, delivered by Satan as a form of retribution,"[206] and "the majority of illnesses arise from sin."[207] His rationale for this belief is rooted in the understanding that ailments did not plague the Garden of Eden, but rather emerged as a result of the sin of Adam and Eve – the inaugural sin in existence

---

[201] Seong-bong Lee, *Malo Mothamyeon Jukeumeuro*, 60. This specific phrase is also found in his preaching. Also see Seong-bong Lee, *Immanuel Gangdan*, 173.

[202] Seong-bong Lee, *Malo Mothamyeon Jukeumeuro*, 102.

[203] However, in Lee's understanding of God's sovereignty, it is hard to find a notion that God must be responsible for evil in the world.

[204] Seong-bong Lee, *Sarangui Gangdan*, 110.

[205] Seong-bong Lee, *Buheungui Bigyeol*, 50

[206] Seong-bong Lee, *Buheungui Bigyeol*, 49.

[207] Seong-bong Lee, *Buheungui Bigyeol*, 46.

– which set the stage for a life of suffering.[208] Lee bolstered this viewpoint by emphasising the ubiquitous nature of sin, asserting:

> It is sin that destroys each individual, family, society, and country. Sin also destroys body and soul. The main cause of downfall is sin whether in the past or the future. It is only by faith in the Lord Jesus that one can be saved from sins while even a small sin cannot be defeated by our power, wisdom, or any means.[209]

According to Lee's interpretation, human beings are living amidst the repercussions of the Fall, enduring pain and the affliction of sickness. This provides a theological backdrop to understand how illness could infiltrate this universe, influencing individuals, families, societies, nations, and even the natural world.

Acknowledging the origins of sickness and death, he underscored divine healing as an exclusive privilege of Christians, granted only to those who confessed their sins and accepted Jesus. In this context, Jeong accurately comprehends that, in Lee's healing theology, achieving salvation from sins is a fundamental task, as "all suffering originates from the issue of sin."[210] This idea led Lee to believe that a theology of healing needed to be established in correlation with salvation, as observed by Noh.[211] Lee perceived divine healing as an extension of God's redemptive work through Jesus:

> The God who created both our spirit and body also wants to save not only our spirit but also our body by sending His Son as flesh. Jesus, who healed many sick people through his words and hands, gave his disciples authority to spread the gospel through signs and wonders. Jesus is the same yesterday, today, and forever. It [divine healing] will be given even today to those who believe and rely on the [healing] power with love as it is.[212]

Within Lee's perspective, healing functions as a physical salvation procured through Jesus. Consequently, divine healing holds equal significance as spiritual salvation and is unveiled as an exhibition of the power and love of Jesus. This reasoning prompted Lee to frequently employ the phrase "salvation of the body" to describe healing.[213]

---

208 Seong-bong Lee, *Buheungui Bigyeol*, 46-47.
209 Seong-bong Lee, *Sarangui Gangdan*, 151.
210 Jin-gyeong Jeong, "Naegabon Lee Seong-Bong Moksa" [Rev. Seong-bong Lee that I observed], edited by The Commemoration Committee of the 100th Anniversary of Lee Seong-Bong's Birth, *Lee Seong-Bong Moksaui Buheungundong Jomyeong* [The Examination of Seong-bong Lee's Revival Movement] (Seoul: Lifebook, 2000): 96.
211 Jae-yang Noh, "A Study on Revival Movement by Rev. Sung Bong Lee," 159.
212 Seong-bong Lee, *Sarangui Gangdan*, 65.
213 Seong-bong Lee, "Revival Tour," 85.

For Lee, divine healing is what "Jesus Christ provided on the Cross."[214] Therefore, he treated healing as a component of the four-fold gospel,[215] an indispensable doctrine that must be promulgated since the central elements of the gospel should encompass divine healing. As Lee elucidated, Jesus' sacrifice on the cross was made for the sick, just as for the salvation of our souls. This was articulated through the Scriptures: 1) "Jesus bore our diseases" (Mt. 8:17); 2) "He provided healing for the sick through his stripes" (2 Pet. 2:24); and 3) "Jesus accepted the curse on our behalf" (Gal. 3:13).[216] Without hesitation, Lee set forth his theological premise that "the completion of salvation lies in divine healing,"[217] implying that salvation solely for our souls is incomplete without the salvation of our bodies. For Lee, the foundation of divine healing is established by the accomplished works of Jesus on the Cross. The importance of these assertions is that they place Jesus as the foundation of divine healing, analogous to the way spiritual salvation is attained through repentance. While the concept of original sin offers a fundamental theological basis for understanding how sickness could infiltrate the world, the remedy for healing is seeking God through repentance and requesting His provision already prepared through Jesus' redemptive works. Therefore, in Lee's healing theology, repentance serves as a vital mechanism to restore the diseased body to its pre-Fall state of completeness.

In examining Lee's hamartiology in the context of divine healing, it is necessary to also discuss actual sin. There are several significant reasons why Lee and his family perceived sickness as divine retribution for personal sins. Lee's parents persistently attributed their ailments to their own sins.[218] Lee, early in his Christian journey, deemed his illness to be a manifestation of his sins and confessed, "I have come to fully comprehend that I am a sinner in the legal, moral, and conscientious sense."[219] This penitential approach to healing was not a transient phase restricted to the period of his spiritual rebirth, but rather a continuous influence over Lee's life and ministry. Each time that he was afflicted by illness, he sought to identify his sins and express remorse. He believed that this contrite prayer eventually facilitated divine healing, regardless of whether it was immediate or delayed.[220]

Lee also attributed the illness and suffering of those around him to their individual sins. For instance, a church member, whom Lee regarded as particularly problematic, succumbed to a severe disease that eventually led to their death.[221] From Lee's perspective, the member's illness was a consequence

---

214 Seong-bong Lee, *Buheungui Bigyeol*, 47.
215 Seong-bong Lee, *Buheungui Bigyeol*, 76-77.
216 Seong-bong Lee, *Buheungui Bigyeol*, 50.
217 Seong-bong Lee, *Buheungui Bigyeol*, 50.
218 Seong-bong Lee, *Malo Mothamyeon Jukeumeuro*, 20-23.
219 Seong-bong Lee, *Malo Mothamyeon Jukeumeuro*, 32.
220 Seong-bong Lee, *Malo Mothamyeon Jukeumeuro*, 60.
221 Seong-bong Lee, *Malo Mothamyeon Jukeumeuro*, 54.

of their sinful nature.[222] Other examples include a female church member who deviated from God through mystical beliefs and consequently suffered, a deacon named Hyeon-ho Kim who met a tragic end following his seduction by the teachings of a heretical group,[223] and a Japanese police officer who had tortured Lee and suffered from eruptive typhus for seven years until his demise, an event Lee attributed to "the retribution of the just God."[224]

However, it is essential to clarify that while Lee correlates illness with sin in his healing theology, it would be a misinterpretation to infer that he propagates the belief that all illnesses are caused exclusively by sin. Lee recognised other potential precipitators, such as Satan, leading an imprudent lifestyle, a means of spiritual training, and the quest for God's glory.[225] From another perspective, he also contemplates that illness can be inflicted by oneself, others, Satan, or even nature.[226] This outlook serves to temper Lee's emphasis on sin as the principal cause of illness. He also alluded to other possible origins of diseases such as "God's will," "a means of spiritual training," and an "outcome of disbelief,"[227] along with "to unveil the divine works of God" and "to humble."[228] While sin is heavily accentuated as the link to sickness in the theological sequence, Lee's healing theology does not exclusively champion the idea that all ailments result from personal sins.

Lastly, it is crucial to investigate how repentance for healing is implemented within Lee's healing ministry. Based on his biblical education, Lee acknowledged that genuine repentance must be accompanied by practical rectification of previous deceitful actions.[229] This message of repentance was also disseminated during his revival meetings, leading to profound joy and transformative changes in the lives of the repentant.[230] Repentance, as a process, commenced not only with the recognition of one's sins but also with the verbal admission of these sins in a personal declaration before Lee.[231] The process of repentance is frequently marked by prayer and the laying on of hands following the confession. Regarding the timing, Lee typically preferred to administer the ministry of repentance during dawn prayer meetings.[232]

---

[222] Seong-bong Lee, *Malo Mothamyeon Jukeumeuro*, 55.
[223] Seong-bong Lee, *Malo Mothamyeon Jukeumeuro*, 56.
[224] Seong-bong Lee, *Malo Mothamyeon Jukeumeuro*, 93.
[225] Seong-bong Lee, *Buheungui Bigyeol*, 48.
[226] Seong-bong Lee, *Sarangui Gangdan*, 30-31.
[227] Seong-bong Lee, *Buheungui Bigyeol*, 48.
[228] Seong-bong Lee, *Buheungui Bigyeol*, 49.
[229] Seong-bong Lee, *Malo Mothamyeon Jukeumeuro*, 38-39.
[230] Seong-bong Lee, *Malo Mothamyeon Jukeumeuro*, 43, and Deuk-hyeon Kim, "Pyeongsindorosseo Naegabon Lee Seong-Bong Moksanim," 28.
[231] Deuk-hyeon Kim, "Pyeongsindorosseo Naegabon Lee Seong-Bong Moksanim," 27-28.
[232] Yong-Gyu Park, *Ibuleul Ggeuji Mara*, 115.

Spiritual Warfare

In a comprehensive interpretation of spiritual warfare, Lee delineated three adversaries: Satan, the world, and sin.[233] These components bear resemblance to Lee's understanding of "our nemeses" as Satan, innate sinfulness, the world (conceived as the realm of individual lust), and death.[234] Nonetheless, in the context of the struggle for healing that Christians must engage in, the primary adversary is Satan. Lee positions Satan as the chief enemy that Christians must confront, with the roles of Satan elucidated as follows:

> The vicious traitor, Satan, enticed Adam and Eve to commit a sin, and continuously attempts to demolish mankind. Although Satan spectacularly failed to compromise Jesus, he caused Judas Iscariot to be spoiled and Peter to be fallen by constantly tempting the disciples. While realising that the last day is coming soon, he at all costs threatens even God's chosen people like a roaring lion and tempts like an angel to delude them.[235]

Lee's conception of spiritual warfare is not narrowly confined to combating illness. Instead, it encapsulates salvific battle where Satan employs disease to hinder the proliferation of God's Kingdom. Lee characterised diseases as "병탄" [Byeongtan], denoting a bullet of illness.[236] In his theology of healing within spiritual warfare, Satan is portrayed as a potent entity causing affliction among believers in tangible ways. Hence, Lee perceived his ailment as a "Satanic test" during his periods of illness.[237] In his revival ministry, disease was also portrayed as an assault by Satan, such as when elder Choe succumbed to an illness.[238]

Within Lee's theological framework, disease is not the enemy but rather a militant tool wielded by Satan to test and assail God's people, obstructing their ultimate salvation.[239] Hence, the combat zone extends beyond our physical bodies to encompass the entire world, necessitating vigilant preparedness by Christians.[240] From the inception of his revival ministry, Lee was cognisant of spiritual warfare, and expressed this in his missive detailing the motivation and plans for his new ministry. He anticipated numerous impediments and guileful tactics employed by Satan.[241]

However, Lee's conviction stemmed from a theological belief that "all wars belong to Jehovah,"[242] and ultimately God's will would prevail despite Satan's

---

[233] Seong-bong Lee, *Buheungui Bigyeol*, 159.
[234] Seong-bong Lee, *Sarangui Gangdan*, 143.
[235] Seong-bong Lee, *Immanuel Gangdan*, 33
[236] Seong-bong Lee, *Malo Mothamyeon Jukeumeuro*, 151.
[237] Seong-bong Lee, *Malo Mothamyeon Jukeumeuro*, 46.
[238] Seong-bong Lee, *Malo Mothamyeon Jukeumeuro*, 137.
[239] This view is commonly shared by animism, which would have a strong appeal to the Korean mindset.
[240] Seong-bong Lee, *Immanuel Gangdan*, 40.
[241] Seong-bong Lee, *Malo Mothamyeon Jukeumeuro*, 65.
[242] Seong-bong Lee, *Malo Mothamyeon Jukeumeuro*, 137; 144.

malevolent acts and humanity's errors or wrongdoings.[243] Lee's role was to wage war against Satan using spiritual weapons while acknowledging that the war fundamentally belongs to God. Lee's arsenal was described metaphorically as "the bullets of praise and worship," "the cannon of prayers," and "the atomic bomb of the Words of God."[244] He credited the conquest of Satan's territories to "the hydrogen bomb of faith," "the bullets" of the full gospel, and "the cannon" of the prayer vigil.[245] Notably, all three spiritual weapons are aggressive tools, highlighting Lee's proactive stance towards healing. Despite Satan's portrayal as a formidable spiritual entity attacking Christians with disease, Lee asserted that the forces of Satan were confined to rudimentary weapons, while believers possess the capacity to wield far more potent armaments, such as the cannon, the atomic bomb, and the hydrogen bomb.

While Lee was not a fervent proponent of the concept of territorial spirits – spiritual entities ruling specific geographical areas – his views allowed room for this belief. For instance, he attributed the prevalence of Satan's malevolent activities in Gunsan Central Church to its former status as a Buddhist temple.[246] Similarly, Gangneung was viewed as a stronghold of Satan due to its association with ancestral rites incorporating shamanistic rituals.[247] It is intriguing to observe how Lee perceived his spiritual warfare in the United States, stating, "I needed to do a long-term ministry for a month in an independent church that welcomed me since I saw the necessity of engaging in an extended war against the enigmatic American Satan."[248] This perspective was influenced by the conception of Satan not merely as a theoretical or solely spiritual entity whose influence is confined to an unseen spiritual world, but rather as a "living" entity within his reality, as posited by Min.[249]

The Baptism of the Holy Spirit

While Lee did not formulate the concept of the Baptism of the Holy Spirit (BHS)[250] as a vital component for divine healing in an explicitly systematic manner, it was nonetheless deemed consequential by him. This was elucidated not only in the context of engendering regeneration and sanctification, but also as the instigator for the power to heal, thus manifesting as signs and wonders promoting the expansion of God's Kingdom. The BHS terminology was

---

243 Seong-bong Lee, *Sarangui Gangdan*, 175.
244 Seong-bong Lee, *Malo Mothamyeon Jukeumeuro*, 131.
245 Seong-bong Lee, *Malo Mothamyeon Jukeumeuro*, 153.
246 Seong-bong Lee, *Malo Mothamyeon Jukeumeuro*, 160.
247 Seong-bong Lee, *Malo Mothamyeon Jukeumeuro*, 129.
248 Seong-bong Lee, *Malo Mothamyeon Jukeumeuro*, 209.
249 Gyeong-bae Min, "Lee Seong-Bong Moksaui Buheungundong Jaejomyeong," 196.
250 The central doctrine of the Wesleyan Methodist is sanctification through the BHS. See Myeong-su Park, "Seonggyeolui Sinhakjeok Ihae" [Theological understanding of Sanctification], [Available at: http://www.sgti.kr/data/person/mspark/5.htm], [Last accessed: 28th October 2023].

frequently employed interchangeably by Lee with "the Baptism of Fire"[251] or "Big Fire,"[252] thereby aiding comprehension of Lee's perception of the phenomenological aspect of the BHS as it transpired in his life. He characterised his BHS experience thus: "As soon as his [Ik-du Kim's] hot hands touched me, an explosion of fire occurred in my body. It was exceedingly hot. I was startled into jumping off the bed, and subsequently realised it was a dream […] It was the Baptism of Fire."[253] According to Lee's personal account, the BHS could coincide with physical manifestations. The BHS encompasses not merely an internal metamorphosis such as regeneration and sanctification, but also external indications, like a sense of fiery filling in his body. It is indeed intriguing to note how frequently Lee pairs the term fire with the BHS.

However, despite his personal encounters with the BHS, Lee dissuaded those who sought to validate the physical symptoms of the BHS.[254] Instead, he urged them to discern the veritable BHS through its resultant effect, which was understood to be an "inner transformation."[255] This caution stemmed from his denominational beliefs, which did not advocate for glossolalia as tangible and initial evidence. In a recounting of his revival meeting in Julpo, Lee documented, "In every session of the revival meetings, the fire of the Holy Spirit descended, and there was a beauty of penitential and repentant testimony."[256] This substantiates that Lee initially interpreted the BHS as a transformative experience ushered in through repentance. Hence, he postulated, "the ones who are not baptised with the Holy Spirit are not Christians," and persistently posited that "those who were already baptised with the Holy Spirit still need to be full of the Holy Spirit."[257] From Lee's perspective, the indwelling Holy Spirit continually sanctifies people through what is understood as the fullness of the Holy Spirit.[258] Accordingly, within Lee's pneumatology, the first two cardinal roles of the Holy Spirit are regeneration and sanctification,[259] concepts integral to Wesleyan theology.

Although Lee's pneumatology centred on regeneration and sanctification, he nevertheless acknowledged that divine healing could be a significant consequence of the BHS. He portrayed the BHS as an experience that engendered divine healing, equating it with the power of the Holy Spirit in a narrower context.[260] A careful analysis of the ten roles of the Holy Spirit delineated by Lee reveals that his pneumatology extends to include the

---

251 Seong-bong Lee, *Buheungui Bigyeol*, 48, and Seong-bong Lee, *Malo Mothamyeon Jukeumeuro*, 62.
252 Seong-bong Lee, *Malo Mothamyeon Jukeumeuro*, 69.
253 Seong-bong Lee, *Malo Mothamyeon Jukeumeuro*, 62.
254 Seong-bong Lee, *Sarangui Gangdan*, 49.
255 Seong-bong Lee, *Sarangui Gangdan*, 56.
256 Seong-bong Lee, "Revival Tour," 39.
257 Seong-bong Lee, *Buheungui Bigyeol*, 34.
258 Seong-bong Lee, *Sarangui Gangdan*, 174.
259 Seong-bong Lee, *Immanuel Gangdan*, 73.
260 Seong-bong Lee, *Buheungui Bigyeol*, 48.

empowerment of the Holy Spirit, which Lee perceived as "the power for evangelism."[261] In this sense, Lee's interpretation of the BHS transcends Wesleyan doctrine to incorporate elements of Pentecostal/Charismatic pneumatology, in terms of the bestowal of spiritual power for missions. When discussing the BHS in the context of divine healing, he referenced its sequential outcome, the spiritual power diffused upon all flesh. Interestingly, neither the Holy Spirit nor the BHS were intended to be viewed as a mechanism for healing in Lee's perspective. Rather, they represent the spiritual power itself, granted through the BHS, which brings about divine healing from the Holy Spirit, who is God:

> When the Holy Spirit who was promised to be sent has come, He has established churches in every place for two thousand years as the era of the Holy Spirit. He made a brazen-faced rascal like me repentant, regenerated, sanctified, and endowed the life and power of heaven to spread the gospel to the ends of the earth.[262]

Lee unambiguously asserted that the BHS was the fulfilment of God's promise for the end times, and that regeneration and sanctification are not the final outcomes of the BHS. He understood that these are succeeded by the spiritual bestowal of "great power" for God's expansion. Therefore, the framework of Lee's healing theology posits that the Holy Spirit is not merely a conduit or means for healing, but rather He Himself is God. This deity empowers individuals to perform acts of healing for the Kingdom of God through the BHS as an experience that is distinct from regeneration and sanctification.

Evaluation of the Contributions of Lee's Healing Ministry

Social Perspective

In a comprehensive appraisal of the Korean Revival Movement, one may inadvertently adopt a reductive perspective, dismissing it as solely a spiritual phenomenon, disconnected from tangible social metamorphosis. Kang postulates that Lee's impact was ostensibly confined to the realm of individual beings, familial units, and ecclesiastical congregations, appearing to have minimal resonance with societal transformations.[263] An examination of Lee's life and ministry may erroneously lead some to infer that his interest was not rooted in a social gospel. This critique may not be completely unfounded, given that Lee's engagement with political structures or social change was not overt. Furthermore, a song frequently performed by Lee lends credence to an interpretation of life as being fraught with futility:

---

261 Seong-bong Lee, *Buheungui Bigyeol*, 30.
262 Seong-bong Lee, *Sarangui Gangdan*, 159.
263 Geun-hwan Kang, "Lee Seong-Bong Moksaui Buheungsayeok," 143.

> When I look at all the things that happen in the world, they look futile. What a waste it is to have wealth, honour, and long life. Fancy house with a fertile rice field will become an empty dream if we once die [...] Alas, it is sad. Where are you people running to? [...] Who can avoid the ordained fate that we all will die one day?[264]

The lyrical persona in this song appears ambivalent towards improving the world through a social gospel. Yet, it is crucial to acknowledge another salient aspect: the song serves as a potent reminder of the existential void and hopelessness that can potentially consume a life devoid of God. It imparts wisdom to those leading Godless lives, exhorting them to lead virtuous lives on Earth, not solely for the promise of a heavenly kingdom. The central tenet is not that the present world is inconsequential, but rather, that it serves as a determinant of our celestial future. In essence, our earthly deeds bear significance in the context of a transformed life aimed at a transcendent future. Through this song, Lee endeavoured to instil the importance of leading a transformed life in the present world, while yearning for the Second Coming of Jesus. Thus, his frequent performance of this song during his revival services should not be misconstrued as reflecting pessimism for the present world.

Lee's ministry was imbued with a sense of hope and solace for the world. He extended encouragement to the distressed populace, urging the entire Korean society to "wait a little more"[265] for a better world.[266] This was a pertinent message of comfort and optimism extended to the downtrodden during one of the most sombre periods in Korean history. Consequently, it is hardly surprising that Lee's revival meetings instilled a sense of jubilation in those who were famished, parched, and subjugated under Japanese rule.[267] Lee's ministry transcended the mere revival of the Korean Church to facilitate a comprehensive restoration of the physically, spiritually, and emotionally wounded. As Park posits, the provision of comfort independent of repentance is paramount to revivalists.[268] Thus, Lee's efforts in instilling hope and comfort in those in need warrant commendation.

While recognising the profound contributions of Lee's healing ministry for the oppressed, another critical facet warrants attention. Despite being one of the oppressed within the desperate context of Korea, he deliberately chose to empower marginalised and socially isolated groups. This was manifest in his decision to commence his itinerant revival ministry, with a ministerial emphasis on aiding small churches and those neglected by society. His efforts extended to specific demographics such as soldiers, policemen, prisoners, the elderly in

---

[264] Seong-bong Lee, *Malo Mothamyeon Jukeumeuro*, 31.
[265] Seong-bong Lee, *Malo Mothamyeon Jukeumeuro*, 109-10.
[266] Regarding this, Lee's eschatology needs to be understood as seeking the "better world" not only in the *Parousia* but also in this age.
[267] Seong-bong Lee, *Malo Mothamyeon Jukeumeuro*, 97.
[268] Myeong-su Park, "Lee Seong-Bong Moksaui Saengaewa Buheungundong," 240.

nursing homes, and lepers. Lee's son-in-law attested to the distinctively nurturing and comforting ministries extended to the despondent.[269] The impetus behind this new ministry was encapsulated in his declaration that "The Lord is the Friend of the weak and the poor."[270] Min interprets this ministry as a distinctive and consequential contribution within the specific context of Korea.[271]

Another significant aspect of Lee's life and ministry involved his earnest endeavours to influence his society by facilitating transformation at the level of individual Korean Christians. As a response to Lee's preaching, which emphasised the importance of thorough repentance, individuals sought to actualise their transformed lives in pragmatic terms. This, Hong argues, contradicts the erroneous attribution of nihilism or pessimism to Lee.[272] Far from advocating withdrawal from worldly concerns or endorsing an isolated existence, Lee urged his followers to remain engaged with the world.[273] In essence, Lee was orchestrating a social revolution in his distinctive manner, a sentiment resonant in his preaching:

> Whether it is individual, society, or country, they first need to be clean in their hearts. This is because all the blessings start from there. What it means by clean does not mean the life of leaving the corrupted world, going to a deep mountain, eating some fruits of trees, and not meeting with the people in the world.[274]

Contrary to espousing a pessimistic worldview, Lee demonstrates concern not just for individuals but also for society and the nation. His strategic approach towards societal transformation involved promoting a sanctified life for believers. From this standpoint, the significance of Lee's contributions should not be underestimated from a social perspective.[275] I posit that Lee's ministry induced societal healing within his community by guiding numerous individuals away from deleterious behaviours towards a transformed existence.

Missional Perspective

The utilisation of divine healing as a catalyst to expedite the evangelism process within mission fields is an undeniable aspect of Lee's healing ministries. An intriguing inquiry arises, one that questions whether the extent of his impact was

---

[269] Dong-su Kim, "Gyeolhonsik Nalui Jeondoseolgyo" [Evangelistic Preaching on a Wedding Day], edited by The Commemoration Committee of the 100th Anniversary of Lee Seong-Bong's Birth, *Lee Seong-Bong Moksaui Buheungundong Jomyeong* [The Examination of Seong-bong Lee's Revival Movement] (Seoul: Lifebook, 2000): 25-26.

[270] Seong-bong Lee, *Malo Mothamyeon Jukeumeuro*, 124-25.

[271] Gyeong-bae Min, "Lee Seong-Bong Moksaui Buheungundong Jaejomyeong," 188.

[272] Chi-mo Hong, "Lee Seong-Bong Moksaui Saengaewa Sinang Sasang," 492.

[273] Seong-bong Lee, *Immanuel Gangdan*, 40.

[274] Seong-bong Lee, *Immanuel Gangdan*, 104.

[275] This attitude of Lee is different from Kim's. Perhaps Lee's emphasis on living in the present world was influenced by the Wesleyan tradition of the sanctified life, which led to the transformation of people in their society.

local or national, denominational or interdenominational. The responses suggest that Lee's influence was both nationwide and interdenominational, although the greatest impact of his healing ministries was prominently observed within the Holiness Church. Given that Lee was a product of a Holiness Bible school and dedicated a significant portion of his life to this denomination, it is hardly surprising that his initial recognition was as a prominent figure of the Holiness Church. His reputation was such that he was regarded as "one of the big stars,"[276] and "the best pastor and revivalist"[277] of the Holiness Church. Many attest to Lee's substantial contributions to the denomination, particularly with regards to his efforts "consolidating the fragmented Holiness Church,"[278] "revitalising the waning Holiness Church" post 1945,[279] "establishing churches that continue to play pivotal roles to date", and to "revive and grow the churches in number."[280] The consensus is that no one can dispute his instrumental role in the denomination's evolution as pastor, revivalist, and healing practitioner.

Despite the inclination of some to confine the scope of Lee's influence strictly to the Holiness Church, his life's work was devoted to the reformation of the Korean Church as a whole. Through his interdenominational background and his noteworthy spiritual gifts as a revivalist, he held the position of a nationwide circulating revivalist, all while maintaining his pastoral duties. He conducted numerous revival meetings and led many individuals to Jesus, particularly through his healing ministry, transcending denominational boundaries. As Noh observes, Lee made visits to approximately sixty-five churches within a span of a year and seven months. The reach of Lee's revival ministry could not have been confined to his denomination alone; indeed, in the initial year of his revival tour, he was hosted not only by the Holiness churches but also by the Presbyterian and Methodist churches. Lee himself expounded on the reasons for the cessation of his revival ministries, stating that as his reputation as a distinguished revivalist grew, he was increasingly solicited by various churches to lead revival meetings within their denominational churches, including Presbyterian and Methodist churches. This circumstance precipitated a dilemma, leading to a request for him to concentrate solely on his ministries within the Holiness Church. Lee's wife also corroborated the extensive solicitations from other denominations, inviting him as their denominational revivalist. Dong-seon Im concurred that Lee conducted numerous revival meetings across almost every denomination of the Korean Church.[281] Considering that numerous eminent pastors and revivalists were nurtured under his influence,[282] and that the structure

---

[276] Chi-mo Hong, "Lee Seong-Bong Moksaui Saengaewa Sinang Sasang," 491.
[277] Shin-chang Kang, "Naega Mannan Geoin Lee Seong-Bong Moksa," 13.
[278] Shin-chang Kang, "Naega Mannan Geoin Lee Seong-Bong Moksa," 16.
[279] Seong-hyeon Kim, *Living Waters* (July 1997): 35.
[280] Myeong-su Park, *Hanguk Gyohoe Buheungundong Yeongu*, 163.
[281] Dong-seon Lim, "Hankuk gidokgyo yeoksaui yeongweonhi bitnal keunbyeol," 77.
[282] Seong-bong Lee, *Sarangui Gangdan*, 119, and Dong-seon Lim, "Hanguk Gidokgyo Yeoksaae Yeongweonhi Bitnal Keun Byeol," 77.

and message of Lee's revival meetings established a distinctly Korean model of revival meetings, it would be unjust to restrict Lee's contributions to the Holiness Church alone. Rather, it should be acknowledged that his contributions extended to the entire Korean Church, which benefitted greatly from his healing ministry and inherited his spiritual legacy.

Theological Perspective

In the context of the Korean revival movement, Ju posits that Lee is an inheritor of the spiritual legacy passed down by Seon-ju Gil and Ik-du Kim.[283] It could be argued that the foundation of the Korean revival movement was solidified by the Wonsan revival in 1903, while the Pyeoyang revival in 1907 marked the pivotal moment for an explosive spiritual awakening, which positioned it at the heart of the movement. Gil is renowned as a leading revivalist within this movement, with Park designating him as a key actor in this context.[284] Gil's movement was characterised by an emphasis on repentance that included material reimbursement,[285] a concept that has been preserved in the Korean Church through Kim and Lee's revival meetings. Particularly noteworthy is Lee's enhancement of the concept of repentance through his application of the term *thorough.* Since 1907, the message of repentance has become central to the Korean Holiness Movement.

While there is a clear continuity between Gil, Kim, and Lee within the revival movement, it is essential to understand that Lee's healing theology did not simply replicate the ideas of his predecessors, but rather evolved its own distinct theological dimension. I agree with Park's assertion that Lee did not just adopt, but also enriched, the traditions of the two revivalists.[286] As this research seeks to trace the theological progression of the divine healing movement in Korea, Lee's role is crucial as he perpetuated the legacy of the divine healing movement inherited from Ik-du Kim and handed it down to Yong-gi Cho.

Lee's theological influence is particularly substantial within the context of the Korean Holiness Movement. His ministry, in collaboration with elder Woon-mong Na, was integrated into the Korean Assemblies of God (hereafter, KAG)

---

283 Seung-min Ju, "Sobokui Buheungundong Gochal" [Examination of Seong-bong Lee's Revival Movement], edited by The Commemoration Committee of the 100th Anniversary of Lee Seong-Bong's Birth, *Lee Seong-Bong Moksaui Buheungundong Jomyeong* [The Examination of Seong-bong Lee's Revival Movement] (Seoul: Lifebook, 2000): 446.

284 Although Gil was not a healing practitioner, his influence over the Korean Church cannot be underestimated, since he took a lead for the first revival movement in Korea, and laid the foundation of the Korean revival movement. See Myeong-su Park, *Hanguk Gyohoe Buheungundong Yeongu*, 56.

285 Myeong-su Park, *Hanguk Gyohoe Buheungundong Yeongu*, 57.

286 Myeong-su Park, "Lee Seong-Bong Moksaui Saengaewa Buheungundong," 216.

from its inception.[287] Undoubtedly, Lee's contributions laid a firm theological groundwork for the Pentecostal movement in Korea. Furthermore, his mentorship of Ja-sil Choe, who later became Yong-gi Cho's mother-in-law, had a profound influence on Cho's life.[288] Given the initial pastoral focus of the Yoido Full Gospel Church's healing ministry under Choe, and Cho's admiration for her spirituality, it seems plausible that Lee's theological viewpoints were transmitted to Cho through Choe. Consequently, it can be concluded that Lee's healing theology has laid the foundation for many contemporary Korean Pentecostals.

Lee's theological contributions to the Korean Church do not stop here. His ideas about the baptism in the Holy Spirit (BHS) in relation to divine healing widened the theological horizons of the Presbyterian and Holiness Churches in terms of pneumatology. Perceiving divine healing as a manifestation of spiritual empowerment for the expansion of God's Kingdom, Lee introduced a more nuanced understanding of pneumatology, asserting that the workings of the Holy Spirit extend beyond regeneration and sanctification.[289]

The balanced theology of Lee also merits evaluation. According to Hong, Lee's theology finds equilibrium between the Wesleyan perspective (on repentance and its fruits) and Calvinism (predestination).[290] This balance underpins Lee's healing theology, highlighting both the divine providence/will and the human plea for healing. The influence of Kim on Lee seems credible, particularly considering that this theological balance is mirrored in Lee's hymns about divine healing. This balance engenders a constructive tension within Lee's healing theology.

Myeong-hyeok Kim categorises Lee's healing theology as a balanced gospel of healing, positioned between cessationists and continuationists.[291] However,

---

[287] Jong-dal Im, *Gidokgyo Daehan Hananimui Seonghoe Osibnyeonsa: Yeoksapyeon* [The 50-Year-History of the Korea Assemblies of God: History 1953-2004 (Seoul: Creation, 2005): 304.

[288] The influence of Lee over Cho will be explored in the following section on Cho. For further information about how Cho appreciated Lee's healing ministry see Yong-gi Cho, "Lee Seong-Bong Moksaui Sayeok Soke Natanan Seongryeong," [The Holy Spirit found in the Ministry of Seong-bong Lee], In The Commemoration Committee of the 100th Anniversary of Lee Seong-Bong's Birth (eds), *Lee Seong-Bong Moksaui Buheungundong Jomyeong* [The Examination of Seong-bong Lee's Revival Movement] (Seoul: Lifebook, 2000): 423.

[289] The traditional view of the Holiness Church on the BHS is limited to regeneration and sanctification. See *The Charter of the Jesus Korea Sungkyul Church* (Seoul: Seongcheongsa, 1989): 28.

[290] Chi-mo Hong, "Lee Seong-Bong Moksaui Saengaewa Sinang Sasang," 504.

[291] Myeong-hyeok Kim, "Lee Seon-Bong Moksaui Samkwa Sinange Daehan Sinhakjeok Jomyeon" [Theological Examination on the Life and Belief of Seong-bong Lee], In The Commemoration Committee of the 100th Anniversary of Lee Seong-Bong's Birth (eds), *Lee Seong-Bong Moksaui Buheungundong Jomyeong* [The Examination of Seong-bong Lee's Revival Movement] (Seoul: Lifebook, 2000): 167.

the validity of this claim is questionable, as Lee's healing theology seemingly leans towards supporting the continuationists. Indeed, the healing theologies of Lee and Ik-du Kim have encouraged the Korean Church, traditionally not Pentecostal, to be more receptive towards Pentecostal perspectives. As Lee's viewpoints on healing unfolded within the Korean Church, they challenged and subdued the sceptical and cynical stance of cessationists to such an extent that numerous Methodist and Presbyterian churches invited Lee to preside over revival meetings within their own denominational settings.

Lastly, as underscored by Min, Lee's position as one of the key revivalists who shaped the Korean Church's revival movement tradition warrants consideration. [292] In relation to both the structure and format of revival meetings,[293] as well as their content and language, which focused primarily on the healing ministry,[294] it is essential to recognise that Lee's revival meetings provided the Korean Church with an exemplar of a Korean healing ministry.

Conclusion

Primarily, in consideration of the context surrounding Lee's healing ministry, it is pertinent to note that he experienced the tumultuous periods of Japanese colonisation and the Korean War. Lee can be seen as a bridge between Kim and Cho, living and ministering through this era of significant transition. Amidst these periods of turmoil, his healing theology was conceived of as a beacon of hope and solace for the beleaguered Korean Church. Moreover, Lee's hamartiology, which postulates that sin engenders sickness, evolved in parallel, ascribing the Korean War to divine chastisement. The idea of spiritual warfare was tangentially influenced by this conflict-ridden context, where illness was perceived as an aggressive onslaught by spiritual adversaries. The crux of Lee's healing theology was integrated into the four-fold gospel of the Holiness Church, positioning divine healing as a component of Jesus' redemptive actions. Furthermore, the belief that divine healing necessitates profound repentance appeared to be an evolution from the heritage of the Pyeoyang Revivals in 1907. Lee's pneumatology regarding healing was also framed in response to mystical groups; it emphasised the centrality of regeneration and sanctification in the Baptism of the Holy Spirit (BHS) over the spiritual gift of healing. Key figures

---

[292] Gyeong-bae Min, "Lee Seong-Bong Moksaui Buheungundong Jaejomyeong," 189.

[293] Min presents five characteristics of Lee's Korean-style revival meetings: 1. Facilitating church building construction; 2. Solving internal problems of churches; 3. Having edified faith and the explosion of emotion; 4. Having miraculous fruits, divine healing; 5. Growing church members. See Gyeong-bae Min, "Lee Seong-Bong Moksaui Buheungundong Jaejomyeong," 206-207.

[294] Lee's revival meetings were believed to be effective because Lee used folksy language and communication skills. See Myeong-su Park, "Lee Seong-Bong Moksaui Saengaewa Buheungundong," 251, Gyeong-bae Min, "Lee Seong-Bong Moksaui Buheungundong Jaejomyeong," 189, Seung-min Ju, "Sobokui Buheungundong Gochal," 457.

such as Ik-du Kim, Myeong-jik Lee, and Seong-bong Lee's parents, particularly his mother, contributed significantly to the practical and theoretical foundation for Lee's development of his healing theology, emphasising the merit of repentant prayer.

Secondly, the framework of Lee's healing theology encapsulates faith, prayer, repentance, spiritual warfare, and the BHS. His perspective on faith underscored two main aspects: 1) the enduring potency and compassion of Jesus, the healer; and 2) the providential control and sovereignty of God, centred on God's will. Prayer, expressed through petitionary, persistent, and sincere supplications, was posited as the fundamental prerequisite for divine healing. As Lee's healing ministry was distinguished by exhaustive repentance, its theological rationale was justified in the context of healing through atonement, which predicates healing on the prior forgiveness of sins. Lee also construed the concept of spiritual warfare in a realistic manner, acknowledging the potency of malevolent spirits causing illness and interpreting sickness as a militant affront from spiritual foes designed to impede the proliferation of God's Kingdom. It was also inferred from Lee's healing ministry that the BHS holds the key to bestowing spiritual power for healing and for the proliferation of God's Kingdom, conceived as an experience distinct from regeneration and sanctification.

Lastly, the merits of Lee's healing ministries were examined from social, missional, and theological perspectives. From a societal standpoint, Lee's first notable contribution lies in his participation in the social gospel in his unique way, encouraging believers to lead a transformed life that benefits not only themselves but also their church, society, and nation. His second social contribution is in providing sustenance for marginalised Korean people to live with hope. His missional contribution is recognised in the revivals of the Korean Church, including the Holiness Church. Lastly, from a theological perspective, Lee expanded the conceptual range of pneumatology beyond the realm of regeneration and sanctification to encompass spiritual empowerment granted for the growth of God's Kingdom.[295]

[295] As my treatment of Lee is synchronic, diachronic research would be a good topic for further investigation.

3. Yong-gi Cho

Life and Ministry

Before Conversion

Yong-gi Cho was born on the 14th February 1936, into a family residing in Gyodong-Li, Samnam-Myeon, Ulju-Gun, as the first son among nine siblings (five brothers and four sisters) to Mr Doo-chun Cho and Mrs Bok-sun Kim.[1] Growing up, Cho exhibited a reserved and emotional demeanour,[2] influenced by his father's intense passion and his mother's calm and reasoned character.[3] Their family was significantly engaged in practicing Buddhism.[4]

Cho's early life was marked by various hardships and struggles as he navigated the challenging societal climate of Korea during the Japanese occupation and subsequent Korean War. His childhood was marred by witnessing the harsh repercussions and "untold suffering" inflicted by Japanese militarism. Furthermore, the imposition of a Japanese identity – Yoshida YoYoki – was a requisite for his admission into an elementary school under Japanese rule.[5] As the conflict with North Korea resulted in widespread devastation, survival became the primary struggle for many, and Cho was not exempt from this struggle.[6] Unfortunately, health issues thwarted his completion of public high school. Nevertheless, his innate interest in the English language served as a catalyst, fostering relationships with numerous missionaries and influential evangelists, thus opening new avenues for his future.

---

[1] Yong-gi Cho, *Widaehan Somyeong: Huimang Mokhoe 50 Nyeon* [Great Call: 50 Years of Hope Ministry] (Seoul: Yoido Full Gospel Church, 2008): 76.

[2] Yong-gi Cho, *Naui Gyohoe Seongjang Iyagi* [The Story of My Church Growth] (Seoul: Seoul Logos, 2005): 285.

[3] Yong-gi Cho, *Naui Gyohoe Seongjang Iyagi*, 346 and N.L. Kennedy, *Dream Your Way to Success*, (Plainfield, NJ: Logos International, 1980): 81.

[4] Yong-gi Cho, *The Fourth Dimension,* vol 2. (Gainesville, FL: Bridge-Logos, 1983): xi; Yong-gi Cho, *To God Be the Glory*, (Seoul: n.s. 1973): 35.
Apart from Buddhism, Confucianism and Eastern studies influenced Cho's childhood. See FGTV, "Biography of Dr. David Yong-gi Cho,"; Yong-gi Cho, *Successful Living* (Seoul: Young San, 1977): 95 and 98; Yong-gi Cho, *To God Be the Glory*, 35.

[5] Hyeong-geun Lim (ed), *Cho Yong-gi Moksa Ildaegi: Yeouidoui Moghoeja* [Biography of Rev. Yong-gi Cho: The Minister of Yoido] (Seoul: Seoul Book, 2008): 45; Yong-gi Cho, *The Fourth Dimension,* vol 2., xi.

[6] Yong-gi Cho, *The Fourth Dimension* (Seoul: Seoul Logos, 1979): xii.

Conversion

Cho's spiritual transformation was indeed a dramatic event. Struggling with tuberculosis, an ailment he contracted in 1954 after a fall from a chin-up bar, he was introduced to Christianity by a friend of his elder sister. Her tireless evangelisation efforts aimed to alleviate Cho's fear of death through the acceptance of Jesus Christ as his Lord and Saviour.[7] This led Cho to delve into the Bible, where he "began to see the beautiful hope" drawn from Christ's self-sacrifice on the Cross – an initial indication of his impending conversion.[8]

In 1956, Cho found himself attending a revival meeting in Pusan, led by Kenneth Tice, an American ex-marine missionary.[9] At the end of the service, overwhelmed by it, he repented of his sins while crying and wailing before God and had a feeling that he had never experienced.[10] It was Cho's experience of real conversion. The following Sunday, through Tice's introduction, Cho visited the World Mission church where Louis P. Richards, an American Assemblies of God (AG) missionary, had been serving from 1953 to 1967.[11] During his interaction with Richards, Cho began to solidify "his own relationship to God [...] for the first time."[12] In fact, it is not quite clear whether it was under Tice or Richards that Cho had the experience of the BHS because there are two different reports on this event: *Widaehan Somyeong: Huimang Mokhoe 50 Nyeon* [Great Call: 50 Years of Hope Ministry] indicates that it was through the influence of Tice[13] while *Dream Your Ways to Success* attributes it to Richards' impact.[14] It seems reasonable to assign a larger influence to Richards since Richards and Cho agreed in their writings. Richards said:

> But in the midst of this human misery [due to the Korean war], God poured out His Spirit upon hungry hearts. Hundreds of precious lost souls were saved. One of these was a young pre-medic student living in Pusan, "Yong-gi Cho." This young man was saved, filled with the Holy Spirit, healed of tuberculosis, and called into the ministry.[15]

More significantly, Cho also stated in the foreword of Richards' book:

---

[7] Yong-gi Cho, *Widaehan Somyeong: Huimang Mokhoe 50 Nyeon* [Great Call: 50 Years of Hope Ministry], 77.
[8] Yong-gi Cho, *Successful Living* (Seoul: Young San, 1977): 97.
[9] Tice came to South Korea as a missionary with the Navigators.
[10] Yong-gi Cho, *Successful Living*, 97.
[11] Myeong-su Park, *Hanguk Gyohoe Buheungundong Yeongu*, 195.
[12] Kennedy was asked by Cho to write Cho's biography. Thus, this Kennedy's book could be considered one of the authenticated books written on the life of Cho. N.L. Kennedy, *Dream Your Way to Success*, 112 and 115-16.
[13] Yong-gi Cho, *Widaehan Somyeong: Huimang Mokhoe 50 Nyeon*, 78.
[14] N.L. Kennedy, *Dream Your Way to Success*, 116-19.
[15] L.P. Richards, *Divine Appointments with God: A Manual for Soul-Winning* (Manila: Evangel, 1967): 53.

> Brother Louis Richards is my own pastor. It was at the Full Gospel Mission in Pusan, Korea in 1956 that I received Jesus Christ as my personal Saviour through a firm "born again" experience. It was through the teaching of God's Holy Word at that time, that my faith in God became strong; I was baptised with the Holy Ghost and received a divine call to preach the gospel.[16]

From the evidence of the historical records of Richards and Cho, it is reasonable to argue that Cho was under Richards' spiritual guidance when he was baptised with the Holy Spirit and his faith was growing in the beginning of his early Christian life.

At the age of 19, Cho received medical training in a hospital, where he was referred to as "Doctor Cho," despite lacking formal licensing.[17] Under Richards' mentorship, he served as an interpreter for a preacher and engaged in the study of the Bible.[18] Even though his faith was in its nascent stages, it incrementally grew as he memorised and absorbed the Word of God from missionaries and his own reading.[19] Cho sought to actualise his faith by participating in days of prayer and fasting, leading to a transformative vision in which he encountered Jesus. Following this encounter, he was baptised with the Holy Spirit, received his ministerial calling, and was promised divine healing from tuberculosis.[20] Inspired by Missionary Richards, Cho relocated to Seoul in September 1956 to attend the Sunbogeum [Full Gospel] Theological Seminary – an Assemblies of God (AG) institution – graduating in March 1958 as part of the fourth cohort.[21] This educational endeavour enabled him to serve as a Classical Pentecostal – Korean Assemblies of God (KAG) – minister, with his formal ordination taking place in 1962.

Ministry

Daejodong Era as the Pioneering Period (1958–1961)

The first church – usually called *Daejodong Cheonmak Gyohoe*, meaning a tent church in the Daejo area of Seoul – started with five members (Cho, Choe[22] and her three children) on 18th May 1958 in an old American service tent. The tent church grew rapidly because of several significant healings. Notably, various recoveries captivated the attention of many sceptics, compelling them to join the church, including: Choe's eldest son, who was afflicted by acute pneumonia; a

---

[16] Yong-gi Cho, in L.P. Richards, *Divine Appointments with God: A Manual for Soul-Winning* (Manila: Evangel, 1967).

[17] N.L. Kennedy, *Dream Your Way to Success*, 106.

[18] N.L. Kennedy, *Dream Your Way to Success*, 118.

[19] N.L. Kennedy, *Dream Your Way to Success*, 119.

[20] Yong-gi Cho, *Widaehan Somyeong: Huimang Mokhoe 50 Nyeon*, 78-79.

[21] Yong-gi Cho, *Widaehan Somyeong: Huimang Mokhoe 50 Nyeon*, 82.

[22] Cho first met Ja-sil Choe in the Bible college. He helped Choe with her ministry after graduation, and they started their church together. Choe became Cho's mother-in-law in 1965.

woman who had been paralysed for seven years; a destitute beggar plagued by physical impairments, and two deaf women.[23] Cho shared with the suffering people what God had previously done for him. As he told them "He would do the same for them," many miracles took place, and the church was soon full of people.[24]

During Cho's military service absence from January to August 1961, the missionary John Hurston, in collaboration with Choe, ensured the continuity of church activities. Notably, a momentous revival gathering held during this period resulted in the recruitment of an additional two hundred adherents.[25] By the time Cho embarked on establishing another church in Seodaemun in 1961, the original church had amassed a congregation of approximately five hundred individuals within a span of three and a half years.[26]

SEODAEMUN ERA AS THE DEVELOPING PERIOD (1961–1973)

The advent of the subsequent phase was heralded by the establishment of the second church, known as *Sunbokeum* [Full Gospel] Revival Centre, situated in Seodaemun of Seoul, which later evolved into *Sunbokeum Jungang Gyohoe* [Full Gospel Central Church].[27] Cho's second ministerial endeavour, initiated through the invitation extended by Hurston, received backing as a "pilot project" from the Department of Foreign Mission of the (US) Assemblies of God, aiming to facilitate mission initiatives in Asian regions proximate to the Seodaemun Intersection, the former headquarters of the Korean Assemblies of God.[28] Notably, the church witnessed significant growth following two revival gatherings conducted under the guidance of Samuel J. Todd, an AG revivalist, resulting in the healing of numerous afflicted individuals. This notable occurrence garnered considerable attention from diverse sectors, including the mother of President Bo-seon Yun.[29] By the time that Cho assumed leadership of the church from Hurston in 1964, the congregation had expanded rapidly to encompass approximately 2,400 members.[30]

During a decade marked by personal physical frailty, Cho laid the groundwork for his flourishing ministry, focusing on two fundamental elements:

---

[23] N.L. Kennedy, *Dream Your Way to Success*, 166; Yong-gi Cho, *Widaehan Somyeong: Huimang Mokhoe 50 Nyeon*, 74; 82-83; Yong-gi Cho, *To God Be the Glory*, 42.

[24] Yong-gi Cho, *To God Be the Glory*, 42.

[25] Kennedy, *Dream Your Way to Success*, 178-80.

[26] International Theological Institute, *Yoido Kyohoei Shinanggwa Shinhak* [The Yoido Full Gospel Church: Its Faith and Theology], vol. II (Seoul: Seoul Books, 1993): 108.

[27] This church was started in October 1961 in the form of the Full Gospel Revival Centre and soon changed to the Full Gospel Central Church in May 1962.

[28] Yong-gi Cho, *Widaehan Somyeong: Huimang Mokhoe 50 Nyeon*, 89; G.B. McGee, *This Gospel Shall Be Preached: A Historical and Theology of Assemblies of God Foreign Missions Since 1959*, vol. 2 (Springfield, MI: Gospel Publishing House, 1989): 72.

[29] Yong-gi Cho, *Widaehan Somyeong: Huimang Mokhoe 50 Nyeon*, 89.

[30] Yong-gi Cho, *Widaehan Somyeong: Huimang Mokhoe 50 Nyeon*, 93.

(1) the formulation of his healing theology and pneumatology, and (2) the establishment of Home Cell Groups. He embarked on an extensive exploration of biblical passages to comprehend the roles of Jesus and the Holy Spirit in the restoration of his ailing body.[31] He was "forced to seek the healing God daily and to search for the promises of healing from Genesis to Revelation,"[32] and it resulted in the publication of his first two books, *Jesus Christ, the Divine Healer* and *The Holy Spirit*.[33] Furthermore, Cho's physical limitations served as the impetus behind the inception of the Home Cell Groups system in 1964, as he recognised the necessity of shared responsibilities within the burgeoning church community.[34] The Home Cell Groups, initially consisting of twenty groups in 1965, experienced ongoing expansion year after year, with a total of 126 groups in 1967 and 296 groups in 1972, encompassing a membership of 10,970 individuals.[35]

Between 1964 and 1973, Cho garnered considerable acclaim within the global church community, leading him to travel extensively to spearhead revival meetings in numerous countries. During this period, he actively engaged in nationwide evangelisation efforts through the publication of a monthly magazine called Weol-Gan-Shin-Ang-Gyei. Additionally, starting in 1968, he disseminated his sermons and shared testimonies from church members through various broadcasting channels.[36] The church, which initially comprised of only two family members, experienced remarkable growth, reaching a membership of approximately 18,000 by 1973.[37]

Yoido Era

The First[38] Expanding Period (1973–1982)

The landmark of this period is the construction and dedication of a new church building that seated 10,000 people on 23rd September 1973, in the developing

---

[31] Yong-gi Cho, *Naui Gyohoe Seongjang Iyagi*, 81-83.

[32] Yong-gi Cho, *Suffering, Why Me?* (Gainesville, FL: Bridge-Logos, 1987): 99.

[33] Yong-gi Cho, *Huimangmokhoe 45 Nyeon* [45 Years of Hope Ministry] (Seoul: Institute for Church Growth, 2004): 73.

[34] Yong-gi Cho, *Suffering, Why Me?* 89; Young-hoon Lee, "Life and Ministry of David Yong-gi Cho," in Wonsuk Ma (ed), *David Yonggi Cho: A Close Look at His Theology and Ministry* (Baguio, Philippines: APTS Press, 2004): 7; Yong-gi Cho, *Widaehan Somyeong: Huimang Mokhoe 50 Nyeon*, 96; International Theological Institute, *Yoido Kyohoei Shinanggwa Shinhak* 2, 107.

[35] Yong-gi Cho, *Widaehan Somyeong: Huimang Mokhoe 50 Nyeon*, 430-31.

[36] Yong-gi Cho, *Widaehan Somyeong: Huimang Mokhoe 50 Nyeon*, 101.

[37] Another statistic of the membership for the period: the church grew from 500 to 18,000 members. Moreover, Cho several times emphasised that the second church was started with two families. Another report indicates that it grew not to 18,000 but to 12,556. See Yong-gi Cho, *Widaehan Somyeong: Huimang Mokhoe 50 Nyeon*, 431 and International Theological Institute, *Yoido Kyohoei Shinanggwa Shinhak*, 2, 108.

[38] As this heading may be misleading since this period started with Cho's third church, I intentionally use "first" to describe the expanding stage, not in the sense of a developing era.

area of Yoido which used to be a desolate place in Seoul. It was the third church that Cho built as a continuation[39] of his second church.[40] One of the outstanding aspects of this time is the explosive church growth, as shown in Table 2.

Table 2: Statistics of the Church Growth of the YFGC[41]

Year	Membership	Cell Group
1973	12,556	394
1974	19,856	542
1975	22,992	755
1976	35,794	1,604
1977	48,975	2,005
1978	75,361	4,818
1979	100,930	6,351
1981	200,144	
1982	230,765	

The exponential growth of the church, which saw an eighteen-fold increase in membership from 1973 to 1982, is undeniably remarkable. As Kennedy noted, "an average of one church member was added every twenty minutes during 1978."[42] By 1981, the church's membership had swelled beyond 200,000, thereby earning the designation of the world's largest church.[43] Such unprecedented growth thrust Cho and his church into the global spotlight, becoming a topic of widespread discussion.

This notable expansion of the church's membership was concomitant with several pivotal factors: 1) the development of the region of Yoido;[44] 2) Christian world events such as the Tenth World Pentecostal Conference in 1973[45] and other conferences of Billy Graham and Campus Crusade for Christ (CCC) in 1974; 3) the establishment of the prayer mountain in Osanri in 1973;[46] 4) the church emphasis on mission projects;[47] 5) conducting lectures on church growth

[39] About 8,000 members were transferred to the Yoido church from Seodeamun. Yong-gi Cho, *Widaehan Somyeong: Huimang Mokhoe 50 Nyeon*, 121.
[40] International Theological Institute, *Yoido Kyohoei Shinanggwa Shinhak*, 2, 109-10.
[41] Yong-gi Cho, *Widaehan Somyeong: Huimang Mokhoe 50 Nyeon*, 122-23.
[42] N.L. Kennedy, *Dream Your Way to Success*, 220.
[43] Yong-gi Cho, *Widaehan Somyeong: Huimang Mokhoe 50 Nyeon*, 123.
[44] Myeong-su Park, "Haebanghu Hangukgyohoesawa Yeoido Sunbokeumgyohoeui Cho Yong-gi Moksa" [Korean Church History and Rev. Yong-gi Cho of the Yoido Full Gospel Church after Japanese Colonization], *JYT*, 23 (2011): 206.
[45] Jae-bum Lee, "Pentecostal Type Distinctives and Korean Protestant Church Growth," (Ph.D. Diss., Fuller Theological Seminary, 1986): 192.
[46] Yong-gi Cho, *Widaehan Somyeong: Huimang Mokhoe 50 Nyeon*, 125.
[47] Yong-gi Cho, *Widaehan Somyeong: Huimang Mokhoe 50 Nyeon*, 127; 132; 136-37.

for world Christians;[48] and 6) efforts to train the church members.[49] An analysis conducted by Cho's International Theological Institute (henceforth referred to as ITI) suggests that the remarkable growth of the church during this period was largely attributable to the spiritual prayer movement, the charismatic leadership and messaging of Cho, and the training provided to the church leaders.[50] Beyond these key elements, divine healing emerged as one of the most crucial driving forces behind the church's growth.

The Second Expanding Period (1983-2008)

The dawn of a new epoch arrived with the renaming of Full Gospel Central Church to Yoido Full Gospel Church in January 1984. The ensuing growth of the church was notably enhanced by the foundation of numerous daughter churches between 1980 and 1990. Consequently, by 1992, the church had achieved a membership of 700,000, thereby meriting its inclusion in the Guinness Book of Records as the world's largest church.[51] Cho's ministry maintained a consistent focus on the accelerative elements of church growth, conceptualised in the previous period. Distinctive components of this era include "world missions," the "utilisation of evangelistic tools," the "formation of Cho's theology," and the "social gospel."

To elucidate further on the distinguishing features of this epoch, Cho's innovative viewpoints on missionary work were the primary instigation for a substantial shift in global missions. Cho strategically steered more missionaries towards non-Western nations and concentrated on evangelistic efforts for indigenous populations, not for immigrant Korean communities.[52] Since the initiation of the first missionary venture to America in 1971, 641 missionaries have been dispatched to an array of 55 diverse countries, with a significant proportion of 43 out of those 55 being non-Western nations. These missionaries had successfully established 775 churches by 2007, thus illustrating the impact of this new approach.[53] Moreover, Cho's ministry leveraged the potent influence of mass media, thereby amplifying its reach and impact. Notable instances include the live broadcast of Cho's sermons and the inception of a Christian daily newspaper named *Kook-Min-Il-Bo*.[54] Lastly, Cho's perspective on holistic salvation including divine healing helped not only to give practical help to the

---

[48] Yong-gi Cho, *Widaehan Somyeong: Huimang Mokhoe 50 Nyeon*, 132-35, and Yong-gi Cho, *Huimangmokhoe 45 Nyeon* [45 Years of Hope Ministry], 142.

[49] As the church was growing so rapidly, Cho needed to train his church members. Thus, he provided them opportunities to study theology, the Bible, systematic theology and in-depth studies of each book of the Bible at Full Gospel Theological Institute in 1978.

[50] ITI, *Yoido Kyohoei Shinanggwa Shinhak 2*, 111.

[51] Yong-gi Cho, *Widaehan Somyeong: Huimang Mokhoe 50 Nyeon*, 160.

[52] Yong-gi Cho, *Widaehan Somyeong: Huimang Mokhoe 50 Nyeon*, 197.

[53] Yong-gi Cho, *Widaehan Somyeong: Huimang Mokhoe 50 Nyeon*, 259-60, 249.

[54] Yong-gi Cho, *Widaehan Somyeong: Huimang Mokhoe 50 Nyeon*, 162; 189.

poor and the weak but also to expand God's Kingdom to include current social affairs.[55]

Theologisation of Cho's perspective is also a crucial characteristic of this era. There was an urgent need to develop Cho's theology and introduce it to Korean Christians, since he was accused of pseudo-Christianity by the major denomination of Korea, the Presbyterian Church of Korea, called *Tonghab* from 1983 on. The debate was concluded when the Presbyterian Church withdrew their objection in 1994. What triggered the problem was multifaceted, but one of the causes was that there had been no specialised effort to conceptualise and form Cho's theology in a systematic way. Realising this felt need, a pre-existing institute, the Full Gospel Research Centre, established in 1978, was changed to the Youngsan Research Centre in 1990, and then in 1993 to the International Theological Institute, which exists for a full-scale study of Cho. Its main tasks are to develop Cho's theology of holistic salvation and to systematise his doctrines. One of the first meaningful fruits of this Institute is the publication of two books, *Faith and Theology of Yoido Full Gospel Church I, II.*[56] These books introduce the history and theology of Cho and the YFGC in order to interact with the *Tonghab* Presbytery and to defend its authenticity. Additionally, Youngsan Theological Institute of Hansei University (the former Full Gospel Theological Research Center in 1990) is another significant organisation endeavouring to establish Cho's theology by conducting seminars and symposia, and by publishing periodical journals like *The Journal of Youngsan Theology* since 2004.

The Formation of the Healing Theology

There exists an extensive body of research pertaining to the origins and formulation of Cho's theology. These studies can be categorised into three principal themes: 1) cultural aspects;[57] 2) the world Pentecostal movement;[58] and

---

[55] Yong-gi Cho, *Widaehan Somyeong: Huimang Mokhoe 50 Nyeon*, 181-91; 284-91 and Gwui-sam Cho, *Youngsan Choyounggi Moksaui Gyohoe Seongjanghak* [The Church Growth of Rev. Yong-gi Cho], 34; Tai-Il Wang, "Dr Yong-gi Cho's Understanding of the Social Salvation," *Journal of Youngsan Theology Supplement Series1: The Spirituality of Fourth Dimension & Social Salvation*, (ed) Mun-hong Choe (Seoul: Hansei University Press, 2012): 205.

[56] ITI, *Faith and Theology of Yoido Full Gospel Church I, II* (Seoul: Seoul Publisher, 1993).

[57] Ig-jin Kim, *History and Theology of Korean Pentecostalism: Sunbogeum (Pure Gospel) Pentecostalism* (Zoetermeer, The Netherlands: Uitgeverij Boekencentrum, 2003): 201.

[58] This group believes that Cho's theology was strongly influenced by world revivalists and Classical Pentecostalism. See V. Synan, "Roots of Yong-gi Cho's Theology of Healing," *JYT* 3 (2006): 7-37; Myeong-su Park, "David Yong-gi Cho and International Pentecostal/Charismatic Movements," 2002 Youngsan International Theological Symposium (Gupo: Hansei University Press, 2002): 219-242; Donald W. Dayton, "The

3) Cho's personal experiences.[59] The first category further bifurcates into two theoretical schools: "Syncretism"[60] and "Contextualisation."[61]

Nevertheless, elucidating the circumstances and mechanisms through which Cho's theology has evolved does not present a simple solution analogous to a multiple-choice question. The complexity arises from the fact that Cho's theology embodies the confluence of various contextual influences. [62]

GOOD GOD and the Theology of Blessings in the Thought of David Yong-gi Cho," *JYT* 7 (2006): 7-39; Dong-Soo Kim and Jang-Hyeon Ryoo, *Yeongsan Cho Yong-gi Moksaui Samgwa Sasang* [Life and Thought of Rev. Yong-gi Cho] (Yongin, Korea: Kingdom Books, 2010).

59 Mun-hong Choe and Pan-ho Kim are the adherents of this school while Hyun-Sung Bae emphasises Cho's personal experiences with contextualisation. See Mun-hong Choe, "Cho Yong-gi Mogsawa Seongryeong" [Rev. Yong-gi Cho and the Holy Spirit], *JYT* 2 (2004): 181-230; Pan-ho Kim, "Yongsan Sinhagui Bangbeoblongwa Teukjing" [Methodology and Characteristics of Yong-gi Cho's Theology] in *Youngsanui Moghoewa Sinhak II* [Ministry and Theology of Yong-gi Cho] (Gunpo, Korea: Hansei University Press, 2008): 373-98; Hyeon-sung Bae, "Full Gospel Theology and a Korean Pentecostal Identity," in A.H. Anderson and Edmong Tang (eds), *Asian and Pentecostal: The Charismatic Face of Christianity in Asia* (Oxford: Regnum, 2004).

60 Boo-woong Yoo, *Korean Pentecostalism: Its History and Theology* (Frankfurt am Main: Peter Lang, 1988): 220-27; Kwang-seon Seo, "Hanguk Gyohoe Seongryeongundonggwa Buheung Undongui Sinhakjeok Ihea" [Theological Understanding of the Holy Spirit Movement and Revival Movement in the Korean Church] in Korea Christian Academy, *Hangukgyohoe Seonglyeongunddongui Hyeonsanggwa Gujo* [Phenomenon and Structure of the Holy Spirit Movement in the Korean Church] (Seoul: Christian Academy, 1981): 22-99; Kwang-il Kim, "Gidokgyo Chibyeong Hyeonsange Gwanhan Jeongsinuihakjeok Josa Yeongu" [A Psychiatric Study of the Phenomenon of Healing Practice in Christianity] in Korea Christian Academy, *Hangukgyohoe Seonglyeongunddongui Hyeonsanggwa Gujo* [Phenomenon and Structure of the Holy Spirit Movement in the Korean Church] (Seoul: Christian Academy, 1981): 233-96; W.J. Hollenweger, *Pentecostalism: Origins and Developments Worldwide* (Peabody, MA: Hendrickson, 1977), 99-105; M.M. Mullins, "The Empire Strikes Back: Korean Pentecostal Mission to Japan," *Japanese Religions*, 17(2), (July 1992): 142-166; D. Hunt and T.A. McMahon, *The Seduction of Christianity: Spiritual Discernment in the Last Days* (Eugene, OR: Harvest House, 1985): 123; D. Martin, *Pentecostalism: The World Their Parish* (Oxford: Blackwell, 2002): 161.

61 A.H. Anderson, "The Contextual Pentecostal Theology of David Yong-gi Cho," *AJPS* 7(1), (2004): 101-123; Hwa Yung, "Missiological Implications of Dr. David Yong-gi Cho's Theology," *2002 Youngsan International Symposium* (Gunpo, Korea: Hasei University Press, 2003): 94-102; Young-hoon Lee, "Sanjungchukbok Sinangui Osunjeol Sinhakjeok Ihae" [A Pentecostal Theological Understanding of the Belief of Three-fold Blessings], *Cho Yong-gi Moksaui Samjungchukboke Deahan Sinhakjeok Ihea* [Theological Understanding of the Three-fold Blessings of Rev. Yong-gi Cho] (Seoul: Seoul Logos, 2000): 29-31; Jae-bum Lee, *Seonglyeong Undongui Yeoksa* [The History of the Pentecostal Movement] (Seoul: Voice, 1985): 8-11.

62 Bon-cheol Bae affirms the need of understanding Cho's theological formation in relation to three factors: socio-political background, traditional aspect, and personal

Consequently, I intend to delve into Cho's healing theology from four distinctive perspectives: the socio-political-economic context, the cultural-religious context, the context of Christianity, and Cho's personal context.

Socio-Politico-Economic Contexts

Driven initially by Korea's dire circumstances, Cho shaped his healing theology to deliver hope to those without any. Numerous scholars have asserted that Cho's hopeful doctrine evolved from the desolation that pervaded Korea post-war, a message tailored for a "despairing and hopeless people."[63] The American AG missionary, Louis P. Richards, who taught and trained Cho in Bible studies until Cho went to a Bible school, vividly depicted the context in which Cho's theology was conceived. Having arrived in Pusan – Cho's city of residence – a mere five months after the 1953 ceasefire,[64] Richards portrayed the shattered city as one consumed by "unspeakable hunger, poverty, suffering, and lack of proper sanitation."[65] Conditions had deteriorated further when Cho inaugurated his initial church in Deajo-dong, Seoul's poorest slum, in 1958. Among Cho's recurrent ministries was guiding the dying towards faith, such as mothers who endured extreme postpartum haemorrhage. Cho succinctly articulated his motivation for his healing ministry, referring explicitly to the suffering in Korea: "I have felt I need the gifts of healing while seeing people dying."[66] Cho's aspirations lay not in testing his theological knowledge but rather in addressing the very real suffering of his fellow citizens, thus, he began to pray for divine healing.

Moreover, Cho's understanding of healing in the *present* context evolved congruently with the theology of the emergence of God's Kingdom. He elucidated how his healing doctrine was shaped by the hardships endured by Korea, remarking, "I was forced to search the Scriptures to find out if our God was a healing God of 'today' or if His healing would only come in the sweet bye and bye when we reached heaven."[67] This urgent necessity for divine intervention prompted a theological evolution that recognises an immanent God, a belief system underpinned by the Kingdom of God and reconciliation of the

---

encounter with foreign missionaries and revivalists. Bon-cheol Bae, "Youngsan Cho Yong-gi Moksa 60 Nyeon Sayeoke Geolchin Seonglyeonglone Natanan Heaksim Nonje Bunseok" [Exploration of the Central Issues of Rev. Yong-gi Cho's Pneumatology in the sixty-year ministry] *JYT* 33 (2015): 7.

[63] A.H. Anderson, "A 'Time to Share Love': Global Pentecostalism and the Social Ministry of David Yong-gi Cho," in Mun Hong Choe (ed), *JYT Supplement: The Spirituality of Fourth Dimension and Social Salvation* (Gunpo, Korea: Hansei University Press, 2012): 150. Also see Sang-yun Lee, *A Theology of Hope: Contextual Perspectives in Korean Pentecostalism* (Eugene, OR: Wipf and Stock, 2019).

[64] The Korean War ceased when the armistice was signed on 27th July 1953.

[65] L.P. Richards, *Divine Appointments with God*, 13-14.

[66] Yong-gi Cho, *Naui Gyohoe Seongjang Iyagi*, 74.

[67] David Yong-gi Cho, "Foreword", In Robert G. Witty, *Divine Healing* (Nashville, TN: Broadman Press, 1989).

tension between *already* and *not yet*. This theological concept materialised as a characteristic feature of Korean healing theology, defined by immediate, present needs.

Notably, the founding period of the Daejodong Church embodied this critical social context. Cho understood the urgency of divine intervention in Korea's tribulations and thus pleaded with God. Nevertheless, it is crucial to acknowledge that Cho's focus on the present did not detract from the significance of the past or future from an eschatological perspective. According to Cho, "God began to manifest Himself not only as the God of the past and the future, but as the God of the present who lives in present time."[68] Evidently, Cho highlighted the present in addition to the established understanding of God of the future and the past to maintain a balance. Therefore, Cho's healing theology can be interpreted as an endeavour to conceptualise the nature of God for contemporary Christians, contrasting with the relatively greater emphasis on the God of the past and future in the Korean Church context.

In a devastated Korea, Cho's healing theology emerged as the "gospel of need"[69] rather than a gospel of prosperity. His theology refuted the notion that God would grant any prayer rooted in greed; instead, it was constructed to address the genuine needs of individuals suffering from hunger and illness. Importantly, Cho's message of blessings was not directed towards those who already lived comfortably in terms of health and wealth. This approach was evidenced by his proclamation, "God wants you to eat three meals every day, wear clean clothes, and sleep in a clean house," aimed at those who frequently lacked meals and wore dirty clothes.[70] Having lived in a shanty and experienced food and clothing scarcity,[71] Cho understood the pressing need for holistic salvation and the notion that "sickness and extreme poverty are not God's blessings."[72] Cho's healing theology was established to deliver the good news of salvation holistically to suffering people. The societal demands significantly influenced Cho's formulation of his healing theology, known today as the three-fold blessings, rooted in 3 John 2.[73]

Finally, Cho's healing theology evolved significantly as his perspective shifted in response to societal transitions. Early in his ministry, the concept of holistic salvation was primarily focused on individual blessings, as these were the most pressing needs. However, as Korea's economy flourished, this concept expanded to encompass the salvation of society and nature.[74] Consequently, Cho

---

68 Yong-gi Cho, *Salvation, Health and Prosperity* (Lake Mary, FL: Creation House, 1987): 11.

69 Hwa Yung, "The Missiological Challenge of David Yong-gi Cho's Theology," 87.

70 Yong-gi Cho, *Naui Gyohoe Seongjang Iyagi*, 49.

71 Yong-gi Cho, *Sa Chawonui Yeongjeok Segye* [Spiritual World of the Fourth Dimension] (Seoul: Logos, 2012): 188.

72 Yong-gi Cho, *Naui Gyohoe Seongjang Iyagi*, 291.

73 Yong-gi Cho, *Salvation, Health and Prosperity*, 11.

74 Hyeong-geun Lim (ed), *Cho Yong-gi Moksa Ildaegi: Yeouidoui Moghoeja*, 563-64.

began to emphasise the church's role in contributing to the social gospel and nature conservation movements.[75] This demonstrates that Cho's theology continually adapts to societal changes to maintain its practical relevance and assist individuals in their lived realities. This includes integrating new societal demands into Cho's healing theology, which now considers healing as extending beyond individuals, encompassing society and even the ecosystem. Thus, Cho's perspective on healing has broadened to encompass restoration in all aspects of human life, beginning with the individual's health.

Cultural-Religious Contexts

From the inception of his ministerial pursuits, Cho recognised the merit in nurturing and conserving Korean Christian traditions, simultaneously incorporating Christianity as transmitted by foreign missionaries.[76] This stance towards his cultural legacy and customs is well elucidated in his remark:

> In the past, missionaries not only brought their religion but also their culture to the countries they evangelised. So it became apparent that the new converts lost much of their natural heritage. I believe that this produced an unnecessary hindrance to the acceptance of the gospel of Jesus Christ, which is for all people. Therefore, church growth is more than just world missions, for it operates on an individual or congregational level, irrespective of nationality or cultural background.[77]

Cho underscores the significance of an individual remaining true to their cultural identity to enhance the efficacy of powerful evangelism for church expansion. Although it remains uncertain whether Cho held this viewpoint at the commencement of his ministry, his theological method appears closely aligned with contextualisation. Keith Warrington, on this topic, designates Cho as "a contextual theologian," by saying that "he [Cho] speaks to given circumstances, offering lessons that are of particular benefit to believers who live in particular settings."[78] Echoing a similar idea, Allan Anderson continues to bring one's attention to another significant task of exploring "to what extent Cho's Pentecostal message is a contextual theology that has adapted to and transformed its cultural and religious environment."[79]

Cho's pneumatology serves as a salient illustration. One of the most singular features of Cho's healing theology pivots around his pneumatology, encapsulated in "the fellowship of the Holy Spirit," as his healing methods

---

[75] Hyeong-geun Lim (ed), *Cho Yong-gi Moksa Ildaegi: Yeouidoui Moghoeja*, 564.
[76] Interestingly, Cho had more exposure to the influence of Western missionaries than Kim and Lee.
[77] Yong-gi Cho, *More than Numbers* (Waco, TX: Word Books, 1984): 9-10.
[78] K. Warrington, "The Fourth Dimension, the Word and the Spirit", In Mun Hong Choe (ed), *The Spirituality of Fourth Dimension & Social Salvation* (Gunpo: Hansei University Press, 2012): 33.
[79] A.H. Anderson, "The Contextual Pentecostal Theology of David Yong-gi Cho," 110.

heavily rely on the Holy Spirit's role.[80] Although Cho's exploration of the indwelling Spirit of God began in 1964, he was inspired to examine the Bible to address a profound question that resonated in the hearts of many Koreans: Where is our God? He expands on how his theology could evolve in association with Asian culture:

> Oriental people, in particular, require the address and location of the god they worship. Most of them grow up under the influence of heathen worship so they need the address of their god in order to go and worship him […] But when I came into Christianity, I could not locate the address of our Heavenly Father God. In those days, it was a great trouble to my heart while I was learning the Christian way of life […] Many new believers would come to me and ask "Pastor Cho, give us at least some picture, or even an image, to address to. You ask us to believe in God but where is He? […] I needed an answer and so in my own way I started seeking the "address" of our God.[81]

Cho's struggle to ascertain God's location derived from his cultural-religious background, most likely influenced by shamanistic belief. Consequently, Anderson views "Cho's Pentecostalism as a contextual form of Korean Christianity interacting with Shamanism" because of Cho's efforts to theologise his "practices" by drawing on the Bible as his primary source.[82] Upon reading 1 Corinthians 3:16 and 2 Corinthians 1:22, Cho "began to comprehend that God the Father and God the Son dwell in me through the Holy Spirit" and that "His address is my address! He resides in my heart."[83] The principal concept of fellowship with the Holy Spirit was forged and expanded at this juncture. Formerly, Cho endeavoured to locate God and maintain connection through prayer on mountains or in valleys and by attending renowned evangelists' revival meetings.[84] However, once he discerned the secret of the indwelling God via the Holy Spirit, he no longer needed to scour every corner to find God. He started inspiring his church members to converse and pray to God and commune with God from within their hearts.[85] He views this enlightening moment as "the actual inception and the cornerstone" of his ministry.[86] It is essential to note that Cho's previous understanding of God's address triggered his search for a biblical truth about God's location, and presented him with the notion that God can be found in specific places. More critically, it ultimately brought a rectification to the authentic shamanistic belief that gods reside in mountains, valleys, trees, rocks,

---

[80] More will be said on this topic under the section dealing with the BHS in Cho's healing theology.
[81] Young-Gi Cho, *The Fourth Dimension*, 173-74.
[82] A.H. Anderson, "The Contextual Pentecostal Theology of David Yong-gi Cho," 114.
[83] A.H. Anderson, "The Contextual Pentecostal Theology of David Yong-gi Cho," 177.
[84] Young-Gi Cho, *The Fourth Dimension,* 178.
[85] Young-Gi Cho, *The Fourth Dimension,* 178.
[86] Young-Gi Cho, *The Fourth Dimension,* 178.

houses, etc. It was a concerted effort not to validate his prior religious beliefs based on Scriptures, but rather to uncover biblical truths and apply them sensitively to the context with corrections, without undermining the worth of Korean culture.

Christian Context

KOREAN CHRISTIAN TRADITION

Cho's theological perspective aligns seamlessly with the long-established heritage of Korean Christianity. His distinct high regard for Christian traditions stems from his unique personal journey:

> Being a Korean and having been saved out of the Buddhist religion, I have been able to appreciate the distinctive position of Christians who come from the Third World. We are coming from a culture which is not traditionally Christian. Korea received its first missionaries from America almost one hundred years ago. Since then, we evangelical Korean Christians have developed our own traditions. This is very important because it makes it possible for us to be Christian without being less Korean.[87]

Cho, celebrated as one of the most prominent Korean Pentecostals, identifies himself as a Korean *evangelical Christian*, all the while acknowledging the Christian traditions passed down from his predecessors. When Cho perceives himself as a custodian of the Korean Church tradition, an intriguing query arises: what spiritual legacies has Cho inherited from his predecessors? Addressing this question, William W. Menzies, a noted Pentecostal historian, asserted that "Cho acquired the value of intercession at an early stage in his ministry [...] [he] embodies what is commonly practiced throughout the churches of Korea."[88] Menzies further elaborated his assertion by stating that Cho is "a faithful steward" of the prayer legacy bequeathed from the significant revivals in 1903 and 1907.[89] Menzies' claims are plausible when considering the unique aspects of Korean prayer traditions that originated in 1903 and have evolved continually throughout Korean church history.

In examining the prayer practices of Korean Pentecostals, distinctions from other global Pentecostal congregations such as the classical Pentecostal group are starkly evident.[90] This is primarily why mountain prayer, daily dawn prayer, and unison prayer are acknowledged as integral components of Korean Christian traditions. The renowned Korean Pentecostal theologian Wonsuk Ma asserts that the prayer mountain movement signifies a "unique feature" of "the

---

[87] Yong-gi Cho, *More than Numbers*, 9.
[88] W.W. Menzies, "Yong-gi Cho's Theology of the Fullness of the Spirit: A Pentecostal Perspective," 31.
[89] W.W. Menzies, "Yong-gi Cho's Theology of the Fullness of the Spirit: A Pentecostal Perspective," 36.
[90] ITI, *Yoido Kyohoei Shinanggwa Shinhak 2*, 232.

Pentecostalisation of Korean Christianity."[91] From an external perspective, John Stetz, an AG missionary, provides an eyewitness account of the distinguishing characteristics of Korean prayer practices:

> This prayer mantle [persistent prayer] was inherited by the Korean Church. At 4:30 o'clock every morning of the year church bells from every church tower ring out the call for the followers to gather for a pre-dawn prayer meeting. They come in the rain and mud; they come before breakfast to meet with their Heavenly Father in their local churches [...] One characteristic feature of their prayer meetings is that they pray audibly all at the same time. Who taught them to pray in this manner? The missionaries didn't [...] In keeping with this tremendous zeal, it comes natural for them to intercede audibly as did the first-century Christians when "they raised their voices in united prayer."[92]

As alluded to by a classical Pentecostal professor above, this *prayer mantle* is a product of the indigenous Korean HSM tradition, developed in its unique cultural context. Acknowledging the origins of these Korean prayer styles, Lee identifies Sun-joo Gil as the initiator of the Early Morning Prayer, while Park emphasises Ja-shil Choe's influential role in fostering fasting prayer in the Korean Church.[93] In this context, Vinson Synan postulates that Cho was profoundly influenced by Korean evangelists such as Sun-joo Gil, Ik-du Kim, and Yong-do Lee.[94] Nevertheless, it remains challenging to single out one or two individuals as Cho's primary influences, given that the Korean Church's prayer tradition is not a heritage suddenly conceived by an individual at a particular time. Instead, it is a persistent tradition, formed and evolved with new emphases and forms throughout Korean church history. It is, therefore, more plausible to perceive Cho's theology of healing prayer as a continuation of the entire Korean church tradition rather than that of select individuals.

Cho has openly acknowledged the profound influence of two other Korean pastors: Gyeong-jig Han and Seong-bong Lee.[95] While Han's influence primarily pertains to ministerial practices rather than to theology,[96] Cho

---

[91] Wonsuk Ma, "Blessing in Pentecostal Theology and Mission," Wonsuk Ma, Veli-Matti Kärkkäinen and J. Kwabena Asamoah-Bydau (eds), *Pentecostal Mission and Global Christianity*, Regnum Edinburgh Centenary Series. Vol. 20. (Oxford: Regnum, 2014), 272-91: 280.

[92] J. Stetz, "The Impact of Christianity on Korea's Culture," (M.A. Thesis, Azusa Pacific College, 1973): 69-70.

[93] Myeong-su Park, "Korean Pentecostal Spirituality as Manifested in the Testimonies of Believers of the Yoido Full Gospel Church," 51.

[94] V. Synan, "Roots of Yong-gi Cho's Theology of Healing," 14.

[95] Sang-in Han, "A Response to Lim's Research on the Pneumatology of Rev. Yong-gi Cho," in Young-hoon Lee (ed), *Osunjeol Sinhak Nondan*, vol. 2, [Forum of Pentecostal Theology] (1999): 37.

[96] Yong-gi Cho, *Widaehan Somyeong: Huimang Mokhoe 50 Nyeon*, 298.

exhibited a profound admiration for Lee,[97] stating that "Lee was walking with the Holy Spirit to preach the gospel, and his ministry became a significant role model for me in terms of pastoring."[98] Considering that Lee was a spiritual father to Ja-shil Choe, who is both Cho's mother-in-law and spiritual mother, Lee's influence on Cho's life is unquestionable. Upon examining the characteristics of Lee and his ministry as recognised by Cho, several shared attributes become evident. Cho views Lee's ministry as exemplifying "the emphasis on the Spirit-led life," "great zeal," "love," and a "message of hope."[99] Particularly, Cho observes that "Lee's message of hope is aligned with the philosophy and objective of his ministry" and that "it is through the power of this message of hope that numerous people were healed at Lee's revival meetings."[100] Thus, he perceives "the secret of the successful ministry of Lee" as "the Spirit-filled life."[101] In summary, Cho acknowledges that both he and Lee emphasise a message of hope for the marginalised and a Spirit-filled/led life in their ministries. Lee's theology of hope and the Holy Spirit, in the context of healing, appears to have been further matured and reinforced by Cho.

Theological Dialogue

Intensive theological debates on Cho's theology took place after he was accused of being a "pseudo-Christian" by the Korean Presbytery of *Tonghab* in 1981. The main issues of the criticism by *Tonghab* were Cho's views on ancestral worship, rumours of a resurrected woman, prayer with laying on of hands for an elder, an issue of ordination, thoughtless participation in holy communion, evidence of the BHS, and evangelism.[102] These accusations required Cho to start having theological interaction with them. It was, of course, not at all a pleasant experience for Cho. The problem with *Tonghab* arose partly because Pentecostal belief was not well-known in the context of Korean Christianity especially at a time when it was dominated by the Presbyterians. The table (Table 3) below shows the breakdown of Pentecostal and Presbyterian groups at that time.

Table 3: Comparison between Pentecostal and Presbyterian Groups in December 1980[103]

	Denominations	Churches	Ministers	Members
Presbyterian	29	12,270	17,613	3,999,137
Pentecostal	7	961	1,585	440,557

[97] As historical sources do not reveal any direct encounter of Cho with Lee, Lee's influence over Cho seems to be primarily through his mother-in-law, Ja-sil Choe.
[98] Yong-gi Cho, "Iseongbong Moksaui Sayeok Soke Natanan Seonglyeong," 423.
[99] Yong-gi Cho, "Iseongbong Moksaui Sayeok Soke Natanan Seonglyeong," 423-44.
[100] Yong-gi Cho, "Iseongbong Moksaui Sayeok Soke Natanan Seonglyeong," 424.
[101] Yong-gi Cho, "Iseongbong Moksaui Sayeok Soke Natanan Seonglyeong," 426.
[102] Yong-gi Cho, *Widaehan Somyeong: Huimang Mokhoe 50 Nyeon*, 155.
[103] Kwang-il Kim, "Gidokgyo Chibyeong Hyeonsange Gwanhan Jeongsinuihakjeok Josa Yeongu," 299.

According to statistical data indicating a ratio of nearly 10:1 between the two groups, it becomes evident that the Korean Presbyterian Church, being the oldest and most dominant denomination, wielded a highly influential role. The attempts made by the Korean Assemblies of God (KAG) to alter their denominational name to the Korean Jesus Presbyterian Church on two occasions in 1973 and 1974 serve as evidence of the Presbyterians' influence.[104] Given the cessationist viewpoint held by the Korean Church[105] and their disapproval of Cho's theological perspectives, as well as the controversial nature of Cho's resurrection episode,[106] it is understandable that Cho was not embraced by the Korean Church. Consequently, due to a lack of understanding of Pentecostal practices and beliefs, combined with Cho's significant errors, he was mistakenly perceived as a heretical Christian akin to Gi-dong Kim.[107] As Cho's ministry primarily centred around spiritual warfare and healing, he could be classified within the same category. Therefore, it becomes apparent that Cho's theological perspectives posed challenges within the mainstream Korean Church, as discernible from Cho's confession: "I endeavoured to soften the impact of the revolutionary principles which I stated."[108]

While the majority of criticisms stemmed from an unfamiliarity with Pentecostal beliefs and the cessationists' perspective, it is also true that Cho incorporated the advice and critiques of *Tonghab* to revise some of his radical concepts. As evident from his statement in 1973, "Never reject the Holy Spirit, for if you do you must die," Cho occasionally employed assertive and radical expressions.[109] As another example of his radical disposition, he had previously permitted his church members to bow before ancestral pictures, albeit not for worship but as an act of filial duty to show respect. However, Cho altered his stance on ancestral worship in an effort to align with the general belief of the Korean Church.[110] During this period, Cho placed increased emphasis on developing and introducing his theology within the Korean Church by establishing theological institutes within his own church. The Institute of

---

[104] The Compilation Committee of the Fifty-Year History of the Korea Assemblies of God, *The 50th History of the Korea Assemblies of God: 1953-2004* (Seoul: Creation, 2005): 345.

[105] As Cho observed that "many today do not believe healing by prayer is possible," most Christians did not believe in the possibility of divine healing. Yong-gi Cho, *To God Be the Glory*, 66.

[106] Cho announced in one of his services that a lady who attended his church was resurrected forty-one hours after her death. However, it was revealed to be false. It is not certain if it was a self-fabricated scenario or a rash act based on the report of the lady's family.

[107] Kwang-il Kim, "Gidokgyo Chibyeong Hyeonsange Gwanhan Jeongsinuihakjeok Josa Yeongu," 235.

[108] Yong-gi Cho, *The Fourth Dimension,* vol 2, vii.

[109] Yong-gi Cho, *To God Be the Glory*, 151.

[110] Ig-jin Kim, *History and Theology of Korean Pentecostalism*, 186.

Theology and the ITI exemplify these endeavours. They sought to further develop and systematise Cho's theology concerning eschatology, revelation, human nature, divine healing, demonology, synergism, and the union between God and humanity.[111]

Another significant theological progression in Cho's work was his expansion of the scope of healing from individuals to encompass society and the environment.[112] In reference to this transformation, Anderson's observations on Pentecostalism can be aptly applied to Cho's case, wherein Anderson affirms that "The subject of 'social theology' is not one that sits easily with Pentecostals. Pentecostals have not always felt comfortable with relating to a wider society, but that is something that is gradually changing."[113] Cho's healing theology has also undergone gradual yet steadfast changes. Since the emergence of criticisms in 1981, he has initiated several noteworthy projects aimed at addressing the needs of the underprivileged. Cho's practical involvement in charitable activities can be observed in his support for heart surgeries for children, aid for parentless children and international refugees, including those from North Korea, assistance for flood victims, impoverished local churches, foreign workers, elderly individuals living alone, Holt International Children's Services, blood donation campaigns, medical services for the indigent, nature conservation efforts, the establishment of the Elim Rehabilitation Center, a heart hospital in North Korea, and the Good People movement. It is also noteworthy that since his retirement in 2008, Cho dedicated his remaining years to assisting marginalised individuals through the establishment of the Sharing Love and Happiness Movement.[114]

Cho exhibits a degree of flexibility in aligning his theology in a practical manner when interacting with diverse individuals, all the while retaining the core values and principles of his theological framework. Cho sought to refine his perspective to be more readily accepted within the context of the Korean Church. In this regard, a significant change can be observed in Cho's preaching throughout different periods of his ministry, as documented by the Institute of Theology (ITI).[115]

Cho's emphasis on the will of God has been apparent since the 1980s, as illustrated in Table 4. Previously, his focus leaned more towards practical principles aimed at seeking blessings from God. However, Cho underwent a significant shift in his theology, redirecting his attention towards understanding God's desires in relation to the blessings and spiritual empowerment bestowed upon believers. This represents a notable transformation wherein God and His will became the central theme of his messages starting from the early 1980s,

---

[111] ITI. *Yoido Kyohoei Shinanggwa Shinhak*, 148-231.

[112] Young-hoon Lee, "The Influence of Dr. Cho's 'God is so good-faith' in the Korean Churches" *JYT* 7 (2006): 107.

[113] A.H. Anderson, "A 'Time to Share Love'," 141.

[114] Yong-gi Cho, *Widaehan Somyeong: Huimang Mokhoe 50*, 181-91 and 284-91.

[115] ITI, *Yoido Kyohoei Shinanggwa Shinhak 2*, 112.

replacing the previous emphasis on what God can provide and how believers can receive such blessings. An additional noteworthy change can be observed in the Korean version of *The Fourth Dimension*, which was translated into Korean in 1999, twenty years after its initial publication in English in 1979. Cho introduced a new sentence, "Strictly speaking, faith is given by God as a gift," to the original argument that "Faith first begins with our own human effort to believe."[116] This alteration highlights Cho's endeavour to strike a balance between human effort and God's sovereignty within his theological framework.

Table 4: The Topics of Cho's Messages by Years

	1958–1961	1961–1973	1973–1982	1982–present
Message	1. Miracles by faith 2. Jesus the healer 3. Good God	1. The works of the Holy Spirit 2. Counsellor, and helper, the Holy Spirit 3. The power of the Cross	1. The power of prayer 2. Law of faith 3. Fullness of the Holy Spirit 4. Positive thinking	1. Sovereignty of God 2. Providence of God 3. Importance of the Law 4. Importance of service

These instances demonstrate Cho's receptive attitude towards critiques, as long as they do not pose a threat to the fundamental tenets of his theology. Cho expressed his intention to publish a book as an official response to the theological critics of *Tonghab*, stating that "the publication of *Faith and Theology of Yoido Full Gospel Church I, II* would be a great opportunity to engage in introspection and self-examination for the maturity of Christian faith."[117] These books serve as a means through which Cho's theology can be clearly communicated and engaged with other theologians, facilitating theological discourse. Consequently, *Tonghab* withdrew their accusations against Cho after realising, through their research, that "most of Cho's theology is based on the characteristics of World Pentecostal beliefs."[118]

It was through Cho's concerted efforts to engage in theological dialogue with his counterparts and incorporate their input that his theology improved and gained broader acceptance.[119] Approximately eleven years after the resolution of the accusations from *Tonghab*, a significant outcome emerged. In 2004, Min, a

[116] Yong-gi Cho, *Sachawonui Yeongjeok Segye*, 173; 184 and Young-Gi Cho, *The Fourth Dimension*, 159; 168.
[117] See the foreword and introduction of ITI, *Yoido Kyohoei Shinanggwa Shinhak* 2.
[118] Yong-gi Cho, *Widaehan Somyeong: Huimang Mokhoe 50 Nyeon*, 158.
[119] One of the good examples of Cho's receptiveness is that Cho added "unity" to his theology of "the fellowship with the Holy Spirit" by accepting a suggestion of a Greek professor in Paris. Yong-gi Cho, *My Church Growth Stories* (Seoul: Seoul Logos, 2006): 84.

prominent historian of the *Tonghab* denomination within the Korean Church, acknowledged Cho's contributions by stating that "Cho has created a new type of Holy Spirit movement while firmly adhering to evangelical tradition and exhibiting flexibility as an indigenous movement."[120] Cho's recognition as an esteemed Korean evangelical theologian today would not have been possible without his proactive engagement with the Korean Church in a positive manner. This process allowed him to further develop the theology of Korean Pentecostalism and exert a substantial influence on the Korean Church as a rational Korean Pentecostal theologian.

Personal Context

Oral Roberts

Among the formative influences shaping Cho's theological disposition, a significant role was played by eminent practitioners of healing, such as Oral Roberts, a fact widely attested by numerous scholars.[121] Ryu's research posits that Cho's theological framework was already well established early in his ministry, before he crossed paths with Roberts.[122] However, careful analysis of historical evidence unequivocally indicates the substantial influence Roberts exerted on Cho's theological orientation. A mutual consensus exists between Cho and Roberts, acknowledging the indebtedness of Cho's theology to Roberts' teachings.[123] Especially, Cho confessed that "Roberts is my spiritual mentor and teacher" and that "the message of 3 John 2 of Roberts has become the basis for my 'every sermon.'"[124] Indeed, Cho's message of hope is focused on the theme of "the Good God"[125] and its practical implication of holistic salvation is based

---

120 Kyoung-bae Min, "ChoYong-gi Maksaui Seonglyeongsinhakgwa Hanguk Gyohoe: Han Yeoksajeok Jeobgeun" [The Theology of Holy Spirit of Rev. Yong-gi Cho and the Korean Church: An Historical Approach," *JYT* 1 (2004): 38.

121 V. Synan, "Roots of Yong-gi Cho's Theology of Healing," 35; Myung-su Park, "David Yong-gi Cho and International Pentecostal/Charismatic Movements," 219-42; Ig-jin Kim, *History and Theology of Korean Pentecostalism,* 193; T.K. Mathew, "O. Roberts and David Yong-gi Cho: A Comparative Evaluation of Their Theologies of Healing," *JYT* 8 (2006): 38-69; W.W. Menzies, "Cho's Theology of the Fullness of the Spirit," 37; Young-hoon Lee, "Oral Roberts and David Yonggi Cho: A Life-long Relationship in Theology and Ministry," *Spiritus: ORU Journal of Theology* 4:1 (Spring 2019), 5-16.

122 Jang-hyun Ryu, "A Theological Study of Dr. Yong-gi Cho's Pneumatology," *JYT* 1 (2004): 167-68.

123 Cho said, "I have been greatly influenced by books of Pastor O. Roberts. As I read those books, the contents in the books have given dreams and hopes in my mind." Yong-gi Cho, *Gyohoeseongjang Jinjeongeuro Wonhasibnigga?* [Do you truly want Church Growth?] (Seoul: Seoul Logos, 1995): 11. Furthermore, Roberts also advocated his influence on Cho in the foreword of Cho's book, *Salvation, Health, and Prosperity*, 8.

124 Yong-gi Cho, *Gyohoeseongjang Jinjeongeuro Wonhasibnigga*? 35.

125 W.W. Menzies, "Cho's Theology of the Fullness of the Spirit," 37; V. Synan, "Roots of Yong-gi Cho's Theology of Healing, 27-28.

on 3 John 2 as was Roberts'. He also adopts the concept of the "seed faith" directly from Roberts, as he indicates in his book.[126]

In stressing the similarities[127] between Cho and Roberts, one needs to pay a great deal of attention to a specific book of Roberts' since Cho admits Roberts' influence on his perspectives especially through *If You Need Healing Do These Things*.[128] It is confirmed through the book that both believe that "everybody has their own faith – a measure of faith,"[129] "your soul governs your physical life,"[130] it is important to "join yourself to companions of faith,"[131] and God has "a better way for you" regarding unanswered prayers.[132]

Beyond these, there exists a plethora of other theological parallels between Cho and Roberts' interpretations of healing, particularly Roberts' assertion that to be effective, faith must first envision God's power manifesting the desired outcome. This perspective bears a striking resemblance to Cho's own coined term, the "Fourth Dimension."[133] Even their views on fasting demonstrate remarkable congruence, with both considering it a means of fostering an intimate relationship with Christ.[134]

Apart from these, there seem to be many shared concepts within their healing theologies. Roberts views that "To be effective, faith must first have a vision held in the heart that sees God bringing to pass what you are believing for […] This [called faith image] lifts the battle from the human level to a new height where God takes over."[135] This concept looks like Cho's invented terminology, the so-called "Fourth Dimension." The concept of fasting is also similar, since

---

[126] Yong-gi Cho, *The Fourth Dimension*, 161.

[127] According to Mathew's observation, the similarities between Cho and Roberts are as follows: Whole person healing, the inter-relationship of human body (spirit, soul, and body), the Good God, God as the ultimate source of every healing (including medical treatment), God's time for healing, death as a natural phenomenon, healing as the nature of God's kingdom, healing as a tool for evangelism, and healing in the atonement. T.K. Mathew, "O. Roberts and David Yong-gi Cho: A Comparative Evaluation of their Theologies of Healing," 61-62.

[128] Yong-gi Cho, *Sachawonui Yeongseong*, 35.

[129] O. Roberts, *If You Need Healing Do These Things*, rev. (Tulsa, OK: Healing Waters, 1951): 27 and Yong-gi Cho, *Successful Living* (Seoul: Young San, 1977): 136.

[130] O. Roberts, *If You Need Healing Do These Things*, 27; Yong-gi Cho, *How can I be Healed?* (Seoul: Seoul Logos, 1999): 38; Yong-gi Cho, *The Fourth Dimension,* vol 2, 73.

[131] O. Roberts, *If You Need Healing*, 149.

[132] O. Roberts, *If You Need Healing*, 63, and Yong-gi Cho, *How can I be Healed?* 136; 139-40.

[133] Cho defines the fourth dimension as the spiritual world, and it is believed to influence the physical world that exists as the first three dimensions. Cho emphasises faith to activating this fourth dimension. See Yong-gi Cho, *Sachawoneui Yeongjeoksegye* [The Fourth Dimension] (Seoul: Seoul Publisher, 1996): 54-86.

[134] O. Roberts, *101 Questions and Answers on Healing and Salvation* (Tulsa, OK: Oral Roberts Evangelistic Association, 1968): 78.

[135] O. Roberts, *101 Questions and Answers*, 35.

Roberts considers fasting as a process of "putting one's mind and heart on seeking Christ and His presence, and of coming into an intimate relationship with Him who is the Answer to all things."[136]

Nonetheless, Cho has his own distinctive perspectives that differentiate him from Roberts in at least seven aspects:

1) God's sovereignty in relation to faith. Cho believes everybody has their own faith, but healings happen only when God's faith comes to human faith, while Roberts argues that "we possess faith, but it will profit us nothing until it is released and sent to God for our particular need [through point of contact]." Even though Roberts also believes that "in salvation the initiative rests with God, but God's initiative must be matched by man's response," he emphasises the human response to show their faith in God for healing.[137]

2) The origin of sickness. Both believe that sickness comes from demons, but Cho separated the direct influence of demons from the indirect by saying, "every illness is not caused by the demons that enter human body." Sometimes, people can be sick because of the careless use of their body, in which case demons just supply the destructive power to the afflicted body in terms of influence not of possession.[138]

3) The understanding of the role of the Holy Spirit. In Cho's perspective, it is quite clear that the Holy Spirit is the One who brings healing and requires believers to have a close and intimate on-going relationship with the Holy Spirit, as Cho frequently uses the concept of the fellowship and partnership with the Holy Spirit. However, Roberts bases his close relationship with God on Christology when he says, "we can visualise God in His Son, Jesus [...] I grew up believing that Jesus lived in our house and was a member of our family."[139] In fact, Cho's understanding of the fellowship with God is more based on the works of the Holy Spirit while Roberts' is more on God and Jesus.[140]

4) Discerning God's time for healing. Both argue that there is God's time to heal. However, Roberts confesses his difficulty to "get people to wait until the time is right for them to receive prayer" whereas Cho articulates that "God's faith [that brings healing] comes to us with peace and conviction in our hearts." In this respect, Cho views that believers would definitely know when the time is right.[141]

5) The sources of healing. Both generally agree that the ultimate healing power comes from God, but Cho advocates another possibility of healing that

---

[136] O. Roberts, *101 Questions and Answers*, 78.

[137] Yong-gi Cho, *Salvation, Health, and Prosperity*, 152; Roberts, *101 Questions and Answers*, 16; 52-53.

[138] ITI, *Yoido Kyohoei Shinanggwa Shinhak 2*, 202.

[139] O. Roberts, *101 Questions and Answers*, 82.

[140] O. Roberts, *101 Questions and Answers*, 40-41.

[141] Yong-gi Cho and Robert Schuller, *Expand Your Horizon: How to make your faith work* (Bladensburg, MD: Dove Christian Books, 1988), 90-102; Yong-gi Cho, *Sachawonui Yeongseong*, 139.

could be brought by demons, since they are believed to be spiritual beings who control the third dimension from the fourth dimension with limited power.[142]

6) The scope of holistic salvation. Both of them emphasise holistic salvation, in which God's blessings for our soul, body, and material things are all prepared by the work of Jesus on the Cross as a finished work. However, Cho expands the concept to his society and nature. In other words, Roberts' understanding is limited to individuals while Cho seeks to deal with a broader territory for God's healing and blessings.[143]

7) Point of contact. Roberts' faith becomes activated when he has a special feeling on his right hand as a point of contact, while Cho does so when God shows him a vision of healing of the sick.[144]

T.L. OSBORN

There are other practitioners whose theologies helped Cho develop his perspectives on healing. T.L. Osborn is acknowledged by several scholars[145] and Cho affirms the influence of Osborn by saying that "I collected Pastor Osborn's book and delivered his healing message."[146] It is interesting that Osborn appreciates Roberts' role in quickening "the message and ministry of deliverance" to Osborn.[147] Osborn's theology of healing is in harmony with Cho's in terms of: 1) God's will to heal,[148] 2) the belief that faith comes by hearing the Word of God,[149] 3) the origin of sickness,[150] 4) the power of our confession,[151] 5) spiritual, mental, and physical healing,[152] and 6) the finished work of Jesus Christ on the Cross.[153]

However, Osborn tends to rely on aggressive concepts in more senses than Cho as he says, "Never pray for faith to be healed […] You don't need to pray

---

142 Yong-gi Cho, *Sachawonui Yeongseong* [The Fourth Dimensional Spirituality], 69-70.
143 Hyeong-geun Lim (ed), *Cho Yong-gi Moksa Ildaegi: Yeouidoui Moghoeja*, 563-64.
144 O. Roberts, *101 Questions and Answers*, 358-59.
145 Myeong-su Park, "David Yong-gi Cho and International Pentecostal/Charismatic Movements," 219-42 and Ig-jin Kim, *History and Theology of Korean Pentecostalism*, 193.
146 Yong-gi Cho, *Gyohoeseongjang Jinjeongeuro Wonhasibnigga*? 84 and D.E. Harrell, Jr., *All Things Are Possible: The Healing and Charismatic Revivals in Modern America* (Bloomington, IN: Indiana University Press, 1975): 63-66.
147 T.L. Osborn, *Divine Healing through Creative Word* (Tulsa, OK: Osborn Foundation, 1949): 6.
148 T.L. Osborn, *Healing the Sick* (Tulsa, OK: Harrison House, 1951), 13.
149 T.L. Osborn, *Healing the Sick*, 32; 81.
150 Osborn asserts that "your sickness came from the devil, your adversary." T.L. Osborn, *Faith's Testimony* (Tulsa, OK: Osborn Foundation, 1956): 63.
151 T.L. Osborn, *Faith's Testimony* (Tulsa, OK: Osborn Foundation, 1956): 65.
152 T.L. Osborn, *Healing the Sick*, 85.
153 Osborn is a strong advocator of healing in the atonement. T.L. Osborn, *Faith's Testimony*, 72.

for it."[154] "When you talk about your sickness and diseases, you are glorifying the adversary who had the ability to put that disease or sickness on you,"[155] and "if you are saved, you should be healed. If you are healed, you should be saved."[156] In this regard, Osborn's healing theology is based on the concept of certainty that it is the definite will of God to heal, so there is "no glory in suffering under post-Calvary epoch" and you must not "ask if it be Your will" to heal.[157] Osborn's belief of healing in the atonement creates an attitude of believing in divine healing with "certainty" and "immediacy."[158] Therefore, Cho's theology can be problematical to Osborn[159] when he stresses the function of prayer to know the will of God, and waiting for God's time to be healed. In this regard, Osborn's impact on Cho's healing theology is limited to the general area of Pentecostal belief in terms of the importance of faith and healing provided on the Cross, not his view of the certainty of divine healing.

OTHERS

Billy Graham is another of the people that Cho considered a role model.[160] Cho listened to Graham's sermons and tried to be like Graham.[161] It is significant that it was not Roberts but Graham who was first invited by Cho to preach in the new sanctuary in 1972,[162] although Cho also invited Roberts to preach at the Church Growth International (CGI) founded by Cho, and received him as an honorary pastor of Cho's church in 1986.[163] Graham's influence, however, is confined to the area of preaching, as Cho could not see the gifts of healing from Graham.[164] In this respect, it can be fairly argued that Cho's healing theology is not directly influenced by Graham in spite of Cho's admiration for him.

---

[154] It is Osborn's argument that believers have a right to claim healing since their healing is already provided by the stripes of Jesus, so he writes that "We no longer try to get healed. God says we were healed. That is ours. We confess it and thank Him for it." T.L. Osborn, *Faith's Testimony,* 55-57.

[155] T.L. Osborn, *Faith's Testimony,* 63.

[156] T.L. Osborn, *Faith's Testimony,* 69.

[157] T.L. Osborn, *Faith's Testimony,* 69; 83.

[158] T.L. Osborn, *Faith's Testimony,* 103.

[159] As well as to the US Assemblies of God from which the Korean AG may have inherited its doctrine of healing.

[160] Yong-gi Cho, *Naui Gyohoe Seongjang Iyagi*, 84; N.L. Kennedy, *Dream Your Way to Success*, 192.

[161] Yong-gi Cho, *Expand your Horizon*, 82 and Hyeong-geun Lim (ed), *Cho Yong-gi Moksa Ildaegi*, 463.

[162] N.L. Kennedy, *Dream Your Way to Success*, 218.

[163] So-heun Lee, "The Passing of Oral Roberts," *The Full Gospel Family Newspaper*, 18th December 2009. [Available at: http://www.fgnews.co.kr/front/view.do?first_category_id=7&second_category_id=49&id=87781], [Last accessed: 3rd November 2023].

[164] Yong-gi Cho, *Gyohoeseongjang Jinjeongeuro Wonhasibnigga?* 19.

The next person is Robert Schuller. Anderson points out that "Cho has shared platforms, in a favourable light with Robert Schuller."[165] In fact, Cho recognises the power of Schuller's preaching in relation to "possibility thinking" as he says, "When I am in the United States and am in a hotel room on a Sunday, and want to watch a Christian programme on television, I turn on Dr Schuller's 'Hour of Power.' I know I can depend on him to put faith, hope and love into my heart. His sermons uplift me."[166] In this regard, Lee is right to contend that "it is through the influence of Schuller that Cho could have preached the messages that meet the needs of people and gave them hope."[167] It is most likely that Cho's message of hope was further developed and systematised with the help of Schuller's perspective of "possibility thinking."

While many have mentioned other names such as Dietrich Bonhoeffer and Paul Tillich,[168] Kenneth Hagin,[169] David du Plessis,[170] and Kathryn Kuhlman,[171] it seems to me reasonable to claim the influences of Tillich[172] with H. Richard Niebuhr, du Plessis and Vincent Peale since Cho himself mentioned those names.[173] Cho tries to signify the importance of having a goal and living "a goal-oriented" life by using an illustration from Peale.[174] However, I believe Peale's role in the formation of Cho's theology is very minimal in spite of Cho's quotation of his illustration. Cho rather appears to use Peale's concept just to support his idea. In the beginning of his ministry, Cho already realised the necessity of a "specific prayer" in terms of having a clear-cut goal from his personal experience: his prayer for a table, a bicycle, and a chair was answered by God when Cho started praying specifically for his prayer requests.[175] It was claimed by Cho to be his own realisation as this experience "became one of several turning points" in his life and ministry.[176]

---

[165] A.H. Anderson, "The Contextual Pentecostal Theology of David Yong-gi Cho," 119-20.

[166] Yong-gi Cho, *Successful Home Cell Groups*, 160.

[167] Jae-bum Lee, *Seonglyeong Undongui Yeoksa*, 212.

[168] Ig-jin Kim, *History and Theology of Korean Pentecostalism*, 193.

[169] V. Synan, "Roots of Yong-gi Cho's Theology of Healing," 33.

[170] N.L. Kennedy, *Dream Your Way to Success*, 196.

[171] V. Synan, "Roots of Yong-gi Cho's Theology of Healing," 35.

[172] Cho admits that his doctrine of humanity was influenced by Tillich in a sense that humans are totally hopeless up to the point that they cannot come out of their despair by themselves, Yong-gi Cho, *Ojung Bokeum Iyagi* [The Story of the Five-fold Gospel] (Seoul: Seoul Logos, 1998): 20.

[173] *Gyohoe Yeonhabsinbo Chuksopan* [Union Newspaper of Church], 1 (13 July 1969) in The Compilation Committee of the Fifty-year History of the Korea Assemblies of God, *The 50th History of the Korea Assemblies of God: 1953-2004* (Seoul: Creation, 2005): 333-34.

[174] Yong-gi Cho, *Salvation, Health, and Prosperity*, 104-105.

[175] N.L. Kennedy, *Dream Your Way to Success*, 172.

[176] N.L. Kennedy, *Dream Your Way to Success*, 172.

It is also interesting to note du Plessis' role in helping Cho to understand a central truth about the gift of healing. In Cho's autobiography, healing is given to the sick through the healing practitioner who is like "a postman delivering the gift from the Giver."[177] Cho learned from du Plessis the idea that the gift of healing in 1 Corinthians 12 is not meant to be that of some individuals but a gift from God.

When it comes to others like Kuhlman and Hagin, these need much more solid support to claim their influences over Cho. Although there is a similarity of "the words of wisdom" between Cho and Kuhlman in terms of their healing practice, Kuhlman's influence can be hardly argued. Cho mentioned that he was confused about his vision as if it came from Satan at first[178] and that the missionaries around him had no idea about his vision of the healing of the sick.[179] These prove that Cho had no idea about Kuhlman's healing ministry which is characterised with the words of wisdom. Additionally, as Anderson nullifies the influence of Hagin,[180] it is unknown whether Cho is resurrecting the idea of *rhema* directly from Hagin, although one cannot ignore their similarities and the indirect connection of Cho to Hagin. Synan's research is considerable since he proves some indirect connections between Cho and Hagin. However, it lacks solid historical data by which Hagin's influence over Cho could officially be acknowledged. In this regard, it is still hard to affirm Hagin's impact on Cho's theology.[181]

Lastly, more attention must be given to Cho and Jurgen Moltmann's relationship, which developed more recently, since Cho mentioned the influence of Moltmann's theology of hope over his ministry. Cho said that "I have practised the theology of hope through my entire life. Your [Moltmann's] theology became the most powerful foundation for my ministry."[182] However, the degree of Moltmann's influence seems to be limited to the message of hope, since most of Cho's theology was already formed before his first encounter with Moltmann in 1995. It is also noticeable that their focal points of theology of hope are different: if Moltmann's message is more on social and political dimensions, Cho has focused more on individual interests. In this regard, Moltmann helped Cho expand his perspective to socio-political matters.

---

[177] N.L. Kennedy, *Dream Your Way to Success*, 196.
[178] Yong-gi Cho, *Sa Chawonui Yeongjeok Segye*, 92.
[179] Yong-gi Cho, *Sa Chawonui Yeongjeok Segye*, 92.
[180] Although it is true that the distinction between *rhema* and *logos* is a well-known theological invention of Hagin, the similarity itself between Cho and this school cannot be an affirmatory clue. See A.H. Anderson, "The Contextual Pentecostal Theology of David Yong-gi Cho," 119-20.
[181] V. Synan, "Roots of Yong-gi Cho's Theology of Healing," 29-32.
[182] Sang-mok Sin, "The theology of hope is still valid," *Kook-Min-Il-Bo*, 30th September 2013 [Available at: http://news.kmib.co.kr/article/view.asp?arcid=0007605710], [Last accessed: 3rd November 2023].

ASSEMBLIES OF GOD

Pan-ho Kim asserts that "the doctrines of healing and blessings were formulated through his own experience of recuperating from tuberculosis prior to the introduction of the theology of the American Assemblies of God (AAG) to Cho." [183] Nevertheless, the considerable influence of the AAG on Cho, substantiated by historical records, should not be dismissed lightly. In accordance with Min's observations, a reasonable inference could be made that the period between 1964 and 1974 marked a significant development of Cho's healing theology and pneumatology.[184] This implies that Cho's theology of healing had not yet fully materialised until his encounters with AAG missionaries and his education at an AG Bible school. Reflecting on his illness in 1964, Cho confesses, "I struggled to augment my faith in my healing. Furthermore, I recognised a lack of precise biblical comprehension regarding divine healing."[185] This distressing experience catalysed Cho's development of healing theology and the publication of his inaugural book on the subject, notwithstanding his healing of numerous individuals prior to this.[186] This pivotal moment substantiates that a systematic conception of Cho's theology of healing was not established until 1964. Hence, the AAG's role should be considered integral to comprehending Cho's theological evolution, given his significant affiliation with the AAG during the foundational stage of his healing theology. This alignment with the AAG is also evident in Cho's endeavours to validate his doctrines as genuine Pentecostal belief in the face of criticism.[187]

What was the extent of AAG's theological influence on Cho? Synan posits that Cho's understanding of healing as part of the atonement, a doctrine widely recognised in classical Pentecostalism, was attained at an AAG Bible school in Seoul subsequent to his conversion to Christianity.[188] Menzies and Park concur with Synan, emphasising the roles of AAG missionaries during Cho's formative years.[189] Ryu's research identifies John Stetz,[190] R.L. Johnston,[191] and John

---

[183] Pan-ho Kim, "Yongsan Sinhagui Bangbeoblongwa Teukjing," 382.

[184] Min articulates that Cho's theology was not clear before 1961. Gyeong-bae Min, "The Theology of Holy Spirit of Rev. Yong-gi Cho and the Korean Church: An Historical Approach," 39-40.

[185] Yong-gi Cho, *Huimangmokhoe 45 Nyeon*, 72.

[186] Yong-gi Cho, *Huimangmokhoe 45 Nyeon*, 64.

[187] ITI, *Yoido Kyohoei Shinanggwa Shinhak 2*, 233.

[188] V. Synan, "Roots of Yong-gi Cho's Theology of Healing," 15.

[189] W.W. Menzies, "Cho's Theology of the Fullness of the Spirit," 30; Myeong-Su Park, "David Yong-gi Cho and International Pentecostal/Charismatic Movements," 107-28.

[190] Stetz as the first AAG missionary to Korea stayed with his family from 1954 to 1977 while he was involved in teaching ministry at the AAG Bible school as president, welfare work, orphAnake ministry, and evangelism for prisoners. He served the KAG as general superintendent and mission director. The Compilation Committee of the Fifty-year History of the Korea Assemblies of God, *The 50th History of the Korea Assemblies of God: 1953-2004*, 314.

[191] Johnston was a missionary to Japan before he came to Korea in 1957. He became the general superintendent for two consecutive years from 1957 and 1958. His ministry was

Hurston as the most influential missionaries, whose impact on Cho's viewpoint became apparent through his interpretation work for them.[192] I propose that Hurston's influence was more profound than that of the other two missionaries. Cho acknowledges Hurston's pivotal contribution to his ministry over approximately a decade until Hurston's departure for Vietnam in 1969.[193] Cho reminisces about his inaugural exorcism alongside Hurston in 1958[194] when he provided interpretation for Hurston during his evangelistic campaign in Korea.[195] It can be reasonably inferred that Hurston initially had more healing experiences than Cho, from which Cho could glean knowledge through interpreting Hurston's preaching and healing ministry.

Comparing the significance of the AAG missionaries in Cho's ministry, Louis P. Richards[196] should be dealt with on a large scale since he led most of Cho's spiritual encounters with God from his conversion until he left Pusan in 1956.[197] In trying to clarify what could be found from Richards' teaching that made an impact on Cho's theology in his early Christian life, one needs to examine Richards' book *Divine Appointments with God: A Manual For Soul-Winning*, which was used as a textbook in the Bible school.[198] There are several important teachings: 1) "God has put all the power and authority of heaven at our disposal to evangelise this lost world;"[199] 2) "Stop trying to make something of yourself – and start letting God do it;"[200] 3) Jesus is "your Saviour, your Sanctifier, your

---

teaching at the AAG Bible school, pioneering churches, and leading Bible studies for some stationary American soldiers in Korea. He died when preparing for his return to the USA in 1960. Cho stayed in Johnston's house while he was planning to go to the States for his further studies. The Compilation Committee of the Fifty-year History of the KAG, *The 50th History of the Korea Assemblies of God: 1953-2004*, 315 and Yong-gi Cho, *Huimangmokhoe 45 Nyeon*, 22.

192 Dong-hee Ryoo, "Younsan ChoYong-gi Moksaui Mokhoe Sasange Deahan Sinhakjeok Jomyeong" [Theological Study on the Philosophy of Cho's ministry] (Ph.D. Diss, Hansei University, 2008): 62.

193 Yong-gi Cho, *Huimangmokhoe 45 Nyeon*, 144.

194 This was also the year when Cho graduated from Bible school and started his tent church.

195 Hyeong-geun Lim (ed), *Cho Yong-gi Moksa Ildaegi*, 320.

196 Richards arrived in Pusan, the southern part of Korea, in 1952 with his wife and worked until 1966. His ministry produced several influential Korean pastors such as Yong-gi Cho, Gyo-min So, and Deok-hwan Jeong. He was involved in evangelism and pioneering churches, and his house functioned as a headquarters for the mission projects in the southern area. The Compilation Committee of the Fifty-year History of the Korea Assemblies of God, *The 50th History of the Korea Assemblies of God: 1953-2004,* 314.

197 L.P. Richards, *Divine Appointments with God*, foreword.

198 See The Compilation Committee of the Fifty-year History of the Korea Assemblies of God, *The 50th History of the Korea Assemblies of God: 1953-2004,* 314, and L.P. Richards, *Divine Appointments with God.*

199 L.P. Richards, *Divine Appointments with God*, 15-16.

200 L.P. Richards, *Divine Appointments with God*, 20.

Lord, and your coming King;"[201] 4) Spiritual gifts are God's message to "a particular person or group of persons at a particular time and for a particular purpose;"[202] 5) "The baptism with the Holy Ghost is a baptism of power" "to witness and disciple for Christ," "to defeat Satan," and "to destroy Satan's works;"[203] and 6) "It is mandatory that we pray according to His will."[204] What Richards taught is clearly in line with Cho's perspectives, especially in terms of the emphasis on the power of the Holy Spirit and the will of God. It is undeniable that Cho experienced the healing of his TB through the teaching of Richards after he heard Richards saying, "the Word of God has tremendous creative power. It will recreate your lungs, it will heal you."[205] Cho came to know the power of God's words in terms of healing though Richards' teaching.

The fact that Cho's early ministry was under the leadership of the AAG allows one to see Cho as an AG minister. In fact, his second church in Seodaemun was started as a pilot project of Global Conquest that the AAG launched to advance worldwide evangelisation. It was a missions project that the AAG launched on 30th August 1959, to target "the need for evangelism in the major cities of the world."[206] As a part of this mission project, several evangelistic revival meetings were conducted in Korea through the support of the AAG, and Samuel J. Todd's[207] revival meetings provided a practical help to pioneer the second church through many people who attended the revival meetings. Todd led two consecutive revival meetings in 1961 throughout the construction of the Full Gospel Revival Centre, where the revival meetings Cho interpreted were so successful that many people joined the church; about two hundred people were healed of their diseases. This event became a great start of a new church in Seodaemun.[208] The church was under the management of the AAG until Cho was ordained and became the senior pastor of the church in 1964.[209] Moreover, Cho's theological perspectives on healing were formed and introduced through an official magazine of the AG called *Weol-Gan-Sun-Bog-Eum*.[210] Knowing that

---

201 L.P. Richards, *Divine Appointments with God*, 20.
202 L.P. Richards, *Divine Appointments with God*, 25.
203 L.P. Richards, *Divine Appointments with God*, 34.
204 L.P. Richards, *Divine Appointments with God*, 83.
205 Yong-gi Cho, *To God Be the Glory*, 39-40; N.L. Kennedy, *Dream Your Way to Success*, 118.
206 G.B. McGee, *This Gospel Shall Be Preached*, 59-74.
207 Todd was an Assemblies of God minister from 1960-1964. His influence was recognised by the Korea Assemblies of God in the 50-year history. He was elected as one of the most honoured revivalists in the church history of the Korea Assemblies of God with three other Korean revivalists. It is meaningful to know that he was the only foreign nominee. Yong-gi Cho, *Widaehan Somyeong: Huimang Mokhoe 50 Nyeon*, 270.
208 Jae-bum Lee, *Seonglyeong Undongui Yeoksa*, 209; Yong-gi Cho, *Huimangmokhoe 45 Nyeon*, 56; G.B. McGee, *This Gospel Shall Be Preached*, 72.
209 Yong-gi Cho, *Widaehan Somyeong: Huimang Mokhoe 50 Nyeon*, 93.
210 The Compilation Committee of the Fifty-year History of the Korea Assemblies of God, *The 50th History of the Korea Assemblies of God*, 331.

the editor-in-chief and the department head were all AAG missionaries,[211] and that the monthly publication of Cho's articles for the magazine later became his first book on healing,[212] one cannot deny the influence of the AAG.

In this regard, many argue that Cho's theology is very close to the Classical Pentecostal position in relation to 1) healing in the atonement;[213] 2) "healing as one of the essential parts of the gospel;"[214] 3) "speaking in tongues as the initial evidence of baptism in the Holy Spirit that is an experience distinct from the new birth;"[215] and 4) the power for service that comes through the BHS.[216] However, Cho's distinctive perspectives that are different from the teaching of the Classical Pentecostals are to be noted as well in his views of 1) suffering;[217] 2) three-fold blessings;[218] 3) "the fourth dimension"; 4) "incubation of faith;"[219] 5) the fullness of the Holy Spirit, and the five-fold gospel;[220] and most importantly, 6) the fellowship with the Holy Spirit who is not a power/experience to heal but the Divine Healer.

Cho's concept of the BHS is one of the most important aspects which has been further developed from the classical Pentecostal perspective. Cho's understanding of the BHS deals with not only the empowerment for service as a powerful evangelistic tool but also with the continuous, intimate, and personal relationship with the Holy Spirit. Thus, Cho makes a distinction between the BHS and the fullness of the Holy Spirit by arguing that the former is a kind of "spiritual experience that the re-born Christians are seized with the Holy Spirit to live victorious lives with the power for service" while the latter means an on-going status of "Spirit-filled life." In this regard, Cho views spiritual baptism as an initial experience of the fullness of the Holy Spirit. Interestingly, this pneumatological concept is not found in Cho's first book on the Holy Spirit in

---

[211] The Compilation Committee of the Fifty-year History of the Korea Assemblies of God, *The 50th History of the Korea Assemblies of God,* 331.

[212] The Compilation Committee of the Fifty-year History of the Korea Assemblies of God, *The 50th History of the Korea Assemblies of God,* 331.

[213] J. Wright, "The Profiles of Divine Healing," *AJPS* 5(2), (2002): 286.

[214] W.W. Menzies, *Osunjeol Seonggyeon Gyoli* [Doctrine of Pentecostalism], trans. The General Council Administration office (Seoul: Korea Assemblies of God, 1994): 235.

[215] Simon K.H. Chan, "The Pneumatology of Paul Yong-gi Cho," In Wonsuk Ma, W.W. Menzies, and Hyeon-sung Bae (eds), *Yong-gi Cho: A Close Look at His Theology and Ministry* (Baguio, Philippines: APTS Press, 2004): 96-119.

[216] W.W. Menzies, "Yong-gi Cho's Theology of the Fullness of the Spirit: A Pentecostal Perspective," 16.

[217] Warrington notices that "he [Cho] differs from many Classical Pentecostals by asserting that suffering not caused by personal sin or folly may be in God's will […] Suffering may be God's best for the believer." K. Warrington, "The Fourth Dimension, the Word and the Spirit," 38.

[218] W.W. Menzies, "Yong-gi Cho's Theology of the Fullness of the Spirit: A Pentecostal Perspective," 37.

[219] Jang-hyeon Ryu, *Hangukui Seonglyeongundonggwa Yeongseong*, 193-95.

[220] Cho adds material blessing to the four-fold gospel of the classical Pentecostal teaching.

1971. The concept of the fullness of the Holy Spirit was developed in line with the fellowship with the Holy Spirit later.[221] In this regard, Menzies says that in Cho's theology "the baptism means the first experience of being filled with the Holy Spirit and fullness refers to a continuous life pattern of the baptism as Spirit-filled life."[222]

Although Cho's theology is influenced by the AAG in various ways, Cho's theological perspectives go beyond the traditional concepts of classical Pentecostalism as examined above. Cho often expressed his scepticism about the education at his Bible school when saying, "While preaching the Word to them and feeding them, I found myself involved in gross self-contradiction, for the God I had learned about at the seminary seemed to be merely the God of the future. I could not find the God of the present to show Him to people who were living in such desolation and poverty."[223] It is evident that Cho was exposed to some classical Pentecostal beliefs from the time of his conversion until his early ministry. However, its influence on Cho's theological formation is limited to the area of healing in the atonement and BHS. In this regard, Kang and Park argue that the AAG provided Cho with "a Pentecostal theological orientation"[224] and "the recent trends of the Pentecostal/Charismatic movements."[225]

Healing Experiences

In the examination of Cho's theological formation within his personal context, the focal point should be his personal experiences of healing and his subsequent efforts to comprehend and theorise them through biblical study, as advocated by Choe. Aligning with this perspective, Synan posits that "what has exerted the most significant influence on Cho's healing theology is his personal experiences."[226] These claims are explicitly validated by Cho himself in his literary works:

> I have gained much by reading books which have illuminated the Word of God to me. However, not being a theological scholar, but rather having my degree in law, I must write from my own personal experience [...] Most of the lessons I have learned have come as a result of passing difficult tests in my life and ministry.[227]

---

221 Yong-gi Cho, *Seonglyeonglon* [Pneumatology], rev, (Seoul: Seoul Logos, 1998): 122.

222 W.W. Menzies, "Yong-gi Cho's Theology of the Fullness of the Spirit: A Pentecostal Perspective," 17.

223 Yong-gi Cho, *Salvation, Health and Prosperity*, 11; N.L. Kennedy, *Dream Your Way to Success*, 230.

224 Chang-soo Kang, "Resources for Studies of David Yong-gi Cho," in Wonsuk Ma, W. W. Menzies, and Hyeon-sung Bae (eds), *David Yong-gi Cho: A Close Look at His Theology and Ministry* (Baguio, Philippines: APTS Press, 2004): 273-302.

225 Myeong-su Park, "David Yong-gi Cho and International Pentecostal/Charismatic Movements," 241.

226 V. Synan, "Roots of Yong-gi Cho's Theology of Healing," 32-33.

227 Yong-gi Cho, *More than Numbers*, introduction.

It is undeniable that Cho's perception of healing was shaped by several texts, although their impact seems rather limited, primarily introducing him to a few biblical healing principles. However, his comprehension of biblical healing intensified when it was corroborated by his personal healing experiences, such as his recovery from various ailments and witnessing healing among his congregation members. A key lesson that Cho assimilated during his struggle with tuberculosis was Christological: he comprehended that Jesus is not only the Redeemer but also the Healer, and remains "the same yesterday, today, and forever."[228] This understanding evolved into a crucial component of Cho's healing theology of faith and was consistently propagated as the linchpin of his healing theology during his initial ministry. The insights that Cho acquired from his personal experiences were implemented in his church setting, initially reinforcing his own conviction and subsequently bolstering his congregation's belief.[229] Witnessing the healing of "countless numbers of people"[230] further matured Cho's healing theology and firmly corroborated his "conviction in the continuous ministry of Christ's divine healing through the Holy Spirit."[231]

Another notable evolution in Cho's healing theology, founded upon his ministerial experiences, is the notion of "fellowship" and "partnership" with the Holy Spirit in the practice of healing.[232] Cho's pneumatology appears to have initially been influenced by the AAG doctrine, particularly during his tenure at a Pentecostal Bible school. As a result, spiritual empowerment is a recurring theme in Cho's early ministry. The widely recognised slogan of Pentecostal theology, the Holy Spirit in power, highlights that the Holy Spirit embodies power for miracles like healing, which serves as a crucial message in opposition to cessationism. However, this pneumatological formula can potentially equate the Holy Spirit to supernatural power alone. Initially, Cho perceived the baptism of the Holy Spirit as a religious experience rather than a relational encounter with the Person of the Holy Spirit. Nonetheless, upon recognising the personhood of the Holy Spirit, who independently seeks to heal the sick, Cho has been relying on the Holy Spirit for healing since 1964.[233]

Occasionally, theological advancements are achieved through costly errors. As Cho developed practical skills for exorcising demons within his ministry, his demonology also matured. Cho concedes that his misinterpretation of the Scripture led to the death of a demon-possessed woman, which served as a significant lesson.[234] As Cho was involved in many healing ministries, his healing theology was gradually formed through various good and bad healing experiences.

---

[228] Yong-gi Cho, *To God Be the Glory*, 43 and Yong-gi Cho, *Suffering*, 91.
[229] Yong-gi Cho, *Suffering*, 104.
[230] Yong-gi Cho, *How can I be Healed?*, 21-22.
[231] Yong-gi Cho, *More than Numbers*, 85-86.
[232] Yong-gi Cho, *Naui Gyohoe Seongjang Iyagi*, 74-75.
[233] Yong-gi Cho, *Naui Gyohoe Seongjang Iyagi*, 74-75.
[234] Hyeong-geun Lim (ed), *Cho Yong-gi Moksa Ildaegi: Yeouidoui Moghoeja*, 320.

Healing Theology

Healing and Suffering

Divine healing can be considered as the core principle of Cho's theology as it forms a significant part of his theological concepts which are summarised as the so-called "seven-fold full gospel faith," "five-fold gospel," and "three-fold blessing."[235] Cho defines divine healing as a "supernatural occurrence" given through "God's divine power and providence"[236] that has nothing to do with medicine or medical treatment.[237] According to him, it is "the will of God," "a part of Jesus' redemptive works," and "a work of the triune God."[238]

Cho perceives divine healing as an indispensable aspect of contemporary church ministry. An analysis of his teachings by one of his disciples highlights that divine healing, as envisioned by Cho, is more than just "the will of God;" it is also deemed as "the task and command" imparted by Jesus.[239] This perspective gains credence from Cho's declaration that "the grace of divine healing is not optional but mandatory in terms of the gospel" and hence, "it should be proclaimed as God's gift provided through the Passion of Christ."[240] In this sense, Cho argues that divine healing is not only what one receives from God as His gift but also what they need to deliver to others as "the duty of the churches."[241]

Over time, Cho's theology of divine healing has evolved in response to shifting societal demands. Critics have highlighted Cho's perceived indifference towards socio-political issues and his association with military dictator-president Park. Shin has expressed a desire for Cho to add depth to his theology, since Cho was considered indifferent to the issues of society, culture, and even the universe.[242] Nevertheless, Cho's theology has shown evident progression. As noted by Hong, Cho's theology of healing transcends individual concerns to encompass familial, societal, and universal spheres.[243] To him, divine healing signifies the restoration of God's creation, which includes addressing human, social, and environmental complications resulting from the fall of humanity. This conceptualisation gradually emerged in the early twentieth century as Cho understood that Jesus' love for "the world" extended beyond humanity. It marked a significant turning point in Cho's theology, helping him confront his

---

235 Yong-gi Cho, *Widaehan Somyeong: Huimang Mokhoe 50 Nyeon*, 361-69.
236 Yong-gi Cho, *Sin Yu Lon* [Healing Theology] (Seoul: Seoul Logos, 2001), 9.
237 Yong-gi Cho, *Byeongeul Jilmeojisin Yesunim* [Jesus who carried our diseases] (Seoul Youngsan Press, 1966): 21.
238 Yong-gi Cho, *Ojung Bokeumgwa Samjung Chukbok*, 81-82.
239 Young-hoon Lee, "Life and Ministry of David Yong-gi Cho," 15.
240 Yong-gi Cho, *Byeongeul Jilmeojisin Yesunim*, 79.
241 Yong-gi Cho, *A Bible Study for New Christians* (Seoul: Seoul Logos, 1997): 58.
242 Hyun-soo Shin, "The God of Shalom in Young San," *JYT* 18 (2006): 160.
243 Lok-young Hong, "Understanding Young San's Divine Healing," *Journal of Youngsan Theology* 5 (2005): 143-44.

own bias towards humanity alone.[244] His conception of divine healing has broadened to include eco-socio-political areas as the needs of society have changed.

Cho portrays divine healing as both "God's grace" and a "human right for Christians."[245] These twin theological pillars generate a tension between divine sovereignty and human free will. Although Cho asserts that "all Christians have the right to experience divine healing"[246] as it is granted as God's grace, it does not infer that every saved Christian will experience physical healing, as "divine healing belongs to God's sovereignty."[247] Indeed, Cho's theological axiom, "man's existence also is controlled by God,"[248] underlines the primacy of God's sovereignty in his healing theology.

Concurrently, Cho places significant emphasis on human agency, asserting that "God's grace and blessing do not come automatically. They should be followed by the human faith and actions from the side of the recipients of God's grace."[249] He maintains that "the blessing of divine healing can also be ours when our hearts are ready to receive it."[250] In this context, Lee aptly discerns Cho's viewpoint on "man's cooperation with God" as follows: "Human actions of obedience play their roles as the preparation and ingredients for God's works."[251] Essentially, while God's grace catalyses the divine healing process, God also invites His people to partake in His divine works through faith and obedience. Thus, Cho's healing theology accentuates God's sovereignty in principle while also valuing human efforts in practice.

Cho initially interprets suffering within his healing theology negatively, identifying it as a weapon wielded by Satan. He asserts that "Satan makes a constant assault on mankind with curses and illness […] to try to crush the gospel of divine healing."[252] Consequently, he often repudiates Satan in his intercessions for the ailing. For instance, when he prayed for a stroke patient, he commanded, "the demon of stroke! I command you to leave her."[253] According to him, not only the suffering of physical illness but also the suffering in the hearts of believers also belong to Satan. In Cho's perspective, it is Satan's work to destroy believers by captivating them with suffering in their hearts.[254] This

---

[244] Hyeong-geun Lim, *Cho Yonggi Moksa Ildaegi: Yeouidoui Moghoeja*, 563.
[245] ITI, *Yoido Kyohoei Shinanggwa Shinhak 2*, 197.
[246] Yong-gi Cho, *A Bible Study for New Christians*, 58
[247] ITI. *Yoido Kyohoei Shinanggwa Shinhak 2*, 197.
[248] Yong-gi Cho, *To God Be the Glory*, 51.
[249] Yong-gi Cho, *Widaehan Somyeong: Huimang Mokhoe 50 Nyeon*, 369.
[250] Yong-gi Cho, *Widaehan Somyeong: Huimang Mokhoe 50 Nyeon*, 369.
[251] Gi-seong Lee, "God's Absolute Sovereignty and Human Free Will: Young San's Understanding of Man's Cooperation with God," *JYT*, 12 (2008): 95.
[252] Yong-gi Cho, *How can I be Healed?*, foreword.
[253] Yong-gi Cho, *Huimangmokhoe 45 Nyeon*, 29-30.
[254] Yong-gi Cho, *Naui Gyohoe Seongjang Iyagi*, 175.

belief easily parallels another theological concept of the vicarious work of Jesus by which he took the suffering of mankind in their place.[255]

However, Cho also acknowledges the constructive effects of suffering. He elucidates:

> When we are facing pain and suffering, we pray to escape from them. However, it is true that the suffering situation that we are going through can be instrumental in helping us to realise the grace of redemption of Jesus and receive the grace of God. It becomes an opportunity to come to God when we overcome the suffering through endurance.[256]

In such circumstances, believers are encouraged not to implore God for healing, but to seek strength to endure their trials.[257] This perspective enabled Cho to confront his personal affliction with gratitude.[258] Nevertheless, this concept does not constitute the crux of Cho's healing theology. He continues to underscore the importance of repentance, stating, "If the suffering comes from Satan's test to destroy our faith, we should come out of the test through repentance."[259] Despite recognising the significance of suffering, Cho consistently warns of the difficulty in discerning the purpose of suffering.[260]

Faith

From the inception of his ministry, Cho underscored the primacy of faith. His inaugural testimonial recounts the healing of his own lungs through the power of faith in God, a turning point that solidified his dedication to disseminating the principle that significant miracles can materialise through faith in God.[261] Interestingly, Cho's initial sermon, based on Mark 16:17, echoed this theme, declaring "signs that will accompany those who believe." He conveyed the transformative power of faith, articulating that belief could metamorphose our hearts, alleviate poverty and illness, and drive away demonic forces.[262] Cho's conviction stands firm, asserting that "faith can heal the sick and raise the dead. Faith is the strongest of all powers."[263] However, Cho emphasises that it is not faith per se that cures the ill, but rather God, as articulated by Hong.[264] Cho posits that God is "the source of all power" and "power comes to us through our faith

---

[255] Jang-hyun Ryu, "A Theological Study of Dr Yonggi Cho's Pneumatology," *JYT*, edited by Huyn-seong Bae (Gunpo: Young San Theology Institute, 2004): 139-171, 169.
[256] Yong-gi Cho, *Sachawonui Yeongseong*, 123.
[257] Yong-gi Cho, *Sachawonui Yeongseong*, 125.
[258] Yong-gi Cho, *Huimangmokhoe 45 Nyeon*, 53.
[259] Yong-gi Cho, *Sachawonui Yeongseong*, 125.
[260] Yong-gi Cho, *Sachawonui Yeongseong*, 125.
[261] Yong-gi Cho, *To God Be the Glory*, 50.
[262] Yong-gi Cho, *Huimangmokhoe 45 Nyeon*, 24.
[263] Yong-gi Cho, *To God Be the Glory*, 52.
[264] Lok-young Hong, "Understanding Young San's Divine Healing," 58.

in God."[265] In essence, Cho believes that "God bestows healing and man receives it through faith."[266]

Cho suggests that the dynamics of faith that facilitate divine healing parallel those of spiritual salvation. He further elucidates this point by stating, "Salvation is not something that can be obtained through the effort of man [...] Similarly, man lacks ability to become a source of divine healing. However, it is faith that becomes the conduit for salvation and divine healing."[267] This concept, according to Cho, underscores the role of faith as a bridge linking divine healing from God to humans.

Cho categorises the requisite faith for divine healing into several facets: 1) Faith in God's forgiveness. As Cho regards sin as the root of sickness, it is important to be forgiven for one to get rid of all sicknesses caused by sin.[268] 2) Faith in Jesus' redemption. Cho views faith in the redemptive works of Jesus as "the basis upon which people can be healed."[269] 3) Faith that the healing has already taken place in the afflicted body. This faith is believed by Cho to lead one to God's dream and vision where God already sees the sick healed.[270] 4) Faith that God will indeed heal. It is Cho's argument that if you "feel that he will perhaps be healed," "the sick one will never be healed."[271] 5) Faith in the everlasting Jesus Christ. He contends that "The same Christ who healed the sick 2000 years ago continues the ministry of healing through the Holy Spirit today."[272] 6) Faith in God's will to heal. Cho's healing theology is based on the theme of the "Good God" who always wants His people to be healed of their diseases and become healthy.[273]

Cho's theological framework incorporates two faith forms: human faith and divine faith. Human faith constitutes "faith that emanates from human beings," while divine faith refers to the "faith that God instils in the human heart."[274] The former is divided into instinctive faith and rational faith. Instinctive faith is what one was born with[275] while rational faith is based on reason like "trusting to

---

[265] Yong-gi Cho, *To God Be the Glory*, 47.
[266] Yong-gi Cho, *Ojung Bokeumgwa Samjung Chukbok*, 136.
[267] Yong-gi Cho, *How can I be Healed?* 71.
[268] Yong-gi Cho, *Byeongeul Jilmeojisin Yesunim*, 67; Yong-gi Cho, *Geonganghan Salmui Gil* [Way of Healthy Life] (Seoul: Seoul Logos, 2012): 20-21; Yong-gi Cho, *How can I be Healed?* 61.
[269] Yong-gi Cho, *How can I be Healed,* 84; Yong-gi Cho, *Sin Yu Lon*, 19.
[270] Yong-gi Cho, *Naui Gyohoe Seongjang Iyagi*, 338; Yong-gi Cho, *To God Be the Glory*, 68.
[271] Yong-gi Cho, *To God Be The Glory*, 68; Yong-gi Cho, *How can I be Healed,* 69; Yong-gi Cho, *Sin Yu Lon*, 83.
[272] Yong-gi Cho, *How can I be Healed?* 93; Yong-gi Cho, *Sin Yu Lon*, 99.
[273] Yong-gi Cho, *Widaehan Somyeong: Huimang Mokhoe 50 Nyeon*, 365.
[274] Yong-gi Cho, *Spiritual Leadership for the New Millennium* (Seoul: ITI, 2002): 14.
[275] Yong-gi Cho, *Seonglyeonglon*, 1998, 156.

natural law and social institutions."[276] Cho posits that human faith lacks the potency to effectuate God's miracles, necessitating the pursuit of divine faith.

Divine faith encompasses the measure of faith and the gift of faith. Despite Thomson Mathew's assertion that Cho downplays the notion that God imparts a measure of faith to every believer,[277] Cho fervently argues that "when one believes in Jesus, God endows one with a measure of faith."[278] This idea is often confirmed by Cho as he believes that "the Holy Spirit must give the measure of faith"[279] and "faith was planted by the Holy Spirit."[280] He acknowledges that whether or not you recognise it, everybody is given God's faith (the measure of faith),[281] and the faith to believe God is already strong enough "to be saved, to be healed, to be baptised with the Holy Spirit and to have miracles in your life right now."[282] That is to say, the faith that leads to divine healing is not a matter of size but of existence.[283] What really matters is whether or not it is alive and active. In Cho's perspective, it is because "many people's faith is dormant" that miracles do not happen.[284] That is why Cho puts his emphasis on how to develop faith.[285]

The gift of faith (another divine faith variant) is deemed a divine endowment accompanying the measure of faith. Cho defines it as a gift from the Lord which always comes from above in a supernatural way. He differentiates the gift of faith from the measure of faith by saying that:

> The gift of faith that is given through the Holy Spirit exceeds other faith. It is poured into the hearts of believers by direct and immediate works of the Holy Spirit. It produces unimaginable miracles that cannot be perceived by human beings. Additionally, this faith is not what believers can possess at all times but what is occasionally given for special time and place according to the will of the Holy Spirit.[286]

This faith was pivotal to the manifestation of numerous healings in Cho's ministry, representing a divine gift facilitated by the power of the Holy Spirit.

---

[276] Yong-gi Cho, *Salvation, Health and Prosperity*, 152.
[277] T.K. Mathew, "O. Roberts and David Yong-gi Cho," 64-65.
[278] Yong-gi Cho, *Seonglyeonglon*, 1998, 156.
[279] Yong-gi Cho, *How can I be Healed?* 71.
[280] Yong-gi Cho and Robert Harold Schuller, *Expand your Horizon*, 79-80.
[281] Cho based this argument on Romans 12:3. See Yong-gi Cho, *Seonglyeonglon*, 1998, 156.
[282] Yong-gi Cho, *Successful Living*, 136.
[283] Yong-gi Cho, *Seonglyeonglon*, 1998, 157.
[284] Yong-gi Cho and Robert Harold Schuller, *Expand your Horizon*, 79-81.
[285] Cho, on the basis of Hebrews 11:1, suggests having "a clear-cut goal" to develop one's measure of faith. Yong-gi Cho and Robert Harold Schuller, *Expand your Horizon*, 81.
[286] Yong-gi Cho, *Seonglyeonglon*, 1998, 157.

While acknowledging the divine origin of faith, Cho frequently emphasises the role of human effort in the Christian life. He asserts that "faith without action is dead," and inaction towards the Word of God signifies faith's death. To invigorate dormant/dead faith, Cho offers four steps: 1) Envision a clear-cut goal; 2) Nurture a burning desire; 3) Pray for assurance; 4) Speak the word.[287] He further incorporates a theological construct termed "the seed faith,"[288] introduced by Oral Roberts, emphasising the importance of expressing faith through action.[289]

Cho insists that Christians must actively engage in receiving divine faith. In his healing theology, the Word of God can be a source of faith for healing, grounded in Romans 10:17: "faith comes from hearing the message, and the message is heard through the word of Christ."[290] Although Cho underscores the human action of reading the Word of God, he perceives the process as awaiting divine faith, affirming God's sovereignty over faith while we strive to receive His gifts.

Faith, in Cho's healing theology, should be examined in conjunction with his theological concept, "the fourth dimension." As indicated by his book title, *The Fourth Dimension: The Key to Putting Your Faith to Work for a Successful Life*,[291] fourth-dimensional faith is posited to lead to a prosperous life, including health. The idea that "faith belonging to the fourth dimension can influence what belongs to the third dimension"[292] informs Cho's healing theology called the "fourth dimension sightseeing." This means a process of projecting "ourselves into the fourth dimension" where people already have what they have prayed for.[293] It is not envisioning what they want in the future but bringing what is already given in the future into the present through dreams and visions.[294] Cho believes that this helps to "constantly supply nutrition" to faith.[295] That is why Cho calls this process "the mother of faith."[296]

In a critical analysis of Cho's work regarding pragmatic methodologies of fostering faith, facilitating its growth, and harnessing it for the materialisation of divine miracles – all while emphasising human endeavours – it could be hastily inferred that Cho aligns with Arminianism. However, a comprehensive appraisal of Cho's theological perspectives uncovers a layer of Calvinistic influence underlying his healing theology. Cho perpetually underscores the theological

---

287 Yong-gi Cho, *Sachawonui Yeongjeok Segye*, 25-45.
288 It is an action by which one proves their faith with material, time, hard work, etc. Yong-gi Cho, *Sachawonui Yeongseong*, 133.
289 Yong-gi Cho, *Sachawonui Yeongjeok Segye*, 175-77.
290 Yong-gi Cho, *How can I be Healed?* 74.
291 Yong-gi Cho, *The Fourth Dimension*, 1979.
292 Yong-gi Cho, *Sachawonui Yeongseong*, 80.
293 Yong-gi Cho and Robert Harold Schuller, *Expand your Horizon*, 90-93.
294 Yong-gi Cho, *Naui Gyohoe Seongjang Iyagi*, 340.
295 Yong-gi Cho and Robert Harold Schuller, *Expand your Horizon*, 90.
296 Yong-gi Cho and Robert Harold Schuller, *Expand your Horizon*, 93.

axiom: "Faith which belongs to the fourth dimension is made to grow by the Holy Spirit. Faith is not our creation but the work of the Holy Spirit and the grace given by God."[297] In relation to this, Lee posits: "In essence, Cho has addressed the prerequisites for God's miracles from the perspective of proactive human engagement. Yet, when dissecting the intricacies of the principles of faith, he strives to interpret it as a symbiosis between divine sovereignty and human free will."[298] The perceived incompatibility between God's sovereignty and human free will does not deter Cho; on the contrary, he strives to reconcile these two theological concepts, establishing them as the unique bedrock of his theology. For Cho, faith – the catalyst for divine healing – is primarily a divine gift, yet its recognition and activation necessitate human initiative. Consequently, humanity is envisioned as an active participant in divine actions, occupying the role of a recipient of God's grace.

Prayer

Cho identifies the practice of prayer as an integral component of the Christian existence, alongside the Word of God and the Holy Spirit.[299] Several reasons are posited for Cho's devotion to prayer, which include seeking "transformation," achieving "victory in spiritual warfare," attaining "God's peace in our mind," and inviting "God's hands to work in our lives."[300] Moreover, he held an unwavering belief that prayer served as "the key solution for our problems."[301] Even before the inception of Cho's ministry, he perceived prayer as an effective instrument to solicit divine healing. This was born from his personal experiences witnessing the potent prayers offered by his mother-in-law and colleagues on his behalf during a near-death experience.[302] It is also understandable that the life of Cho, especially his early ministry, was prayer-centred because his life was full of hardships as he lived in his war-torn country after the Korean War. He prayed every day for almost ten hours from 4:30 in the morning.[303] It seems to me that Cho could do nothing except pray when most of his church members including himself were from slum areas and were sick people.

In the initial phase of his ministry, he diligently sought spiritual power through fervent prayer,[304] seemingly understanding the Holy Spirit as a conduit for miraculous acts such as supernatural healing. From his early perspective, the spiritual gift of healing could potentially serve as an indicator of an individual's spiritual maturation or condition. However, his viewpoint underwent gradual

---

[297] Yong-gi Cho, *Sachawonui Yeongseong*, 148.
[298] Gi-seong Lee, "God's Absolute Sovereignty and Human Free Will," 81.
[299] Yong-gi Cho, *Ten-minute Broadcast Sermon,* vol.3, *Dousineun Seongryeongnim* [The Holy Spirit who helps us] (Seoul: Seoul Logos, 2011): 86.
[300] Yong-gi Cho, *Ten-minute Broadcast Sermon,* 88-98.
[301] Yong-gi Cho, *A Bible Study for New Christians*,78-79.
[302] Yong-gi Cho, *Huimangmokhoe 45 Nyeon*, 26 and 50-53.
[303] Yong-gi Cho, *Huimangmokhoe 45 Nyeon*, 25.
[304] Yong-gi Cho, *Naui Gyohoe Seongjang Iyagi*, 74.

evolution, broadening to encompass additional aspects. He discusses the significant role of prayer in terms of asking God for healing:

> Prayer is not to draw God into you, but to draw yourself closer to God […] The more we pray, the more our hopes and motivations become pure enough to live a Christ-centred life and pray according to God's will, then God will open the door of heaven and show us unimaginable miracles."[305]

According to Cho's healing theology, the purpose of prayer is to inspire the supplicant to live in accordance with God's will, consequently prompting the manifestation of divine miracles. He posits that prayer serves as a mechanism to gain insight into the nature of God's heart.[306] Therefore, in Cho's theological framework, a prayer for healing commences with the establishment of a correct relationship with the divine Healer. He believes that "divine healing flows from God" and it represents "a blessing that we receive when we remain in Christ."[307] The cultivation and preservation of a close relationship with God, he argues, must be mediated through prayer.[308] This viewpoint appears to be congruent with Cho's interpretation of the origins of sickness. As discussed earlier, the fall of humanity precipitated illnesses and disrupted the bond with God. Thus, for Cho, the re-establishment of this divine relationship via prayer constitutes a crucial precondition for healing.

Underscoring the significance of the divine will in the context of prayer, Cho elucidates two critical factors. First, he asserts that if we solicit in accordance with God's will, we will obtain what we have requested.[309] In this light, Cho appears to perceive a knowledge of God's will as a vital element in human petitions for healing, thereby enhancing the potency of the prayers. Second, he reminds us that "We cannot force or command God to help us, but we ought to realise God's will and obey it,"[310] adding that "His will is always best for our lives."[311] Cho thus accentuates the role of prayer as not only a means of addressing God but also of heeding His voice. Within this dialogue, God responds to prayer "in a way and time appropriate to Him."[312] Consequently, in Cho's healing theology, responses that require patience, demonstrate disapproval, or provide unexpected answers can all be considered forms of divine responses.[313]

On a practical note, Cho proposes various strategies for eliciting responses to prayers for healing. He maintains that prayer for healing should not be

---

305 Yong-gi Cho, *Ten-minute Broadcast Sermon*, 88-98.
306 Yong-gi Cho, *Huimangmokhoe 45 Nyeon*, 224.
307 Yong-gi Cho, *How can I be Healed?* 130-31.
308 Yong-gi Cho, *How can I be Healed?* 131.
309 Yong-gi Cho, *To God Be the Glory*, 102.
310 Yong-gi Cho, *Naui Gyohoe Seongjang Iyagi*, 303.
311 Yong-gi Cho, *To God BetThe Glory*, 131.
312 Yong-gi Cho, *A Bible Study for New Christians*, 80.
313 Yong-gi Cho, *A Bible Study for New Christians*, 80.

interpreted as an appeal for sympathy, but rather as a request for health and a cure, which are preordained by Jesus' sacrifice.[314] As such, it should be recognised as a "basic right" conferred upon Christians.[315] For Cho, the ailing can express a prayer of faith, acknowledging that healing is integral to the redemptive works of Jesus Christ. Individuals are encouraged to persist in prayer until they are endowed with divine faith.[316] Hence, prayer and faith are inextricably linked, with prayer offering the afflicted an opportunity to anticipate the divine faith that facilitates healing. In relation to the process of awaiting God's faith through prayer, Cho insists on the need for "earnest"[317] and "fervent"[318] prayers. Unsurprisingly, Cho has instituted various prayer programmes for his church, including overnight and early morning prayers.

Fasting

In the context of Cho's healing theology, the practice of fasting retains significant prominence, despite being perceived as an integral facet of ordinary Christian life within his church.[319] His emphasis on fasting for healing can be observed from his ministries. Remarkably, his prayer mountain emerged as the pioneering institution to incorporate the term "fasting" within its name. He also instituted a formal structure for a 21-day "Daniel Prayer" and a 40-day fast, inspired by the precedent set by Jesus. Fasting, in this view, is interpreted as a crucial mechanism for resolving myriad problems. Based on Cho's empirical observations, it was noted that approximately 90% of those suffering from ailments, who undertook a fasting regimen on Cho's prayer mountain, experienced healing from their respective diseases.[320] It is intriguing to note that Cho frequently couples the act of fasting with prayer. He regards fasting as a conduit to amplify the intensity of prayer and foster "greater faith."[321] This concept finds clear expression in Cho's assertion that "In instances where faith is elusive through ordinary prayer, it becomes imperative to partake in all-night prayer and fasting services to instil this faith within our hearts."[322] Within the spiritual framework of Cho's church, fasting prayer is perceived as an elevated modality of prayer, given its degree of urgency.[323]

---

[314] Yong-gi Cho, *Sin Yu Lon*, 212.
[315] Yong-gi Cho, *Huimangmokhoe 45 Nyeon*, 223.
[316] Yong-gi Cho, *Sin Yu Lon*, 239; Yong-gi Cho, *Sachawonui Yeongseong*, 139; Yong-gi Cho, *Miteumkwa Silsang* [Faith and the Substance of Things] (Seoul: Youngsan Press, 1967): 132.
[317] Yong-gi Cho, *Ten-minute Broadcast Sermon*, 218; Yong-gi Cho, Sachawonui Yeongseong, 140.
[318] Yong-gi Cho, *How can I be Healed*? 137.
[319] ITI, *Yoido Kyohoei Shinanggwa Shinhak 2*, 121.
[320] Yong-gi Cho, *Huimangmokhoe 45 Nyeon*, 174.
[321] Yong-gi Cho, *Successful Living*, 132.
[322] Yong-gi Cho, *Salvation, Health, and Prosperity*, 152-54.
[323] ITI, *Yoido Kyohoei Shinanggwa Shinhak 2*, 121.

Cho used to believe that fasting leads one to a deeper level of Christian life. That is why he often tried to make his body suffer through fasting and all-night prayer.[324] Nevertheless, Cho eventually came to the realisation that his health problems could be attributed, at least partially, to this ascetic lifestyle. This experience was instrumental in changing Cho's theology of fasting. He no longer motivated himself to do fasting prayer in order to enter a deeper level of Christian life, but he still stresses the value of fasting in relation to divine healing. In his healing theology, Cho asserts that fasting does not inherently possess healing properties, yet those who invoke healing prayers could amplify their efficacy through fasting. According to Cho, "Though God remains perpetually prepared to respond to our prayers, they often remain unanswered due to our erroneous attitudes in prayer."[325] He contends that the correct prayer attitude should originate from God's will, leading subsequently to God's answer.[326] This God-centric paradigm serves as a fundamental component in comprehending Cho's healing theology with respect to fasting. Cho strives to rectify misconceptions concerning the value of fasting, emphasising that "Some individuals harbour the belief that they can sway God through fasting and prayer. However, the reality is that when we engage in prayer and fasting, it is we who are persuaded by God."[327] Fasting thus serves to enhance the intensity of prayer, leading to greater comprehension of God's will rather than increasing appeal. Cho perceives fasting as a means to discern God's will, not a way to enhance pleas to God for healing. Cho's perspective unambiguously asserts that fasting's principal purpose is not to influence God, but rather to effect change within ourselves and understand God's will.[328]

Atonement

Many have recognised that the underpinnings of Cho's theology reside in Christology.[329] The achievements of Jesus on the Cross provide the theological bedrock for Cho's interpretation of healing. As Ryu points out, Cho's conceptualisation of divine healing does not originate from the supernatural capabilities of Jesus or his dominion over disease, but from the potency of his suffering.[330] The Atonement's role in healing constitutes a pivotal component of Cho's healing theology, as indicated in the introduction of his debut book, primarily devoted to exploring divine healing.[331] Cho intended for the readers to perceive the same Jesus who sacrificed his life for their ailments, as suggested

---

[324] Yong-gi Cho, *Obunganui Myeongsang* [5 Minute Devotion] (Seoul: Seoul Logos, 1976): 111.
[325] Yong-gi Cho, *Huimangmokhoe 45 Nyeon*, 174.
[326] Yong-gi Cho, *Huimangmokhoe 45 Nyeon*, 174.
[327] Yong-gi Cho, *Naui Gyohoe Seongjang Iyagi*, 168.
[328] Yong-gi Cho, *Sachawonui Yeongseong*, 84.
[329] Dawk-mahn Bae, "Healing Jesus: A Study on Young San's Christology Focusing on Jesus Christ as a Healer," *JYT* 5 (2005): 136.
[330] Jang-hyun Ryu, "A Theological Study of Dr Yong-gi Cho's Pneumatology," 169.
[331] This concept is also the official "truth" of the US Assemblies of God.

by the book's title *Jesus Who Carried Sickness*.[332] Jesus, with whom Cho had a personal encounter, is portrayed as the redeemer and healer.[333]

In Cho's theological construct, the forgiveness of sins is conjoined with healing, leading him to assert that where there is forgiveness of sin, there is healing, and when one preaches on repentance, healing must occur.[334] While the simplicity of Cho's notion might generate the misconception that he views healing as a prerequisite for salvation, he unequivocally declares that healing is not a salvation condition but a privilege granted to the redeemed.[335]

Cho's healing theology is predicated upon several biblical foundations. Primarily, he regards the suffering servant of God in Isaiah 53 as Christ, a viewpoint reaffirmed by Matthew 8:16-17, stating that Jesus offered his blood to liberate not only our spirits but also our bodies.[336] Consequently, he persistently contends that "if someone believes that there is no healing in the atonement, it signifies they also lack faith in its forgiveness."[337] Psalm 103:3 is employed to depict God not only as the absolver of all transgressions but also the curer of all maladies.[338] Secondly, Cho underscores the notion that healing occurred roughly two thousand years ago, an idea derived from 1 Peter 2:24. He maintains that Peter intentionally employed past tense to declare "you were healed."[339] Therefore, from Cho's perspective, it is crucial to acknowledge that healing has already been arranged through Jesus' redemptive acts and to claim it. Cho argues that divine healing is "a matter of our knowledge and faith,"[340] as he believes many individuals deny the completed works of Jesus that formed the cornerstone of divine healing.

A significant scripture for Cho is 3 John 1:2, which led him to embrace the concept of multiple blessings. This passage gifts Cho with the comprehension that God's blessings extend beyond the spiritual realm and encompass physical and material aspects, an idea encapsulated in his Threefold Blessing. He holds that each blessing facet is interdependent, suggesting that they are intricately linked.[341] When emphasising these three blessings, he tends to prioritise spiritual elements. According to Cho, all aspects of human life are significantly associated with and affected by the state of their spirit.[342] This viewpoint accentuates the

---

[332] Yong-gi Cho, *Byeongeul Jilmeojisin Yesunim*, preface 2.
[333] Yong-gi Cho, *The Fourth Dimension,* vol 2. preface, xvii.
[334] Yong-gi Cho, *Sin Yu Lon*, 277.
[335] ITI, *Yoido Kyohoei Shinanggwa Shinhak 2*, 196.
[336] Yong-gi Cho, *Geonganghan Salmui Gil*, 82-83.
[337] Yong-gi Cho, *Geonganghan Salmui Gil*, 84.
[338] Yong-gi Cho, *Sin Yu Lon*, 211.
[339] Yong-gi Cho, *Geonganghan Salmui Gil*, 86.
[340] Yong-gi Cho, *Geonganghan Salmui Gil*, 86.
[341] Yong-gi Cho, *Ojung Bokeumgwa Samjung Chukbok* [Five-fold Gospel and Three-fold Blessings] (Seoul: Seoul Logos, 1988): 143.
[342] Yong-gi Cho, *Widaehan Somyeong: Huimang Mokhoe 50 Nyeon*, 367.

importance of spiritual blessings, which are anticipated to accompany physical and material blessings in Cho's theology.

Despite Cho's inclination to overstate the physical and material aspects, he clarifies that "the healing of the physical body is not the Spirit's primary objective. It is crucial to recognise the hierarchy of priorities. His primary goal is the healing of your soul."[343] In Cho's healing theology, physical healing serves as a conduit for the healing of souls. This perspective enables a distinction between Cho's theology of blessings and the prosperity gospel. In Cho's theology, blessings are not the primary objective of Christian existence, but rather an outcome that stems from spiritual salvation.

Repentance

Broadly construed, Cho's theology of healing draws heavily upon the theological foundations of healing as embodied within the Atonement. This framework extends to underscore another crucial element – repentance. Cho brings into sharp relief the significance of repentance as it pertains to healing. This is encapsulated succinctly in his assertion that "anyone who harbours a sincere desire for healing must undertake repentance and receive forgiveness for their sin."[344] Cho's treatise is focused on the subject of divine healing, articulating this through the delineation of seven stages of prayer intended for healing: 1) Regeneration; 2) Repentance; 3) Comprehension of God's healing promises; 4) Praying until conviction is achieved; 5) Receiving prayer with the imposition of hands; 6) Believing in and proclaiming God's healing; and finally, 7) Offering gratitude to God for healing.[345] Notably, the initial two stages of the healing prayer address humanity's inherent sinful nature. For Cho, it is an axiomatic concept that a robust relationship exists between sin and sickness in the context of divine healing. This is reflected in his declarations that "sickness is always related to sin,"[346] "where there is forgiveness of sin there always is healing,"[347] and "forgiveness of sin and healing always go together [...] And they are inseparable."[348]

Understandably, this perspective risks being misconstrued, as though Cho is a vehement proponent of the belief that sin invariably precipitates sickness. Kwang-il Kim critiques Cho for his equivocation concerning the association between illness and sin, articulating that "it remains ambiguous whether Original Sin or individual sin is the catalyst for illness."[349] However, Cho elucidates his stance unequivocally:

---

343 Yong-gi Cho, *The Fourth Dimension,* 108.
344 Yong-gi Cho, *How can I be Healed?* 59.
345 Yong-gi Cho, *Sin Yu Lon*, 229-48.
346 Yong-gi Cho, *Sin Yu Lon*, 272.
347 Yong-gi Cho, *Sin Yu Lon*, 85.
348 Yong-gi Cho, *Sin Yu Lon*, 97.
349 Kwang-il Kim, "Gidokgyo Chibyeong Hyeonsange Gwanhan Jeongsinuihakjeok Josa Yeongu," 238.

> Of course the Bible tells of sicknesses which are not caused by sin [...] This means that a person's sickness is not necessarily caused by sin. But sickness came into being and reached all mankind because of the original sin of Adam and Eve, with whom we have joint responsibility. Therefore, a man should first receive forgiveness of sins before he is healed of his illness.[350]

As illustrated above, Cho's interest in healing, in relation to repentance, leans predominantly towards Original Sin, believed to be the harbinger of death and sickness in the world. Therefore, Cho's assertion that when we are assailed by a seemingly fatal illness, we must initially repent for our sins and beseech God for healing, primarily addresses the origin of sickness in a broad sense, not the causality of sickness in individuals. This notion is buttressed by his concept of spiritual salvation. The principle that repentance should precede regeneration given our collective sinfulness resulting from Adam and Eve remains applicable in Cho's interpretation of divine healing. If the forgiveness of our sins is a prerequisite for our spiritual salvation, this same principle must be operative within the context of divine healing.

Although Cho's healing theology underscores the relationship between Original Sin and the redemptive works of Jesus on the Cross through repentance, it is apparent that Cho does not downplay the impact of individual sins that engender sickness. In this regard, Cho employs two terms: 1) "direct" cause of sickness for individual sins, and 2) "indirect" cause of sickness from the Original Sin.[351] For Cho, sickness and death are attributed either to individual sins or to Original Sin.[352] Whether the cause is direct or indirect, repentance is an essential component of Cho's healing theology, as he posits that "no man can be born and remain sinless."[353]

While the central role of repentance as a precondition for divine healing in Cho's healing theology cannot be disputed, Cho's emphasis on the role of repentance for healing prayer should also be understood within the framework of prayer efficacy. Cho offers two reasons for this: 1) divine healing is conferred exclusively upon God's children on the basis of Matthew 15:21-28, and repentance allows individuals to be recognised as God's children and "entitles them to request healing from their Father"[354] and 2) Sin obstructs "all things which God desires to provide us (Jer. 5:25)."[355] Cho maintains that "our sins preclude God from responding to our prayers"[356] as outlined in Isaiah 1:15. It is Cho's interpretation that repentance itself does not elicit God's healing upon the

[350] Yong-gi Cho, *Salvation, Health and Prosperity*, 123.
[351] Yong-gi Cho, *Sin Yu Lon*, 31.
[352] Yong-gi Cho, *Sin Yu Lon*, 31-32.
[353] Yong-gi Cho, *How can I be Healed?* 60.
[354] Yong-gi Cho, *Sin Yu Lon*, 230.
[355] Yong-gi Cho, *How can I be Healed?* 59.
[356] Yong-gi Cho, *How can I be Healed?* 59.

sick but empowers them to petition God for healing and offer prayers that are more likely to be heard by God.

Spiritual Warfare

In a broader context, spiritual warfare constitutes a pivotal component of Cho's healing theology, owing to his conviction that Satan is the primary source of all illness. Cho perceives Satan, curses, and punishment as the principal origins of disease,[357] although he does not adopt a systematic approach in understanding them, acknowledging that they do not equate in terms of the origin of illness. Such an approach might cause misunderstandings about Cho's perspective, as Hong proposes a dichotomous understanding of the roots of illness in Cho's theology – God and Satan.[358] However, this perspective proves incompatible with Cho's healing theology, which regards Satan as the perpetuator of illness, whereas God symbolises life and "true healing."[359] As such, God should not be considered the root of illness, even though sickness may occasionally serve as His "curse"[360] and "punishment."[361] It would be more apt to distinguish between the origins and functional factors of illness, as the root cause of a disease is distinct from its mode of causation. In this context, Bae's effort to distinguish the origin and supplier of illness provides a valuable perspective. According to Bae's scrutiny of Cho's theology, sin represents the genesis of sickness, while Satan serves as its propagator.[362] This aligns with Cho's belief that the devil "ceaselessly infuses illness with life and strength, leading to an incessant loss of life through pain and suffering" through sin.[363] Consequently, Satan is not the creator of sickness but is viewed as its deliverer, spreading the disease engendered by sin among humans.

A comprehension of the roots of disease in relation to Original Sin unveils the inherent connection between illness and spiritual warfare, as evident in Cho's assertion:

> Since our struggle is spiritual in nature, we must bind the authority of the devil and provide spiritual peace in the name of Jesus Christ wherever we go […] Therefore, this world is a battleground between the Holy Spirit and the devil.[364]

Cho is unequivocal in his stance: our combat is spiritual, even in the face of physical maladies. This theological notion of Cho was further developed into the concept of "territorial spirits" as he argued that "Wherever we go, we meet the

---

[357] Yong-gi Cho, *Widaehan Somyeong: Huimang Mokhoe 50 Nyeon*, 365.
[358] Lok-young Hong, "Understanding Young San's Divine Healing," 144.
[359] Yong-gi Cho, *How can I be Healed,* 100.
[360] Yong-gi Cho, *How can I be Healed?* 32.
[361] Yong-gi Cho, *Suffering,* 58.
[362] Dawk-mahn Bae, "Healing Jesus," 118-19.
[363] Yong-gi Cho, *Suffering*, 13; Dawk-mahn Bae, "Healing Jesus," 118-19.
[364] Yong-gi Cho, *Spiritual Leadership*, 51.

strongholds of the enemy – of Satan. Every town has its own devil."[365] Thus, it was a necessary process to challenge the power of his spiritual enemies when Cho needed to establish a church in some areas.[366]

To elucidate the direct and indirect causes of sickness in relation to Satan, Cho proposes two concepts: influence and possession. While he consistently ascribes the destructive power in every sickness to Satan, he emphasises that sickness does not always result from Satan's invasion of the human body.[367] When Satan's entry into a human body causes sickness, this is interpreted as "possession," whereas "influence" denotes illness arising from non-spiritual causes. This differentiation has led to misconceptions about Cho's demonology, as though he advocates Gi-dong Kim's doctrine.[368] Yet, Cho's understanding of demons diverges from Kim's in that Cho sees demons as fallen angels rather than the spirits of the deceased, and does not agree with Kim's notion that humans were created solely to destroy demons.[369] Regardless of whether it is possession or influence, Cho upholds the belief that Satan is invariably associated with disease, necessitating the confrontation and denouncement of Satan during prayers for the sick.[370]

A crucial aspect of Cho's healing theology, in the context of spiritual warfare, is his understanding of sickness. There are several words referring to sickness in Korean: 병 *Byeong*, 질병 *Jil-Byeong*, 병마 *Byeong-Ma*. Although Cho has used two words interchangeably, the word that Cho more frequently[371] uses is 병마 (病魔), *Byeong-Ma*. Interestingly, this term has two different meanings: 1. serious "sickness," "illness," "disease," 2. "the demon of ill health," "the curse of a disease,"[372] or "sickness as demon, in a metaphorical sense."[373] In fact, the literal translation is the latter, as the first syllable *Byeong* means sickness while the second *Ma* refers to a demon.[374] This concept is partially in line with Cho's

---

365 Yong-gi Cho, *Expand Your Horizon*, 52.
366 Yong-gi Cho, *Expand Your Horizon*, 52.
367 ITI, *Yoido Kyohoei Shinanggwa Shinhak 2*, 202.
368 This demonology of Cho was criticised by *Tonghab* Presbytery. See ITI, *Yoido Kyohoei Shinanggwa Shinhak* 2, 199.
369 ITI, *Yoido Kyohoei Shinanggwa Shinhak 2*, 199.
370 Yong-gi Cho, *Sin Yu* [Divine healing] (Seoul: Hansei University Press, 2012): 96.
371 Cho tends to use the term with the idea that demons directly and indirectly influence sickness. Hyeong-geun Lim (ed), *Cho Yong-gi Moksa Ildaegi*, 379-80.
372 *Gyohoeyongeo Sajeon* [Church Glossary], *Naver. Glossary of Church Terms: The Right Glossary* [Available at: http://terms.naver.com/entry.nhn?docId=2380561&ref=y&cid=50762&categoryId=51371], [Last accessed: 4th November 2023].
373 *Pyojun Gukeo Deasajeon* [Standard Korean Language Dictionary], https://stdict.korean.go.kr/search/searchResult.do?pageSize=10&searchKeyword=%EB%B3%91%EB%A7%88.
374 This terminology was broadly used not only by Cho and Lee, but also the Korean people, including non-believers. Furthermore, many Korean people have been using this word until today.

perspective, as he healed many sick people through spiritual warfare against evil powers. For instance, while praying for a stroke patient, Cho rebuked the evil spirit causing the affliction, commanding it to leave in the name of Jesus Christ.[375] Cho typically employs words of command and rebuke in his spiritual warfare for healing,[376] signifying that even medical conditions like high blood pressure are subject to spiritual confrontation.[377]

However, it would be a misconception to perceive Cho's theology as a syncretism of shamanistic beliefs and Christianity. His theology is rooted in biblical principles, specifically Romans 6:23 and Hebrews 2:14, which affirm that sin is the invisible root of illness and death, and the devil ceaselessly infuses sickness with life and strength through sin.[378]

It is worth noting the evolution of Cho's perspectives on spiritual warfare. Initially, Cho staunchly asserted that sickness was prevalent among those serving Satan, those who did not believe in Jesus Christ.[379] In the first two healing performances that set the stage for church growth, Cho directly attributed the stroke of a woman and the severe stomach-ache of a man to demons, and during that time, Cho tended to consider every healing as spiritual warfare against demons.[380] However, Cho gradually began to differentiate the direct causes of illness from the indirect. Although he believed, in general and in principle, that it is a demon that confers its destroying power to all sickness since the Fall, "it does not mean that every sickness is directly caused by evil spirits or demons,"[381] and there could be other causes such as "overwork," "overeating," "intemperate life," "punishment of God" and "thoughtless partaking of the holy communion."[382]

As Cho traces the onset of illness and death to Adam and Eve's fall,[383] it follows that sickness must be addressed in the context of Original Sin, and its resolution sought in Christ's atonement.[384] Cho's understanding of spiritual warfare emerged from his awareness of demons as formidable spiritual entities who bring sickness to humans. It evolved further, rectified through biblical perspectives, to acknowledge demons as both direct and indirect causes of

---

375 Yong-gi Cho, *Huimangmokhoe 45 Nyeon*, 29.
376 Knowing that the Third Wave theorised that the naming or revealing of the adversary is essential in a power encounter, some may argue that Third Wave groups influenced Cho. However, Cho already used this method in the beginning of his ministry before the Third Wave movement started in the 1980s.
377 Yong-gi Cho, *Naui Gyohoe Seongjang Iyagi*, 111.
378 Yong-gi Cho, *Suffering,* 13.
379 Yong-gi Cho, *Suffering,* 13.
380 While praying for healing for two deaf women, Cho directly commands the demon to come out since he believed it caused the lady to be deaf. Hyeong-geun Lim, 270-82 and 298.
381 ITI, *Yoido Kyohoei Shinanggwa Shinhak 2*, 202.
382 Yong-gi Cho, *Widaehan Somyeong: Huimang Mokhoe 50 Nyeon*, 365.
383 Yong-gi Cho, *Suffering, Why Me?* 3-6.
384 Yong-gi Cho, *Suffering, Why Me?* 4.

sickness, which could be overcome through God's grace and power manifested in Christ's sacrifice on the Cross.

Evaluation of the Contribution of Cho's Healing Ministry

Social Perspective

In a study collaboratively conducted by the Christian newspaper, *Gi-Dok-Gyo-Yeon-Hab-Sinmun*, and the Christian broadcast network C3TV in 2003, Cho was recognised as the most influential Korean church leader in terms of social impact (46.7%), leadership (28.7%), integrity (20.7%), and church size (3.9%).[385] Notably, the primary catalyst for his top ranking was his societal influence. Ahn robustly postulates that Cho's significant contribution was his ability to illuminate the importance of societal service through active participation in society.[386] His societal contributions have been recognised not only by his immediate community but also by outsiders. In 2007, the United States Congress honoured Cho with a certificate for his contributions to societal development, while the United States legislature awarded him an international leadership award.[387] Cho and his church have been featured by numerous media outlets such as the BBC (1993), *The Guardian* (1994), *Cutting Edge* (1995), *Korea Post* (1999), and *Weol-Gan-Jung-Ang* [monthly magazine] (1999). Most of these features spotlighted Cho's active role in relief work and welfare.[388]

Nevertheless, Cho has been frequently criticised for his perceived indifference towards societal change. In the early 1980s, critiques emerged in various forms, culminating in a book criticising Cho's theology for overemphasising individual aspects and lacking a socio-political change perspective. Seo opined that Cho's focus on physical healing as a form of Christian salvation and its limitation to the physical body is problematic.[389] He further argued that divine healing should be related to the matter of *Minjung* and of its "socio-politico-economic structure."[390] Both Kwang-il Kim and Wan-sang Han concurred, expressing concern that Cho's healing ministries may divert people's attention towards the supernatural realm, consequently reducing their involvement in social participation.[391] Wan-sang Han presented a similar idea:

---

385 Yong-gi Cho, *Widaehan Somyeong: Huimang Mokhoe 50 Nyeon*, 299.

386 Myung-jun Ahn, "The Theological Understanding of Young San to the Salvation of the Society," *Journal of Yongsan Theology* 15 (2008): 102.

387 Yong-gi Cho, *Widaehan Somyeong: Huimang Mokhoe 50 Nyeon*, 238-40.

388 Yong-gi Cho, *Widaehan Somyeong: Huimang Mokhoe 50 Nyeon*, 238-40.

389 Kwang-seon Seo, "Hanguk Gyohoe Seongryeongundonggwa Buheung Undongui Sinhakjeok Ihea," 66.

390 Kwang-seon Seo, "Hanguk Gyohoe Seongryeongundonggwa Buheung Undongui Sinhakjeok Ihea," 70.

391 Kwang-il Kim, "Gidokgyo Chibyeong Hyeonsange Gwanhan Jeongsinuihakjeok Josa Yeongu," 291-4.

Cho's emphasising of individual matters can make people undervalue social salvation and environmental reformation.[392]

The assessment of Cho's approach towards societal affairs necessitates a differential approach across time periods. During the early stages of his ministry, Cho did not place a significant emphasis on social service as his focus was primarily on addressing basic human necessities in the wake of the Korean War. Cho's societal engagement, in fact, emerged later in his career, particularly from the early 1980s onwards. Consequently, there could be grounds for criticising Cho for his initial indifference towards social issues. However, upon a thorough examination of the societal contributions made by Cho's church over the past three decades, such criticisms may not hold up. Anderson astutely observed, "This contribution has not received sufficient attention in many things that have been written about Dr Cho and his church."[393] This observation aligns with my belief that Cho's involvement in social relief work presents a strong case for acknowledging him as a proponent of societal involvement in the context of a social gospel. Cho's pragmatic efforts in assisting individuals encompasses support for: cardiac surgeries, orphaned children, international refugees including North Koreans, victims of natural disasters, impoverished local churches, foreign workers, the elderly living alone, disabled individuals, Holt International Children's Services, a blood donation campaign, medical services for the impoverished, environmental conservation initiatives, the establishment of the Elim Rehabilitation Centre, and a cardiac hospital in North Korea. Furthermore, Cho, since retiring in 2008, has consistently directed his efforts towards aiding marginalised communities through the initiation of the Sharing Love and Happiness Movement.[394] It is indisputable that Cho's societal engagement has facilitated the advancement of social welfare and environmental conservation, and has stimulated an awareness among Korean Christians regarding the pressing need for societal involvement.

The arguments advocating Cho's societal contributions are tangible, yet the commencement of his societal impact and the emergence of criticisms against him can be studied without in-depth analysis. Notable criticisms were raised against Cho in the early 1980s, after which he began to engage significantly in societal activities. Hence, such prior criticisms may contain elements of validity. However, when the YFGC emerged as the world's largest church by 1981,

---

392 Wan-sang Han, "Gyohoe Yangjeok Geubseongjange Deahan Saheohakjeok Gochal" [Sociological Study of the Explosive Growth of the Korean Church], in Korea Christian Academy (eds), *Hangukgyohoe Seonglyeongunddongui Hyeonsanggwa Gujo* [Phenomenon and Structure of the Holy Spirit Movement in the Korean Church] (Seoul: Christian Academy, 1981): 216-31.

393 A.H. Anderson, "A 'Time to Share Love,'" 156.

394 Yong-gi Cho, *Widaehan Somyeong: Huimang Mokhoe 50 Nyeon*, 181-91 and 284-91; Gwui-sam Cho, *Youngsan Choyounggi Moksaui Gyohoe Seongjanghak*, 34; Tai-il Wang, "Dr Yong-gi Cho's Understanding of the Social Salvation," 205.

amassing approximately 200,000 members,[395] Cho's perception of the social gospel underwent a transformation, evolving gradually in response to the escalating demands on his church.

An intriguing aspect of this narrative is the internal critique within Cho's church. Young-hoon Lee, Cho's successor and a Korean Pentecostal historian, asserts that:

> YFGC [Yoido Full Gospel Church] must broaden its interests to include wider social concern and social reformation. Previous HS movements have been more concerned with personal salvation and church growth, and YFGC will have to make a critical choice for its future.[396]

Lee cautiously puts forth his notion that societal concern has often been secondary to individual matters, although this does not negate Cho's previous social engagement efforts. Cho himself acknowledged this in a late confession in 2005:

> I recently began to realise some shortcomings of my 47-year ministries. The Bible clearly says that God so loved *the world* that he gave his one and only Son. It does not say that God gave his Son for God so loved *the man* [...] My evangelistic ministries have been man-centred without including the world.[397]

At this point, Cho substantiates his belief that the gospel should serve not only humankind but also society and the ecosystem. Another disciple points out that, since 2005, Cho has actively advocated for society and the ecosystem.[398] In light of this self-examination, Lee rightly suggests that Cho's theology should evolve to incorporate Cho's perspective on the Good Father God's relevance to the salvation of society and the ecosystem.[399]

While evaluating Cho from a societal viewpoint, it is pertinent to question whether there are other aspects that warrant consideration apart from Cho's engagement in a social gospel. Korean scholar Dong-sik Yoo notes that the ministries of Cho, as a leader of the "maternal" Holy Spirit movement, undeniably played a critical role for marginalised individuals.[400] Cho, in his early ministries, recognised the significance of the Church's role in societal

---

395 Yong-gi Cho, *Widaehan Somyeong: Huimang Mokhoe 50 Nyeon*, 123.
396 Young-hoon Lee, "Life and Ministry of David Yong-gi Cho," 22-23.
397 Hyeong-geun Lim, *Cho Yonggi Moksa Ildaegi*, 563.
398 Hyeong-geun Lim, *Cho Yonggi Moksa Ildaegi*, 564-65.
399 Young-hoon Lee, "Influence of Dr Cho's 'God is so good – faith' in the Korean Churches," *JYT* 7 (2006): 107.
400 Yoo defines the Korean Holy Spirit movement with two concepts: a paternal one unfolded mostly by the Presbyterian Church based on Confucianism and a maternal one formed by the Korean Pentecostal movement with special reference to Cho. Dong-Sik Yoo, "Hanguk Gyohoe wa Seongryeong Undong," 20.

transformation. He outlined his vision for societal transformation in a 1969 interview with a Christian newspaper:

> The Holy Spirit movement is misunderstood as if it seeks to receive the Holy Spirit in a deep mountain while being away from the world. The true Holy Spirit movement must snuggle into the society to reform and change it […] The solution for social problems, the problems between the rich and the poor, and ethical problems can be found in the efforts to change individuals.[401]

Cho advocated that societal reformation commences with individual transformation and that personal change precedes societal change.

Cho's conceptualisation of a successful life was never individualistic, but altruistic. It appears unjust to criticise Cho for a lifestyle removed from society when he frequently emphasised the importance of compassion for one's neighbours, suggesting that "whatever you do, you must think of the happiness of others first," "Your attitude throughout life should be to serve others," and "you should seek to find opportunities to serve God, the church, and your brothers and sisters."[402] It is noteworthy that Cho has attempted to participate in societal reform in various ways. He endeavoured to bring about change in society by transforming the hearts of the sick, hopeless, and marginalised on an individual basis. This initiative commenced with preaching a gospel that related to the present life in order to "help the people rehabilitate their thinking, to help their present life,"[403] which was fraught with post-Korean War hardships.

Cho explores the motivations behind his early ministries in a book commemorating his 50 years of service:

> We were so poor. The bitter winds gusted about the tent church where we were having worship services. There seemed to be no hope at all in the eyes of my church members but only the groans of the sick, worries about foods, and ragged clothes. I needed to do something for them. I wanted to give them hope and dream as Jesus did. The preaching with tears started saturating them with the hope and dreams.[404]

His foremost pastoral priority was to address societal needs in terms of hope, a universal and immediate concern. In this regard, Cho's efforts to instil hope in a war-ravaged nation and his contributions to Korean society deserve reconsideration.

---

[401] Gyohoe Yeonhab Sinbo [the United Christian Newspapers], 13th July 1969, quoted in Jong-dal Im, *Gidokgyo Daehan Hananimui Seonghoe Osibnyeonsa: Yeoksapyeon* [The 50-Year-History of the Korea Assemblies of God: History 1953-2004] (Seoul: Creation, 2005): 333-34.

[402] Yong-gi Cho, *Successful Living*, 23.

[403] N.L. Kennedy, *Dream Your Way to Success*, 165.

[404] Yong-gi Cho, *Widaehan Somyeong: Huimang Mokhoe 50 Nyeon*, 5.

Missional Perspective

Since Cho's church has been recognised as the "world's largest" church, a deeper exploration into its missional value is merited. The initial contribution from Cho was in breathing spiritual vivacity into the Korean Church under the auspices of the Holy Spirit, thus accelerating the expansion of God's Kingdom. Intriguingly, Cho's contribution has been frequently scrutinised in conjunction with the works of the Holy Spirit. It was foreseeable, therefore, that Cho would be considered one of the cardinal leaders in the centenary history of the Holy Spirit movement in Korea.[405] A distinguished historian of the Korean Church, Gyeong-bae Min, likewise ascribes the resurgence in vitality of the contemporary Korean Church to Cho's influential stewardship, which was intimately associated with "the era of the Holy Spirit", a period believed to have been inaugurated under Cho's leadership since the 1960s.[406] Correspondingly, Jae-bum Lee posits that Cho was instrumental in illuminating the role of the Holy Spirit within the context of church growth.[407]

It is important to explore the interconnection between the workings of the Holy Spirit and church growth, particularly when seeking to understand the significance of divine healing as the nexus between these two aspects, from Cho's viewpoint. In line with this, I concur with Lee's assertion that the development of YFGC as the fulcrum of the Holy Spirit movement pivots around healing,[408] an idea substantiated robustly by Cho's statements. In his seminal book, *The Story of My Church Growth*, Cho elucidates the rapid expansion of his church, attributing this growth to the work of the Holy Spirit as the central driver.[409] From Cho's viewpoint, it is unequivocal that "It was divine healing that turned many toward God," a sentiment that resonates through his narrative:

> In the morning I got word that the young man had run out of the house and began to tell all of the neighbours what had happened. All of the Buddhists and other non-Christians in the town knew the situation, and they were amazed at the power of God. Since then most of the people in that part of town have been saved because of the healing power of God.[410]

The integral role of divine healing in the growth of Cho's church must be acknowledged as a result of the Holy Spirit's work. It is distinctly clear from Cho's theology that divine healing is "the manifestation of the Spirit."[411] Therefore, based on the above discussion, Cho's missional contribution has

---

[405] Yong-gi Cho, *Widaehan Somyeong: Huimang Mokhoe 50 Nyeon*, 295-96.
[406] Gyeong-bae Min, "The Theology of Holy Spirit of Rev. Yong-gi Cho and the Korean Church: An Historical Approach," 59-60.
[407] Jae-bum Lee, "Pentecostal Type Distinctives and Korean Protestant Church Growth," 219-20.
[408] Young-hoon Lee, "Life and Ministry of David Yong-gi Cho," 15.
[409] Yong-gi Cho, *Naui Gyohoe Seongjang Iyagi*, 75.
[410] Yong-gi Cho, *More than Numbers*, 87-89.
[411] Yong-gi Cho, *Salvation, Health, and Prosperity*, 136.

clearly enabled the spiritual rejuvenation of the Korean Church, empowering it via the Holy Spirit for the proliferation of God's Kingdom and employing divine healing as an influential evangelistic tool.

Recognising Cho's personal influence over the Korean Pentecostal groups, particularly the KAG, where Cho was ordained and served for over six decades, his contribution to its growth, as evidenced in numerous statistical surveys, is irrefutable.

Table 5: Population Comparison between KAG and the YFGC

Year	KAG[412]	YFGC[413]	Percentage[414]
1958	3,684	5	0.13%
1964	4,261	2,000	46.93%
1970	17,172	8,252	48.05%
1980	199,916	132,940[415]	66.49%
2001	1,225,512	752,401	61.39%
2003	1,192,514	788,441	66.11%

As discernible from Table 5, the membership of the KAG demonstrated consistent growth in parallel with Cho's church. It is plausible to postulate that the growth trajectory of YFGC has exerted a significant impact on the KAG population since 1964, when it accounted for almost half of the denominational populace. It is noteworthy that despite its late arrival in the sphere of Korean Christianity, the KAG has become one of the three predominant denominations in Korea, alongside the Presbyterian and Methodist churches, within a span of just forty years.[416] It is, therefore, understandable that the KAG attributes its progress in its half-century history to Cho, equating his contribution with that of early Korean Pentecostal missionaries.[417]

Cho's contribution has elicited nationwide recognition beyond the confines of the KAG due to his significant influence over the Korean Church. In 1999, the Korean Christian Newspaper Association bestowed upon Cho the Korean Church Leadership Award, acknowledging his contributions to church growth.[418] Moreover, Cho's endeavours to engage in diverse mission projects – encompassing global missions, the NGO Good People's Relief Works, and

---

[412] The numbers include the membership of the YFGC. Jong-dal Im, *Gidokgyo Daehan Hananimui Seonghoe Osibnyeonsa: Yeoksapyeon* [The 50-Year-History of the Korea Assemblies of God: History 1953-2004] (Seoul: Creation, 2005): 434.

[413] Yong-gi Cho, *Widaehan Somyeong: Huimang Mokhoe 50 Nyeon*, 431.

[414] This indicates the YFGC's percentage of the Assemblies of God population.

[415] Kwang-il Kim, "Gidokgyo Chibyeong Hyeonsange Gwanhan Jeongsinuihakjeok Josa Yeongu," 299.

[416] Jong-dal Im, *Gidokgyo Daehan Hananimui Seonghoe Osibnyeonsa: Yeoksapyeon* [The 50-Year-History of the Korea Assemblies of God: History 1953-2004] (Seoul: Creation, 2005): 376.

[417] Yong-gi Cho, *Widaehan Somyeong: Huimang Mokhoe 50 Nyeon*, 270.

[418] Yong-gi Cho, *Widaehan Somyeong: Huimang Mokhoe 50 Nyeon*, 224.

extending support to impoverished churches in farming and fishing villages – were met with appreciation when he was granted the *Yujib*[419] award for his evangelistic efforts.[420] Of further interest is the evaluation of Cho by an American Pentecostal historian. Cho is acknowledged as a central figure in the revival movement of Korean Christianity, which, starting as a modest minority after the Korean War, quickly ascended to become the dominant religion.[421] Such an assertion does not appear hyperbolic when considering the influence of the Pentecostal/Charismatic movements in Korea.

Table 6: Population Comparison between Pentecostals/Charismatics, and Evangelicals[422]

	Pentecostals/ Charismatics	**Evangelicals**
1900	500 (1.17%)[423]	6,400 (14.9%)
1970	250,000 (4.28%)	2,130,000 (36.54%)
Mid-1990	6,550,000 (38.32%)	7,940,000 (46.46%)
Mid-2000	7,580,000 (39.69%)	9,142,000 (47.87%)

A salient feature embodied by the statistics provided pertains to the marked shift in the Korean Christian population from 1970 to the mid-1990s. Notably, this period saw an increment of 21.6% in the Korean population identifying as Christian within a span of merely two decades. A particularly noteworthy development is the growth rate of the Pentecostals/Charismatics sector during this period. Data analysis can readily illuminate the primary factors contributing to this substantial increase. Indeed, it is quite astonishing to observe that this group expanded by a factor of 26.2, in stark contrast to the Evangelicals (whose population still tripled in size). Barrett's findings indicate that during the 1990s, Pentecostals/Charismatics continued to experience exponential growth, eventually surpassing 7.5 million adherents. This total comprised 32% Pentecostals, 27% Charismatics, and 42% Independents.[424] To gain a nuanced understanding of the dynamics during this period, it could prove beneficial to scrutinize the data for the year 1980, which represents the midpoint. The data reveals that by 1980, Pentecostals alone had amassed 440,557 adherents, spanning 961 churches across seven distinct Pentecostal groups. Concurrently,

---

[419] This award is normally given to the people whose contribution is made in evangelism.
[420] Yong-gi Cho, *Widaehan Somyeong: Huimang Mokhoe 50 Nyeon*, 297.
[421] W.W. Menzies, "Yong-gi Cho's Theology of the Fullness of the Spirit," 12.
[422] D.B. Barrett, G.T. Kurian, and T.M. Johnson, *World Christian Encyclopedia: A Comparative Survey of Churches and Religions in the Modern World*, vol. 1, 2nd ed. (New York: Oxford University Press, 2001): 682.
[423] The percentages for Pentecostals/Charismatics and Evangelicals indicate its portion of the Korean Christian population.
[424] D.B. Barrett, G.T. Kurian, and T.M. Johnson, *World Christian Encyclopedia*, 684.

the Korean Assemblies of God (KAG) had 408 churches. Cho's role in fostering the development of the KAG is unequivocally critical. Furthermore, it is vital to underscore that the ripple effects of Cho's missional initiatives permeated the KAG and consequently influenced the Korean Church significantly. In light of this, Myeong-su Park posits that Cho and his church have become emblematic of the Korean Church at large.[425]

Cho's contributions to the broader sphere of Christianity, encompassing global Pentecostalism, are manifold and widely recognised. A particularly noteworthy accolade received was the prestigious Family of Man Medallion in 2005. This award, usually conferred upon individuals exemplifying exceptional utilisation of divine talents in service to humanity,[426] has previously been awarded to eminent personalities such as John F. Kennedy, Dwight D. Eisenhower, Richard M. Nixon, and Jimmy Carter. The absence of any recipient since 1986 further underlines Cho's influential stature as a world leader. His selection primarily hinges on his profound spiritual leadership that has significantly impacted the global landscape, particularly in the domains of world missions and church growth.[427] Cho's influence on global Christianity and the expansion of God's Kingdom is profound. Furthermore, his tenure as chairman of the World Assemblies of God Fellowship from 1992 to 2000, which boasted a membership of 30 million across 60 nations, is considered a milestone signalling that the main impetus of the Holy Spirit movement was passed on to Korea.[428] Cho's prolific publications also merit attention when assessing his global impact. He is credited with publishing 621 books in 40 languages, distributed by 58 different publishers worldwide.[429] While celebrating Cho's influential leadership, it is also important to recognise his significant contributions to the field of church growth.

Nonetheless, my primary apprehension regarding Cho, from a missional viewpoint, revolves around personal issues involving his family members – namely, his son implicated in financial malpractice, and his younger brother and brother-in-law involved in the KAG schism. These incidents may potentially mar his remarkable influence over world Christianity, as they have left many feeling betrayed and disheartened by their religious leader through the actions of his

---

[425] Myeong-su Park, "Haebanghu Hangukgyohoesawa Yeoido Sunbokeumgyohoeui Cho Yong-gi Moksa," 225.

[426] Yong-gi Cho, "Dr. Cho awarded the Family of Man Medallion," *David Cho Website* [Available at http://www.davidcho.com/journal/jbody.asp?id=729], [Last accessed: 23rd November 2023].

[427] Yong-gi Cho, "Dr. Cho awarded the Family of Man Medallion," *David Cho Website* [Available at http://www.davidcho.com/journal/jbody.asp?id=729], [Last accessed: 23rd November 2023].

[428] FGTV, "The Church at Yoido (1973-present)," at http://www.davidcho.com/neweng/ba-1.asp.

[429] Yong-gi Cho, *Widaehan Somyeong: Huimang Mokhoe 50 Nyeon*, 319.

immediate family. I also need to express my ambivalent attitude toward Cho since with great power comes great responsibility.

Theological Perspective

While the social and missional aspects of Cho's work are often the subject of discussion, his theological contributions appear underappreciated relative to their merit. Vinson Synan posits that Cho's contribution to the development of the so-called Three-Fold blessing warrants heightened scrutiny, as its theological framework is singular and virtually non-existent outside of Korea.[430] In Synan's perspective, it is in this context that Cho's distinctive contributions to global Pentecostal theology can be fully appreciated.[431] Furthering this discussion, William Menzies has advocated for a comprehensive examination of Cho's theology, with particular emphasis on its roots in the social and historical landscapes of Korea. Such an approach would serve to dispel potential misinterpretations stemming from its uniquely theological attributes.[432]

Initially, Cho's theology was a cause for contention, leading to its rejection by the mainstream Korean Church. In fact, Cho was denounced as a heretic in 1983.[433] However, by 1994, the *Tonghab* Presbyterian Church retracted its accusations against Cho, acknowledging that his perspectives were rooted in the theological uniqueness of Pentecostal beliefs.[434] This event served to highlight the unfamiliarity of the Korean Church with Pentecostal theology, creating confusion and posing significant challenges for Korean Christians. Mun-chul Shin underscores that, through Cho's work, a burgeoning understanding of the continuity of the Holy Spirit's deeds from the apostolic churches to contemporary churches emerged amongst Korean pastors and theologians. Consequently, the doctrine of cessationism began to be challenged and dismantled by Cho.[435] This is widely regarded as one of Cho's key contributions to the Korean Church. His secondary contribution is identified as the introduction of the concept of the "second blessing," in reference to the Baptism of the Holy Spirit (BHS) within the Korean Church. As a dedicated classical Pentecostal, Cho fervently proposed that the BHS is a spiritual event subsequent to regeneration which brings a fuller experience of the Spirit's power.[436] Min and Kwon posit that Cho's teachings have fostered a deeper understanding within the Korean Church of an immanent God who is actively engaged in our practical

430 V. Synan, "Roots of Yong-gi Cho's Theology of Healing," 8.

431 V. Synan, "Roots of Yong-gi Cho's Theology of Healing," 8.

432 W.W. Menzies, "Yong-gi Cho's Theology of the Fullness of the Spirit: A Pentecostal Perspective," 13.

433 Yong-gi Cho, *Widaehan Somyeong: Huimang Mokhoe 50 Nyeon*, 158.

434 Yong-gi Cho, *Widaehan Somyeong: Huimang Mokhoe 50 Nyeon*, 158.

435 Mun-chul Shin, "A Trinitarian Pneumatology of Youngsan Yong-gi Cho," *Journal of Yongsan Theology* 2 (2004): 68.

436 Jae-bum Lee, "Pentecostal Type Distinctives and Korean Protestant Church Growth," 214-15.

lives,[437] thus broadening the theological perspectives of the Holy Spirit Movement.[438]

As Cho laboured to integrate Pentecostal beliefs into the Korean Church, the initial scepticism surrounding his theological perspective gradually metamorphosed into acceptance and even admiration. On the evolution of the Korean Church's perspective, Min postulates that Cho's Holy Spirit movement has been positively and actively embraced within both Korean society and the church.[439] Min goes so far as to suggest that the second wave of the Holy Spirit movement in Korea was spearheaded by Cho, following the major revivals that transpired between 1905 and 1907.[440] Jang-hyun Ryu, a distinguished systematic theologian at Hansin University,[441] concurs with this sentiment, emphasising that "Cho has sculpted a novel belief system for the Korean Church through leading the Korean Holy Spirit movement."[442]

However, criticism has often been directed towards Cho, especially for his message on blessings, which some perceive as prosperity gospel or shamanistic belief. Misunderstandings in this regard can largely be attributed to confusion in three broad areas: 1) Discussions on Cho's theology have predominantly focused on his pneumatology, healing, and blessings, without sufficiently scrutinising his Christology, which is a critical aspect of his beliefs.[443] 2) Some critiques have relied heavily on secondary sources, leading to potentially skewed perspectives. In his book, *Fire from Heaven*, Harvey Cox criticised Cho as a Korean shaman,[444] later admitting that this was an error prompted by reliance on secondary sources about Cho. Cox pledged to rectify this misrepresentation.[445] 3) Certain aspects of Cho's teaching exhibit theological imprecision, often resulting in paradoxical teachings due to his theological adaptability. Simon Chan suggests that "Some of Cho's teachings are easily misunderstood because

---

[437] Gyeong-bae Min, "The Theology of Holy Spirit of Rev. Yong-gi Cho and the Korean Church: An Historical Approach," 60.

[438] Oh-seong Kwon, "Seongryeong undongeui sae jipyeongeul yeon Choyonggi moksanimeui seongyeok osibjunyeoneul chukadeuribnida" [Congratulations on Rev. Yonggi Cho's 50 year ministry], in Yong-gi Cho, *Widaehan Somyeong: Huimang Mokhoe 50 Nyeon* [Great Call: 50 Years of Hope Ministry] (Seoul: Yoido Full Gospel Church, 2008): 7.

[439] Gyeong-bae Min, "The Theology of Holy Spirit of Rev. Yong-gi Cho and the Korean Church: An Historical Approach," 52.

[440] Gyeong-bae Min, "The Theology of Holy Spirit of Rev. Yong-gi Cho and the Korean Church: An Historical Approach," 39-40.

[441] It is very meaningful that Cho's evaluation came from a prominent theologian of Hansin University which has played a significant role in developing and maintaining the spirit of Minjung theology in Korea.

[442] Jang-hyun Ryu, "A Theological Study of Dr Yong-gi Cho's Pneumatology," 140.

[443] Dawk-mahn Bae, "Chiryohasineun Yesunim" [Healing Jesus], in Pan-ho Kim (ed), *Yongsanui Mokhoewa Sinhak* 1 [The Ministries and Theology of Yongsan 1] (Seoul: Hansei University Press, 2008): 222.

[444] H. Cox, *Fire from Heaven*, 219-55.

[445] Yong-gi Cho, *Widaehan Somyeong: Huimang Mokhoe 50 Nyeon*, 211.

they are not well integrated into the broader framework of his own teaching."[446] I concur with Chan in recognising that Cho has endeavoured to reconcile divergent theological paradigms, exemplified by the tension between Calvinism and Arminianism. This tension is evident even within Cho's healing theology, where healing is regarded as both a divine gift and a human right. Cho's theology grapples with these paradoxical tensions in myriad ways. Regarding the role of prayer for healing, Cho underscores two aspects: God's will and the fervent desire of humanity.[447] As such, Cho's theology is frequently characterised by terms like "holistic,"[448] "creative adaptations,"[449] and "moderate theological neutrality."[450] This suggests an evolving theology that oscillates, much like a pendulum, and a theological stance striving for neutrality. Cho's theological ambiguity is understandable considering his lack of formal training in academic theology and his primary role as a healing practitioner. His theology occasionally exhibits inconsistencies and paradoxes, as Cho has demonstrated an openness to various theological concepts that are challenging to reconcile. Despite his attempts to adapt his theology to his society's changing needs, there remains a scholarly obligation to offer a systematic explanation synthesising all of his theological perspectives.

While there are occasional ambiguities arising from the diversity of Cho's theology, he has indeed formulated a robust contextual theology of blessings. Allan Anderson's article entitled "The Contextual Pentecostal Theology of Cho" substantiates the justification of Cho's theology on the basis that his conclusion is sound and it is vitally important that "The success of Cho's Pentecostalism should not be attributed to a conscious syncretism, but should be seen as a response to the influence of the worldview of Shamanism that permeates and underlies Korean society."[451] This perspective can be substantiated by the following arguments: 1) Cho's theology is to be understood in the proper biblical context of the theology of blessings.[452] The aspiration for blessings is not estranged from the biblical worldview. 2) Cho's theology was shaped through

---

[446] Simon K.H. Chan, "The Pneumatology of Paul Yong-gi Cho," 117.
[447] Yong-gi Cho, *To God Be the Glory*, 102 and 132-37.
[448] Hong-gyu Park, "Youngsan's Theology of Happiness," *JYT* 16 (2009): 72, and also see Young-hoon Lee, "Dr Yong-gi Cho's Influence on the Korean Church in Relation to His Pneumatology," *JYT* 2 (2004): 144.
[449] A.H. Anderson, "The Contextual Pentecostal Theology of David Yong-gi Cho," 122-23.
[450] Veli-Matti Kärkkäinen, "March Forward to Hope: Dr Yong-gi Cho's Pentecostal Theology of Hope," *JYT* 4 (2005): 45.
[451] A.H. Anderson, "The Contextual Pentecostal Theology of Cho," In Wonsuk Ma, W.W. Menzies, and Hyeon-sung Bae (eds), *David Yong-gi Cho: A Close Look at His Theology and Ministry* (Baguio, Philippines: APTS Press, 2004): 110.
[452] Regarding this discussion, see Wonsuk Ma, "David Yong-gi Cho's Theology of Blessing: Basis, Legitimacy, and Limitations," *ERT* 35(2), (2011): 140-59.

his careful study of the Bible.[453] He did not seek to justify Korean religiosity by selectively interpreting biblical references, but rather, he endeavoured to interpret the Korean context through the lens of the Bible, bringing about critical corrections to the context. 3) There are fundamental differences between Shamanism and Cho's practices. Lee contends that Cho's theology diverges from Shamanism in its soteriological, eschatological, and ethical values.[454] 4) Cho's theology is rooted in a God-centred existence, as opposed to a blessing-focused, human-centred existence. Cho argues that shamanistic belief springs from a human-centric worldview, where God is reduced to an instrument for procuring blessings, whereas for him, "the most important thing to us is to surrender every aspect of our lives to God, and to let God use us."[455] In Cho's theology, receiving blessings is not the terminus of Christian life but the commencement of a missional call for God's Kingdom. Cho's innovative theological concepts of the Five-Fold Gospel with the Three-Fold Blessing merit appreciation as contextual theology tailored specifically for post-Korean War society. Synan identifies these two theological pillars as an "original contribution"[456] of Cho's theology to global Pentecostal theology, remarking that "Cho's theology is not simply following the Western theology; it is Korean type of theology which is relevant to the Korean context."[457]

As Cho's theology appears focused on his pneumatology, his understanding of the Holy Spirit's nature and actions constitutes a significant part of his theological contribution. Cho has further developed the classical Pentecostal teaching that "the primary purpose of the Baptism is to give greater power for witnessing (Acts 1:8)."[458] Cho was greatly influenced by this idea in his early ministry, which is why he prayed so hard to receive the Holy Spirit as power.[459] However, he came to realise the importance of the personhood of the Holy Spirit, and started having a personal relationship with the Holy Spirit. Cho believes that this realisation brought about great changes in his life and that new power manifested in terms of anointed preaching and healing.[460] It was viewed by Cho to be the real beginning of his ministries. This theological paradigm shift is recognised as the central component of Cho's pneumatology and even his entire theology, with its influence permeating many Korean pastors and theologians.[461]

---

[453] Gyeong-bae Min, "The Theology of Holy Spirit of Rev. Yong-gi Cho and the Korean Church: An Historical Approach," 42.

[454] Young-hoon Lee, "Dr Yong-gi Cho's Influence on the Korean Church in Relation to His Pneumatology," 144.

[455] Yong-gi Cho, *Naui Gyohoe Seongjang Iyagi*, 232.

[456] V. Synan, "Roots of Yong-gi Cho's Theology of Healing," 9.

[457] Yeol-soo Eim, "The Influence of Dr. Cho's Goodness of God Theology Upon His Ministry," *JYT* 7 (2006): 83.

[458] Eun-cheol Kim, *Hananimui Seonghoe Gyori* [Doctrine of the Assemblies of God] (Suwon, Korea: Moses, 2011): 79.

[459] Yong-gi Cho, *Naui Gyohoe Seongjang Iyagi*, 73-74.

[460] Yong-gi Cho, *Naui Gyohoe Seongjang Iyagi*, 101.

[461] Mun-chul Shin, "A Trinitarian Pneumatology of Youngsan Yong-gi Cho," 68.

While Cho's theological contributions have undeniably impacted many Christians in Korea and globally, there are areas within his perspective that require refinement. First, a critical evaluation from a social perspective is necessary, as mentioned earlier. I concur with Bae's belief that Cho's socio-politico-economic theology requires further development to address issues grounded in his healing theology, soteriology, and Christology.[462] Second, Cho's Five-Fold Gospel should better address ethical issues, given the absence of the gospel of sanctification and the inclusion of the gospel of blessing. In this regard, according to Park, "the modern Pentecostal movement has experienced serious ethical problems so that the Pentecostal movement should emphasise again the message of holiness, which was the central theme of the early Pentecostal movement."[463] Third, Cho's missiology must be revisited to broaden its narrowly defined conception of preaching the gospel and planting churches, as discussed by Ma.[464] Lastly, Cho needs to elucidate more systematically how divine healing operates in conjunction with human participation, taking into account divine sovereignty and human freewill. Given Cho's receptivity to various ideas in his efforts to harmonise different theological schools, it could potentially culminate in paradoxical theology or merely an accumulation of disparate theologies.

Conclusion

Cho cultivated his unique perspective on healing, conceptualising it as a form of practical theology that is highly adaptive to the evolving needs of his society. In the first context, the socio-political-economic landscape significantly influenced Cho's formation of his healing theology. This theology emerged as a segment of the theology of hope and the theology of the Kingdom of God in contemporary times, designed to address the needs of marginalised populations in the aftermath of Japanese colonisation and the Korean War. The second context is the prevalent religiosity deeply ingrained within the Korean populace. Concepts like continuous fellowship with the Holy Spirit as a source of healing, and the notion of spiritual warfare as a healing process, were framed and elaborated with particular reference to the *address of gods*. In the third context, Cho found himself in the Korean Christian tradition of prayer and a Spirit-filled existence, drawing specific influences from Ik-du Kim and Seong-bong Lee. Furthermore, Cho's healing theology solidified into an established theology through inter-denominational dialogues with Korean Christian groups such as the Presbyterian *Tonghab*. Finally, Cho's personal encounters with global Pentecostal figures and his own healing experiences significantly influenced his theological

[462] Dawk-mahn Bae, "Healing Jesus: A Study on Young San's Christology Focusing on Jesus Christ as a Healer," 137.
[463] Myeong-su Park, "Haebanghu Hangukgyohoesawa Yeoido Sunbokeumgyohoeui Cho Yong-gi Moksa," 238.
[464] Won-suk Ma, "David Yong-gi Cho's Theology of Blessing: Basis, Legitimacy, and Limitations," 140-59.

development. The Assemblies of God (AAG) imparted a theological orientation centred on healing through the Atonement and the power of the Holy Spirit. Other Pentecostal leaders, including Roberts, Osborn, and Schuller, furnished Cho with novel insights. Concepts such as possibility thinking, the good God, and healing through faith were incorporated into Cho's healing ideology. Particularly, Roberts' concept of holistic salvation as presented in 3 John 2 and seed faith became the theological backbone of Cho's healing practices and messages.

Cho's theology is an empirical theology that has been shaped in the historical contexts of Korea and entailed Spiritual experiences of world Pentecostal revivalists. However, Cho established a unique variant of Pentecostal theology predicated on his biblical studies and healing experiences. Aspects such as the three-fold blessing, the five-fold gospel, the fourth dimension, and fellowship with the Holy Spirit underscore Cho's theological divergence from those who influenced him. Cho's healing theology of faith emphasises two fundamental aspects: the divine faith that ultimately leads to healing and the human faith that needs to be activated to respond to God's grace of healing. Additionally, the belief that God is a good Father whose will is to heal the sick is another significant pillar of Cho's healing theology. Prayer is envisaged to fulfil dual objectives: developing an intimate relationship with God, allowing healing to emanate naturally from the divine Healer, and invoking God's intervention in our lives.

Practices such as fasting, mountain prayer, and dawn prayers were deemed particularly effective in offering meaningful prayers and inducing personal transformation. The principle of healing in the Atonement underpins Cho's healing theology, as healing is considered a fundamental privilege granted to believers. In this light, healing is perceived not as the objective of Christian life but as a by-product of following Jesus. This theological notion places great importance on repentance for original and individual sins as a healing avenue, underscoring the belief that sickness is primarily a product of sin, constantly nourished by Satan. Hence, spiritual warfare becomes essential to counteract the sources of illnesses.

Cho's contributions to his society have been manifold. The most noteworthy include his late engagement in social relief works, and his inspiring messages of hope for the disillusioned Korean populace. Despite some ethical dilemmas that may have dampened his societal contributions, Cho's greatest influence has undeniably been his missional role. He led the world's largest church, imparting spiritual vitality to the Korean Church through the Holy Spirit Movement, both practically and theologically. Furthermore, Cho's paradigm shift in theology for his personal growth and for the Korean Church demands considerable commendation. His pneumatology, with its focus on the personhood of the Holy Spirit, the Korean form of theology of blessings, and the growing theological interests in and messages for the environment, have drawn significant attention.

4. A Korean Healing Theology

Faith

The Immutable Divine Healer and Cessationism

The theological anchor shared among Kim, Lee, and Cho in the healing movement can be succinctly represented by belief in the immutable God. This theological notion accentuates the steadfast characteristic of God as the ever-present divine Healer. As a result, the distinct hallmark of the Korean healing movement resides in the belief that the divine healing witnessed during biblical eras extends into the contemporary age, with its potency and core nature remaining steadfastly unchanged.

Undoubtedly, this belief in the perpetual occurrence of divine healing became indispensable for the Korean Church, particularly in an environment where cessationism was pervasive, posing a potential dampener to the vitality of the healing movement. As a result, a persistent tension, dilemma, and challenge have been maintained between the cessationism of Western theology and the Asian religious acceptance of divine healing. Within this context, the assertion by Julie Ma appears particularly insightful:

> Historical records attest that in the majority world, there had been religious anticipation of healing. Hence, healing is a part of religious practice and expectancy in Christianity and in other religions. Such belief systems and experiences help people to anticipate the Christian God to heal when healing is warranted. In this environment, supernatural healing occurs more frequently across Christian traditions.[1]

Initially, Korean indigenous Christians were captivated by the healing narratives in the Scriptures and responded to them from the framework of their own belief systems. However, when Christianity was introduced to Korea by Western missionaries, there was scant or no knowledge about divine healing because of the influence of cessationist beliefs amongst the missionaries. This led to a degree of disarray among the indigenous Christian leaders.[2]

---

[1] Julie C. Ma, "Miraculous Divine Activity and religious Worldviews," *Carl F.H. Henry Center For Theological Understanding Website*. 2020. [Available at: https://henrycenter.tiu.edu/2020/01/miraculous-divine-activity-and-religious-worldviews/], [Last accessed: 24th November 2023].

[2] The confusion reigns not only among Korean Christians but also among Western missionaries. In fact, some of the missionaries changed their perspectives on cessationism when they could witness some healing events with their own eyes. See

A salient example of this predicament was Ik-du Kim's departure from his initial belief in cessationism. At first, Kim struggled with this theological preoccupation brought by the Western missionaries, as he used to believe that the healing anointing was only for apostles and prophets in Scripture rather than for individuals at the present time.[3] However, Kim's healing ministries later became sensational enough to draw a great deal of attention to his healing practices up to the point that the Presbyterian Church formed a team called the Miracle Witness Committee to investigate him. As a result, theological conflicts arose from different perspectives between Korean Christians and Western missionaries, and cessationists eventually overpowered the indigenous belief in divine healing despite the influence that Kim made when he became the moderator of the Korean Presbyterian Church, leading numerous healing ministries after 1920.[4] Unfortunately, Kim's effort to amend the Constitution of the Presbyterian Church on cessationism was rejected by the Western missionaries in 1924.[5] This theological tension existed not only in Kim's time but also for the entire Korean Church history until recently. It is not surprising that Cho's theology fell victim of this Western theological misconception judged as cultic by the largest Korean Presbyterian group, *Tonghab,* in 1983. It took approximately eleven years for the judgement to be withdrawn in 1994.[6]

In this specific Korean Church context, Kim felt an urgency to establish his healing theology on the belief that if God's power to heal great diseases applied to the believers in the Bible, there would be no reason for the immutable God to refuse giving him the power to heal the sick *in his time.*[7] Although this theological notion of the immutable divine Healer seems very simple, it is fundamental in terms of challenging the cessationists' perspectives. According to B.B. Warfield,[8] the so-called "greatest of the cessationist scholars"[9] who laid the foundational work on which other cessationists have developed their

---

Sung-deuk Oak, "Healing and Exorcism: Christian Encounters with Shamanism in early Modern Korea," 107-19.

[3] Taek-kwon Im, *Joseon Yesugyohoe Ijeogmyeongjeung*, 1921, 1.

[4] Yong-gyu Park, *Anak Sangol,* 90.

[5] Gyeong-bae Min, *Taehan Yesugyo Changnohoe baeknyonnsa* [A Centennial History of the Presbyterian Church in Korea] (Seoul: General Assembly of the Presbyterian Church in Korea, 1984): 354.

[6] *Christian Newspaper*, 1994, 9, 17.

[7] This was the first motivation of Kim's healing ministry on which his healing theology was first built in terms of faith. See Taek-kwon Im, *Joseon Yesugyohoe Ijeogmyeongjeung*, 1921, 2-3.

[8] Warfield's influence over the Western missionaries in Korea, especially the number one denomination, the Presbyterian Church, cannot be treated lightly, since many of the missionaries to the early Korean Church were the graduates of the Princeton Seminary where Warfield taught systematic theology. See Deok-ju Lee, *Hanguk Tochag Gyohoe Hyeongseongsa Yeongu*, 57.

[9] J. Deere, *Surprised by the Power of the Spirit* (Grand Rapids: Zondervan, 1993): 268, n.9.

theologies, "the Apostolic Church was characteristically considered a miracle-working church." Furthermore, miracles were "the characterising peculiarity of specifically the Apostolic Church, and it therefore belonged exclusively to the Apostolic age."[10] The cessationists' view rejected the continuity of divine healing and sought to confine the validity of divine healing only to the time of the early Church in the New Testament while suggesting that "they [charismata] subsisted through the first three centuries, and then ceased in the beginning of the fourth, or as soon as Christianity came to be established by the civil power."[11]

However, this perception leads to the difficulty of defining what is meant by the "foundational" period and "established" church. When many cessationists believe that the Edict of Milan in 313 or "the triumph of Athanasianism in 381" is normally mentioned as the end of the foundational period,[12] it seems to me that the case of the foundational period can hardly be understood as *foundational* since it covers about three hundred years, not only for the early establishment of the Church. In fact, this inversely helps clarify that miraculous gifts like divine healing were used not only for planting the Church but also for the rebuilding, growing, and empowering of the established Church as an on-going action.[13] In regard to this, Grudem notes, "If ministry in the power and glory of the Holy Spirit is characteristic of the new covenant age (2 Cor. 3:1-4:18)", we "would also have the ability to minister the gospel [...] with accompanying miraculous demonstrations of God's power."[14] Even though it is partly true that the charismatic ministry appeared to decrease after the Apostolic period, it was not "wholly extinguished" in church history.[15] It is, therefore, to be marked as a monumental event that Kim, through his stance on the unchanging God, challenged cessationism to the extent that he attempted to amend the constitution of the cessationists' view in the Church although the proposal was rejected by a vote of 10 to 6 in 1923.[16] From the beginning of Kim's healing ministry, it was crystal-clear that there is no exegetical evidence to reject the continuation of divine healing, and divine healing served him as a simple yet important reminder of the unchanging nature of God's power and love.

---

[10] B.B. Warfield, *Counterfeit Miracles* (Carlisle, PA, Banner of Truth Trust, 1918): 5-6.

[11] B.B. Warfield, *Counterfeit Miracles*, 6.

[12] B.B. Warfield, *Counterfeit Miracles*, 8.

[13] Burgess' research indicates that throughout church history, the Holy Spirit was always at work to bring renewal to the Church, although it is also acknowledged that in the Western tradition the Holy Spirit was "subordinated" to Jesus in the sense of "applying the salvation accomplished by Christ to mankind." See S. M. Burgess, *The Holy Spirit: Ancient Christian Traditions* (Peabody, MA: Hendrickson 1984), 5.

[14] W. Grudem, *Systematic Theology: An Introduction to Biblical Doctrine* (Andhra Pradesh, India: OM Books, 1964): 368.

[15] The charismatic gifts were often observed in the tradition of the Eastern Church. See T. Ware, *The Orthodox Church* (London: Penguin, 1993): 249-50.

[16] *Joseon Yesugyo Jangrohoe Je 13hoe Hoerok* [The Minutes of the 13th Korean Presbytery] (1924): 10-20.

Lee's theology of healing also posits a belief in the perpetuity of divine healing, although his emphasis differs slightly from Kim's. Lee augmented Kim's theological understanding of the immutable God through his Christocentric perspective. As Lee underscored the power of God, his theological basis was deeply grounded in the Christological conviction that "Jesus is the same yesterday, today, and forever."[17] The unwavering nature of Jesus, the supreme divine healer, is the cornerstone of Lee's theology of healing. In his sermon addressing "how to receive healing," Lee persistently proclaimed, "have faith in divine healing. Let it manifest as per your belief. Jesus remains unaltered."[18] The critical concept underscoring Lee's healing theology is the notion that Jesus is the same and unchangeable, implying that the healing ministry of Jesus as described in the Bible continues in the present day.

Cho's theology of healing is fundamentally intertwined with the same theological concept of the everlasting Jesus Christ, thereby expressing a belief in the immutability of God. He argues that "the same Christ who healed the sick 2,000 years ago perpetuates the ministry of healing through the Holy Spirit today."[19] Notably, he endeavours to construct a pneumatology predicated on Christology to advocate for the ongoing nature of divine healing. Cho's healing theology accentuates the role of the Holy Spirit, without negating the significance of Christology and the invariable God. The Korean healing theology of the immutable God, first introduced by Kim, further developed by Lee, and consolidated by Cho, formed the foundational understanding of the Trinitarian God as an unwavering divine Healer. Although the three theological perspectives exhibit nuanced differences, they all fundamentally assert the continued healing power of the immutable God. The shared backbone of their healing movement posits an unwavering faith in the perpetual healing power of the Trinitarian God.

Addressing the conventional defence of cessationism, it is crucial to recognise that the central tenet of cessationism lies in a theological concept of what Gaffin describes as the "history of salvation" as follows:

> In theological terms, the phrase "history of salvation" refers to events that are part of Christ's once-for-all accomplishment of his work of earning our salvation. The events in the history of salvation (such as Christ's death and resurrection) are finished, nonrepeatable events that have importance for all of God's people for all time.[20]

It is Gaffin's essential point that the event of Pentecost in Acts 2 (which is normally adopted by the Pentecostals to support the continuation of *charismata*) should be viewed as one of the events in the history of salvation when

---

[17] Seong-bong Lee, *Sarangui Gangdan*, 65.
[18] Seong-bong Lee, *Buheungui Bigyeol*, 50.
[19] Yong-gi Cho, *How can I be Healed?* 93; Yong-gi Cho, *Sin Yu Lon*, 99.
[20] R.B. Gaffin, Jr, "A Cessationist View," in W.A. Grudem (ed), *Are Miraculous Gifts for Today?* (Grand Rapids, MI: Zondervan, 1996): 31.

emphasising Pentecost as the "climax"[21] of the redemptive work of Jesus. Hence, the event of Pentecost is seen as a completed work, not intended for repetition in the present day. However, Gaffin's argument may be contentious when he strives to interpret the pneumatology of Luke-Acts through the prism of Pauline Christology. There is insufficient evidence for cessationists to presume that the applications of these completed works are primarily soteriological. This theological notion risks undermining Christology by excessively emphasising the completed works and restricting their applications to the soteriological realm.

The shared theology of Kim, Lee, and Cho allows for a concentrated focus on the unwavering divine power of healing, with their healing theologies revolving around the roles of the Trinitarian God. The Korean healing theology fosters a productive tension among the three Divine Persons by recognising their individual roles in healing. When God sent Jesus to redeem the world, Jesus' ministry was empowered by the Holy Spirit, and the full-scale works of the Holy Spirit were later endorsed by Jesus. Consequently, the Jesus who healed the sick according to the Bible is the same Jesus who is fervently healing the sick today through the Holy Spirit. Thus, faith in the ongoing nature of divine healing can be convincingly argued by affirming that Jesus, the incarnated God, remains unchanged – yesterday, today, and forever – the divine Healer is present among his people through the Holy Spirit to this very day.

God's Will to Heal

The secondary tenet of the Korean healing movement rests on the premise that it is within God's will to heal the sick, although this form of healing may not always satisfy all human requests. Lee and Cho understand divine healing according to a broad theological concept that most modern scholars call "healing in the Atonement." Their theological interpretations were nurtured and expanded within a theological discourse where the redemptive actions of Jesus are considered to address not only the spirit but also the soul and body.[22] The shared belief that God provides His children with opportunities to request healing enabled by Jesus' salvific works on the Cross is prominent, although it is also recognised that healing may not always manifest immediately or that God may express His will through denial of certain prayers. Lee postulated that divine healing is realised through "faith in the promise and power of God, and God's will to heal,"[23] while Cho upheld the belief that the "Good God" always wants His people to be healed of their diseases and become healthy.[24] Despite Lee's and Cho's admission that healing may sometimes be absent from God's will, it

---

[21] R.B. Gaffin, Jr, "A Cessationist View," 32.

[22] This idea is well extracted from the theological frameworks of Lee and Cho. Divine healing is one facet of the four-fold Gospel for Lee and of the five-fold Gospel for Cho. See Seong-bong Lee, *Malo Mothamyeon Jukeumeuro*, 100; Yong-gi Cho, *Ojung Bokeum Iyagi*.

[23] Seong-bong Lee, *Buheungui Bigyeol*, 47.

[24] Yong-gi Cho, *Widaehan Somyeong: Huimang Mokhoe 50 Nyeon*, 365.

is unequivocal that their healing theology emphasises faith in God's desire to heal the afflicted.

Intriguingly, Kim's healing theology aligns with the conviction that God's will is to heal the ill. This is borne from the belief that "God would certainly answer prayers of faith."[25] Kim viewed that "God will heal every kind of sickness when prayer of faith is offered" regardless of the requests presented during prayer. Kim's healing theology is anchored on the conviction that "God will certainly heal the sick."[26] Nevertheless, the practical question arises: "Is divine healing always God's will?" The answer to this could be extrapolated from James 5:15, which forms the basis of Kim's perspective on divine healing. Yet, it is a misconception to suggest that this passage provides an unconditional guarantee of healing; rather, James' healing theology emphasises a conditional assurance prompted by the will of God,[27] as alluded to in James 4:15. Korean healing practitioners must address the theological challenge posed by the tension between the concepts of *God will certainly heal the sick* and *the sick require God's will to be fulfilled.*

In response to the Korean healing movement's inclination to underscore the certainty of divine healing, Andrew Murray's perspective serves as an important caveat. He warns that healing "is only possible when we are certain that we are asking according to the will of God."[28] The certainty of the prayer of faith should be first predicated on the assurance of God's will to heal. Simply put, God's will should be the deciding factor in every healing event, not personal psychological certainty or the straightforward belief that healing is invariably God's will. Deere's argument presents a thought-provoking perspective: if God's will is "to heal all sickness in this life [...] all we have to do is to confess and claim our healing, and God is obligated to heal."[29] It may indeed be the case that sometimes, or even often, healing practices are enacted by simply proclaiming God's healing power in the name of faith and not His will. However, God heals according to His will, not on the basis of His obligation or our own will. This leads to the question: does God unilaterally impose His will? The answer is no, as God's will operates through human faith: "God will provide a gift of faith that will enable us to pray in the assurance that the prayer will be answered in the way that it has been offered."[30]

The conundrum of how our prayer, offered in faith, aligns with the divine will of God, is indeed perplexing. Scrutinising the intricacies of faith's principles, Cho ventures to elucidate this dilemma by delving into the dynamics of divine-

---

[25] Ik-du Kim, "Samui Pilyowa Seonggyeong", 56.
[26] Ik-du Kim, *Anak Sangol*, 84.
[27] K. Warrington, *Healing & Suffering: Biblical and Pastoral Reflections* (Milton Keynes, Bucks: Paternoster Press, 2005): 178.
[28] A. Murray, "Divine Healing," in L.G. Jonathan (ed), *Healing: The Three Great Classics on Divine Healing* (Pennsylvania, PA: Christian Publications, 1992): 84.
[29] J. Deere, *Surprised by the Power of the Spirit*, 126.
[30] K. Warrington, *Healing & Suffering*, 132.

human interactions.[31] In Cho's perspective, the faith inspiring divine healing is initially imparted as a spiritual gift from God, but necessitates acknowledgement and activation via human response to this God-bestowed faith. Humans, in this divine schema, are mandated to partake in God's plan as vessels through which His will is manifested and accomplished. As elucidated in 1 Corinthians 12:9, faith is essentially a spiritual endowment from God. "If it is God's faith, it must be God Himself thinking His thoughts through my mind with His own certainty."[32] The nature of this relationship is not dictatorial; God does not impose one's faith, nor does the faith compel God into action. The divine faith is imparted "so that we can partner Him in ensuring that His will is accomplished."[33]

Nevertheless, the divine phenomenon of God's healing is beyond the comprehension of human intellect because "Healing is a mystery of God's love."[34] Healing can be perceived as a divine enigma, a product of God's sovereignty operating in the lives of individuals. It is essential to recognise that God's plan may not always be disclosed, nor is there an obligation for it to be so. This notion serves as a reminder for the Korean healing movement that God's sovereignty is absolute. While figures like Kim, Lee, and Cho acknowledge suffering as a potential divine tool for shaping His people, their theological emphasis is prominently placed on the faith that illnesses do not align with God's will, considering that sin is often perceived as the primary instigator of diseases. Consequently, the collective theology of the Korean healing movement should make room for the belief that, depending upon His sovereignty, healing may not always align with God's will. Suffering can be seen as "God's way of refining believers" and He possesses "the capacity to use it, on occasions, to serve his purposes on our behalf."[35] It is therefore more judicious to consider that "when prayers for healing appear unanswered, as in the case of Paul's 'thorn in the flesh' (2 Cor. 12:7-9), it is crucial not to succumb to resentment and bitterness but to acknowledge God's sovereignty." The thoughts and ways of God are distinct and higher than ours (Is. 55:8-9), but they remain the optimal course.

Absolute Faith

The exploration of a shared theology between the triumvirate has hitherto focused on two theological facets: 1) an enduring belief in the divine healing perpetrated by the same Trinitarian God; and 2) conviction regarding the divine intent to restore health to the ailing. Nonetheless, it is vital to investigate further pivotal elements in the progressive construction of Korean healing theology. The

---

[31] Gi-seong Lee, "God's Absolute Sovereignty and Human Free Will," 81.
[32] R.M. Sipley, *Understanding Divine Healing* (Colorado Springs, CO: Victor Books, 1986): 125.
[33] K. Warrington, *Healing & Suffering*, 131.
[34] F. MacNutt, *Healing* (Notre Dame, IN: Ave Maria Press, 1974): 261.
[35] K. Warrington, *Healing & Suffering*, 196.

initial consideration centres on the indispensability of faith in divine healing: "Is faith an intrinsic attribute of every act of healing?" Lee's perspective provides the initial response, a decisive "No." In his healing theology, faith is considered merely as one of the "conditions"[36] and "methods"[37] of divine healing, whereas Cho and Kim vehemently underscore the inevitability of God's response stemming from a faith-infused prayer. Kim's healing theology proposes the traditional defence that healing is unattainable without faith,[38] while asserting that healing is experienced exclusively by "those with fervent desire and faith, and those who earnestly anticipate their healing."[39] Cho reiterates Kim's premise, positing that, if a person merely entertains the possibility of healing, they will invariably remain afflicted.[40]

However, the conclusion drawn by Kim and Cho appears tentative when one scrutinises the reality that Jesus healed not only those who professed faith in their appeals for aid. Wilkinson's discourse on biblical healing discloses that "out of the twenty-six accounts of individual healing miracles recorded in the Gospels, faith is mentioned in only twelve."[41] Moreover, it has been noted that Jesus' motivation to heal was linked not solely to human faith but also to "compassion," "mercy," "manifestation of glory," "fulfilment of Scripture,"[42] and occasionally, no discernible rationale. This scriptural testimony suggests that faith, while significant, should not be construed as an absolute prerequisite for divine healing.

Assuming faith were mandatory for each act of healing performed by Jesus, He would be reduced to "a servant of faith" and His healing ministry reliant on the human expression of faith to restore the ill.[43] Healing would thus no longer be anchored in divine grace but instead become a mechanistic response elicited by human faith. God does not necessitate human faith as an expression to manifest His divine mercy in healing; rather, He heals in accordance with His divine will. Faith, while crucial, is not intended to be the solitary ultimate conduit for every healing. No human endeavour can be identified as an absolute principle that catalyses divine healing. It can be inferred that God does not intend to offer any absolute pathway to divine healing other than Jesus, so that the faith of the ill will rely on nothing more than God's grace and mercy as conveyed through Jesus.

---

[36] Seong-bong Lee, *Buheungui Bigyeol*, 47.
[37] Seong-bong Lee, *Buheungui Bigyeol*, 48.
[38] A. Murray, "Divine Healing," 27.
[39] A. Murray, "Divine Healing," 27.
[40] Yong-gi Cho, *To God Be The Glory*, 68; Yong-gi Cho, *How can I be Healed?* 69; Yong-gi Cho, *Sin Yu Lon*, 83.
[41] J. Wilkinson, *The Bible and Healing: A Medical and Theological Commentary* (Edinburgh: Handsel, 1998): 101.
[42] J. Wilkinson, *The Bible and Healing*, 97.
[43] K. Warrington, *Healing & Suffering*, 32.

Insufficient Faith

The subject warranting substantive consideration is "Does insufficient faith limit the divine healing power of God?" Initially, Kim assigned his inability to cure a disabled mendicant to his lacklustre faith.[44] At the heart of Kim's theology of healing resides the postulate that God's curative power aligns directly with the extent of an individual's faith.[45] That is to say, from Kim's standpoint, the scale of healing corresponds with the depth of faith. It is inferred, on the basis of Kim's viewpoint, that a certain magnitude of faith is a prerequisite to attain healing. Intriguingly, Kim's theology of healing is intertwined with the concept that faith can be nurtured to reach higher levels,[46] typically attributing this growth potential to human encounters with healing evangelism.[47] In other words, the frequency of engagement in healing practices can augment the faith one has for healing. Hence, Kim's theological framework could potentially evoke a sense of trepidation or guilt that unfulfilled prayers for healing are indicative of a lack of faith or unatoned sin. It is not a baseless supposition that a greater exertion in "cultivating sufficient faith to procure healing" might be the predominant aim of unwell Christians, but then, "one's faith is in faith, not in God."[48] Nevertheless, "there is no suggestion in the gospel that a certain amount of faith is needed to receive healing."[49] The Parable of the Mustard Seed in Luke 17:6 serves as a significant reference, emphasising the "existence of faith" not the "amount of faith."[50] Consequently, a simple openness to beseech God for assistance is sufficient to experience a divine miracle. The notion that God demands high (or strong or sufficient) levels of healing faith could potentially lead to a misconstrued belief that God's power is contingent upon the measure of one's faith, and seems to confine God's healing capability. Thus, irrespective of how feeble or deficient one's faith may appear, the simple act of seeking God's help for healing is sufficient assurance of His benevolence.

Prayer

Earnest Prayer

The efficacy of earnest prayer constitutes a standard paradigm in the context of the Korean healing movement. The three practitioners of healing underscore its pivotal role. Kim employed an exegetical approach, using Luke 11:5-13 as a foundational text to affirm the effectiveness of earnest prayer in soliciting and

---

44 Yong-gyu Park, *Anak Sangol*, 75.

45 Yong-gyu Park, *Anak Sangol*, 84; 172.

46 See F. MacNutt, *Healing*, 249; D. Dunkerley, *Healing Evangelism* (Grand Rapids, MI: Chosen Books, 1995): 81-82.

47 D. Dunkerley, 83.

48 R.A.N. Kydd, *Healing through the Centuries: Models for Understanding* (Peabody, MA: Hendrickson, 1998): 16.

49 K. Warrington, *Healing & Suffering*, 31.

50 K. Warrington, *Healing & Suffering*, 32.

receiving divine interventions.[51] Lee echoes this sentiment, positing that prayer, when offered earnestly and wholeheartedly, possesses efficacy, as God responds to those ardently seeking divine aid.[52] Interestingly, Lee's understanding of effective earnest prayer surpasses Kim's initial proposition by advocating that prayers lacking genuine fervour are unlikely to be answered.[53] This aspect of Kim's healing theology was later embraced and further refined by Lee, eventually regarding earnest prayer as a requisite for effective supplication. Moreover, Cho offers a comprehensive elucidation of the operational mechanism through which earnest prayer contributes to divine healing.[54] For Cho, prayers that are "earnest"[55] and "fervent"[56] play a crucial role while awaiting God's faith that actualises healing. Kim's conception of earnest prayer was later expanded upon by Lee and Cho, transforming it into a vital component of divine healing. Hence, the palpable emotional intensity in prayer meetings across Korean churches – often characterised by vocal exclamations and crying – seems only logical. Such emotional eruptions are a distinctive feature of Korean revival meetings, particularly visible during Kim's revival gatherings marked by "penitent weeping,"[57] "earnest prayer", and "beating of chests, weeping in repentance."[58]

It is essential to recognise that earnest prayer serves as a universal principle underpinning effective supplication. Western systematic theology also underscores "praying earnestly" as a critical ingredient in efficacious prayer, often highlighting that "it will be natural to pray with intense emotional involvement and to expect God, as a merciful Father, to respond to heartfelt prayer."[59] Yet, it is important to acknowledge that expressions of earnest or fervent prayer can differ greatly, dependent on various contextual factors. For instance, the Korean Church's style of earnest prayer typically involves vocalisations, arm flailing, and bodily movements. While these expressions may be construed as excessively emotional and as due to cultural misunderstandings regarding the conventional practice of emotionally charged, petitionary prayers, Hernandez's insights are enlightening in comprehending the cultural diversity inherent in prayer:

> Just as we converse with different people through a variety of different means, we also talk with God in a number of ways that inevitably reflect our unique culture,

---

[51] Ik-du Kim, *Gidoui Jonggyo*, 9.

[52] Seong-bong Lee, *Immanuel Gangdan*, 21.

[53] Seong-bong Lee, *Sarangui Gangdan*, 87.

[54] Choe, as much as Cho, was responsible in developing the theology of prayer and fasting. She was directly influenced by Lee.

[55] Yong-gi Cho, *Ten-minute Broadcast Sermon*, 218; Yong-gi Cho, *Sachawonui Yeongseong*, 140.

[56] Yong-gi Cho, *How can I be Healed?* 137.

[57] Taek-kwon Im, *Joseon Yesugyohoe Ijeogmyeongjeung*, 1921, 46.

[58] Taek-kwon Im, *Joseon Yesugyohoe Ijeogmyeongjeung*, 1921, 70.

[59] W. Grudem, *Systematic Theology*, 1994, 388.

> our tradition, our depth of experiences, our own personalities and even our temperamental mix – none of which should be construed to be automatically right or wrong. Some cultures may be very vocal and repetitive in the way they verbalise their prayers, others might tend to be passionate and loud when they come together as a community, engaging in simultaneous outbursts of intercessory prayer.[60]

Hernandez's perspective cautions against the grave danger of prematurely judging individuals from different cultural backgrounds on the basis of one's cultural norms. It is important to consider the unique cultural, socio-political, and economic contexts of the Korean Church, which has endured considerable historical suffering. Without this understanding, the intense and earnest prayer tradition of the Korean Church – often marked by emotional outbursts – may be misconstrued as overly emotional or sorrowful. Nevertheless, this approach to prayer emerged from a desperate cry for immediate divine intervention amidst the hardships faced by the Korean Church.[61] The urgency associated with this style of earnest prayer is connected to a sense of immediate need. The afflicted Korean Christians prayed emphasising the present, not pleading for prosperity, but for their most basic necessities.

Fasting Prayer

The solemnity inherent in fervent prayer is often intertwined with the practice of fasting, constituting a distinct form of devotional exercise within Korean Christian traditions. This practice of fasting prayer stands as an emblem of Korean Christianity's fervour,[62] although it is generally not a common observance among Western Christians.[63] The necessity of fasting prayer is recognised within the theological context of the Korean healing movement. Cho's observations corroborate the effectiveness of this practice, suggesting that roughly 90% of the individuals who undertook fasting at his prayer mountain witnessed significant health improvements.[64] Kim and Lee further argued that the fervour of prayer must be amplified when prayers remain unanswered or during times of extreme difficulty. They propose fasting as an effective method to enhance the sense of urgency intrinsic to fervent prayer.[65] Similarly, within Cho's congregation, fasting prayer is considered an elevated form of prayer, largely because of its inherent urgency.[66] However, this practice does not imply

---

[60] W. Hernandez, "Prayer" in W.A. Dyrness and Veli-Matti Kärkkäinen (eds), *Global Dictionary of Theology* (Nottingham: Inter-Varsity Press, 2008): 701.
[61] It is also interesting to know that this is often observed in African Pentecostal prayer meetings in much more emotional ways.
[62] Yeol-soo Eim, "South Korea" in Stanley M. Burgess (ed), *International Dictionary of Pentecostal and Charismatic Movements* (Grand Rapids, MI: Zondervan, 2002): 240.
[63] W. Grudem, *Systematic Theology*, 391.
[64] Yong-gi Cho, *Huimangmokhoe 45 Nyeon*, 174.
[65] Taek-kwon Im, Joseon Yesugyohoe Ijeogmyeongjeung, 1921, 4-5; Deuk-hyeon Kim, "Pyeongsindorosseo Naegabon Lee Seong-Bong Moksanim," 30.
[66] ITI, *Yoido Kyohoei Shinanggwa Shinhak* 2, 121.

a higher spiritual standing for those who partake in fasting. In delineating the purpose of fasting prayer, Cho underscores the concept of "greater intensity". He conveys his belief that we can propel the urgency of our plea to appear before God's throne with such fervour that He will listen and respond.[67] The theological underpinning of fasting, in relation to the urgency of prayer, can be articulated thus:

> Fasting expresses earnestness and urgency in our prayers: if we continued to fast, eventually we would die. Therefore, in a symbolic way, fasting says to God that we are prepared to lay down our lives that the situation be changed rather than that it continued. In this sense fasting is especially appropriate when the spiritual state of the church is low.[68]

As indicated above, the necessity for fervent healing prayers became a focal point for Korean Christians while navigating the turbulent historical landscape characterised by Japanese persecution and the Korean War. Within this specific context, Korean healing movement theology frequently emphasised the aspect of *speaking to God* over *listening to God* within prayer's functional framework. The act of speaking to God in prayer typically serves to present human petitions to God. This is the rationale behind Cho's definition of "petitioning God" as the fundamental purpose of prayer, substantiating his belief that "God is our Father, and as a father, He enjoys giving to His children […] God is a good God! He desires to give all good things to us if we just ask Him."[69]

Persistent Prayer

The discussion progresses towards a key theological concept, termed "persistent prayer." As posited by Kim, when individuals approach the divine with a particular request such as healing, it is often necessary to persistently and fervently pray, foregoing food and sleep, until their petitions are acknowledged.[70] Lee's exegetical interpretation of Mark 2:1-12 parallels Kim's, underscoring the importance of insistent prayer.[71] It is Lee's main argument that the heart of the Lord can be moved by persistent requests.[72] Moreover, the perspective of Cho is significant as he systematised persistent prayer programmes in the Korean Church, such as Overnight Prayers, Daniel Prayers, and Congregational Unison Prayer with the triple shout of "Lord!" Cho's healing theology of prayer signifies another aspect of persistent prayer as he argues that "we need to pray until the

---

[67] Yong-gi Cho, *Prayer that Brings Revival* (Lake Mary, FL: Creation House, 1998): 99.
[68] W. Grudem, *Systematic Theology*, 1994, 391.
[69] According to Cho, prayer is petitionary, devotional, and intercessory. See Yong-gi Cho, *Prayer that Brings Revival*, 45.
[70] Ik-du Kim, *Gidoui Jonggyo*, 15.
[71] Seong-bong Lee, *Sarangui Gangdan*, 88.
[72] Seong-bong Lee, *Sarangui Gangdan*, 88.

faith and conviction of God's healing comes."[73] In other words, the notion of persistent prayer is not like an aimless repetition of words in prayer. The sense of persistence depends on the arrival of divine faith that healing is to take place within the sick body. It is not a human effort to make a great appeal to God but to draw near to the will of the divine healer through persistent prayer. According to Cho:

> Prayer is not to draw God into you, but to draw yourself closer to God [...] The more we pray, the more our hopes and motivations become pure enough to live a Christ-centred life and pray according to God's will, then God will open the door of heaven and show us unimaginable miracles.[74]

Thus, it is suggested in the Korean healing theology that the petitioner should come to God persistently until God answers.[75] This theological notion of prayer supports Grudem's claim that "When we are earnestly seeking God for an answer to a specific prayer, we may repeat the same request several times."[76] While in some cultures repetition may sound too demanding or unnecessary, persistent prayer needs not to be viewed as a means to annoy God for what one wants. It is an effective means for the sick to be continually dependent on the divine Healer for His mercy. This persistent prayer is only possible when the petitioners are aware that God is the only hope and that He has the power and authority to heal.

Yet, it is noted that this practice of persistent prayer, predominantly by Pentecostal churches, has drawn substantial criticism from non-Pentecostal circles due to a perceived lack of biblical foundation.[77] Occasionally, petitionary prayer is misconstrued as based on the prosperity gospel. This could potentially suggest that petitioning for human needs in prayer might be considered immature, while listening to God is deemed more significant. Nevertheless, it is crucial to recognise that "prayer involves a loving dialogue between two parties: an individual and/or a believing community and God."[78] Hence, conversational prayer should equally emphasise the two main components: speaking to and listening to God. This facilitates the understanding that without verbalising to God, prayer cannot facilitate a bilateral conversation between believers and God but would rather serve as a mere revelation of God's will. In the Korean healing movement, individuals approach God with petitions because petitionary prayer is ultimately God-centric, not centred on human needs or desires. Contrarily, it is prudent to caution that, without understanding God's will in prayer, it could

---

[73] Yong-gi Cho, *Sinyu* [Divine Healing], 229-248; Yong-gi Cho, *Sachawonui Yeongseong* [The Fourth Dimensional Spirituality], 41.
[74] Yong-gi Cho, *Dousineun Seongryeongnim* [The Holy Spirit Who Helps Us], 97-98.
[75] Yong-gi Cho, *Prayer that Brings Revival*, 119.
[76] W. Grudem, *Systematic Theology*, 387.
[77] Dong-soo Kim, "Lukan Pentecostal Theology of Prayer: Is Persistent Prayer Non-Biblical?" *Asian Journal of Pentecostal Studies* 7(2), (2004): 205.
[78] W. Hernandez, "Prayer," 701.

be misinterpreted as a spell from a fairytale to fulfil desires. The balance between articulating to God and heeding His word should be preserved.

The value of petitionary prayer can be further expounded from a biblical standpoint. As reflected in Lee's endeavour to substantiate the validity of persistent prayer based on Luke 11:8, Dong-soo Kim, utilising the same passage, lays an exegetical foundation on the parable of the friend, commenting that "the main focus of the parable of the friend at midnight is not on God's generous character, but on human attitude in prayer, i.e., persistence."[79] The theological concept of persistent prayer is not alien to biblical studies and is indeed prevalent in Lukan theology, since "Luke stresses persistence in human prayer, as is also shown in the parable of the importunate widow (Luke 18:1-8)."[80]

These exegetical interpretations permit us to understand that God's miraculous intervention in this world is not solely dictated by His sovereignty. God still encourages His children to participate in His plan, a response to His unconditional love, which is not predicated on human merits. In this context, the role of petitionary prayer in potentially influencing God's heart can be discussed, even as many Christians remain sceptical about the plausibility of influencing God's decision-making process. If prayer is viewed as a relational conversation, it is conceivable that it can impact not only the supplicants but also God. In this regard, Hernandez's assertion is pertinent:

> Prayer is where we intimately encounter God and God encounters us. And in such an encounter, transformation inevitably happens. Prayer does change things. For one, it changes us. But it changes God too. A responsive, loving God attends to our prayers even as we ourselves learn to respond to God's overtures of love.[81]

The overarching intent of Hernandez's argument is to propose the idea that God is not compelled to act out of human merits but, because of His responsive and loving nature, He chooses to heed the petitions of His children. Consequently, it is logical that prayers we offer can potentially move and alter the heart of God. That is, prayer can serve as a medium not to generate healing but to receive the grace God wishes to bestow.

Relational Prayer

Another significant aspect of the healing theology of prayer for Kim, Lee, and Cho lies in its foundation upon the relationship with God. According to Kim, prayer serves as a means to "rely on God" and "deepen the relationship with God."[82] Lee shares a similar perspective, examining the role of prayer in times of suffering: prayer's primary objective in the context of illness is not solely to restore physical health, but rather to attain a greater understanding of, gratitude

---

[79] Dong-soo Kim, "Lukan Pentecostal Theology of Prayer," 215.
[80] Dong-soo Kim, "Lukan Pentecostal Theology of Prayer," 215.
[81] W. Hernandez, "Prayer," 703.
[82] Ik-du Kim, *Gidoui Jonggyo*, 10.

towards, and love for God.[83] Cho also regards prayer as a devotional act aimed at seeking God "in deep fellowship and communion."[84] Consequently, in Cho's theological framework, prayer for healing commences with the restoration of a proper relationship with the Divine Healer. For him, "divine healing flows from God" and it is "a blessing that we receive when we remain in Christ."[85] The cultivation and sustenance of a close relationship with God are thus fostered through prayer.[86] Consequently, it is within the realm of Korean healing theology to acknowledge that prayer initially serves as a tool to approach the divine Healer with personal pleas for healing, while simultaneously aiding the sick in the development of their personal relationship with God, ultimately leading to an understanding of God's will. In this respect, the prayer for healing is intended to act as a facilitator of God's will, ensuring that "we will receive what we have asked for"[87] and even what is deemed best for us in accordance with God's will.

Mountain Prayer

The Korean healing theology necessitates continual focus on several unique modes of prayer, such as the dawn prayer and mountain prayer. These methods serve as distinct theological elements intrinsic to the Korean healing movement. As postulated by Yeol-soo Eim, "the prayer mountain movement is an indigenous Korean Pentecostal movement."[88] The three practitioners in the field of healing engaged energetically with these prayer modes in their healing ministries. Kim, as an example, routinely visited mountains to prime himself with prayer in preparation for leading revival meetings.[89] Through mountain prayer, his ailing wife achieved healing.[90] Intriguingly, documentation exists of multiple individuals receiving healing from various diseases after persistently praying on a mountain after Kim's revival meeting.[91] Mountain prayer also constitutes a portion of Lee's ministries. His engagement with mountain prayer commenced during his childhood, subsequently leading to the establishment of a weekly prayer meeting on a mountain with church congregants.[92] Mountain prayer was invoked during times of critical necessity for divine intervention within Lee's ministry. The value of mountain prayer is echoed in the practices of Cho, who systematically adopted the phenomenon following the founding of the prayer mountain movement by Woon-mong Rah, in proximity to Independence. Indeed, Cho further perpetuated Rah's legacy, elevating it to a

---

[83] Seong-bong Lee, *Sarangui Gangdan*, 123.
[84] Yong-gi Cho, *Prayer that Brings Revival*, 59.
[85] Yong-gi Cho, *How can I be Healed*, 130-31.
[86] Yong-gi Cho, *How can I be Healed*, 131.
[87] Yong-gi Cho, *To God Be the Glory*, 102.
[88] Yeol-soo Eim, "South Korea," 240.
[89] Yong-gyu Park, *Anak Sangol*, 95.
[90] Yong-gyu Park, *Anak Sangol*, 75-77.
[91] Taek-kwon Im, *Joseon YesuGyohoe Ijeogmyeongjeung*, 1921, 93.
[92] See Seong-bong Lee, *Malo Mothamyeon Jukeumeuro*, 17; Seong-bong Lee, *Malo Mothamyeon Jukeumeuro*, 51-52.

higher echelon.[93] However, this integration drew sceptical views due to the possible influences of Shamanism in the genesis of mountain prayer.

Shamanism's association with mountains has occurrences throughout Korean history. Numerous national cults thrived on mountaintops having originated there.[94] There are some reasons why such national cults had been practiced in mountainous places, rather than on the plains. According to Christopher Pae, Korean culture was formulated by *Cheon shin* (heavenly god), who was the supreme god, and the centre for worshiping *Cheon shin* was on the mountain because Koreans have believed that the heavenly god descended to these very mountains from heaven and dwells there.[95] Consequently, many Koreans consider mountains as the holiest of places.

This notion of sacred mountains has influenced not only national cults but also other Korean religions. Buddhists have a specific cult (*San Sin Gak*), which is practiced once a year at *Tong Do* Temple, one of the largest temples in Korea. The specific term, *San Sin*, means mountain god[96] and it is obvious that this religion has been influenced by Korean Shamanism, since *San Sin Gak* originated from mountain worship. *Chun Do Kyo*, another Korean folk religion has the concept of the sacred mountain. The pioneer of *Chun Do Kyo*, Jae-woo Choe, was called by a god at Mount *Gumi* on 5th April 1860[97] which marks the beginning of *Chun Do Kyo*.

Taking into account the multifaceted historical and religious contexts of Korea, where the notion of sacred mountains originates, the current data appear inadequate to conclusively argue that mountain prayer is solely a product of shamanistic traditions. Furthermore, the concept of sacred mountains is not alien to people in biblical times. Mountains held great significance as symbols in the religious fabric of Israel's life, spanning from the most ancient times until the culmination of the Second Temple period and beyond. Abundant evidence supports the assertion that the Israelites preserved the concept of the sacred mountain. In this context, Donaldson provides insightful details: 1) Bethel, a hilly region, served as a vital cultic centre, 2) the northern city of Shechem, situated near Mount Gerizim, was revered as a worship site, 3) Mount Ebal was the location of a covenant renewal ceremony (Dt. 11:29, 27:1-13; Josh. 8:33),

---

93 Yong-gi Cho, *Prayer that Brings Revival*, 92.

94 Regarding this issue, Yo-han Lee presents some significant information in his dissertation: In the period of the Buyeo Dynasty (about 4200 years ago), Yong Go, in the Ko Ku Ryo Dynasty (37 BCE–668 CE), Dong Mang, in the Jin Han Dynasty, So Du, and in the Ko Ryo Dynasty (918–1392 CE), and Pal Kwan Hae were important national cults that were practiced. See Yo-han Lee, "The analysis of the Christian prayer mountain phenomenon in Korea" (Ph. D. diss., Fuller Theological Seminary, 1985): 83.

95 Christopher Pae, "A Study of the Influence of Shamanism in the 100 Years' History of the Koreans" (Ph. D. diss., Fuller Theological Seminary, 1995): 74.

96 Yo-han Lee, "The analysis of the Christian prayer mountain phenomenon in Korea," 85.

97 Yo-han Lee, "The analysis of the Christian prayer mountain phenomenon in Korea," 85.

and 4) Mount Carmel was perceived as the locus of a local religious centre during the times of Elijah (1 Kings 18:30) and Elisha (2 Kings 2:25, 4:25).[98] These local mountains were deemed sacred, given the prevalent belief that they were sites of divine worship.

As this study further explores the critical assessment of religious practices associated with mountains, it is imperative to consider the parallels and distinctions between the Christian prayer mountain movement and shamanic practices. Yo-han Lee argues convincingly that Korean mountain prayer has been influenced by shamanistic precursors,[99] while Allan Anderson cautiously notes the association between Christian prayer mountains and ancient spirituality.[100] Anderson explores how mountains have been viewed as locations where pioneering pilgrims and Shamans could obtain spiritual powers, premised on the belief that benevolent gods inhabit these specific mountains. It is evident that mountains have historically been revered by Koreans as the quintessential sacred sites for divine encounters and experiences of supernatural powers. This perception is evident in Cho's portrayal of his prayer mountain, where he posits, "In this [mountainous] atmosphere of concentrated prayer, healings and miracles are a common occurrence."[101] In Cho's theology, mountain prayer continues to offer Christians the opportunity to experience divine power, attributing miracles and healings to "concentrated prayer," rather than the sanctity of the mountain. Its link to Shamanism must therefore be perceived as a contextualised expression of Korean theology, influenced by the collective religiosity of the Korean populace. Cho explains the purpose of mountain prayer when he states, "At these prayer grottos, people can get very still and quiet before God. In my own prayer closet, I can shut the door and commune with my heavenly Father in concentrated and prolonged prayer."[102] Cho's primary focus lies not in the sacredness of the mountain, but in the intensity and duration of prayer.

This understanding facilitates the progression from the shamanistic belief in the geographical sanctity of mountains as abodes of gods to the contextualised belief in mountains as conducive environments for contemporary Christians to engage in uninterrupted quality time with God. Consequently, the value of mountain prayer resides in the effectiveness of prayer in solitude. This solitary nature serves as a critical factor in comprehending why Korean Christians pray on mountains. This concept aligns with Grudem's proposition, "When we are truly alone with God, in the privacy of a room to which we have 'shut the door'

---

[98] T.L. Donaldson, *Jesus on the Mountain: A Study in Matthean Theology* (Sheffield: Sheffield Academic Press, 1990): 30.
[99] Yo-han Lee, "The analysis of the Christian prayer mountain phenomenon in Korea," 131.
[100] A.H. Anderson, "The Contextual Pentecostal Theology of David Yong-gi Cho," 104.
[101] Yong-gi Cho, *Prayer that Brings Revival*, 92.
[102] Yong-gi Cho, *Prayer that Brings Revival*, 92.

(Mt. 6:6), then we can pour out our hearts to him."[103] Therefore, the Korean Church primarily views the value of mountain prayer as an efficient means to enhance readiness to focus on God in solitude.

This analysis clarifies that the practice of mountain prayer scarcely aligns with the shamanistic belief, particularly when considering the purpose of mountain prayer, as explained by Cho:

> I believe there are many Christians who are longing for a place where they can meet God in a dynamic way. Not that God can't be found everywhere men seek Him in spirit and in truth, but there is no place on earth that has more concentrated prayer than a prayer mountain. Christians are not satisfied with just hearing about the moving of God; they desire to see what God is doing.[104]

Despite the apparent similarity of forms between mountain prayer and Shamanism, it is untenable to argue that mountain prayer is redundant because of its ties to Shamanism. Shamanistic beliefs have played merely a supplementary role in shaping Korean prayer practices. Cho, in this respect, proposed an innovative alternative by redefining prayer on the sacred mountain as more concentrated prayer in a secluded location. This form of mountain prayer was contextualised as an intensified expression of urgent prayer. Many Korean Christians found mountain prayer appealing and effective, especially for specific requests such as healing. Prayer mountains are often perceived by visitors as the optimal locations for focused, fervent prayer with various intentions, such as to "receive physical and spiritual healings" and to experience spiritual phenomena akin to the BHS.[105]

Early Morning Prayer

Discerning the essence of daily early morning prayer is comparable to comprehending the concept of mountain prayer. It is a common tradition among Korean Churches to convene early morning prayer meetings each day, typically from 4:30 to 5:30 a.m.[106] This ritual is equally manifested in other religious domains such as Buddhism, Confucianism, Taoism, and Shamanism.[107] Kyum-il Na elucidates the significance of early morning prayer by drawing connections to the symbolic dawn, which is potent with notions of "creation" and "nativity." Dawn is traditionally perceived as a potent period of the day, especially in the context of Shamanism.[108] Nonetheless, Na underscores the importance of

---

[103] W. Grudem, *Systematic Theology*, 389.
[104] Yong-gi Cho, *Prayer that Brings Revival*, 93.
[105] Yeol-soo Eim, "South Korea," 243.
[106] The Christian origin of this prayer is often attributed to the Pyeongyang Revival in 1907. It was a spontaneous development after an overnight vigil.
[107] Kyum-il Na, "Early morning prayer and church growth: based on the case study of Inchun Juan Presbyterian Church" (D. Min. diss., Asian Center for Theological Studies and Mission and Fuller Theological Seminary, 1941), 23-24.
[108] Kyum-il Na, "Early morning prayer and church growth," 23-24

morning prayer through a distinct lens of spiritual edification, positing that Christians can foster their spirituality through this ritual.[109] Another prominent aspect of early morning prayer resides in its potential to act as a catalyst for both spiritual and physical rejuvenation, extending its utility to praying for the unwell, as exemplified in Lee's revival meetings. Numerous instances of healing have been reported and witnessed in these dawn prayer gatherings, as articulated by Lee.[110] This is not merely a result of the Korean Church's continued belief in the sacred and powerful nature of dawn, but rather, its significance has evolved to encapsulate a novel concept of persistent prayer, defined as "continuing in prayer over time."[111] Morning prayer is thus an expression of the Korean Church's fervent pursuit of God. As such, culturally rooted prayer forms like dawn prayer and mountain prayer should not be dismissed on account of their historical and shamanistic ties. Rather, they are employed in the contemporary context as a means of prayer that encourages a focus on God while offering a dedicated timeframe and space for intensified prayer.

On the other hand, as the contextualised forms of mountain prayer and dawn prayer provided avenues for the expansion of prayerful life in the Korean Church, they also provided obstacles and even dangers to a certain degree. What Sipley mentions below is a significant reminder and lesson for today's Korean Christians who desire to come to God for requests in their prayers:

> If fasting is carried on as a religious exercise to gain merit or persuade God, it will not produce divine healing [...] However, fasting under the leadership of the Holy Spirit and coupled with earnest, persistent prayer, may be very effective in the matter of physical healing. Fasting is not so much for God as it is for the person who is praying. The withdrawal from satisfying the desires of the body seems to strengthen the inner human spirit. It makes the person more sensitive to God, sin and demonic powers. The will and guidance of God becomes more clear. Fasting has an inner purifying effect that makes the one who is fasting and praying a cleaner channel for the will and working of God.[112]

Although Sipley's observation primarily pertains to the practice of fasting for healing, its theological implications extend to morning and mountain prayers, contributing to the evolution of the Korean healing movement. It serves as a call for introspection for those who place excessive emphasis on their religious rituals to fulfil their needs. The intensified forms of prayer such as mountain prayers, fasting, and early morning prayers should not be the primary focus as religious practices. Instead, they should be utilised as tools to bring individuals closer to God, aiding the unwell to rely on and strengthen their relationship with the divine Healer. Koreans are often prone to treat their gods in a functional manner rather

---

109 Kyum-il Na, "Early morning prayer and church growth," 23-24.

110 Seong-bong Lee, *Malo Mothamyeon Jukeumeuro*, 118, 121, and 159; Heui-beom Choe, "Malo Mothamyeon Jukeumeuro," 466.

111 W. Grudem, *Systematic Theology*, 387.

112 R.M. Sipley, *Understanding Divine Healing*, 158.

than relational because of the pervasive influence of shamanistic beliefs. Without a conscious effort by Korean Christians to strike a balance between both aspects of prayer (speaking and listening to), Korean Christianity risks devolving into a quasi-Christian religion or a modernised form of Shamanism imitating Christianity.

Repentance

Relationship between Sin and Sickness

One of the prominent characteristics of Korean healing theology prevalent in the Korean Church since the significant revivals of 1903 and 1907 is the emphasis on repentance. During the initial revivals, repentance emerged as a crucial aspect and continued to influence Korean healing theology. This Christian tradition of repentance quickly evolved into the belief that sin is the primary cause of sickness. The theological perspective of the three healing practitioners highlights two aspects: 1) Sin is not the sole cause of sickness; and 2) Most illnesses are attributable to sin. Kim, Lee, and Cho consistently associated sickness with sins, while exhibiting some minor differences in their approaches. Kim shed light on the occasional connection between sin and illness, considering sin as a major factor in the onset of sickness. Consequently, Kim's prayers for the sick were preceded by a simple question: "Do you believe in God and do you know your sins?"[113] His prayer was often followed by the advice: "See, you are well again. Stop sinning or something worse may happen to you."[114] Kim's healing ministry revealed a notable correlation between relapses of illnesses and sins.[115] Lee strongly supported this concept, asserting that when people are sick, they must identify the sin causing the sickness.[116] Similarly, Cho emphasised the significance of repentance for healing, stating that "anyone who has an earnest hope of being healed must repent and be forgiven of their sin."[117] Lee and Cho's perspective, initially derived from Kim's theological notion, later became associated with another theology, known as healing in the Atonement. Viewing sin as the primary cause of sickness, Lee and Cho regarded the sin of Adam and Eve as the underlying source of illness. This allowed for differentiation between the consequences of Original Sin and individual sins, as Cho asserted that "illness is always related to sin" either directly or indirectly.[118] Individual sin was understood as a direct cause and original sin as an indirect one. There is a strong intrinsic connection between sin and sickness in the Korean healing theology of all three men, not in the sense that illness is always *caused* by individual sin but

---

[113] Yong-Gyu Park, *Anak Sangol*, 173.
[114] Myeong-su Park, *Hanguk Gyohoe Buheungundong Yeongu*, 84.
[115] See Taek-kwon Im, *Joseon Yesugyohoe Ijeogmyeongjeung*, 1921, 31; 114; 137.
[116] Seong-bong Lee, *Buheungui Bigyeol*, 49.
[117] Yong-gi Cho, *How can I be Healed,* 59.
[118] Yong-gi Cho, *Sin Yu Lon*, 97.

in the sense that "most sicknesses come from sins"[119] and that every sickness began to exist in the world through Original Sin.

A theological notion emerges suggesting that sickness exists in the world because of Original Sin, and personal ailments can be triggered by individual sins. In such cases, the forgiveness of sins through repentance becomes a means to bring healing to the sick. Interestingly, this idea finds support within the Bible. Warrington highlights the connection between healing and repentance in his discussion of the confession of sins based on James 5:16, which states, "Therefore confess your sins to each other and pray for each other so that you may be healed. The prayer of a righteous man is powerful and effective." According to Warrington, "the practices of private and public confession of sin were common in Judaism [...] the tense of the verb (present imperative) [of "confess" your sins] in 5:16 suggests that it was expected that confession should form a regular part of life in the community."[120] This allows one to note that sickness was often attributed to sin, although he cautions that this theology must work only for the case of the suffering caused by sin.[121] This theological notion is supported by another theologian, Erickson, who writes that "Apparently there is not as intimate a connection between sickness and individual sin,"[122] and reluctantly admits that "this is what we would expect if sickness is the result of individual sin, for in that case physical healing would require forgiveness of sin causing the sickness."[123] While both Warrington and Erickson understand that sickness can be caused by sins, in which case repentance should be first practised, their main argument is the rejection of the idea that every sickness is caused by sin or most sicknesses come from sins. In a similar way, the Korean healing theology is not in favour of the idea that sickness is always caused by sin but is carefully supportive of the idea that sickness is always *related* to sins whether directly or indirectly.[124]

However, it is essential to acknowledge that this belief can lead to a destructive misconception about people and God. The Korean Church must be cautious not to attribute all or most causes of suffering to sins, as it can distort the image of a loving and merciful God. God is not to be always treated as a punisher. In this regard, Lee's judgement is still untenable when he said:

> Korea has been beaten with the bat of the 36-year Japanese colonisation because of the sins committed by the Choseon Dynasty for five hundred years. We are being

---

[119] Seong-bong Lee, *Buheungui Bigyeol*, 46.
[120] K. Warrington, *Healing and Suffering*, 173.
[121] K. Warrington, *Healing and Suffering*, 173.
[122] M.J. Erickson, *Christian Theology*, 3rd edn. (Grand Rapids, MI: Baker Academic, 1983): 765-66.
[123] M.J. Erickson, *Christian Theology*, 765.
[124] An extensive discussion was previously made in Chapters 2 to 4 under the sections of repentance in healing theology.

> beaten with the bat of communists since we are not grateful to God for giving us independence and we have continued to live a sinful life.[125]

This type of theological orientation can lead many to hurtful situations where the image of a loving and merciful God fades away. Although suffering can be an instrument for God to get the sick person's attention and to refine them for a more intimate relationship with Him, the link between personal sin and subsequent suffering is not always necessary. Moreover, the Korean healing theology requires further discussion regarding the fact that the suffering of sickness is often purely physiological, and its causes can be explained through medical diagnosis. The strong association between sin and sickness in the Korean healing theology arose from a focus on practical questions regarding the underlying reasons for sickness and its causation, while fundamental questions about divine healing and suffering necessitate more extensive exploration. Thus, there is a pressing need for the Korean Church to delve into the theological foundation of healing by addressing core questions regarding sickness and healing.

Despite the inclination to attribute illnesses to sins, it should not be assumed that repentance for sins is always mandatory for every healing process in the Korean healing movement. Lee and Kim acknowledged other possible causes apart from sin. Lee identified four factors: 1) Satan, 2) a careless and intemperate lifestyle, 3) spiritual training, and 4) God's glory.[126] He also believed that sickness can be caused by "oneself," "others," "Satan," or "nature."[127] Cho similarly listed additional causes, such as Satan, curses, and punishment,[128] as well as lifestyle factors like overwork, overeating, inappropriate dietary habits, alcoholism, smoking, and intemperate and careless lifestyles.[129] Considering all the possible causes of illness mentioned above, apart from sin, there is no concrete evidence to argue that the Korean healing theology exclusively attributes the cause of sicknesses to sins.[130]

Preconditions for Healing

The theological locus of the Korean healing movement is predicated on the conviction that repentance serves as an indispensable prerequisite for healing, not only in instances where illness is engendered by sin, but also in ensuring the efficacy of prayers for healing proffered by righteous individuals. The exegetical

---

[125] Seong-bong Lee, *Malo Mothamyeon Jukeumeuro*, 108.
[126] Seong-bong Lee, *Buheungui Bigyeol*, 48.
[127] Seong-bong Lee, *Sarangui Gangdan*, 30-31.
[128] Yong-gi Cho, *Widaehan Somyeong: Huimang Mokhoe 50 Nyeon*, 365.
[129] Yong-gi Cho, *Ojung Bokeumgwa Samjung Chukbok*, 145; Yong-gi Cho, *Sin Yu Lon*, 56; Yong-gi Cho, *How can I be Healed*? 34-35.
[130] However, it is undeniable that there is an emphasis on repentance for healing prayer. It is believed that most sicknesses come from sins and people suffer from disease and death as the punishment for the original sin.

evidence that repentance is necessary for efficacious prayer for healing is grounded in James 5:16-18, a text which encourages "the readers to recognise the power available through prayer and the necessity of a righteous lifestyle to experience it."[131] However, the Korean healing theology supplements this perspective by laying additional exegetical groundwork for the healing potency of repentant prayer. This perspective is further developed through an examination of other scriptural passages invoked by the three healing practitioners as a basis for the formulation of their healing theology. In interpreting Isaiah 1:15 and 59:1-2, Kim subtly shifts the theological discourse by positing that prayers proffered by sinful individuals would likely remain unanswered by God.[132] This perspective thereby establishes repentance as a prerequisite for healing, or at least in terms of efficacious prayer. Lee, meanwhile, postulates "God does not answer the prayers of sinners since they cannot fellowship with God because of sin blocking the relationship with God."[133] As Lee suggests, there is a particular emphasis on the nexus between the supplicants and the divine Healer in the healing process. Korean healing theology thus appears to underscore not the prayer of the righteous, but rather the role of God. It suggests that spiritual purity or a godly life is not the direct agent of healing; rather, within the Korean healing theology, it is perceived as a necessary preparation for divine healing which stems from an intimate communion with God. As the necessity of repentance for healing is examined within the framework of efficacious prayers by righteous individuals, the focus is placed on the essentiality of a sound relationship with the divine Healer. This concept is subsequently evolved by Cho to an advanced plane. Cho employs Isaiah 1:15 and Jeremiah 5:25 to articulate a perspective akin to that of Kim and Lee.[134] However, he extends his argument by integrating another biblical reference – Matthew 15:21-28 – to substantiate his assertion that divine healing is accorded exclusively to the children of God. From Cho's viewpoint, repentance enables one to be accepted by God as His children, and consequently "have a right to ask their Father for healing."[135] Cho's healing theology is principally focused on the belief that repentance does not directly heal the diseased body, but rather serves to mend the severed relationship with the divine Healer.

However, the question arises as to whether it is a valid argument to view repentance as an obligatory prerequisite for every healing process. If conversion or repentance is posited as a precondition for every healing, it would imply that only believers can receive healing, a premise not universally supported in biblical accounts, or even in observed real-world instances. It is irrefutable that Jesus healed many sinners who did not confess their sins. Erickson sagaciously

---

[131] K. Warrington, *Healing and Suffering*, 176.
[132] Ik-du Kim, *Gidoui Jonggyo*, 17.
[133] Seong-bong Lee, *Immanuel Gangdan*, 60.
[134] Yong-gi Cho, *How can I be Healed?* 59.
[135] Yong-gi Cho, *Sin Yu Lon*, 230.

asserts that Jesus' healing ministry was not "always connected with the forgiveness of sin."[136] Therefore, while repentance is undeniably an important facet of Christian life, it is not to be viewed as an obligatory prerequisite for divine healing.

What is Sin?

Another problematical point in connection with repentant prayer for healing is the definition of sin. The three healing practitioners held strict legalistic views of their ethical values. Kim construed the withholding of loyalty to God, the discontinuation of prayer, and non-compliance with the Sabbath as instances of sin. Explicitly, the observance of the Sabbath extends beyond merely attending church services on Sundays. Kim indoctrinated believers to abstain from purchasing goods, performing labour, or hosting any events, such as birthday celebrations, funerals, weddings, and even the commemoration of Jesus' birth, on Sundays. However, as Erickson articulates, "many people are unable to grasp the concept of sin as an inner force." Kim's conceptualisation of sin revolves around an "external act."[137] From this standpoint, one might postulate that Kim's conception of sin engendered a legion of followers who, rather than relying on God's grace to guide their actions internally, became adherents of a legalistic form of worship. Indeed, legalistic judgement tends to be based on external acts called an "ethical system" which is "governed primarily by obedience to prescribed laws or rules."[138]

Sin is characterised as "not only individual acts such as stealing, lying, or committing murder, but also attitudes contrary to what God requires of us."[139] As per McKim, sin denotes the "human condition of separation from God that arises from opposition to God's purposes. It may, thus, be breaking God's Law, failing to do what God wills, or rebellion."[140] This illuminates the integral role of God's will and purpose in relation to Kim's viewpoint. The fulfilment of God's will in actions should serve as the cardinal determinant in the categorisation of sin. If the impetus for an individual's conduct is rooted in the will of God, even acts that appear to transgress the Ten Commandments may not be classified as sinful. Examples include Jesus healing the infirm on the Sabbath (John 9:9-10) and dining at Matthew's residence amidst tax collectors and sinners (Matthew 9:10). In light of these biblical accounts, the classification of sin should focus more on the question of "why are we doing what we are doing?" as opposed to merely adhering to the outward manifestation of Christian life.

---

136 M.J. Erickson, *Christian Theology*, 765.
137 M.J. Erickson, *Christian Theology*, 582.
138 D.K. McKim, *Westminster Dictionary of Theological Terms* (Louisville, KY: Westminster John Knox, 1996): 159.
139 W. Grudem, *Systematic Theology*, 490.
140 D.K. McKim, *Westminster Dictionary of Theological Terms*, 260.

Atonement

Healing as Physical Salvation

The topic of repentance is further examined through the lens of "healing in the Atonement," offering significant discourse. Kim does not share their viewpoint but Lee and Cho, drawing from their denominational backgrounds, staunchly advocate for the concept of healing in the Atonement. They attribute sickness to the consequences of Adam and Eve's fall, aligning with their belief system. Consequently, their objective is to address the role of Original Sin as the primary cause of illness. Lee and Cho agreed that healing as "the salvation of body"[141] must work in the same way as it does for spiritual salvation.[142] In trying to deepen his understanding, Cho deals with the theological sequence of "sin leads to sickness" from two broad perspectives: 1) "direct" cause of sickness from individual sins, and 2) "indirect" cause of sickness from Original Sin.[143] For Cho, it could be either because of individual sins or Original Sin that people get sick and die.[144] Whether it is a direct or indirect cause, repentance is, therefore, mandatory in Cho's healing theology, viewing that "no man can be born and remain sinless."[145] As it is noted that "when sin entered the human race, a curse (actually a series of curses) was pronounced on humanity; diseases were part of that curse,"[146] this theology of Cho and Lee does not sound untenable at least in a theological sense with special reference to its origin.

Biblical Foundations

Then, what is the biblical foundation for healing in the Atonement? There have been numerous views and critiques on the position that healing should be a part of Christ's redemptive works. Those discussions mostly centre on three specific passages: Isaiah 53:4-6, Matthew 8:17, and 1 Peter 2:24. A counter-argument is often made to the effect that the passage in Isaiah 53 does not support healing in the atonement for several reasons: 1) the suffering servant in Isaiah is not Jesus and the passage is not even a prophecy about him,[147] 2) Isaiah 53 should be interpreted figuratively (meaning that it deals with a spiritual sickness and not a

---

[141] Seong-bong Lee, "Revival Tour," 85.

[142] This is an essential dividing line between Kim and Lee-Cho. Healing is one of the four cardinal doctrines of both the Korean Holiness Church and the worldwide Assemblies of God. On the other hand, Kim had to negotiate with the cessationist Presbyterian Church of Korea.

[143] Yong-gi Cho, *Sin Yu Lon*, 31.

[144] Yong-gi Cho, *Sin Yu Lon*, 31-32.

[145] Yong-gi Cho, *How can I be Healed,* 60.

[146] M.J. Erickson, *Christian Theology*, 763.

[147] J.N. Oswalt, "Who is the suffering servant in Isaiah 53?" *Zondervan Academic* 7th March 2019 [Available at: https://zondervanacademic.com/blog/suffering-servant-isaiah-53], [Last accessed: 17th November 2023].

physical one,[148] and 3) Isaiah 53 is referring to "actual physical and mental illnesses and distresses, but not necessarily to a vicarious bearing of them."[149]

As a response to the critique of the first group, Oswalt's study is perceptive as he concludes that "surely this Servant is not the recipient of God's redemption for his people, but the agent of it."[150] The passage evidently shows that the suffering servant should be someone who "suffered in our place (Is. 53:4)," bears "the punishment for our sins and even the sin itself (Is. 53:5, 11, 12)," and intercedes "on our behalf (Is. 53:12)." As another important argument, Matthew's quotation of this passage was adopted to support the ministry of Jesus as the fulfilment of Isaiah's prophecy. The redemptive works of the suffering servant in Isaiah should be credited on the basis of Matthew's authority even if there might be disputes on the historical figure of the suffering servant in Isaiah 53. The idea, therefore, that the suffering servant in Isaiah 53 does not refer to Jesus does not suffice for anyone to deny how Matthew 8:17 interprets Isaiah 53.

As a supporter of the second critique, Warrington remarks that "The context in Isaiah indicates that the infirmities referred to are of a spiritual kind."[151] However, the Hebrew word referring to infirmity is חֳלִי meaning "sickness" and "disease"[152] and according to the linguistic data it is not common for the word to be used figuratively. It was only three times out of thirty-four that the metaphorical usage occurred (as of distress of land in Hosea 5:13, Isaiah 1:5, Jeremiah 10:19), and in context of land not humanity.[153] This seems to support the idea that the suffering of the servant observed in v.6 must be a physical not a spiritual suffering since it fits well with "the typical ancient Near Eastern understanding of the source of suffering" that physical sickness is a normal consequence of individual sins.[154] People first considered the servant to be suffering because of his own sin, on the basis of their belief that the sick are sinners. But the reality is that "surely he took up our infirmities and carried our sorrows" in our place. As a matter of fact, it is pointless to attempt to provide biblical evidence for the figurative interpretation of the passage whose context is strongly and explicitly associated with physical suffering.

The last dispute must involve a longer discussion. Erickson's attempt to nullify the idea of healing in the atonement generally focuses on the linguistic data from Isaiah 53. His main point is that "the emphasis is on what the suffering servant has carried rather than on how he has carried it." According to his

---

[148] K. Warrington, *Healing and Suffering*, 52.
[149] M.J. Erickson, *Christian Theology*, 766.
[150] J.N. Oswalt, "The Book of Isaiah: Chapter 40-66," in R.K. Harrison and R.L. Hubbard, Jr. (eds), *The New International Commentary on the Old Testament* (Grand Rapids, MI: William B. Eerdmans, 1998): 323.
[151] K. Warrington, *Healing and Suffering*, 52.
[152] F. Brown, S. Driver, and C. Briggs, A. *The Brown-Driver-Briggs Hebrew Lexicon* (Peabody, MA: Hendrickson, 1996): 318.
[153] F. Brown, S. Driver, and C. Briggs, *The Brown-Driver-Briggs Hebrew Lexicon*, 318.
[154] J.N. Oswalt, "The Book of Isaiah: Chapter 40-66," 386.

analysis of the passage, the major Hebrew verbs such as נָשָׂא and סָבַל carry little or no "connotation of vicariousness."[155] Some confusion is introduced, however, when what Erickson sought to justify appears to be a non sequitur, since his research is contradictory to his idea that there are six references to a vicarious bearing of guilt for נָשָׂא.[156] Additionally, the research of Freedman and Willoughby substantially undergirds the concept of vicariousness as they affirm that "in view of the rite of the scapegoat, one can attribute the following connotations to נָשָׂא in these texts: The Servant suffers as a result of our sickness (cf. v. 3), he bears its burden, carries it away, and heals us from it (cf. v. 5)."[157] This allows us to see the representative work of the suffering servant in place of "our sickness." Oswalt also concurs that the two main verbs are "the language of the cult" which is normally associated with the idea of "substitutionary."[158] The concept of representative atonement, thus, needs to be intentional in terms of the authorial intent when the main verb is used together with the scapegoat (vv. 6-7). Lastly, in Motyer's treatment of "the vicarious suffering of the Servant," particular attention is given to the emphatic usage of the independent pronouns *he* and *we* in order for him to develop his assertion that "Yet *we* is an emphatic pronoun, contrasting with *he* and isolating him in his substitutionary work [in v.4]."[159] Even verse 6 employs a special technique called "palistrophe which begins with *All we* (כֻּלָּנוּ *kullanu*) and ends with *us all* (כֻּלָּנוּ *kullanu*)"[160] as they make a beautiful rhyme. These studies show that the focal point is on the contrasting pronouns: *him* on which the LORD has laid the iniquity for *us all*. Therefore, it is tenable and even more convincing to put its emphasis on the underlying theme, "the vicarious suffering of the Servant" for all. In fact, this idea is what can be clearly found from the quotation in 1 Peter 2:24. According to Jobes:

> As a matter of style, Peter seems deliberately to change the pronouns from the wording of Isa. 53:5 LXX, which he otherwise follows. If his readers are primarily Gentiles, perhaps he is underscoring their inclusion in the people of God by excluding himself as a Jew. In other words, Peter is saying, "The Suffering Servant died not just for us Jews, but also for you Gentiles.[161]

---

[155] M.J. Erickson, *Christian Theology*, 766.
[156] M.J. Erickson, *Christian Theology*, 766.
[157] D.N. Freedman and B.E. Willoughby, "נָשָׂא" in G. Johannes Botterweck, Helmer Ringgren, and Heinz-Josef Fabry (eds), *Theological Dictionary of the Old Testament, vol. 10* (Grand Rapids, MI: William B. Eerdmans, 1999): 36.
[158] J.N. Oswalt, "The Book of Isaiah: Chapter 40-66," 386.
[159] J.A. Motyer, *The Prophecy of Isaiah: An Introduction and Commentary* (Downers Grove, IL: InterVarsity Press, 1993): 430.
[160] J.A. Motyer, *The Prophecy of Isaiah: An Introduction and Commentary*, 430.
[161] K.H. Jobes, *1 Peter* (Grand Rapids, MI: Baker Academic, 2005): 198.

From the perspective of Peter, the foundation of healing laid in Jesus' atonement in Isaiah 53 is intentionally extended to the Gentiles from the Jews. This means that healing as the redemptive work of Jesus embodied in Isaiah 53 strikes a markedly universal note. The passage is strongly suggestive of universal grace for everybody. The resulting theory is supported by many in arguing that Matthew 8:17, which was recorded with special reference to Jesus' healing of the sick – obviously physical healing – evidently concludes that there is healing in the Atonement.[162]

Theological Foundations

However, it is crucial to acknowledge the inherent risks associated with the potential misinterpretation or misuse of the aforementioned passages, particularly in their application, to advocate for "the unconditional promise that all believers should be able to claim healing for their illnesses before death."[163] This raises an important theological concern regarding misconceptions surrounding the concept of healing in relation to the Atonement. A commonly asked question further highlights this issue: "If healing operates in a manner similar to spiritual salvation, why is it that healing sometimes does not occur despite fervent requests, whereas spiritual salvation is instantaneously granted through faith?" Such an argument cannot be easily dismissed. Recognising that the question is theological rather than exegetical, it becomes imperative to engage in a comprehensive discussion encompassing two significant topics: 1) immediate or progressive salvation and 2) right or privilege.

Erickson asserts that the process of forgiveness is both unconditional and immediate, as he posits that "we cannot expect, then, that in every case healing is to be granted upon request, as is forgiveness of sins."[164] While this perspective holds some validity, it is reasonable to conclude that spiritual salvation is simultaneously progressive and conditional. Grudem supports this notion by stating:

> Both faith and repentance continue throughout life. Although we have been considering initial faith and repentance as the two aspects of conversion at the beginning of the Christian life, it is important to realise that faith and repentance are not confined to the beginning of the Christian life.[165]

---

[162] Many New Testament scholars agree that Matthew 8:17 deals with physical healing in light of Isaiah 53. See D.A. Carson, "Matthew" in F. Gaebelein (ed), *The Expositor's Bible Commentary*, vol. 12 (Grand Rapids, MI: Zondervan, 1984): 207; C.L. Blomberg, "Matthew," in D.S. Dockery (ed), *The New American Commentary* (Nashville, TN: Broadman Press, 1992): 145; C.S. Keener, "Matthew," in G.R. Osborne (ed), *The IVP New Testament Commentary* (Downers Grove, IL: InterVarsity Press, 1997): 178.

[163] K. Warrington, *Healing and Suffering*, 52.

[164] M.J. Erickson, *Christian Theology*, 768.

[165] W. Grudem, *Systematic Theology*, 712.

This idea is not much different from Erickson's perspective when he seeks to define salvation with three key words: the "beginning," "continuation," and "completion of salvation."[166] He is aware of three perspectives in defining salvation: 1) "we have been saved," "we are being saved," and "we shall be saved."[167] According to Erickson's theological perception, it is inadequate to choose only one of these descriptions to elucidate salvation. This is because salvation originates from a singular point – the experience of regeneration – yet its scope extends far beyond that initial encounter. It is more fitting to conceptualise salvation as a collection of numerous interconnected elements such as effectual calling, conversion, regeneration, union with Christ, justification, adoption, sanctification, and glorification. Even within the process of conversion and regeneration, repentance and faith play pivotal roles. This understanding allows us to comprehend that spiritual salvation is both immediate and progressive. Consequently, it becomes paramount to recognise that healing, as an integral part of salvation, exhibits characteristics of both instant and progressive manifestations. Thus, healing may occur instantly, progressively, or ultimately be realised in the *parousia.* In this regard, Blomberg concurs, stating that:

> Inasmuch as the healings consistently function as pointers to God's in-breaking kingdom, one should expect the present blessings of God's reign at times to include miraculous recovery from illness. But to require such healing of God this side of eternity loses sight of the future aspect of the kingdom. Only in the world to come will sickness and death be banished altogether from believers' lives.[168]

Blomberg's perspective helps to elucidate that healing has *already* commenced through the advent of God's Kingdom and the works of Jesus but is still *not yet* accomplished as a perfect healing since it will eventually be realised with the Second Coming of Jesus in a perfect way. This perspective aligns with the emphasis in the Korean healing movement on the belief that individuals can still experience healing today, similar to the healings witnessed in the apostolic church, with ultimate and complete healing awaiting the Second Coming of Jesus to remove "all the tears of sicknesses."[169]

While salvation must be unconditional in the sense that it is bestowed freely on the basis of God's sovereignty rather than human merit, it is still conditional in the sense that an individual needs to acknowledge, accept, and trust in the grace provided by God.[170] Erickson logically argues that a person participates in salvation passively, as seen in his claim that "salvation is mediated by faith. Faith appropriates the work accomplished by Christ. The recipient is, in a sense,

---

166 M.J. Erickson, *Christian Theology*, 825-948.
167 M.J. Erickson, *Christian Theology*, 827.
168 C.L. Blomberg, "Matthew," 145.
169 Seong-bong Lee, *Immanuel Gangdan*, 78-79.
170 W. Grudem, *Systematic Theology*, 709-17.

passive in this process."[171] Acknowledging the complexity of salvation, it becomes evident that healing, as a component of salvation, also requires the faith of the sick individual, extending beyond a mere cognitive awareness of the work accomplished by Christ. In other words, receiving healing is not akin to a mechanical reaction that can be unconditionally granted upon every request. It necessitates the presence of faith and trust, whereby sick individuals willingly and trustingly seek healing. Moreover, it is inappropriate to view healing in the Atonement as providing a foundation for the so-called instant and unconditional healing upon request. Additionally, one must recognise that numerous factors contribute to the healing process, including faith, repentance, spiritual warfare, forgiveness, and God's will, among others. Therefore, the notion of healing in the Atonement should not be misconstrued as supporting unconditional and instant healing. When proponents of healing in the Atonement emphasise that healing has already been provided at Calvary's Cross, it does not imply that healing is automatically physically manifested in the bodies of the sick. Instead, it entails a process wherein petitioners desire and trust in the fact that the price for healing has already been paid. Healing does not occur unconditionally through a mere verbal declaration.

Finally, if healing is believed to be conferred through the Atonement, the question arises as to whether it should be considered a right for the sick to claim. Lee and Cho assert that it is indeed a right bestowed upon the children of God.[172] Notably, the concept of healing as a right lies at the core of the "Pentecostal" movement. Simpson, the founder of the four-fold Gospel upon which Lee and Cho[173] base their healing theology, similarly regards healing as a right. He articulates this by stating, "There is no longer need that we should suffer what Christ has sufficiently borne. Thus, our healing becomes a great redemption right that we simply claim as our purchased inheritance through the blood of Christ's cross." Simpson further substantiates his viewpoint by asserting:

> Do not merely ask for it, but humbly and firmly claim healing as His covenant pledge, as your inheritance, as a purchased redemption right. Claim it as something already fully offered you in the gospel and waiting only your acceptance to make good your possession.[174]

This statement appears to possess sufficient sensationalism to engender numerous disputes. Undeniably, Simpson's utilisation of assertive expressions such as "don't merely ask for it" and "firmly claim healing" establishes a

---

[171] M.J. Erickson, *Christian Theology*, 828.
[172] Seong-bong Lee, *Buheungui Bigyeol*, 49; Yong-gi Cho, *Sin Yu Lon*, 230.
[173] The influence of the Christian & Missionary Alliance (founded by Simpson) was strong in forming the non-Wesleyan Pentecostal denominations. However, his focus is slightly different from the "Pentecostal" ones. The latter's set has the substantial addition of the spiritual baptism.
[174] A.B. Simpson, *The Gospel of Healing*, 66.

fundamental framework within which proponents of healing in the Atonement could be misconstrued as asserting an unconditional guarantee that any supplicant seeking healing will invariably receive it. While there may be some truth to this assertion, it is also evident that these conviction-laden words do not convey an extreme notion that God is treated as a vending machine, dispensing whatever desires are sought. Simpson's expression introduces a quandary concerning the interplay of God's sovereignty and human desire through the juxtaposition of the terms "humbly" and "firmly." In truth, Simpson's strong conviction does not exceed his prerogative to request that which is not granted. He believed, in a general sense, that it is God's intention to heal the infirm, both presently and in the *parousia*. However, this does not imply an unconditional healing upon request, as it is inherently conditional that the afflicted individuals humbly beseech God for healing. This idea remains viable only because God continues to be regarded as the ultimate authority who bestows healing – a final arbiter. Otherwise, there would be no reason for the afflicted to seek healing from God if they held the belief that healing operates unconditionally. Even in the form of a request, the process for the infirm to obtain the ultimate authorisation from God is still a part of the equation.

It is crucial to highlight that Simpson's theology of healing also firmly rests on the grace of God, rather than human merits, as evidenced by his statement that "Everything that comes through Christ must come as grace [...] If Christ heals, He must do it alone,"[175] rather than due to human supplications or faith. Therefore, the healing within the Atonement remains inherently rooted in grace and necessitates human appropriation. Specifically, what Simpson meant by claiming healing on request does not necessarily guarantee that every afflicted individual will instantaneously receive healing, but rather refers to the fundamental privilege bestowed upon Christians to approach God and rely on His willingness to heal either instantaneously or progressively. Nevertheless, I concur that the adoption of the term *right* does not align with the intended theological notion, primarily because of its negative connotation suggesting that the divine Healer lacks a personal voice in the healing process. Thus, it would be more appropriate to comprehend this concept as a privilege rather than a right. This interpretation is evident in Cho's teachings as he explores various approaches to ensure one's prayers for healing are answered. According to Cho, praying for healing is not a plea for sympathy but a request for health and a cure that God desires to provide through the sacrificial death of Jesus.[176] Consequently, it is regarded as an inherent "privilege" and a "basic right" afforded to Christians.[177] Thus, within Korean healing theology, healing in the Atonement must be understood as a privilege bestowed upon God's children,

[175] A.B. Simpson, *The Gospel of Healing*, 31.
[176] Yong-gi Cho, *Sin Yu Lon*, 212.
[177] Yong-gi Cho, *Huimangmokhoe 45 Nyeon*, 223.

enabling them to request *what God wants to give* in terms of *what He has already prepared for them on the cross.*

Spiritual Warfare

Power of Satan and Shamanism

The first principle of healing theology in the context of spiritual warfare revolves around the conviction that Satan and evil spirits possess the capability to inflict ailments upon individuals. Kim's theological framework assigns considerable power to evil spirits, depicting them as potent spiritual entities. According to his perspective, evil spirits exist and can manifest in both mental and physical diseases, as exemplified in the case of Su-eun Park. Kim asserts that her sudden collapse resulted from her refusal to participate in a shamanic ritual, attributing the problem to the malevolent spirit of the Shaman.[178] Lee, in his discussion on the role of Satan, also contends that sickness can be caused by Satan.[179] Similarly, Cho maintains that illness is always induced by Satan, who wields a destructive influence, while ascribing life and "true healing" to God.[180] Initially, Cho regarded every physical ailment as a manifestation of spiritual warfare against demons,[181] but gradually recognised the existence of other causes of sickness.

The belief in the ability of evil spirits to inflict illness upon individuals was a widely held shamanistic belief, as well as one documented in the New Testament. Consequently, numerous afflicted individuals sought to expel demons through shamanic rituals until the widespread adoption and dissemination of Christianity in Korea. Cho elucidates this belief in his autobiography, stating:

> Among the common people, sickness was largely attributed to evil spirits […] the belief that evil spirits caused illness was the basis for stabbing hot needles into an afflicted part to kill the evil spirit supposed to have caused the problem.[182]

Because of the dominance of shamanistic beliefs within Korean society, the destructive power of evil spirits was often conceptualised in tangible terms, with their spiritual existence being physically confined to this world. Consequently, people harboured superstitious notions that evil spirits could be affected by physical materials, just as they could exert a pernicious impact on the physical realm. Various elements were widely employed in shamanic practices to ward

---

[178] In-seo Kim, *Kim Ik-Du Moksa SoJeon,* 161.
[179] Seon-bong Lee, *Buheungui Bigyeol*, 48.
[180] Yong-gi Cho, *How can I be Healed?* 100.
[181] While praying for healing for two deaf women, Cho directly commanded the demons to come out since he believed demons caused the women to be deaf. Hyeong-geun Lim, *Cho Yonggi Moksa Ildaegi: Yeouidoui Moghoeja*, 270-282 and 298.
[182] N.L. Kennedy, *Dream Your Way to Success*, 101-102.

off sickness and seek healing from diseases, including the use of red and yellow colours, the resonance of drums and metal, vocalisation, pungent aromas and flavours, as well as the application of hot and sharp stimuli.[183] It is evident that this notion originates from the distinct cultural and religious context of Asia.

Shamanism encompasses numerous deities, including ancestral spirits, as well as benevolent and malevolent gods believed to inhabit the material world, residing within rocks, trees, the ground, sky, and sea.[184] The diagram below (Figure 6) illustrates the information, underscoring the significance of Shamanism as a crucial key to comprehending the essence of Korean culture.

Figure 6: Comparison of Korean Religions in 1962 and in 2015[185]

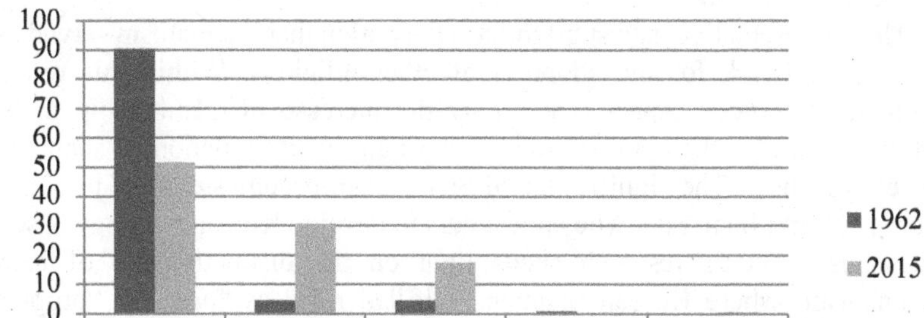

	No religion	Protestantism & Catholicism	Buddhism	Confucianism	Others
1962	90.25	4.3	4.5	0.7	0.25
2015	51.58	30.45	17.29	0.17	0.51

Figure 6 illustrates intriguing data, challenging Shearer's assertion from 1962 that "ninety percent of the Korean people are not religious is far from the

---

[183] According to a Korean book written in 1849 by Seok-mo Hong to explain Korean monthly events and their traditions, this ritual is believed to have originated from a tradition in the Warring States in ancient China which dates to 770-221 BC. Seok-mo Hong, *Dongguksesigi* [Monthly Events and Tradition of Korea] (1849) in "Aekmagi" [Exorcism] *Wikipedia* [Available at: https://ko.wikipedia.org/wiki/%EC%95%A1%EB%A7%89%EC%9D%B4], [Last accessed: 19th November 2023].

[184] R.E. Shearer, *Wildfire: Church Growth in Korea*, 30.

[185] The statistics indicate the population percentages of Korean religions in the years of 1962 and of 2015. The data in 1962 is based on R.E. Shearer, *Wildfire: Church Growth in Korea*, 29, and the data in 2015 is based on "2018 Hangukeu jonggyo hyeonhwang" [The statistics of Korean religions in 2018] issued by Ministry of Culture, Sports and Tourism [Available at: https://www.mcst.go.kr/kor/s_policy/dept/deptView.jsp?pSeq=1731&pDataCD=0406000000&pType=03], [Last accessed: 19th November 2023].

truth."[186] According to Canadian missionary James Gale, Shamanism, the most influential religious belief system, remained largely unrecognised by many missionaries because of its deep entrenchment in the daily lives of most Koreans.[187] Lillias S.H. Underwood, an American physician and the wife of the first Presbyterian missionary to Korea, H.G. Underwood, keenly observed the pervasive influence of Shamanism and regarded it as the most potent and widespread superstition among the Korean people.[188] These findings provide compelling evidence that most Koreans did not perceive Shamanism as merely a religion but rather as an integral part of their existence, despite their belief in supernatural forces.[189] Such evidence is pivotal in understanding the prevalence of Shamanism in Korea, considering its presence within the *minjung* (the masses).

This representative data substantiates the notion that Shamanism served as an ideal groundwork for the adoption of other religions. Within this religious context, the crucial aspect is not only the increase in membership in these religions but also their transformation through the assimilation of shamanistic belief systems.[190] The significance of Shamanism becomes evident through the words of Sung-bum Yun, who endeavours to develop Korean theology based on Shamanism. Yun's research sheds light on the distinctiveness of Korean Shamanism, where Korean Shamans fulfilled roles as "priests," "prophets," "medicine people," and "entertainers,"[191] surpassing the limited functions performed by Shamans in other countries. This enduring tradition of entertainment has, for centuries, demonstrated the Shamans' commitment to the satisfaction of the *minjung*. Korean Shamans have not merely served as religious authorities but have also been companions who profoundly influenced Korean society in countless ways. Thus, it is evident that the significance of shamanistic influences on the Korean Church cannot be disregarded through mere denial or rejection.

While the understanding of evil spirits and their powers seems intricately linked to the specific context of Shamanism, the biblical concept of demons as entities capable of inflicting spiritual, emotional, and physical harm remains relevant. It is certain that "the reality" and "activity of demons" are clearly

---

[186] R.E. Shearer, *Wildfire: Church Growth in Korea*, 30.

[187] James S. Gale, *Korian Seukechi* [Korean Sketch], trans. Mun-pyeong Jang (Seoul: Hyeonamsa, 1979): 252-53.

[188] Lillias S.H. Underwood, *Eondeoudu Buinui Joseon Saenghwal* [The life of Mrs. Underwood in Korea], trans., Cheol Kim (Seoul: Tree deeply rooted Publisher, 1984): 22.

[189] "No religion" in 2015 can also be understood in the same manner in the sense that many Korean people may be still religious, and their faith centres on idols such as money and ego as a result of the growth of materialism and secularism in South Korea.

[190] D.J. Adams, *Christ and Culture in Asia*, 67.

[191] Sung-bum Yun, *Hankuk Jongkyowa Hankukjeok Kidockyo* (Korean Religion and Indigenous Christianity), vol. 1, *Yun Sungbum chunjib* (Seoul: Gam Sin, 1998): 146.

witnessed in the Bible.[192] Ryle's interpretation of Matthew 8:28-34 exemplifies this, as he considers it as evidence that "There is an unseen spirit always near us, very powerful and full of endless malice against our souls."[193] However, some argue against overemphasising the power of demons, contending that "Demons are real, but their reality is mere illusion in the presence of the ontological absoluteness of God. They can only be but the mere whisper of reality [...] Demons can only terrorise those who attribute to them the power to do so."[194] This perspective is taken to an extreme by Gilbert, who regards the demonic power as symbolic, claiming that "the image of spiritual warfare is but one of a number of metaphors that are used in Scripture to characterise the Christian life."[195]

Kim, Lee, and Cho share three key beliefs in spiritual warfare: 1) ministry as salvific spiritual warfare (Kim and Lee), 2) the acknowledgement that Christians can be demon-possessed (Kim and Cho), and 3) the understanding that Satan is not the originator but a mere purveyor of sickness (Lee and Cho). Further exploration reveals practical challenges faced by these three healing practitioners – challenges believed to be instigated by evil spirits. Kim's conversion experience was linked to a spiritual battle against an evil spirit called *Cheonjadaegam*.[196] His ministry in Sincheon was described as "a holy fight."[197] Moreover, Kim encountered spiritual warfare when spreading the gospel among idolaters who adhered to shamanistic beliefs. Lee perceives spiritual warfare not solely as a battle against sickness but as an inclusive approach that encompasses salvific works. He posits that Satan utilises sickness as a tool to hinder the expansion of God's Kingdom. Cho echoes Lee's perspective, stating:

---

[192] C.F. Dickason, *Demon Possession & The Christian*, 21.

[193] J.C. Ryle, *Matthew: Expository Thoughts on the Gospels* (Wheaton, IL: Crossway, 1993): 61.

[194] P.J. Gilbert, "Spiritual Warfare," in W.A. Dyrness & Veli-Matti Kärkkäinen (eds), *Global Dictionary of Theology* (Nottingham: Inter-Varsity Press, 2008): 850.

[195] P.J. Gilbert, "Spiritual Warfare," 850.

[196] *Cheonjadaegam* is one of gods who were worshipped in the shamanistic context of Korea. The word *daegam* appears to have originated from the vocational term referring to those officers who had at least the third position of the eighteen ranks of the *Joseon* dynasty. This was later developed into a religious word that was combined with other modifying terms to name various gods with their distinctive roles of conferring fortune, misfortune, protection, health, wealth and so on, as in ancestor worship. See In-seo Kim, *Kim Ik-Du Moksa SoJeon*, 144; [Daegum Play] *Encyclopedia of Korean Folk Culture Website* [Available at: http://folkency.nfm.go.kr/kr/topic/detail/1273], [Last accessed: 19th November 2023]; and "Jung Yi Poom" *Encyclopedia of Korean Ethnic Culture Website* [Available at: https://terms.naver.com/entry.nhn?docId=547620&cid=46622&categoryId=46622], [Last accessed: 19th November 2023].

[197] According to In-seo Kim, the process of the propagation of the gospel is like a holy fight for early Christians. See In-seo Kim, *Kim Ik-Du Moksa SoJeon*, 161-64.

> Wherever we go, we meet the strongholds of the enemy – of Satan. Every town has its own devil. If I ever would like to establish a church in a certain area, I have to challenge that power first. If I can defeat the devil, then I can build a church.[198]

Throughout the discussions on spiritual warfare by Kim, Lee and Cho, it is commonly observed that when the gospel is proclaimed in areas with limited exposure to Christianity or where it has not yet been introduced, the level of disturbance caused by spiritual enemies is significantly higher. This perception does not sound like a preposterous idea in the sense that demons were usually associated with the idolatry of non-believers[199] and that "idolatrous activity is energised by demons" to oppose the "reception of the gospel that Christians are to spread" (Lk. 8:12).[200] While this theological notion may share similarities with the concept of "territorial spirits,"[201] the key point is that Satan's efforts to impede evangelists from spreading the gospel are tangibly felt and amplified in such circumstances. This raises theological questions regarding the confinement of Satan to specific geographic locations. The concept of territorial spirits tends to visually depict the presence of evil spirits in physical terms, although they remain spiritual entities. Therefore, doubts arise regarding the idea that spiritual beings are bound to certain geographical regions. However, this concern does not negate the theological notion that a heightened sense of spiritual enemy attacks and hindrances may be experienced, particularly in mission fields where Christianity is unfamiliar or not widely accepted. Just as Jones previously noted the tendency in Korean culture to spiritualise all natural phenomena through Shamanism,[202] it could be argued that this carries the risk of blurring the distinction between the spiritual and physical realms. Whether spiritual entities are considered like physical ones or the other way around, either idea can easily lead Korean Christians to a much simplified belief where God or Satan are considered to be physically finite entities confined to this world. Despite the help of a territorial spirit to feel the reality of spiritual warfare against Satan in a practical way, this often comes at the expense of virtually confusing believers. There, apparently, is a theological imprecision that still necessitates an exhaustive study in a much more systematic way to provide a clear understanding of how the entire hierarchy of demons can be present in this physical world as they are still spiritual ones.

---

[198] Yong-gi Cho, *Expand Your Horizon*, 52.
[199] C.S. Keener, *A Commentary on the Gospel of Matthew* (Grand Rapids, MI: William B. Eerdmans, 1999): 281.
[200] C.F. Dickason, *Demon Possession & The Christian*, 67.
[201] This idea is developed and introduced by Peter Wagner. A territorial spirit refers to an entire hierarchy of demons whose power is over the people of a region. It is believed that those demons are hovering and dwelling in specific geographical territories. See C.P. Wagner, *Territorial Spirits* (Shippensburg, PA: Destiny Image Publishers, 2012).
[202] G.H. Jones, "The spirit worship of the Koreans," *Transactions of the Korea Branch of the Royal Asiatic Society* 2 (1901): 37-58.

Supplier of Sickness

The secondary theological tenet shared between Lee and Cho, yet deemed irrelevant by Kim,[203] pertains to their perception of Satan as the sole distributor of affliction, rather than its progenitor. Advocating this perspective, Lee contended that "sickness is the wage of sins and it comes from Satan."[204] This interpretation coincides with Cho's exegesis of Romans 6:23, wherein he observes that the scripture "teaches us that the invisible root of sickness and disease is sin [...= Through this sin, 'the power of death, that is, the devil' (Heb. 2:14) incessantly provides sickness with life and strength, to drain life by endless amounts of pain and suffering."[205] Lee and Cho, therefore, unequivocally perceive Satan not as the architect of disease and death but their provider. This conceptualisation assists in alleviating the fear of Satan, instead portraying him merely as a courier of agony, while God retains control over the entire situation. Such a lesson ought to serve as a reminder for those who frequently emphasise the destructive capabilities of Satan, indicating that the superior power to confine him has already been procured through Jesus's completed work on the Cross.

In the context of spiritual warfare, another concordance between Kim and Cho implies that Christians, particularly from Kim's viewpoint, are susceptible to demonic possession. When detailing Kim's healing of a man possessed by a demon, it was reported that "although the son believed in the Lord, such symptoms appeared because he had harboured corrupt thoughts in his heart."[206] This instance served as validation for Kim's assertion that believers in God – typically referred to as Christians – are susceptible to demonic possession. Despite this constituting another topic warranting comprehensive discourse, Cho's theology briefly grazes the crux of the matter. Cho identifies two designations for the maladies inflicted by Satan. He explicates that, while Satan invariably provides the destructive potency behind each ailment, "it is seldom because Satan enters the human body that people get sick."[207] When Satan enters a human body, inducing illness, it is perceived as possession, whereas influence

---

[203] It is hard to argue that Kim believed it is always evil spirits who supply the destructive power of sickness. His healing theology of suffering appears to be more associated with the notion that "sin always leads to sickness" rather than "Satan always leads to sickness" in spite of his awareness that Satan can bring sickness to people. In this respect, it needs to be observed that Lee and Cho's healing theologies laid a concrete argument that there must be something between sin (the cause) and sickness (the consequence), and Satan is believed to be its supplier, while Kim's attention was not substantially given to the topic.

[204] See Seong-bong Lee, *Buheungui Bigyeol* [The Secret of Revival] (Seoul: Word of Life Books, 1993): 49; Seong-bong Lee, *Sarangui Gangdan* [The Pulpit of Love], 151. However, Lee also presented other causes of sickness such as carelessness, overwork, immoderation, God's punishment, training for blessings, for God's glory. See Seong-bong Lee, *Buheungui Bigyeol*, 48.

[205] Yong-gi Cho, *Suffering, Why Me?* 13.

[206] Taek-kwon Im, *Joseon Yesugyohoe Ijeogmyeongjeung*, 2008, 49.

[207] ITI, *Yoido Kyohoei Shinanggwa Shinhak 2*, 202.

pertains to instances of sickness arising from causes other than spiritual. In essence, it is consistently Satan/demons who supply mental and physical sickness, however, the notions of direct and indirect must be separately scrutinised to discern whether illnesses may stem from an indirect influence or a direct possession of Satan over a human body.

Pneumatology

The Holy Spirit in Power

In a broad sense, the theological underpinnings of the Korean healing movement, particularly in relation to the Baptism of the Holy Spirit (BHS), rest on two fundamental precepts: 1) the conception of healing as a divine empowerment conferred by the Holy Spirit to further the reach of God's Kingdom, and 2) the portrayal of the Holy Spirit not as an inherent healing power, but as the divine Healer. A recurrent theme discernible among the three healing practitioners under study is the accentuation of the roles of the Holy Spirit, culminating in a spiritual bestowal of signs and wonders, intended for the enhancement of God's Kingdom. Kim, whose healing practice was predominantly linked with "the power of the Holy Spirit,"[208] maintained that the BHS is granted for the purpose of serving God. This perspective is epitomised in his sermon, "Let's serve the Lord by receiving the BHS,"[209] where he construed the BHS as a critical tool for disseminating the gospel. On the other hand, for Lee, the BHS was initially perceived as a conduit for divine healing.[210] This notion is explicit in his postulation:

> When the Holy Spirit who was promised to be sent has come, He has established churches in every place for two thousand years as the era of the Holy Spirit. He made a brazen-faced rascal like me to repent, to be regenerated, sanctified, and endowed with the life and power of heaven to spread the gospel to the ends of the earth.[211]

While the Holy Spirit has been traditionally perceived in the Christian context as a vital force connected with a life of repentance, regeneration, and sanctification, it is Lee's final contention that divinely bestowed gifts, such as healing, serve a purpose beyond personal sanctification – specifically for the expansion of the Kingdom of God. This view finds resonance in Cho's assertion that "Special power to serve God comes with the BHS […] It is given to empower the process of spreading the gospel to save souls."[212] The healing theology propounded by these figures situates the Holy Spirit in a central role.

---

208 "Pyeongyang Gwadung" *Yesugyosinbo*, 15th December 1908, 218.
209 Seong-ho Lee (ed), *Kim Ik-Du Moksa Seolgyo Mit*, 62-63.
210 Seong-bong Lee, *Buheungui Bigyeol*, 48.
211 Seong-bong Lee, *Sarangui Gangdan*, 159.
212 ITI, *Yoido Kyohoei Shinanggwa Shinhak* 2, 70.

This significance is further underscored by the observable impact in the mission field where numerous individuals have been drawn to God via their healing ministries. Thus, it becomes crucial to understand that, within Korean healing theology, the Baptism of the Holy Spirit (BHS) serves a multifaceted function. It does not solely participate in the processes of regeneration and sanctification, but it also empowers individuals to become effective advocates for the expansion of the Kingdom of God.

The Holy Spirit not as Power

Despite their conviction in the healing potential of the Holy Spirit, the three healing practitioners contested the oversimplified notion of the Holy Spirit serving merely as a specialised conduit for healing. They proposed a distinct theological construct, encapsulated in the phrase *in* not *as*, signifying that the Holy Spirit arrives in potency but does not exist solely as a healing power. Kim underscored the Holy Spirit as the Supreme Entity, from whom ultimate authorisation for healing should be sought.[213] This perspective reframes the Holy Spirit not as an impersonal healing mechanism, but as a sentient Being, presiding over the healing process as an authoritative divine figure. In this context, the rapport between the Holy Spirit and the healing practitioners is instrumental in soliciting successful healing outcomes.[214] Lee's assertion that the gospel can be disseminated through miraculous signs and wonders drew specific focus to the clarifying phrase: the Holy Spirit.[215] From Lee's standpoint, the Holy Spirit is recognised as the Divine Giver of the extraordinary healing signs and wonders. Consequently, Lee does not view communion with the Holy Spirit as a spiritual phenomenon requiring tangible validation, such as "shaking of the body, seeing, smelling, or hearing something special."[216] Instead, Lee perceives the Holy Spirit as a guiding Person in his spiritual life.[217] Adding to Kim's and Lee's discourses on the Holy Spirit, Cho's perspective matured to deliver a significant revelation:

> But I said, "O God, I have the Holy Spirit. I'm born again. I have the Holy Spirit in me. I've received the fullness of the Holy Ghost so I have the experience, too. But,

---

[213] KIATS, *Kim Ik-Du: The D.L. Moody of Korea*, 116-17.

[214] It is also interesting that there are minimal relational aspects between gods/spirits and Shamans. The healing process in Shamanism is not relational but functional. The Shamanistic rituals are a borrowing of power, which is supposed to be much stronger than that of the evil spirits believed to cause sickness. See Eun-seok Yun, "Hanguk Godokgyoui Musoksinange Daehan Taedo Yeongu" [A Study on the Attitude of the Korean Christians toward Shamanism] (Ph.D. Thesis, Seoul Theological Seminary, 2017): 340.

[215] Seong-bong Lee, *Sarangui Gangdan*, 48.

[216] Seong-bong Lee, *Sarangui Gangdan*, 48.

[217] Seong-bong Lee, *Malo Mothamyeon Jukeumeuro*, 65.

> Holy Spirit, do I need more?" Then the stern rebuke came to me [...] The Holy Spirit is more than an experience. The Holy Spirit is an awesome Person.[218]

As plainly elucidated by Cho, while the Korean healing movement extensively acknowledges the Holy Spirit's role in divine healing, the Holy Spirit is not merely a source of healing power, but a divine *Healer*. Cho, Kim, and Lee collectively enriched Korean pneumatology by shifting the focus from spiritual empowerment, such as signs and wonders, to fellowship with the Holy Spirit as the Bestower of these signs and wonders.

Korean healing theology recognises that the Holy Spirit is often sought functionally to facilitate healing. It acknowledges the occasional misinterpretation of the Holy Spirit as an impersonal entity, symbolised by elements like wind, breath, or fire. Thus, during healing practices, there is a potential risk of the Holy Spirit being misconstrued as a force manipulable by human will or command. In this context, the arguments presented by Kim, Lee, and Cho serve as poignant reminders for Pentecostal/Charismatic groups about the true essence of the Holy Spirit. Cho's elucidation on this topic is particularly enlightening:

> Many people do not know the meaning of fellowship with the Holy Spirit. They say they are born again and have received the baptism in the Holy Spirit. They have experienced the power of the Holy Spirit in ministry [...] But God changed my attitude and showed me that the Holy Spirit is more than the Spirit of being born again, more than the Spirit of power. He's a person – but a person who lives inside me. To live with a person means to have fellowship with the person. It means recognition of each other. It means intimate fellowship and communication.[219]

The BHS should not be construed as a transitory spiritual encounter. The spiritual experiences, occasionally accompanied by supernatural signs and wonders, are the outcomes of interaction with the Holy Spirit. Common interpretations of "But you will receive power when the Holy Spirit comes on you (Act 1:8)" should not precipitate an overly simplified belief that the Holy Spirit comes only in/for power. The peril lies in a disproportionate focus on the healing power over its Giver, leading to a temptation to indulge in the BHS as religious ecstasy. Korean healing theology strongly asserts that the BHS should be perceived relationally rather than functionally. It is a strong reminder of the Korean healing theology that the BHS must be understood as relational not functional. The Korean healing theology of "in not as" must continue to remind the cessationists that the Holy Spirit comes *in* power and the Pentecostals/Charismatics that the Holy Spirit does not come *as* power to heal. The Holy Spirit is the divine healer.

---

[218] Yong-gi Cho, *Expand your Horizon*, 62-63.

[219] Yong-gi Cho, *Successful Home Cell Groups* (Seoul: Seoul Logos, 1997): 120.

Han and Emotional Healing

Comprehending the circumstances surrounding the Korean Church is paramount, as the investigation delves into the terminal theological nucleus of the Korean healing movement. This movement has fostered a crucial dimension of divine healing, asserting that it extends beyond mere physical recuperation to constitute a comprehensive restoration that also incorporates the emotional healing of *Han*. Such an all-encompassing perspective on divine healing was conceived within the unique environment of the Korean Church, a setting characterised by significant suffering. The chart below (Figure 9) illuminates the backgrounds of the three practitioners within the healing movement. I will comment on the chart in the following section.

Figure 9: Biographical Data and Brief Social Context of Korea

Year	Kim	Lee	Cho	Social Context
1870	Birth (1874)			
1890	Failure in the state Exam (1890) Marriage (1893)			
1895				
1900	Conversion (1900) Pastoring: 1st Jaeryeong church (1901) 2nd Sinchoen church (1901–23)	Birth (1900)		Wonsan Revival (1903)
1905	B-School(1906–10)			Pyeongyang Revival (1910)
1910	300 members, Revival meetings started, B-school graduation (1910) Ordination (1910) Healing ministries started (1911)			Japanese Occupation (1910–45)
1915	Many Revival meetings started (1919)	Marriage (1918)		* Failure of the Independence Movement followed by severe persecution on the Korean Church (1919)

1920	800 members (1920) General sup. (1920) Left Shinchoen Church (1923)	Peristitis contracted (1920) Conversion (1920)		
1925		B-School (1925–28) 1st Suwon church (1928)		
1930		2nd Mokpo church (1930)		
1935	3rd Namdeamun church (1936) 4th Sungdong church (1939)	Ordained (1932) 3rd Sineuju church (1936–37) Circulating National Revival Meetings (1937–39) Study in Japan(1939)	Birth (1936)	
1940	Joined Shrine Worship (1940) Forced to resign (1942–45)	Evangelism in Manju (1941-45)		
1945	Joined KCF (1946)			Communist Persecution (1945–1950)
1950	General Sup. of KCF (1949) Death as martyred (1950)	Immanuel Commando (1954–55)		The Korean War (1950–53)
1955		Jubilee Revival (1955–56) Jubilee evangelism (1957) U.S.A evangelism (1959)	T.B. contracted & conversion (1955) B-school (1956–58) 1st tent church (1958)	The war-torn context
1960			2nd Seodeamun church (1961) Ordained (1962) 3rd Central church (1962) Cell group (1964) Marriage (1965)	
1965		Last sermon at the general council (1965) Death (1965)	7,750 members (1967) General Sup. (1966)	
1970			10,000 members (1973)	

1975			New Church building at Yoido (1973) Pray Mountain (1973)	
1980			World Largest Church with 200,144 members (1981) Daughter churches (1980)	
1985			Church name changed (1984) Cult dispute started (1983) World Missions, Media evangelism, Social gospel,	
1990			Guinness as the world largest church with 700,000 (1992)	
1995			Withdrawal of cult dispute (1994)	
2000				
2005			Step down as emeritus (2008)	
2010				

The Suffering Context and Emotional Healing

In examining the theological underpinnings of the Korean healing movement, a notable and essential characteristic lies in the significant role healing has played in supporting the oppressed and marginalised. The Korean Church faced numerous trials precipitated by Japanese colonisation and the Korean War. Kim, Lee, and Cho interpret healing not merely as a physical phenomenon but as a holistic restoration emanating from the miraculous works of the immanent God, the Holy Spirit. Consequently, the healing ministries of these practitioners should not be perceived as mere accounts of healing but require contextual understanding within the framework of the Korean Church to acknowledge divine intervention amid suffering. The circumstances shaping the Korean healing movement markedly differ from those of the North American Pentecostal/Charismatic movement. The Korean Church has endured a history characterised by profound suffering and disappointment.

As Figure 9 shows, Kim started leading numerous revival meetings from 1919 although he was already engaged with some healing ministries since his Bible school year in 1910. The year of 1919 when the Independence Movement failed is depicted as a crisis for the Korean Church[220] and a hopeless time filled with frustration caused by "a sense of emptiness," "sufferings," and "anxiety"[221] due to the persecution growing fiercer and more widespread soon after. In this regard, it was proved by the Miracle Witness Committee[222] that Kim's healing was the revelation of God's special comfort and strength that testified of God's presence for the persecuted and marginalised people struggling with poverty, tribulation, and suffering during this time.[223] In this context, Kim's healing movement helped not only the suffering people with their physical diseases but also the broken-hearted who had lost hope since the loss of their country.[224] The healing movement of Kim brought mental and spiritual relief and cure of the sufferers together with physical healing.

The circumstances faced by Lee and Cho were even more dire, with people bearing the burden of both the Japanese occupation (1910–1945) and the Korean War (1950–1953). When Lee launched his revival ministries in 1938, the populace was suffering under oppressive Japanese policies such as shrine worship, mandatory manpower drafts, military sexual slavery, compulsory labour, and forced name changes. Kang delineates Lee's ministry as bringing "joy," "peace," "courage," and "hope" to the oppressed.[225] This was fairly observed in the report of Lee on his revival meetings conducted right after the Independence Day in 1945. He said, "all the oppressed with hunger and thirst under the Japanese rule were filled with joy, and wherever I went spiritual fire was kindled" resulting in bringing people to Jesus.[226] Lee provided an appropriate ministry for the oppressed people to be healed not only of their physical illness but also of emotional wounds experienced in their hearts.

Cho's mission began under even more challenging circumstances when he established his first church in Daejo-dong, Seoul's poorest slum, in 1958. His ministry often involved providing spiritual guidance to dying individuals, including mothers suffering from postpartum haemorrhage. This context led Cho to develop a healing theology that encompassed a holistic salvation message, as he noted: "I have felt I need the gifts of healing while seeing people dying."[227] What Cho endeavoured to show the suffering Korean Church was not a simple event of divine healing but a message of hope. His message of hope was developed from the desolate situation of Korea after the War for "a despairing

---

220 Seong-Ho Lee, *Kim Ik-Du Moksa Seolgyo Mit Yakjeonjib*, 123.
221 Doek-ju Lee, *Saerosseun Hanguk Geuriseudoinui Gaejong Iyagi*, 424.
222 The first part of the full text of the foreword that Im wrote after the investigation on Kim's healing ministries is provided in Appendix 4.
223 Taek-kwon Im, *Joseon Yesugyohoe Ijeogmyeongjeung*, 1921, 3-4.
224 Jang-hyun Ryu, *Hangukui Seonglyeongundonggwa Yengseong*, 95.
225 Geun-hwan Kang, "Lee Seong-Bong Moksaui Buheungsayeok," 138.
226 Seong-bong Lee, *Malo Mothamyeon Jukeumeuro*, 97.
227 Yong-gi Cho, *Naui Gyohoe Seongjang Iyagi*, 74.

and hopeless people"[228] and eventually brought emotional healing together with physical comfort.

To have an understanding of the emotional healing for the suffering Korean Church, one needs to examine a key term, underlying the suffering souls of the oppressed in Korea, called *Han*.[229] *Han*, the typical soul of the Korean, translates as "wandering souls," which are filled with anger, bitterness, and resentment, because of the unjust death of people.[230] In his broad definition, Adams explains *Han* as "an accumulation of suppression" and "condensed experiences of oppression," and he continues to list four socio-political factors that historically have induced *Han*: 1) oppression by powerful nations, 2) tyrannical rulers, 3) oppression of women because of Neo-Confucian laws and customs, and 4) hereditary slavery.[231] Jeong also presents a similar view in defining *Han* "as the diseased hearts of people who are physically or psychologically associated with the suffering of survival created by wars, patriarchal suppression, poverty, and sicknesses in Korean history."[232] Throughout Korean history, *Han* has been culturally, socially, politically, and economically formed. As Adams points out above in the way *Han* could have formed, one can understand the reason why *Han* has broadly spread into most Koreans' minds. The significance of *Han* can be noticed when one pays special attention to its uniqueness. According to Kwon's claim, *Han* appears in no other Asian countries, only in Korea.[233] This argument is, of course, not entirely true because minorities in countries like Myanmar (and even in China) have also suffered in a similar national way. However, nowhere else has a whole nation experienced this suffering in recent years, so that *Han* is a uniquely Korean concept that is not easily translated into other contexts.

The Healer of the Suffering Souls

After investigating the unique spirit of *Han* formed in the suffering context of Korea, one still needs to ask how this *Han* could be healed in Korea. The role of the Holy Spirit is the key to bringing this emotional healing to the oppressed Koreans. As there can be many approaches to this topic, the concept of the immanent God through the Holy Spirit is the first to be discussed. God is the

---

[228] A.H. Anderson, "A 'Time to Share Love,'" 150.

[229] For *Minjung* theologians, *Han* often has a political connotation, as has Liberation Theology. As an exemplary work written on the incorporation of *Minjung* theology to Pentecostalism concerning Han, see Dong-yun Koo, *Baptism in the Holy Spirit: An Ecumenical Theology of Spirit Baptism* (Lanham, MD: University Press of America, 2003).

[230] Soo-young Kwon, "How Do Korean Rituals Heal? Healing of *Han* As Cognitive Property," *Journal of Pastoral Theology* 14 (2004): 31.

[231] D.J. Adams, *Christ and Culture in Asia*, 97.

[232] Chong-hee Jeong, "The Korean Charismatic Movement as Indigenous Pentecostalism," 555.

[233] Soo-young Kwon, "How Do Korean Rituals Heal?" 31.

Creator who constantly takes care of nature since creation, and the Holy Spirit is dwelling in that creation to sustain people in their lives. As a supporter of this idea, Prichard, in referring to the Hebrew word *Shekhinah*, precisely states that "the indwelling presence of God is, indeed, the very Spirit of God."[234] Towns echoes the same idea, stating that "as the Spirit of the Lord, the Holy Spirit is the Key to our having a vital relationship with God [...] The Holy Spirit is the means by which God dwells in and among people."[235] In dealing with a similar idea, Moltmann further explains how this indwelling Spirit sustains life. He believes that God is "in all things" and that the idea of "all things in God" relates to a theological understanding of the Holy Spirit "as the power of creation and the wellspring of life."[236] Such an immanent perception of the Holy Spirit helps us to understand how the Holy Spirit could help the suffering Korean Church. Most importantly, Moltmann's concept of God as "immanent transcendence" leads to another cognisance of the role of the Holy Spirit. He asserts that we can experience this "immanent transcendence" and we can experience everything that we are experiencing today through the Holy Spirit.[237] This idea enables one to envision the possibility that God was suffering together with the Korean people by sympathising with her suffering through the Holy Spirit.

In exploring the role of the Holy Spirit for the suffering Korean Church, Oden's statement contributes to the second point:

> Through directly touching, meeting, and indwelling within the human spirit, God the Spirit gives new life to the sinner, sustains the soul through the hazards of moral bankruptcy, and works to draw human freedom without coercion back to its original purpose of refracting the goodness of God.[238]

As Oden presents the Holy Spirit as the One who is with His people to give new life, sustaining them, and working for human freedom, such that the Holy Spirit is dwelling in this world to set the captives (the Korean Church) free. That is why Moltmann in a similar way contends that where the Spirit is, there exists freedom[239] by drawing our attention to the interpretation of the Hebrew word *ruach*. For him, Yahweh's *ruach* – which can be translated as the Spirit – has its significance in "God's own creative power to give life, and the created ability to live enjoyed by all the living."[240] In fact, the Holy Spirit is the One who strives to grant all people the freedom of life.

---

[234] R.B. Prichard, *Sensing the Spirit: The Holy Spirit in Feminist Perspective* (St. Louis, MO: Chalice, 1999): 87.
[235] E.L. Towns, *The Name of the Holy Spirit* (Ventura, CA: Regal Books, 1994): 31.
[236] J. Moltmann, *The Spirit of Life: A Universal Affirmation* (Minneapolis, MN: Fortress, 1992): 35.
[237] T.C. Oden, *Systematic Theology*, 34.
[238] T.C. Oden, *Systematic Theology*, vol. 3, *Life in the Spirit* (New York: HarperCollins, 1992): 37.
[239] T.C. Oden, *Systematic Theology*, 270.
[240] J. Moltmann, *The Spirit of Life: A Universal Affirmation*, 41.

Additionally, "God's Spirit is a living energy[241] that interpenetrates the bodies of men and women and drives out the germs of death."[242] That is why we can perceive the Holy Spirit to be the ultimate power of healing. Then, is it not possible that the Spirit sets captives free not only *physically*, but also *emotionally* and *spiritually*? The Holy Spirit can work for liberation in multifarious ways. As Comblin points out: "freedom is a gift of the Spirit, the effect of the Spirit's presence in men and women,"[243] and one of the essential roles of the Spirit is to free people and communities. Therefore, it can be conjectured that the Holy Spirit, who takes care of the Korean people, enabled them to be liberated from oppression as He brought emotional healing for *Han*. As Park observes, whenever people were filled with the Holy Spirit, they became filled with joy because of their changed hearts.[244] Even heart disease could be cured through the powerful work of the Holy Spirit. In this regard, Jeong more directly connects the healing of *Han* with the rapid growth of the church, by saying that "the fire of the Spirit quickly spread through all parts of the land and brought about a powerful zeal for the healing of *Han*, and a resulting 'explosive' growth in the church."[245] It is quite understandable that many Korean people have come into the Korean Church to be comforted and strengthened by the Holy Spirit. The Holy Spirit has been attractive to many Koreans since the immanent God has worked for the oppressed as our friend, counsellor, comforter, and healer. This should be evaluated as a tremendous contribution of the healing movement in the Korean Church.

As the Holy Spirit so powerfully set the oppressed free out of the bondage of *Han*, Jeong takes the view that "the healing of *Han* as the contextualisation of Korean Pentecostalism is one of the characteristics through 'the work of the Holy Spirit.'"[246] That is why he considers the first spiritual revival in Pyeongyang in 1907 as "the climax of the Charismatic Movement" which brought forth "the healing of *Han*."[247] When this argument contributes to the point that the Holy Spirit works to bring emotional healing, it should be admitted that the spiritual

---

[241] There are several studies on the Asian concept of Gi/Chi and the life-giving Spirit. See Dong-yun Koo, *The Holy Spirit and Ch'I (Qi): A Chiological Approach to Pneumatology* (Eugene, OR: Pickwick, 2012).
[242] J. Moltmann, *The Spirit of Life: A Universal Affirmation*, 190.
[243] J. Comblin, *The Holy Spirit and Liberation* (New York: Orbis, 1989), 63.
[244] Myeong-su Park, "Korean Pentecostal Spirituality as Manifested in the Testimonies of Believers of the Yoido Full Gospel Church," in Wonsuk Ma, W.W. Menzies, and Hyeon-sung Bae (eds), *David Yong-gi Cho: A Close Look at His Theology and Ministry* (APTS and Hansei University Press), 55-56.
[245] Chong-hee Jeong, "The Korean Charismatic Movement as Indigenous Pentecostalism," 558.
[246] Chong-hee Jeong, "The Korean Charismatic Movement as Indigenous Pentecostalism," 556-57.
[247] Chong-hee Jeong, "The Korean Charismatic Movement as Indigenous Pentecostalism," 557.

vitality of the revival movement has been continually passed down to others and even fortified throughout Korean Church history. Nonetheless, the Korean revival movement has not come to an end. One needs to understand that the revival movement in 1907 was the output of the Holy Spirit not of the Charismatic Movement. It needs to be understood as an on-going process that the Holy Spirit has kindled in the Korean Church and that still brings her holistic restoration. In this regard, one of the most urgent tasks given to the Korean Church is to re-define what is meant by suffering for today's Christians. What healing of the Holy Spirit does the Korean Church need today? Perhaps this is not an easy question to answer since the context of the Korean Church has more rapidly changed than ever before because of globalization with its remarkable socio-politico-economic growth. Despite this challenge, the people still have *Han* probably in another form and the liberating Spirit of God is still at work. This is, therefore, a high time for the Korean healing movement to revive the Church by helping those who are suffering from another type of *Han* transformed under modernization. The liberating work of the Holy Spirit still needs to be continued in a holistic way.

Conclusion

In delving into the unique contextual dimensions of the Korean Church, Chapters 1 through 3 put forth several key arguments. The Korean healing movement emerges as a venerable cornerstone in the Korean Church history, intricately moulded by the nation's complex socio-religious-politico-economic landscape. Moreover, the origins of the divine healing movement in Korea can be traced back to indigenous traditions that predate the arrival of the first Pentecostal missionaries in 1928. This underscores the distinct lineage of the Korean Holy Spirit movement, broadening its theological purview to be more inclusive of traditions beyond the Pentecostal faith.

Eminent healing practitioners such as Ik-du Kim, Seong-bong Lee, and Yong-gi Cho formulated a representative healing theology that resonated with the hope and comfort required in the tumultuous environments of 20th century Korea. Such challenging contexts mandated fervent, continuous prayers for divine intervention.

The spiritual worldview within the Korean Church also led indigenous leaders to challenge the imported doctrine of cessationism, which had its roots in the early Protestant Church of the Global North. In this discourse, two critical cultural-religious elements were highlighted: belief in a supreme god known as *Hanuel*, and the practice of Shamanism. Particularly, *Hanuel* was conceptualised as an omnipotent deity whose limitless healing power oversees all situations. Shamanism, serving as a pivotal belief system, enriched the spiritual lives of Korean Christians through the practices of mountain and dawn prayers, intensifying the urgency for divine healing. Furthermore, it heightened awareness of spiritual warfare and the notion that illness could be a tactic employed by Satan to hinder the gospel's spread.

Within the Christian context, practitioners like Kim, Lee, and Cho inherited a tradition of comprehensive repentance as a prerequisite for healing. However, an excessive focus on repentance and the emergence of occultism seemed to narrow Korean pneumatology only to regeneration and sanctification, inadequately addressing the spiritual gift of healing.

On a personal level, individual interactions with missionaries, bible school teachers, family members and others reaffirmed the relevance of these diverse beliefs for the three healing practitioners. The considerable influence of the Global North's Pentecostal movement in shaping Korean healing theology is undeniable. Particularly, the theological education these practitioners received enabled them to systematise their primal understanding of divine healing as manifested in the Korean Church's practices.

Moreover, the initial three chapters culminate in an assessment that highlights the healing movement's multiple contributions: 1) societal contributions of offering hope, comfort, and emotional healing for the collective Han, 2) missional contributions that include spurring church growth and spiritual revitalisation, and 3) theological contributions in the form of a pneumatological framework that allows for divine healing to serve the expansion of God's Kingdom.

Chapter 4 conceptualises the theological underpinnings of the Korean Healing Movement through the investigation of seven critical elements: faith, prayer, repentance, spiritual warfare, baptism of the Holy Spirit, and emotional healing. These elements collectively offer a comprehensive understanding of the movement's theological foundations.

The Korean healing theology has evolved from its initially formation by Kim, later refined by Lee, and crystallised by Cho, evolving into a holistic model for individual, societal, and even ecological restoration. Given that the Korean healing movement transcends denominational lines and serves as the spiritual patrimony of the Korean Church, ongoing collective efforts are imperative for addressing emerging needs and ensuring holistic restoration in a continually evolving landscape.

Bibliography

Primary Sources

1) IK-DU KIM

Kim, Ik-du. "Cheotsarangeul Ilchimalja" [Do Not Lose Your First Faith], 1924. In Jae-hyun Kim, Ed. *Kim Ik-du: The D.L. Moody of Korea*. Translated by Woong G. Kim. Seoul: KIATS Press, 2008.

—. "Chiljungeui Jobeunmun" [Seven Narrow Gates], 1939. In Seong-Ho Lee, Ed. *Kim Ik-du Mogsa Seolgyo Mit Yagjeonjib* [The Sermons and Biography of Ik-Du Kim]. Seoul: Hyemunsa, 1977.

—. "Discerning How to Receive the Holy Spirit" In Jae-hyun Kim, Ed. *Kim Ik-du: The D.L. Moody of Korea.* Translated by Woong G. Kim. Seoul: KIATS Press, 2008.

—. "Gidoeui Jonggyo" [Religion of Prayer]. In Seong-Ho Lee, Ed. *Kim Ik-du Mogsa Seolgyo Mit Yagjeonjib* [The Sermons and Biography of Ik-Du Kim]. Seoul: Hyemunsa, 1977.

—. "Hananimi Gibbeohaneun Adeul Ddalidoeja" [Let Us Become Sons and Daughters with Whom God is Pleased], 1940. In The Korea Institute for Advanced Theological Studies, Ed. *Kim Ik-Du: The D.L. Moody of Korea*. Translated by Woong G. Kim. Seoul: KIATS Press, 2008.

—. "Hoegaehara Cheonguki Gaggaunira" [Repent, for the kingdom of heaven is at hand]. In Seong-Ho Lee, Ed. *Kim Ik-du Mogsa Seolgyo Mit Yagjeonjib* [The Sermons and Biography of Ik-Du Kim]. Seoul: Hyemunsa, 1977.

—. "Insaengeui Yoguwa Seongseo" [The need of life and the Bible]. *Hwalcheon*, August (1937): 53-56.

—. "Juileul Geolukheui Jikija" [Keep the Lord's Day Holy]. In Seong-Ho Lee, Ed. *Kim Ik-du Mogsa Seolgyo Mit Yagjeonjib* [The Sermons and Biography of Ik-Du Kim]. Seoul: Hyemunsa, 1977.

—. "Juileul Geolukheui Jikija" [Keep the Lord's Day Holy]. In *Kim Ik-Du*. Edited by KIATS. Seoul: Hongseongsa, 2008.

—. "Receive the Holy Spirit". In Jae-hyun Kim, ed., *Kim Ik-du: The D.L. Moody of Korea*. Translated by Woong G. Kim. Seoul: KIATS Press, 2008.

—. "Sameui Pilyowa Seonggyeong" [The Needs of Life and the Bible]. Hwalcheon. August and September, 1937.

—. "Seoro Saranghara" [Love One Another]. In Seong-Ho Lee, Ed. *Hankug Sinang Jeojakjib* [Collected Writings of Korean Beliefs]. Seoul: Hyemunsa, 1977.

—. "Seoro Saranghara" [Love One Another]. In The Korea Institute for Advanced Theological Studies, Ed. *Kim Ik-Du: The D.L. Moody of Korea.* Translated by Woong G. Kim. Seoul: KIATS Press, 2008.

—. "Seonggyeongeun Hananimeui Malsseum" [The Bible is God's Word], 1938. In Seong-Ho Lee, Ed. *Hankug Sinang Jeojakjib* [Collected Writings of Korean Beliefs]. Seoul: Hyemunsa, 1977.

—. "Seongryeongeui sere" [the Baptism of the Holy Spirit]. In Seong-Ho Lee, Ed. *Kim Ik-du Mogsa Seolgyo Mit Yagjeonjib* [The Sermons and Biography of Ik-Du Kim]. Seoul: Hyemunsa, 1977.

—. "Seongryeongsereeui yeoseokgaji hyeongtae" [Six types of the baptism of the Holy Spirit]. In Seong-Ho Lee, Ed. *Kim Ik-Du Mogsa Seolgyo Mit Yagjeonjib* [The Sermons and Biography of Ik-Du Kim]. Seoul: Hyemunsa, 1977.

—. "Seongryeongeul bateura" [Receive the Baptism of the Holy Spirit]. In Seong-Ho Lee, Ed. *Kim Ik-Du Mogsa Seolgyo Mit Yagjeonjib* [The Sermons and Biography of Ik-Du Kim]. Seoul: Hyemunsa, 1977.

—. "Seongsin Serye" [the Baptism of the Holy Spirit] *Hwalcheon* (July 1934): 18-22.

—. "Seongsin Batneun Bunbyeol" [Discerning the Baptism of the Holy Spirit]. In *Kim Ik-Du*. Edited by KIATS. Seoul: Hongseongsa, 2008.

—. "Seoro Saranghara" [Love One Another]. In The Korea Institute for Advanced Theological Studies, Ed. *Kim Ik-Du: The D.L. Moody of Korea*. Translated by Woong G. Kim. Seoul: KIATS Press, 2008.

—. "The Servant of Christ". In Jae-hyun Kim, Ed. *Kim Ik-Du: The D.L. Moody of Korea*. Translated by Woong G. Kim. Seoul: KIATS Press, 2008.

—. "Urineun seongryeoneui sere bata damyeongeul gamdanghayeoboja" [Let's cope with our mission by receiving the Baptism of the Holy Spirit]. In Seong-Ho Lee, ed., *Kim Ik-du Mogsa Seolgyo Mit Yagjeonjib* [The Sermons and Biography of Ik-Du Kim]. Seoul: Hyemunsa. 1977.

2) SEON-BONG LEE

Lee, Seong-bong. "Bokheungsaeob Sunhoe Yakbo" [Report on Revival Ministry]. *Hwal Cheon* (June 1939): 37.

—. *Buheungeui Bigyeol* [The Secret of Revival]. Seoul: Word of Life Books, 1993.

—. *Immanuel Gangdan* [The Pulpit of Immanuel]. Seoul: Word of Life Books, 1993.

—. *Malo Mothamyeon Jukeumeuro* [If You cannot Preach in Words, Preach by Death]. Seoul: Word of Life Books, 1993.

—. "Miguk Sunhoe Jeondogi" [Report on Revival Tour in the United States] *Living Waters* (October 1959): 28-29.

—. "Myeongsimdo Ganghwa" [The Heart of Man], 1949. In *Cheolroyeokjeongganghwa, Myeongsimdoganghwa, Yonaseoganghwa*. Edited by Seongbonghoe. Seoul: Lifebook, 1993.

—. "Revival Tour." *Living Waters* (October 1938).

—. *Sarangeui Gangdan* [The Pulpit of Love]. Seoul: Word of Life Books, 1993.

—. "Sowi Sinyu Godojareul Jueuihal Il" [Be Careful with the so-called Healing Practitioners] *Living Water* (March 1938): 1.

—. "Yonaseoganghwa" [Jonah], 1957. In *Cheolroyeokjeongganghwa, Myeongsimdoganghwa, Yonaseoganghwa*. Edited by Seongbonghoe. Seoul: Lifebook, 1993.

3) YONG GI CHO

Cho, Yong-gi. *A Bible Study for New Christians*. Seoul: Seoul Logos, 1997.

—. *Byeongeul Jilmeojisin Yesunim* [Jesus who carried our diseases]. Seoul Youngsan Press, 1966.

—. *Dousineun Seongryeongnim* [The Holy Spirit who Helps Us]. In *Ten-Minute Broadcast Sermon.* Vol. 3. Seoul: Seoul Logos, 2011.

—. "Dr Cho awarded the Family of Man Medallion," *David Cho Website* [Available at http://www.davidcho.com/neweng/ba2005-eng.asp], [Last accessed: 23rd November 2023].

—. *Geonganghan Salmui Gil* [Way of Healthy Life]. Seoul: Seoul Logos, 2012.

—. *Gyohoeseongjang Jinjeongeuro Wonhasibnigga?* [Do You Truly Want Church Growth?]. Seoul: Seoul Logos, 1995.

—. *How Can I Be Healed?* Seoul: Seoul Logos, 1999.

—. *Huimangmokhoe 45 Nyeon* [45 Years of Hope Ministry]. Seoul: Institute for Church Growth, 2004.

—. "Iseongbong Moksaui Sayeok Soke Natanan Seonglyeong" [The Holy Spirit revealed in the Ministry of Rev. Seong-bong Lee]. In *Iseongbong Moksaui Buheungundong Jomyeong* [Evaluation of Rev. Seong-bong Lee's Revival Movement]. Seoul: Lifebook, 2000.

—. "Lee Seong-bong Moksaeui Sayeok Soke Natanan Seongryeong," [The Holy Spirit found in the Ministry of Seong-bong Lee]. In *Lee Seong-bong Moksaeui Buheungundong Jomyeong* [The Examination of Seong-bong Lee's Revival Movement]. Edited by The Commemoration Committee of the 100th Anniversary of Lee Seong-bong's Birth. Seoul: Lifebook, 2000: 423-429.

—. *Miteumkwa Silsang* [Faith and The Substance of Things]. Seoul: Youngsan Press, 1967.

—. *More than Numbers*. Waco, TX: Word Books, 1984.

—. *My Church Growth Stories*. Seoul: Seoul Logos, 2006.

—. *Naui Gyohoe Seongjang Iaygi* [The Story of My Church Growth]. Seoul: Seoul Logos, 2005.

—. *Obunganui Myeongsang* [5 Minute Devotion]. Seoul: Seoul Logos, 1976.

—. *Ojung Bokeum Iyagi* [The Story of the Five-Fold Gospel]. Seoul: Seoul Logos, 1998.

—. *Ojung Bokeumgwa Samjung Chukbok* [Five-Fold Gospel and Three-Fold Blessings]. Seoul: Seoul Logos, 1998.

—. *Ojungbokeumkwa Samjung Guweoneui Chukbok* [Five-Fold Gospel and the Blessing of the Three-Fold Salvation]. Seoul: Seoul Logos, 1988.

—. *Prayer that Brings Revival*. Lake Mary, FL: Creation House, 1998.

—. *Sachawonui Yeongjeok Segye* [The Spiritual World of the Fourth Dimension]. Seoul: Seoul Logos, 1999.

—. *Sachawonneui Yeongseong* [The Fourth Dimensional Spirituality]. Seoul: Institute of the Church Growth, 2012.

—. *Salvation, Health and Prosperity*. Lake Mary, FL: Creation House, 1987.

——. *Sambagja Guwon* [Three-Fold Blessings]. Seoul: Youngsan Press, 1977.
——. *Seonglyeonglon* [Pneumatology]. Seoul: Youngsan Press, 1980.
——. *Seonglyeonglon* [Pneumatology]. Rev. ed. Seoul: Seoul Logos, 1998.
——. *Sin Yu* [Divine Healing]. Seoul: Hansei University Press, 2012.
——. *Sin Yu Lon* [Healing Theology]. Seoul: Seoul Logos, 2001.
——. *Spiritual Leadership for the New Millennium.* Seoul: International Theological Institute, 2002.
——. *Successful Home Cell Groups*. Seoul: Seoul Logos, 1997.
——. *Successful Living.* Seoul: Young San, 1977.
——. *Suffering, Why Me?* Gainesville, FL: Bridge-Logos, 1987.
——. *The Fourth Dimension.* Seoul: Seoul Logos, 1979.
——. *The Fourth Dimension.* Vol 2. Gainesville, FL: Bridge-Logos, 1983.
——. *The Leap of Faith.* South Plainfield, NJ: Bridge Publishing, 1984.
——. *To God Be The Glory*. Seoul: n.p. 1973.
——. *Widaehan Somyeong: Huimang Mokhoe 50 Nyeon* [Great Call: 50 Years of Hope Ministry]. Seoul: Yoido Full Gospel Church, 2008.
Cho, Yong-gi and R.H. Schuller. *Expand your Horizon: How to Make Your Faith Work.* Melbourne, FL: Dove Christian Books, 1988.

Secondary Sources

Adams, D.J. *Christ and Culture in Asia.* Quezon City, Philippines: New Day, 2002.
Albrecht, D.E. *Rites in the Spirit: A Ritual Approach to Pentecostal/Charismatic Spirituality.* Sheffield: Sheffield Academic Press, 1999.
Alexander, K.E. *Pentecostal Healing: Models in Theology and Practice.* Leiderdorp, Netherlands: Deo, 2007.
Allison, G.R. *Historical Theology.* Grand Rapids, MI: Zondervan, 2011.
Anderson, A.H. "A 'Time to Share Love': Global Pentecostalism and the Social Ministry of David Yonggi Cho", Journal of Youngsan Theology Supplement Series. *The Spirituality of Fourth Dimension and Social Salvation.* Edited by Mun-hong Choe. Gunpo, Korea: Hansei University Press, 2012: 141-161.
——. "Revising Pentecostal History in Global Perspective", In A. Anderson and E. Tang, Eds. *Asian and Pentecostal: The Charismatic Face of Christianity in Asia.* Oxford: Regnum Books International, 2005: 147-173.
——. *An Introduction to Pentecostalism: Global Charismatic Christianity.* Cambridge: Cambridge University Press, 2004.
——. "The Contextual Pentecostal Theology of Cho", In Wonsuk Ma, W.W. Menzies, and Hyeon-sung Bae, Eds. *David Yonggi Cho: A Close Look at His Theology and Ministry.* Baguio, Philippines: APTS Press, 2004.
——. "Introduction: World Pentecostalism at a Crossroads", In A.H. Anderson and W.J. Hollenweger, Eds. *Pentecostals after a Century: Global Perspectives on a Movement in Transition.* Sheffield: Sheffield Academic Press, 1999.
Anderson, A., and E. Tang, Eds. *Asian and Pentecostal: The Charismatic Face of Christianity in Asia.* Oxford: Regnum Books International, 2005.

Anderson, A.H., and W.J. Hollenweger, Eds. *Pentecostals After A Century: Global Perspectives on a Movement in Transition.* Sheffield: Sheffield Academic Press, 1999.

Babbie, E.R. *The Practice of Social Research.* 4th ed. Belmont, CA: Wadsworth, 1986.

Bae, Hyeon-sung. "Full Gospel Theology and a Korean Pentecostal Identity", In A.H. Anderson and Edmond Tang, Eds. *Asian and Pentecostal: The Charismatic Face of Christianity in Asia.* Oxford: Regnum Books International, 2004.

Baird, R. H. *William M. Baird of Korea: a Profile.* Oakland, CA: Richard H. Baird, 1968.

Barrett, D.B., G.T. Kurian and T.M. Johnson, Eds. *World Christian Encyclopedia: A Comparative Survey of Churches and Religions in the Modern World.* 2nd ed. Oxford: Oxford University Press, 2001.

Berg, L.B. *Qualitative Research Methods for the Social Sciences.* 4th ed. Boston, MA: Allyn and Bacon, 2000.

Blomberg, C.L. "Matthew", In D.S. Dockery, Ed. *The New American Commentary* 22. Nashville, TN: Broadman Press, 1992.

Bromiley, G.W. *Historical Theology: An Introduction.* Edinburgh: T&T Clark, 2000.

Brown, F., S. Driver and R. Briggs. *The Brown-Driver-Briggs Hebrew Lexicon.* Peabody, MA: Hendrickson, 1996.

Burgess, S.M., Ed. *Encyclopedia of Pentecostal and Charismatic Christianity.* London, Routledge, 2006.

—. *The Holy Spirit: Ancient Christian Traditions.* Peabody, MA: Hendrickson, 1984.

Burgess, S.M., and E.M. Maas, Eds. *New International Dictionary of Pentecostal and Charismatic Movements.* Grand Rapids, MI: Zondervan, 2002.

Burgess, S.M., and G.B. McGee, Eds. *Dictionary of Pentecostal and Charismatic Movements.* Grand Rapids, MI: Zondervan, 1988.

Byeon, Jong-ho. *Hangukeui Ohsunjeol Sinangundongsa* [The History of Korean Holy Spirit Movement]. Seoul: Sinsaenggwan, 1978.

Carson, D.A. "Matthew", In F. Gaebelein, Ed. *The Expositor's Bible Commentary.* Vol. 12. Grand Rapids, MI: Zondervan, 1984.

Chan, Simon K.H. "The Pneumatology of Paul Yonggi Cho", Wonsuk Ma, Ed. *Yonggi Cho: A Close Look at His Theology and Ministry.* Baguio, Philippines: APTS Press, 2004: 96-119.

Chase, S.N. "Inquiry: Multiple lenses, approaches, voices", In N.K. Denzin and Y.S. Lincoln, Eds. *The SAGE Handbook of Qualitative Research.* 3rd ed. London: Sage Publications, 2005: 651-679.

Cho, Gwui-sam. *Youngsan Choyounggi Moksaui Gyohoe Seongjanghak* [The Church Growth of Rev. Yong-Gi Cho]. Gunpo, Korea: Hansei University Press, 2009.

Choe, Heui-beom. "Malo Mothamyeon Jukeumeuro" [If You Cannot Preach in Words, Preach by Death], In The Commemoration Committee of the 100th Anniversary of Lee Seong-bong's Birth, Eds. *Lee Seong-bong Moksaeui*

Buheungundong Jomyeong [The Examination of Seong-bong Lee's Revival Movement]. Seoul: Lifebook, 2000: 461-476.

Choe, Mun-hong. "A Response to Dr Myung Sook Park's David Yonggi Cho and International Pentecostal/Charismatic Movements", In *2002 Youngsan International Theological Symposium*. Gupo: Hansei University Press, 2003: 266-272.

Choe, Hyeon. *Daebuheungsa Kim Ik-Du* [Great Revivalist Ik-du Kim]. Seoul: Jerusalem, 2000.

Choe, Seon. *Seongdoeui Jeulgeoum* [The Pleasure of Believers]. Seoul: Grisim, 2008.

Chung, Sung-kuh. "Reverend Ik-Du Kim (1874–1950): The D. L. Moody of Korea", In The KIATS, Eds. *Kim Ik-du*. Translated by Woong G. Kim. Seoul: KIATS Press, 2008.

Clark, M.S., and H.I. Lederle. *What Is Distinctive About Pentecostal Theology?* Muckleneuk, Pretoria: University of South Africa, 1983.

Comblin, J. *The Holy Spirit and Liberation*. New York: Orbis Books, 1989.

Corbin, J. *Basics of Qualitative Research: Grounded Theory Procedures and Techniques*. Newbury Park, CA: Sage, 1990.

Cox, H.G. *Fire From Heaven: The Rise of Pentecostal Spirituality and the Reshaping of Religion in the Twenty-First Century*. Boston, MA: Da Capo, 1995.

Daunton-Fear, Andrew. *Healing in the Early Church: The Church's Ministry of Healing and Exorcism from the First to the Fifth Century*. Milton Keynes: Paternoster Press, 2009.

David, E.G. *Doing Research in the Real World*. 2nd ed. London: Sage Publications, 2009.

Dayton, D.W. *Theological Roots of Pentecostalism*. Grand Rapids, MI: Baker Academic, 1987.

—. "Toward a Theological Analysis of Pentecostalism", In Society For Pentecostal Studies Fifteenth Annual Meeting: The Distinctiveness of Pentecostal-Charismatic Theology. Gaithersburg, MD: Mother of God Community, 1985.

Deere, J. *Surprised by the Power of the Spirit*. Grand Rapids, MI: Zondervan, 1993.

Dempster, M.W., B.D. Klaus and D. Petersen, Eds. *Globalization of Pentecostalism: A Religion Made to Travel*. Oxford: Regnum Books International, 1999.

Dickason, C.F. *Demon Possession & the Christian: A New Perspective*. Wheaton, IL: Crossway, 1987.

Donaldson, T.L. *Jesus on the Mountain: A Study in Matthean Theology*. Sheffield: Sheffield Academic Press, 1990.

Dunkerley, D. *Healing Evangelism*. Grand Rapids, MI: Chosen, 1995.

Eim, Yeol-soo. "The Roots of Korean Pentecostalism", In Young-hoon Lee, Ed. *The 18th Pentecostal World Conference Seoul: Asian Issues on Pentecostalism*. Seoul: Republic of Korea 21 September, 1998.

Elliott, J. *Using Narrative in Social Research: Qualitative and Quantitative Approaches*. London: Sage, 2005.

Erickson, M.J. *Christian Theology.* 3rd ed. Grand Rapids, MI: Baker Academic, 1983.

Gaffin, R.B. Jr. "A Cessationist View", In W.A. Grudem, Ed. *Are Miraculous Gifts for Today?* Grand Rapids, MI: Zondervan, 1996.

Gale, J.S. *Korea in Transition.* New York: Eaton and Mains, 1909.

—. *Korian Seukechi* [Korean Sketch]. Translated by Mun-pyeong Jang. Seoul: Hyeonamsa, 1979.

Gifford, D.L. *Joseoneui Pungsokgwa Seongyo* [The Tradition of Korea and Mission]. Translated by Hyun-nyo Shim. Seoul: Society of the History of Christianity in Korea, 1995.

Graf, M.A. Jr., and A.B. Simpson. *Healing: The Three Great Classics on Divine Healing.* Camp Hill, PA: Christian Publications, 1992.

Grudem, W. *Systematic Theology: An Introduction to Biblical Doctrine.* Leicester: Inter-Varsity Press, 1994.

Han, Sang-in. "A Response to Lim's Research on the Pneumatology of Rev. Yong-Gi Cho", In Yong-Hoon Lee, Ed. *Osunjeol Sinhak Nondan* 2, [Forum of Pentecostal Theology 2] (1999): 33-37.

Han, Wan-sang. "Gyohoe Yangjeok Geubseongjange Deahan Saheohakjeok Gochal" [Sociological Study of the Explosive Growth of the Korean Church], In Korea Christian Academy, Eds. *Hangukgyohoe Seonglyeongunddongui Hyeonsanggwa Gujo* [Phenomenon and Structure of the Holy Spirit Movement in the Korean Church]. Seoul: Christian Academy, 1981.

Harrell, D.E. Jr. *All Things Are Possible: The Healing and Charismatic Revivals in Modern America.* Bloomington, IN: Indiana University Press, 1975.

Higgins, J.R., M.L. Dusing and F.D. Tallman. *An Introduction to Theology: A Classical Pentecostal Perspective.* Dubuque, IA: Kendall Hunt, 1993.

Hollenweger, W.J. *Pentecostalism: Origins and Developments Worldwide.* Peabody, MA: Hendrickson, 1977.

—. "From Azusa Street to the Toronto Phenomenon: Historical Roots of the Pentecostal Movement", In J. Moltmann and K.J. Kuschel, Eds. *Pentecostal Movements: As An Ecumenical Challenge.* New York: Orbis, 1996: 3-14.

Hong, Chi-mo. "Lee Seong-bong Moksaeui Saengaewa Sinang Sasang" [Seong-bong Lee's Life and Religious Belief], In The Commemoration Committee of the 100th Anniversary of Lee Seong-bong's Birth, Eds. *Lee Seong-bong Moksaeui Buheungundong Jomyeong* [The Examination of Seong-bong Lee's Revival Movement]. Seoul: Lifebook, 2000: 491-513.

Hong, Sung-wook. *Naming God in Korea: The Case of Protestant Christianity.* Oxford: Regnum Books International, 2009.

Hunt, D. and T.A. McMahon. *The Seduction of Christianity: Spiritual Discernment in the Last Days.* Eugene, OR: Harvest House, 1985.

Huntley, M. *To Start A Work: The Foundations of Protestant Mission in Korea, 1884–1919.* Seoul: Presbyterian Church of Korea, 1983.

Hurston, J.W., and K.L. Hurston. *Caught in the Web.* Seoul: Mountain Press, 1977.

Hwa, Yung. "Missiological Implications of Dr David Yong-gi Cho's Theology", In *2002 Youngsan International Symposium.* Gunpo, Korea: Hasei University Press, 2003.

——. "Pentecostalism and the Asian Church", In A.H. Anderson and E. Tang, Eds. *Asian and Pentecostal: The Charismatic Face of Christianity in Asia.* Oxford: Regnum Books International, 2005.

Hyatt, E.L. *2000 Years of Charismatic Christianity: A 21st Century Look at Church History from a Pentecostal/Charismatic Perspective.* Lake Mary, FL: Charisma House, 2002.

Lim, Hyeong-geun, Ed. *Cho Yonggi Moksa Ildaegi: Yeouidoui Moghoeja* [Biography of Rev. Yong-Gi Cho: The Minister of Yoido]. Seoul: Seoul Book, 2008.

Im, Jong-dal. *Gidokgyo Daehan Hananimui Seonghoe Osibnyeonsa: Yeoksapyeon* [The 50-Year History of the Korea Assemblies of God: History 1953-2004]. Seoul: Creation, 2005.

Im, Taek-kwon. *Joseon Yesugyohoe Ijeogmyeongjeung* [A Testament of Miracles in the Joseon Jesus Church]. Seoul: Christian Literature Society of Korea, 1921.

——. *Joseon Yesugyohoe Ijeogmyeongjeung* [A Testament of Miracles in the Joseon Jesus Church]. Translated by D.J. Torrey. Seoul: KIATS Press, 2008.

International Theological Institute. *Yoido Kyohoei Shinanggwa Shinhak* 2 [The Yoido Full Gospel Church: Its Faith and Theology 2]. Seoul: Seoul Logos, 1993.

——. *Faith and Theology of Yoido Full Gospel Church I, II.* Seoul: Seoul, 1993.

Jeong, Chong-hee. "The Korean Charismatic Movement as Indigenous Pentecostalism", In A.H. Anderson and E. Tang, Eds. *Asian and Pentecostal: The Charismatic Face of Christianity in Asia.* Oxford: Regnum Books International, 2005: 551-571.

Jeong, In-gyo. *Sindeok Gyohoe 70 Junyeon Haksul Nonmunjib* [Symposium Paper for the 70th Anniversary of Sindeok Church]. Seoul: Sindeok Church, 1997.

Jeong, Jin-gyeong. "Naegabon Lee Seong-bong Moksa" [Rev. Seong-bong Lee that I observed], In The Commemoration Committee of the 100th Anniversary of Lee Seong-bong's Birth, Eds. *Lee Seong-bong Moksaeui Buheungundong Jomyeong* [The Examination of Seong-bong Lee's Revival Movement]. Seoul: Lifebook, 2000: 79-87.

Jeong, Seung-il. "Guryeongkwa Jeondoeui Yeolro Taoreusin Lee Seong-bong Moksanim" [Rev. Seong-bong Lee who was set on Fire for Evangelism], In The Commemoration Committee of the 100th Anniversary of Lee Seong-bong's Birth, Eds. *Lee Seong-bong Moksaeui Buheungundong Jomyeong* [The Examination of Seong-bong Lee's Revival Movement]. Seoul: Lifebook, 2000: 79-87.

Jobes, K.H. *1 Peter*. Grand Rapids, MI: Baker Academic, 2005.

Johnson, T.M., and K.R. Ross, Eds. *Atlas of Global Christianity.* Edinburgh: Edinburgh University Press, 2009.

Jones, G.H. *The Korea Mission of the Methodist Episcopal Church.* New York: Board of Foreign Missions of the Methodist Episcopal Church, 1910.

Ju, Seung-min. "Sobokeui Buheungundong Gochal" [Examination of Seong-bong Lee's Revival Movement], In The Commemoration Committee of the 100th Anniversary of Lee Seong-bong's Birth, Eds. *Lee Seong-bong Moksaeui*

Buheungundong Jomyeong [The Examination of Seong-bong Lee's Revival Movement]. Seoul: Lifebook, 2000: 430-460.

Kang, Chang-soo. "Resources for Studies of David Yonggi Cho", In Wonsuk Ma, Ed. *David Yonggi Cho: A Close Look at His Theology and Ministry*. Baguio, Philippines: APTS Press, 2004: 273-302.

Kang, Geun-hwan. "Lee Seong-bong Moksaeui Buheungsayeok" [The Revival Ministry of Seong-bong Lee], In The Commemoration Committee of the 100th Anniversary of Lee Seong-bong's Birth, Eds. *Lee Seong-bong Moksaeui Buheungundong Jomyeong* [The Examination of Seong-bong Lee's Revival Movement]. Seoul: Lifebook, 2000: 117-145.

Kang, Shin-chan. "Naega Mannan Geoin Lee Seong-bong Moksa" [Seong-bong Lee, The Giant that I have met], In The Commemoration Committee of the 100th Anniversary of Lee Seong-bong's Birth, Eds. *Lee Seong-bong Moksaeui Buheungundong Jomyeong* [The Examination of Seong-bong Lee's Revival Movement]. Seoul: Lifebook, 2000: 13-18.

Kay, W.K. *Pentecostalism: A Very Short Introduction*. Oxford: Oxford University Press, 2011.

Kay, W.K., and A.E. Dyer. *Pentecostal and Charismatic Studies: A Reader*. London: SCM Press, 2010.

Kennedy, N.L. *Dream Your Way to Success*. Plainfield, NJ: Logos International, 1980.

Keener, C.S. *A Commentary on the Gospel of Matthew*. Grand Rapids, MI: William B. Eerdmans, 1999.

—. "Matthew", In G.R. Osborne, Ed. *The IVP New Testament Commentary*. Downers Grove, IL: InterVarsity Press, 1997.

Kelsey, M.T. *Healing and Christianity: A Classic Study*. Augsburg, MN: Fortress, 1995.

KIATS, Eds. *Kim Ik-doo*, Seoul, Korea: Hongseongsa, 2008.

Kim, Deuk-hyeon. "Pyeongsindorosseo Naegabon Lee Seong-bong Moksanim" [Rev. Seong-bong Lee that I have met as a Layperson], In The Commemoration Committee of the 100th Anniversary of Lee Seong-bong's Birth, Eds. *Lee Seong-bong Moksaeui Buheungundong Jomyeong* [The Examination of Seong-bong Lee's Revival Movement]. Seoul: Lifebook, 2000: 27-33.

Kim, Dong-su. "Gyeolhonsik Naleui Jeondoseolgyo" [Evangelistic Preacing on a Wedding Day], In The Commemoration Committee of the 100th Anniversary of Lee Seong-bong's Birth, Eds. *Lee Seong-bong Moksaeui Buheungundong Jomyeong* [The Examination of Seong-bong Lee's Revival Movement]. Seoul: Lifebook, 2000: 23-26.

Kim, Dong-su, and Ryoo, Jang-hyeon. *Yeongsan Cho Yonggi Moksaui Samgwa Sasang* [Life and Thought of Rev. Yong-gi Cho]. Yongin, Korea: Kingdom, 2010.

Kim, Eun-cheol. *Hananimui Seonghoe Gyori* [Doctrine of the Assemblies of God]. Suwon, Korea: Moses, 2011.

Kim, Ig-jin. *History and Theology of Korean Pentecostalism: Sunbogeum (Pure Gospel) Pentecostalism*. Zoetermeer, The Netherlands: Uitgeverij Boekencentrum, 2003.

Kim, In-seo, *Hanguk Gidokgyohoeeu Yeoksa* [The History of the Korean Church]. Seoul: Janglohoe Sinhak Deahakgyo Press, 1997.

Kim, In-seo, *Kim Ik-Du Moksu Sojeon* [A Short Biography of Ik-Du Kim], 1932, In Seong-ho Lee, Ed. *Kim Ik-du Mogsa Seolgyo Mit Yagjeonjib* [The Sermons and Biography of Ik-Du Kim]. Seoul: Hyemunsa, 1977.

Kim, Jae-hyeon, Ed. *Joseon Yesugyohoe Ijeok Myeongjeung* [A Testament of Miracles in the Joseon Jesus Church]. Seoul: KIATS Press, 2008.

Kim, Kwang-il. "Gidokgyo Chibyeong Hyeonsange Gwanhan Jeongsinuihakjeok Josa Yeongu" [A Psychiatric Study of the Phenomenon of Healing Practice in Christianity], In Korea Christian Academy, Ed. *Hangukgyohoe Seonglyeongunddongui Hyeonsanggwa Gujo* [Phenomenon and Structure of the Holy Spirit Movement in the Korean Church]. Seoul: Christian Academy, 1981: 233-296.

Kim, Myeong-hyeok. "Lee Seon-Bong Moksaeui Samkwa Sinange Daehan Sinhakjeok Jomyeon" [Theological Examination on the Life and Belief of Seong-bong Lee], In The Commemoration Committee of the 100th Anniversary of Lee Seong-bong's Birth, Eds. *Lee Seong-bong Moksaeui Buheungundong Jomyeong* [The Examination of Seong-bong Lee's Revival Movement]. Seoul: Lifebook, 2000: 146-169.

Kim, Pan-ho. "Yongsan Sinhagui Bangbeoblongwa Teukjing" [Methodology and Characteristics of Yong-Gi Cho's Theology], In *Youngsanui Moghoewa Sinhak II* [Ministry and Theology of Yong-Gi Cho]. Gunpo, Korea: Hansei University Press, 2008: 373-398.

Koo, Dong-yun. *Baptism in the Holy Spirit: An Ecumenical Theology of Spirit Baptism*. Lanham, MD: University Press of America, 2003.

——. *The Holy Spirit and Ch'I (Qi): A Chiological Approach to Pneumatology*. Eugene, OR: Pickwick, 2012.

Korea Christian Academy, Eds. *Hangukgyohoe Seonglyeongunddongui Hyeonsanggwa Gujo* [Phenomenon and Structure of the Holy Spirit Movement in the Korean Church]. Seoul: Christian Academy, 1981: 22-99.

Kwon, Oh-seong. "Seongryeong undongeui sae jipyeongeul yeon Choyonggi moksanimeui seongyeok osibjunyeoneul chukadeuribnida" [Congratulations on Rev. Yonggi Cho's 50 year ministry]. In Yong-gi Cho, *Widaehan Somyeong: Huimang Mokhoe 50 Nyeon* [Great Call: 50 Years of Hope Ministry]. Seoul: Yoido Full Gospel Church, 2008.

Kydd, R.A.N. *Healing through the Centuries: Models for Understanding*. Peabody, MA: Hendrickson, 1998.

Ladd, G.E. *A Theology of the New Testament*. Grand Rapids, MI: William B. Eerdmans, 1974.

Lawler, S. "Narrative in Social Research", In T. May, Ed. *Qualitative Research in Action*. London: Sage, 2002: 242-258.

Lee, Deok-ju. *Hanguk Tochag Gyohoe Hyeongseongsa Yeongu* [A Study of the Historical Formation of Korean Indigenous Churches]. Seoul: Institute of the History of Christianity in Korea, 2000.

——. *Saelosseun Hanguk Geuriseudoineu Gaejong Iyagi* [Revision of The Conversion Stories of Korean Christians]. Seoul: Institute of the History of Christianity in Korea, 2003.

Lee, Jae-bum. *Seonglyeong Undongui Yeoksa* [The History of Pentecostal Movement]. Seoul: Voice, 1985.

Lee, Sang-yun. *A Theology of Hope: Contextual Perspectives in Korean Pentecostalism*. Eugene, OR: Wipf and Stock, 2019.

Lee, Seong-ho, Ed. *Kim Ik-Du Mogsa Seolgyo Mit Yagjeonjib* [The Sermons and Biography of Ik-Du Kim]. Seoul: Hyemunsa, 1977.

Lee, Yong-gyu, *Hanguk Gyohoewa Shinyu Undong* [Divine Healing Movement and the Korean Church]. Seoul: Qumran, 2006.

Lee, Young-hoon, "Life and Ministry of David Yonggi Cho", In Wonsuk Ma, Ed. *David Yonggi Cho: A Close Look at His Theology and Ministry*. Baguio, Philippines: APTS Press, 2004.

—. "Oral Roberts and David Yonggi Cho: A Life-long Relationship in Theology and Ministry", *Spiritus: ORU Journal of Theology* 4(1), (Spring 2019): 5-16.

—. "Sanjungchukbok Sinangui Osunjeol Sinhakjeok Ihae" [A Pentecostal Theological Understanding of the Belief of Three-Fold Blessings], In *Cho Yong-gi Moksaui Samjungchukboke Deahan Sinhakjeok Ihea* [Theological Understanding of the Three-fold Blessings of Rev. Yong-Gi Cho]. Seoul: Seoul Logos, 2000.

—. *The Holy Spirit Movement in Korea: Its Historical and Theological Development*. Oxford: Regnum Books International, 2009.

Lim, Dong-seon. "Hanguk Gidokgyo Yeoksaae Yeongweonhi Bitnal Keun Byeol" [The Big Star that will always Shine in the History of the Korean Christianity], In The Commemoration Committee of the 100th Anniversary of Lee Seong-bong's Birth, Eds. *Lee Seong-bong Moksaeui Buheungundong Jomyeong* [The Examination of Seong-bong Lee's Revival Movement]. Seoul: Lifebook, 2000: 74-78.

Macchia, F.D. "The Struggle for Global Witness: Shifting Paradigms in Pentecostal Theology", In M.W. Dempster *et al.*, Eds. *Globalization of Pentecostalism: A Religion Made to Travel*. Oxford: Regnum Books International, 1999: 8-29.

MacNutt, F. *Healing*. Notre Dame, IN: Ave Maria Press, 1974.

Maitlis, S. "Narrative Analysis", In G. Symon and C. Cassell, Eds. *Qualitative Organizational Research: Core Methods and Current Challenges*. London: Sage, 2012: 492-512.

Martin, D. *Pentecostalism: The World Their Parish*. Oxford: Blackwell, 2008.

Ma, Wonsuk. "Asian (Classical) Pentecostal Theology in Context", In A.H. Anderson and E. Tang, Eds. *Asian and Pentecostal: The Charismatic Face of Christianity in Asia*. Oxford: Regnum Books International, 2005: 59-91.

—. "Blessing in Pentecostal Theology and Mission", In Wonsuk Ma, Veli-Matti Kärkkäinen and J. Kwabena Asamoah-Bydau, Eds. *Pentecostal Mission and Global Christianity*. Regnum Edinburgh Centenary Series. Vol. 20. Oxford: Regnum Books International, 2014: 272-291.

—. "Hollenweger's Pentecostalism: An Asian Reflection", In Yong-hoon Lee., Ed. *The 18th Pentecostal World Conference Seoul: Asian Issues on Pentecostalism*. Seoul: Republic of Korea, 21st September 1998.

——, Ed. *The Fourth General Assembly Asia Pacific Theological Association: Facing the Theological Issues of the Twenty-First Century*. Sydney, Australia. 28th September–1st October 1999. Manila: Asia Pacific Theological Association, 1999.

Ma, Wonsuk, and R.P. Menzies, Eds. *Pentecostalism in Context: Essays in Honor of William W. Menzies*. Sheffield: Sheffield Academic Press, 1997.

McGavran, D.A. *Understanding Church Growth*. Grand Rapids, MI: William B. Eerdmans, 1990.

McGee, G.B. *This Gospel Shall Be Preached: A History and Theology of AG Foreign Missions Since 1959*. Vol. 2. Springfield, MI: Gospel, 1989.

McGuire, M. *Ritual Healing in Suburban America*. New Brunswick, NJ: Rutgers University Press, 1988.

McGrath, A.E. *Historical Theology: An Introduction to the History of Christian Thought*. 2nd ed. Oxford: Wiley-Blackwell, 2012.

Menzies, W.W. "Facing Theological Issues of the Twenty-First Century." In *Facing Theological Issues of the Twenty-First Century: Conference Papers*. The Proceedings of the Fourth General Assembly Asia Pacific Theological Association. Sydney: Southern Cross College, 28th September–1st October 1999.

——. "Frontiers in Theology: Issues at the Close of the First Pentecostal Century", In Yong-hoon Lee, Ed. *The 18th Pentecostal World Conference Seoul: Asian Issues on Pentecostalism*. Seoul: Republic of Korea, 21 September 1998.

——. *Osunjeol Seonggyeon Gyori* [Doctrine of Pentecostalism]. Translated by The General Council Administration office. Seoul: Korea Assemblies of God, 1994.

Menzies, W.W., and R.P. Menzies. *Spirit and Power: Foundations of Pentecostal Experience*. Grand Rapids, MI: Zondervan, 2000.

Merriam, S.B. *Qualitative Research: A Guide to Design and Implementation*. San Francisco, CA: Jossey-Bass, 2009.

Min, Gyeong-bae. "Lee Seong-bong Moksaeui Buheungundong Jaejomyeong" [Re-examination of Seong-bong Lee's Revival Movement], In The Commemoration Committee of the 100th Anniversary of Lee Seong-bong's Birth, Eds. *Lee Seong-bong Moksaeui Buheungundong Jomyeong* [The Examination of Seong-bong Lee's Revival Movement]. Seoul: Lifebook, 2000: 187-214.

——. *Hanguk Gidokgyohoesa* [The History of Korean Christianity]. Seoul: Yense University Press, 1993.

——. *Iljehaeui Hanguk Gidokgyo Minjog Sinang Udongsa* [The History of Korean Christian Beliefs under Japanese Colonization]. Seoul: Christian Literature Society of Korea, 1991.

——. *Taehan Yesugyo Changnohoe baeknyonnsa* [A Centennial History of the Presbyterian Church in Korea]. Seoul: General Assembly of the Presbyterian Church in Korea, 1984.

Moltmann, J. *The Spirit of Life: A Universal Affirmation*. Minneapolis, MN: Fortress Press, 1992.

Moltmann, J., and K.J. Kuschel, Eds. *Pentecostal Movements: As An Ecumenical Challenge*. New York: Orbis, 1996.

Motyer, J.A. *The Prophecy of Isaiah: An Introduction and Commentary*. Downers Grove, IL: InterVarsity Press, 1993.

Murray, A. "Divine Healing", In L.G. Jonathan, Ed. *Healing: The Three Great Classics on Divine Healing*. Camp Hill, PA: Christian Publications, 1992.

Na, Kyum-il. "Early morning prayer and church growth: based on the case study of Inchun Juan Presbyterian Church", D. Min. diss., Asian Center for Theological Studies and Mission and Fuller Theological Seminary, 1941.

Neuman, L. *Social Research Methods: Qualitative and Quantativve Approaches*. Boston, MA: Allyn & Bacon, 2000.

Nichol, J.T. *Pentecostalism*. New York: Harper & Row, 1966.

Oak, Sung-deuk. "Healing and Exorcism: Christian Encounters with Shamanism in Early Modern Korea", *Asian Ethnology* 69(1), 2010: 95-128.

Oden, T.C. *Systematic Theology*. Vol. 3. Life in the Spirit. New York: HarperCollins, 1992.

Osborn, T.L. *Divine Healing Through Creative Word*. Tulsa, OK: Osborn Foundation, 1949.

—. *Faith's Testimony*. Tulsa, OK: Osborn Foundation, 1956.

—. *Healing The Sick*. Tulsa, OK: Harrison House, 1951.

Oswalt, J.N. "The Book of Isaiah: Chapters 40-66", In R.K. Harrison and R.L. Hubbard, Jr., Eds. *The New International Commentary on the Old Testament*. Grand Rapids, MI: William B. Eerdmans, 1998.

Park, Jeong-ryeol. *Ohsunjeol Sinhak* [Pentecostal Theology]. Gunpo, Korea: Sunshin University Publishing, 1996.

Park, Myeong-su. "David Yonggi Cho and International Pentecostal/Charismatic Movements", 2002 Young San International Theological Symposium. Gunpo: Hansei University Press, 2002: 219-242.

—. *Hanguk Gyohoe Buheungundong Yeongu* [A Study on the Revival Movement in Korean Church]. Seoul: Institute of the History of Christianity in Korea, 2003.

—. "Lee Seong-bong Moksaeui Saengaewa Buheungundong" [Seong-bong Lee's Life and Revival Movement], In The Commemoration Committee of the 100th Anniversary of Lee Seong-bong's Birth, Eds. *Lee Seong-bong Moksaeui Buheungundong Jomyeong* [The Examination of Seong-bong Lee's Revival Movement]. Seoul: Lifebook, 2000: 215-256.

—. "Korean Pentecostal Spirituality as Manifested in the Testimonies of Believers of the Yoido Full Gospel Church", In Wonsuk Ma, Ed. *David Yonggi Cho: A Close Look at His Theology and Ministry*. Baguio, the Philippines: APTS Press, 2004, 43-67.

—. "Seonggyeoleui Sinhakjeok Ihae" [Theological Understanding of Sanctification], *SGTI Website* [Available at: http://www.sgti.kr/data/person/mspark/5.htm], [Last accessed: 25th November 2023].

Park, Yong-gyu. *Anak Sangol: Hanguk Gyohoe Buheung Mogsa Kim Ik-Du Jeongi* [The Backwoods of Anag: The Biography of Korean Revivalist Rev. Ik-Du Kim]. Seoul: Christian Sinmunsa, 1968.

——. *Haguk Gidok Gyohoesa 2: 1910–1960* [The Korean Church History 2: 1910–1960]. Seoul: Lifebook, 2004.

——. *Ibuleul Ggeuji Mara* [Do Not Quench This Fire]. Seoul: Seoul Cultural Publishers, 1968.

Pearson, M. *Christian Healing*. Grand Rapids, MI: Fleming H. Revell, 1990.

Plessis, L.D. "A Proprium for Pentecostal Theology", In M.S. Clark *et al.*, Eds. *What is Distinctive about Pentecostal Theology?* Pretoria: University of South Africa, 1989: 143-152.

Poewe, K. *Charismatic Christianity as a Global Culture*. Columbia: University of South Carolina Press, 1994.

Prichard, R.B. *Sensing the Spirit: The Holy Spirit in Feminist Perspective*. St. Louis, MI: Chalice, 1999.

Punch, D.K.F. *Introduction to Social Research: Quantitative and Qualitative Approaches*. 2nd ed. London: Sage, 2005.

Rhodes, H.A. *History of the Korea Mission, Presbyterian Church USA vol. 1, 1884–1934*. Seoul: The Chosen Mission Presbyterian Church U.S.A., 1934.

Richards, L.P. *Divine Appointments with God: A Manual For Soul-Winning*. Manila: Evangel, 1967.

Riessman, C.K. *Narrative Methods for the Human Sciences*. London: Sage, 2008.

Roberts, O. *If You Need Healing Do These Things*. Rev. ed. Tulsa, OK: Healing Waters, 1951.

——. *101 Questions and Answers on Healing and Salvation*. Tulsa, OK: Oral Roberts Evangelistic Association, 1968.

Robins, R.G. "Pentecostal Movement", In D.G. Reid *et al.*, Eds. *Dictionary of Christianity in America*. Downers Grove, IL: InterVarsity Press, 1990: 885-891.

Ryu, Jang-hyun. *Hangukui Seonglyeongundonggwa Yeongseong* [The Holy Spirit Movement and Spirituality in Korea]. Seoul: Preaching Academy, 2004.

Ryle, J.C. *Matthew: Expository Thoughts on the Gospels*. Wheaton, IL: Crossway, 1993.

Ryle, J.C., A. McGrath and J.I. Packer. *Matthew: Expository Thoughts on the Gospels*. Wheaton, IL: Crossway, 1993.

Seo, Kwang-seon. "Hanguk Gyohoe Seongryeongundonggwa Buheung Undongui Sinhakjeok Ihea" [Theological Understanding of the Holy Spirit Movement and Revival Movement in the Korean Church], In The Korea Christian Academy, Eds. *Hangukgyohoe Seonglyeongunddongui Hyeonsanggwa Gujo* [Phenomenon and Structure of the Holy Spirit Movement in the Korean Church]. Seoul: Christian Academy, 1981: 22-99.

Seong, Gi-ho. "Sajung Bokeumgwa Lee Seong-bong Moksaeui Buheungundong" [The Four-Fold Gospel and the Revival Movement of Seong-bong Lee's Revival Movement], In The Commemoration Committee of the 100th Anniversary of Lee Seong-bong's Birth, Eds. *Lee Seong-bong Moksaeui Buheungundong Jomyeong* [The Examination of Seong-bong Lee's Revival Movement]. Seoul: Lifebook, 2000: 278-300.

Seybold, K., and U.B. Mueller, *Sickness & Healing: Biblical Encounters Series*. Translated by D. W. Stott. Nashville, TN: Abingdon, 1981.

Shearer, R.E. *Wildfire: Church Growth in Korea*. Grand Rapids, MI: William B. Eerdmans, 1966.

Sho, J.W. *Toward Inner Freedom: A Missiological Approach to Root Healing of Han in Korea*. Pasadena, CA: Fuller Theological Seminary, 1996.

Simpson, A.B. *The Gospel of Healing*. Camp Hill, PA: Christian Publications, 1994.

Sipley, R.M. *Understanding Divine Healing*. Wheaton, IL: Victor Books,1986.

Sudman, S., and N.M. Bradburn. *Asking Questions: A Practical Guide to Questionnaire Design*. San Francisco, CA: Jossey-Bass, 1982.

Synan, V. *The Holiness-Pentecostal Tradition: Charismatic Movements in the Twentieth Century*. 2nd ed. Grand Rapids, MI: William B. Eerdmans, 1997.

Synan, V. "Roots of Yonggi Cho's Theology of Healing", In Young San Theological Institute, Eds. *Dr Yonggi Cho's Ministry & Theology I*. Seoul: Hansei University Logos, 2008: 263-284.

The Compilation Committee of the Fifty-year History of the Korea Assemblies of God. *The 50th History of the Korea Assemblies of God: 1953-2004*. Seoul: Creation, 2005.

The Society of the History of Christianity in Korea, Eds. *Korean Christian Classics Series*. Vol. 2. *Joseon Yesugyohoe Ijeok Myeongjeung: A Testament of Miracles in the Joseon Jesus* Church. Seoul: KIATS Press, 2008.

The Society of the History of Christianity in Korea. *Hanguk Gidokgyoeui Yeoksa* 2, [The History of Korean Christianity 2]. Seoul: Christian Literature Press, 2012.

Towns, E.L. *The Name of the Holy Spirit*. Ventura, CA: Regal, 1994.

Underwood, L.S.H. *Eondeoudu Buineui Joseon Saenghwal* [The Life of Mrs. Underwood in Korea]. Translated by Kim, Cheol. Seoul: Tree Deeply Rooted Publisher, 1984.

Vanhoozer, K.J. "Theological Method", In W.A. Dyrness *et al.*, Eds. *Global Dictionary of Theology: A Resource for the Worldwide Church*. Downers Grove, IL: IVP Academic, 2008: 889-897.

Wagner, C.P. *Signs and Wonders Today*. Altemonte Springs, FL: Creation House, 1987.

——. *Territorial Spirits*. Shippensburg, PA: Destiny Image, 2012.

Wang, Tai-il. "Dr. Yonggi Cho's Understanding of the Social Salvation", *Journal of Younsan Theology Supplement Series 1: The Spirituality of Fourth Dimension & Social Salvation*. Edited by Mun-hong Choi. Seoul: Hansei University Press, 2012.

Ware, T. *The Orthodox Church*. London: Penguin, 1993.

Warfield, B.B. *Counterfeit Miracles*. Carlisle, PA: Banner of Truth Trust, 1918.

Warrington, K. *Healing & Suffering: Biblical and Pastoral Reflections*. Milton Keynes, Bucks: Paternoster Press, 2005.

——. *Pentecostal Theology: A Theology of Encounter*. Edinburgh: T. & T. Clark, 2008.

——. "The Fourth Dimension, the Word and the Spirit", In Mun Hong Cho, Eds. *The Spirituality of Fourth Dimension & Social Salvation*. Gunpo, Korea: Hansei University Press, 2012: 27-55.

White, T.B. *The Believer's Guide to Spiritual Warfare*. Ann Arbor, MI: Servant, 1990.

Wilkinson, J. *The Bible and Healing: A Medical and Theological Commentary*. Edinburgh: Handsel Press, 1998.

Williams, J.R. "A Pentecostal Theology", In *Society for Pentecostal Studies Fifteenth Annual Meeting: The Distinctiveness of Pentecostal-Charismatic Theology*. Gaithersburg, MD: 14th-16th November 1985.

Wilson, E.A. "They Crossed the Red Sea, Didn't They?: Critical History and Pentecostal Beginnings", In M.W. Dempster *et al.*, Eds. *Globalization of Pentecostalism: A Religion Made to Travel.* Oxford: Regnum Books International, 1999: 85-115.

Wimber, J. *Signs and Wonders and Church Growth*. Redlands, CA: Vineyard Ministries International, 1984.

Wimber, J., and Springer, K. *Power Healing*. New York: HarperOne, 1991.

Witty, R.G. *Divine Healing*. Nashville, TN: Broadman Press, 1989.

Yang, Jae-cheol. *Hanguk Ohsunjeol Gyohoeeui Sinanggwa Sinhak* [Belief and Theology of Pentecostal Church in Korea]. Seoul: Haneulmogjang, 2005.

Yin, R.K. *Applications of Case Study Research*. 3rd ed. Thousand Oaks, CA: Sage, 2011.

——. *Case Study Research: Design and Methods*. 3rd ed. Thousand Oaks, CA: Sage, 2002.

Yoo, Boo-woong. *Korean Pentecostalism: Its History and Theology*. Paris: Lang, 1988.

Yoo, Dong-sik. "Hanguk Gyohoewa Seongryeong Undong" [The Korean Church and the Holy Spirit Movement], In The Korea Christian Academy, Eds. *Hangukgyohoe Seonglyeongunddongui Hyeonsanggwa Gujo* [Phenomenon and Structure of the Holy Spirit Movement in the Korean Church]. Seoul: The Korea Christian Academy, 1981: 9-21.

Yung, Hwa. "Missiological Implications of Dr David Yonggi Cho's Theology", In *2002 Youngsan International Symposium*. Gunpo, Korea: Hansei University Press, 2003: 94-102.

——. "The Missiological Challenge of David Yonggi Cho's Theology", In Wonsuk Ma, Ed. *David Yonggi Cho: A Close Look at His Theology and Ministry*. Baguio, Philippines: APTS Press, 2004: 70-93.

Yun, Sung-bum. *Hankuk Jongkyowa Hankukjeok Kidockyo* [Korean Religion and Indigenous Christianity]. Vol. 1, Yun Sungbum chunjib. Seoul, Korea: Gam Sin, 1998.

Articles

Adams, D.J. "Reflections on an Indigenous Movement: The Yoido Full Gospel Church", *The Japan Christian Quarterly* 57(1), (Winter 1991): 36-45.

Ahn, Myung-jun. "The Theological Understanding of Young San to the Salvation of the Society", *Journal of Yongsan Theology* 15 (2008): 78-104.

Anderson, A.H. "The Contextual Pentecostal Theology of David Yonggi Cho". *AJPS* 7(1), (2004): 101-123.

Bae, Bon-cheol. "Youngsan Cho Yonggi Moksa 60 Nyeon Sayeoke Geolchin Seonglyeonglone Natanan Heaksim Nonje Bunseok" [Exploration of the Central Issues of Rev. Yong-Gi Cho's Pneumatology in the sixty-year ministry]. *JYT* 33 (2015): 7-36.

Bae, Dawk-mahn. "Healing Jesus: A Study on Young San's Christology Focusing on Jesus Christ as a Healer", *JYT* 5 (2005): 114-138.

—. "Chiryohasineun Yesunim" [Healing Jesus], In Pan-ho Kim, Ed. *Yongsanui Mokhoewa Sinhak* 1 [The Ministries and Theology of Yongsan 1]. Seoul: Hansei University Press, 2008.

Choe, Mun-hong. "Cho Yonggi Mogsawa Seongryeong" [Rev. Yong-Gi Cho and the Holy Spirit], *JYT* 2 (2004): 181-230.

Dayton, D.W. "The GOOD GOD and the Theology of Blessings in the Thought of David Yonggi Cho", *JYT* 7 (2006): 7-39.

Eim, Yeol-soo. "The Influence of Dr Chos Goodness of God Theology Upon His Ministry", *JYT* 7 (2006): 58-83.

Gale, J.S. "The Revival in Seoul", *Korea Mission Field* 1 (January 1921): 4-5.

Heo, Myeong-seob. "Chogi Haguk Gyohoeui Sinyu Ihae" [Understanding Healing in the Early Korean Church], *Seonggyeol Gyohoewa Sinhag* 11 [The Holiness Church and Theology 11], (Spring 2004): 140-170.

Hong, Lok-young. "Understanding Young San's Divine Healing", *JYT* 5 (2005): 139-160.

Wright, J. "The Profiles of Divine Healing", *AJPS* 5(2), (2002): 271-28.

Jones, G.H. "The Growth of the Church in the Mission Field", *The International Review of Missions* 1(3), (1912): 416-421.

—. "The Spirit Worship of the Koreans", *Transactions of the Korea Branch of the Royal Asiatic Society* 2 (1901): 37-8.

Kang, Byeong-oh. "A Study on Yongsan's Clergy and Ministry in Pastoral Ethics", *JYT* 23 (2011): 171-202.

Kärkkäinen, Veli-Matti. "March Forward to Hope: Dr Yonggi Cho's Pentecostal Theology of Hope", *JYT* 4 (2005): 30-46.

Kim, Dong-su. "Lukan Pentecostal Theology of Prayer: Is Persistent Prayer Non- Biblical?" *AJPS* 7(2), (2004): 205-217.

Kim, Ig-jin. "A Prominent Woman in Early Korean Pentecostal Movement: Gui-Im Park (1912-1994)", *AJPS* 9 (2), (2006): 199-218.

Kwon, Soo-young. "How Do Korean Rituals Heal?: Healing of *Han* As Cognitive Property," *Journal of Pastoral Theology* 14 (2004).

Lee, Gi-seong. "God's Absolute Sovereignty and Human Free Will: Young San's Understanding of Man's Cooperation with God", *JYT* 12 (2008): 64-96.

Lee, Jae-bum. "Chiyumokhoeui Hyunjanglon" [A Practical Theory of Healing Ministry]. *Mokhoewa Sinhak* [Ministry and Theology], (April 1993): 80-95.

Lee, Myeong-jik. "Gyeongnameseo Iljugan" [A Week in Gyeongnam] *Living Water* (October 1924): 47.

—. "Seongsineui Yeoksawa Akyeongeui Yeoksa" [The Works of the Holy Spirit and the Evil Spirit]. *Living Water* (April 1933): 1-4.

Lee, Young-hoon. "Dr Yonggi Cho's Influence on the Korean Church in Relation to His Pneumatology", *JYT* 2 (2004): 125-149.

—. "Hanguk Osunjeol Undonggwa Sinyu" [Korean Pentecostalism and Divine Healing], *Seonggyeol Gyohoewa Sinhak* [The Holiness Church and Theology]. (Spring 2004): 171-193.

—. "The Influence of Dr. Cho's 'God is so good-faith' in the Korean Churches", *JYT* 7 (2006): 84-112.

Mathew, T.K. "Oral Roberts and David Yonggi Cho: A Comparative Evaluation of Their Theologies of Healing", *JYT* 8 (2006): 38-69.

Ma, Wonsuk. "David Yonggi Cho's Theology of Blessing: Basis, Legitimacy, and Limitations", *Evangelical Review of Theology* 35(2), (2011): 140-159.

Menzies, W.W. "Yong-gi Cho's Theology of the Fullness of the Spirit: A Pentecostal Perspective", *JYT* 1 (2004): 11-31.

Min, Gyeong-bae. "Choyonggi Maksaui Seonglyeongsinhakgwa Hanguk Gyohoe: Han Yeoksajeok Jeobgeun" [The Theology of Holy Spirit of Rev. Yonggi Cho and the Korean Church: An Historical Approach", *JYT* 1 (2004): 32-60.

Moose, J.R. "What Do the Korean Worship?" *The Korea Mission Field* (May 1905).

Mullins, M.M. "The Empire Strikes Back: Korean Pentecostal Mission to Japan", *Japanese Religions* 17(2), (July 1992): 142-166.

Myeong, Seong-hoon. "Sinyuwa Gyohoeseongjang" [Divine Healing and Church Growth], *Ministry and Theology* [Mokhoewa Sinhak] (April 1993): 69-79.

Noble, M.W. "After the Cholera: Native Testimonies in a Korean prayer meeting", *Woman's Missionary Friend* (January 1903): 4.

Oak, Seong-deuk. "Healing and Exorcism: Christian Encounters with Shamanism in Early Modern Korea", *Asian Ethnology* 69(1), (2010): 95-128.

Park, Hong-gyu. "Youngsan's Theology of Happiness", *JYT* 16 (2009): 69-97.

Park, Myeong-su. "David Yonggi Cho and International Pentecostal/Charismatic Movements", *Journal of Pentecostal Theology* 12(1), (2003): 107-28.

—. "Haebanghu Hangukgyohoesawa Yeoido Sungogeumgyohoeui Cho Yonggi Moksa" [Korean Church History and Rev. Yong-Gi Cho of the Yoido Full Gospel Church after Japanese Colonization], *JYT* 23 (2011): 203-239.

Rhodes, H.A. "Some Results of the Kim Ik Tu Revival Meeting in Seoul", *The Korea Mission Field* (June 1921).

Ryu, Jang-hyun. "A Theological Study of Dr Yonggi Cho's Pneumatology", *JYT* 1 (2004): 139-171.

Shin, Cheol-kwang. "Minjokjeok Sileui Geukbokhan Ijeokeui Sado Kim Ik Du Moksa" [The apostle of signs and wonders who overcome the national despair], *Mokhoewa Sinhak* 79 [Pastoral Ministry and Theology 79], (January 1996): 196-99.

Shin, Hyun-soo. "The God of Shalom in Young San", *JYT* 18 (2006): 135-164.

Shin, Mun-chul. "A Trinitarian Pneumatology of Youngsan Yonggi Cho", *JYT* 2 (2004): 41-78.

Swallen, W.L. "God's Work of Grace continued in Pyeong Yang, Korea", *The Korea Mission Field* 3 (1907): 77-80,

Synan, V. "Roots of Yonggi Cho's Theology of Healing", *JYT* 3 (2006): 7-37.

Vinton, C.C. "Obstacles to Missionary Success in Korea", *MRW* (December 1894): 837-43.

Yoo, Boo-woong. "Response to Korean Shamanism by the Pentecostal Church", *International Review of Mission* 75 (1986): 70-4.

Yong, Amos. "Salvation, Society and the Spirit: Pentecostal Contextualization and Political Theology from Cleveland to Birmingham, from Springfield to Seoul", *JYT* 17 (200): 35-64.

Theses

Cho, Il-koo. "Healing in the Context of Korean Pentecostalism, 1950s to the Present: Historical and Ethnographic Approaches", Ph. D. thesis. Claremont, CA: Claremont Graduate University, 2002.

Kim, Ahn-sik. "Kim Ik-Du Mogsaeui Seolgyosayeogeh Daehan Bunseokgwa Pyeongga" [The Analysis and Evaluation of Ik-du Kim's Preaching Ministry]. Th. M. Seoul: Presbyterian Seminary.

Kim, Cheol-woong. "Kim Ik-du moksae daehan yeongu: saenge, sinyu buheungundong, sinhakeul jongsimeuro" [A Study of Rev. Ik-du Kim: with special reference to his life, healing movement, and theology], Th. M. diss. Seoul: The Presbyterian University and Theological Seminary, 2001.

Kim, S.Y. "Lessons from the Pentecostal Movement in Korea in the Twentieth Century", D. Miss. Pasadena, CA: Fuller Theological Seminary, 1990.

Lee, Jae-bum. "Pentecostal Type Distinctives and Korean Protestant Church Growth", Ph. D. diss. Pasadena, CA: Fuller Theological Seminary, 1986.

Lee, Yo-han. "The analysis of the Christian prayer mountain phenomenon in Korea", Ph. D. diss. Pasadena, CA: Fuller Theological Seminary, 1985.

Noh, Jae-yang. "A Study on Revival Movement by Rev. Sung Bong Lee", Ph.D. diss. Asan: Hoseo Divinity School, 2004.

Pae, Christopher. "A Study of The Influence of Shamanism in the 100 Years' History of The Korean", Ph. D. diss. Pasadena, CA: Fuller Theological Seminary, 1995.

Ryoo, Dong-hee. "Younsan Choyonggi Moksaui Mokhoe Sasange Deahan Sinhakjeok Jomyeong" [Theological Study on the Philosophy of Cho's ministry], Ph. D. diss. Gunpo City: Hansei University, 2008.

Stetz, J. "The Impact of Christianity on Korea's Culture", M.A. thesis. Azusa, CA: Azusa Pacific College, 1973.

Yun, Eun-seok. "Kim Ik-Du Mogsaeui Sinyu Buheung Undong Yeongu" [An Investigation on the Healing Movement of Ik-du Kim], Th. M. thesis. Seoul: Seoul Theological Seminary, 2012.

—. "Hanguk Godokgyoeui Musoksinange Daehan Taedo Yeongu" [A Study on the Attitude of the Korean Christians toward Shamanism], Ph. D. thesis. Seoul: Seoul Theological Seminary, 2017.

Dictionary and Encyclopedia Entries

Dyrness, W.A. *et al.*, Eds. *Global Dictionary of Theology: A Resource for the Worldwide Church*. Downers Grove, IL: IVP Academic, 2008.

Eim, Yeol-soo. "South Korea", In S.M. Burgess, Ed. *International Dictionary of Pentecostal and Charismatic Movements*. Grand Rapids, MI: Zondervan, 2002.

Freedman, D.N., and B.E. Willoughby. "נָשָׂא", In G.J. Botterweck, H. Ringgren and Heinz-Josef Fabry, Eds. *Theological Dictionary of The Old Testament. Vol. 10.* Grand Rapids, MI: William B. Eerdmans, 1999.

Gilbert, P.J. "Spiritual Warfare", In W.A. Dyrness and Veli-Matti Kärkkäinen, Eds. *Global Dictionary of Theology*. Nottingham: Inter-Varsity Press, 2008.

Hernandez, W. "Prayer", In W.A. Dyrness and Veli-Matti Kärkkäinen, Eds. *Global Dictionary of Theology*. Nottingham: Inter-Varsity Press, 2008.

Ma, Wonsuk. "Asia, East", In S.M. Burgess, Ed. *Encyclopedia of Pentecostal and Charismatic Christianity*. London: Routledge, 2006.

McGee, G.B. "Pentecostalism", In S.W. Sunquist, Ed. *A Dictionary of Asian Christianity*. Grand Rapids, MI: William. B. Eerdmans, 2001: 646-650.

McKim, D.K. "Spiritual Warfare", *Westminster Dictionary of Theological Terms*. Grand Rapids, MI: Zondervan, 1996.

Sunquist, S.W., Ed. *A Dictionary of Asian Christianity*. Grand Rapids, MI: William. B. Eerdmans, 2001.

Newspaper Articles

"Asialeul Hwibseun Seongryeong Undong" [The Holy Spirit movement that swept over Asia], Gyohoe Yeonhab Sinbo [The United Christian Newspapers], 13th July 1969: 13.

"Cheonwadae, Cho Young-gi moksa harabaleone danghok" [The Blue House was perplexed by Rev. Cho's words to lead to the removal of the president from office]. *Dong A Il Bo*, 28th February 2011. [Available at: http://news.donga.com/Politics/3/00/20110225/35129558/1], [Last accessed: 24th November 2023].

"Cho Young-gi Moksa, Baeim Yuzoehwakjeong" [Yong-gi Cho proven guilty of breach of trust]. *News and Joy*, 17th May 2017, [Available at: http://www.newsnjoy.or.kr/news/articleView.html?idxno=210940], [Last accessed: 24th November 2023].

Gyohoe Yeonhabsinbo Chuksopan [Union Newspaper of Church], vol I, (13 July 1969). In The Compilation Committee of the Fifty-year History of the Korea Assemblies of God. *The 50th history of the Korea Assemblies of God: 1953-2004*. Seoul: Creation, 2005.

"Gyeongseong gyohwoi hwaserye", *Gi-Dok-Shin-Bo* [Christian Newspaper], 3rd November 1902.

"Hamheung Gyohoe Daebuheung" [The Great Revival at Hamheung Church], *Gi-Dok-Shin-Bo* [Christian Newspaper], 19th January 1921.

"Hyeondaeineui Sinangsaeanhwal" [Today's Christian Life], *Dong-A-Il-Bo*, 21st May 1926.

"Janyeo Gyoyugeul Uihayeo Osibgaeeui Geumjihwan", [Fifty Pieces of Gold for Children's Education], *Dong-A-Il-Bo*, 92, 3rd July 1920: 3.

"Kim Mogsaeui Ijeok" [The Miracles of Pastor Kim], *Dong-A-Il-Bo*, 30th May 1920.

"Misinjeok Hogisimeul Iyonghaneun Jeondo" [Using Superstitious Curiosity for Evangelism], *Maeilsinbo* [Daily Newspaper], 28th October 1920.

"'Yujoe' Cho Yong-gi moksa, 'Jinju mandeulryeogo gonanjusyeo,'" ["Rev. Yong-gi Cho found guilty," "God gave me suffering to train as a process of making a pearl"], *News and Joy*, 24th February 2014, [Available at: http://www.newsnjoy.or.kr/news/articleView.html?idxno=196193], [Last accessed: 24th November 2023].

"Pyeongyang Gwandong" [Gwandong province in Pyeongyang], *Yesugyo Sinbo* [Christian Messenger], 15th December 1908: 218.

Online Sources

Encyclopedia of Korean Culture. "천도교" [*Cheondogyo*]. [Available at: https://encykorea.aks.ac.kr/Contents/Item/E0055819], [Last accessed: 24th November 2023].

—. "동학" [*Donghak*]. [Available at: https://encykorea.aks.ac.kr/Contents/SearchNavi?keyword=%EB%8F%99%ED%95%99%EC%9A%B4%EB%8F%99&ridx=1&tot=1411], [Last accessed: 24th November 2023].

Gatolic sajeon [Chatolic Dictionary], "Oriental Missionary Society." https://maria.catholic.or.kr/dictionary/term/term_view.asp?ctxtIdNum=1610&keyword=Oriental+Missionary+Society&gubun=01.

Gyohoeyongeo Sajeon [Church Glossary], Glossary of Church Terms: The Right Glossary, *Naver.* [Available at: http://terms.naver.com/entry.nhn?docId=2380561&ref=y&cid=50762&categoryId=51371], [Last accessed: 24th November 2023].

Hankukminjokmunhwadaebaekgoa [Encyclopedia of Korean Ethnic Culture]. "정이품." *Naver.* [Available at: https://terms.naver.com/entry.nhn?docId=547620&cid=46622&categoryId=46622], [Last accessed: 24th November 2023].

Hong, Seok-mo. *Dongguksesigi* [Monthly Events and Tradition of Korea], 1849. Quoted in "Aekmagi" [Exorcism] *Wikipedia* [Available at: https://ko.wikipedia.org/wiki/%EC%95%A1%EB%A7%89%EC%9D%B4], [Last accessed: 24th November 2023].

International Theological Institute. "Ministry of ITI." http://iti.fgtv.com/default.asp.

Luog, L. "Spirit and Power: A 10-Country Survey of Pentecostals", *Pew Research Center Website.* 5th October 2016. Washington: Pew Research Center, 2006. [Available at: https://www.pewresearch.org/religion/2006/10/05/spirit-and-power/], [Last accessed: 24th November 2023].

Ma, Julie C. "Miraculous Divine Activity and Religious Worldviews", *Carl F.H. Henry Center For Theological Understanding Website*. 2020. [Available at:

https://henrycenter.tiu.edu/2020/01/miraculous-divine-activity-and-religious-worldviews/], [Last accessed: 24th November 2023].

Ministry of Culture, Sports and Tourism. "2018 Hangukeu jonggyo hyeonhwang" [The statistics of Korean religions in 2018]. [Available at: https://www.mcst.go.kr/kor/s_policy/dept/deptView.jsp?pSeq=1731&pDataCD=0406000000&pType=03], [Last accessed: 24th November 2023].

National Folk Museum. "대감놀이" [Play of High Officer]. [Available at: http://folkency.nfm.go.kr/kr/topic/detail/1273], [Last accessed: 24th November 2023].

Oak, Seong-deuk. "The disbandment of the Holiness Church on the 29th of December in 1943", *Prof. Ok Sung-Deuk's History of Christianity in Korea,* 25th November 2019. [Available at: https://koreanchristianity.tistory.com/749], [Last accessed: 24th November 2023].

Oswalt, J.N. "Who is the suffering servant in Isaiah 53?" *Zondervan Academic Blog* 7th March 2019 [Available at: https://zondervanacademic.com/blog/suffering-servant-isaiah-53], [Last accessed: 24th November 2023].

Pyojun Gukeo Deasajeon [Standard Korean Language Dictionary]. https://stdict.korean.go.kr/main/main.do (accessed on March 2, 2016).

World Health Organization. "Foodborne parasitic infections: Paragonimiasis (Lung fluke)", *WHO Website* [Available at: https://www.who.int/publications-detail-redirect/WHO-UCN-NTD-VVE-2021.5], [Last accessed: 24th November 2023].

The Korean Methodist Church, "*Seongyochogi Mi,Namgamrihoe Joseonyeonhoe Gyosehyeonhwang (~1930)*" [The total number of believers of the Korean Methodist Church in the beginning of its missions until 1930], *KMC Website* [Available at: https://kmc.or.kr/head-quater-kmc/resources-history-of-kmc/historical-resources?uid=62239&mod=document&pageid=1], [Last accessed: 24th November 2023].

Young San Theological Institute of Hansei University. [Available at: http://www.ysti.co.kr/], [Last accessed: 24th November 2023].

Other

Joseon Yesugyo Jangrohoe Je 13hoe Hoelok [The Minutes of the 13th Korean Presbytery] (1924).

The Charter of the Jesus Korea Sungkyul Church. Seoul: Seongcheongsa, 1989.

Appendix 1

Summary of Biography (Ik-du Kim)

1874 Birth on 3rd November
1880 Studied *Yuseo* and *Sanbeob* for ten years
1886 Death of Kim's father
1890 Failed state examination & start of business
1893 Married Ik-jin Kim
1900 Entered the *Geumsan* Church through the help with his friend Tae-hwan Park
1900 Water baptism by missionary W. L. Swallen in July
1901 Conversion
1901 First holy communion 20 months after his water baptism
1901 Reading the Bible 100 times for 20 months until his first holy communion
1901 Worked as a teacher in *Jaeryeong* while running a medical store for 6 months
1901 First healing of Su-eun Park
1901 Assigned by Swallen to another church in *Sincheon* area in October
1902 Started fasting prayer in a mountain for 3 church members
1906 Started theological education at the Pyeongyang Theological Seminary
1910 Constructed a new church building for *Sincheon Seobu* Church
1910 Graduated from the Seminary as the 3rd batch
1911 Ordained
1911 Started healing the sick upon assuring himself of the healing of Mark 9:23
1911 Started leading revival meetings to heal the sick
1911 Co-pastored a church outside the South Gate with Jae-hyeong Lee
1919 Started leading full-scale healing ministry upon healing an incurable disease at *Gandong Yeompa* Church
1919 The Miracle Witness Committee formed in July
1920 Led *Pyeongyang* union revival meeting, about 6,000 people gathered on June 30.
1920 Elected as the 9th moderator of the Presbyterian Church
1920 Led a union revival meeting for 2 weeks at *Sungdong* Church for 10,000 people
1921 Publication of *Ijeokmyeongjeung* as a result of an investigation by the Miracle Witness Committee from December 1919 to January 1921
1923 Resigned from Sincheon Church and started national tour revival meetings

1923 Made a proposal to amend the Presbytery Constitution chapter 3 Article 1 on cessationism
1924 The proposal to amend the Constitution was rejected
1936 Pastored *Namdaemun* Church
1939 Pastored *Sungdong* Church
1940 Was forced by Japanese police to participate in Shrine worship after revival meeting at *Sineuiju Jeil* Church
1942 Was tortured at Japanese *Jongro* Police station for 15 days
1942 Was forced by Japan to step down from his pastoral works and confined to an orchard in *Jigjeon-li*
1942 Stopped pastoral work because of the Pacific War until 1945
1946 Entered the KCF
1947 Led tour revival meeting in North Korea
1949 Was appointed to be the general superintendent of KCF
1950 Was martyred after dawn service by the withdrawing North Korean People's Army on 14th October
1950 Funeral service was conducted by about 50 churches in *Sincheon* area

Sources

In-seo Kim, *Kim Ik-Du Moksa Sojeon* [A Short Biography of Ik-Du Kim], 1932, In Seong-ho Lee, Ed. *Kim Ik-du Mogsa Seolgyo Mit Yagjeonjib* [The Sermons and Biography of Ik-Du Kim] (Seoul: Hyemunsa, 1977): 177; Seon Choe, *Seongdoeui Jeulgeoum* [The pleasure of Believers] (Seoul: Grisim, 2008), 10-12; Deok-ju Lee, *Saerosseun Hanguk Geuriseudoinui Gaejong Iyagi* [Revision of The Conversion Stories of Korean Christians] (Seoul: The Institute of the History of Christianity in Korea, 2003): 413-17.

Appendix 2

Summary of Biography (Seong-bong Lee)

1900	Birth on 4th July
1905	Conversion of Lee and his family to Christianity
1918	Married Eun-sil Lee on 10th February
1920	Contracted periostitis on his right thigh, and it lasted for about 3 years
1920	Experienced real conversion after he contracted disease on 24th June
1925	Started theological education at the Holiness Bible School in March
1928	Graduated from the Bible School in March
1928	Planted and pastored *Suweon* Church, and constructed a new church building
1930	Pastored Mokpo Church, and constructed a new church building
1932	Ordained
1936	Pastored *Sineuiju* Church
1938	Was appointed as national tour revivalist
1939	Study and tour evangelism in Japan
1941	Embarked on evangelistic ministry in *Manju*
1941	Was imprisoned and tortured in *Sariweon* Police Station for 1 month, and resumed revival meetings in *Manju*
1945	Focused on reconstruction of the poor Holiness Church in Northern area of Korea
1946	Crossed the 38th parallel to the South, and started tour revival meetings
1950	Started new ministries such as Immanuel Prayer Centre and Immanuel Publisher, and was imprisoned and tortured by the North Korean People's Army
1954	Embarked on Immanuel Commando to help poor and weak churches
1955	Planted and pastored a new church at his house in *Sinchon* area
1955	Led revival meetings for Jubilee Celebration in 1956 for about 11 months to establish 1,000 churches
1957	Formed the Jubilee Evangelistic Team and led tour revival meetings for 7 months while focusing on city churches
1958	Led seven revival meetings in *Jeju* Island
1959	Started tour evangelism in the United States for 8 months
1961	Led tour revival meetings for 480 churches for 17 months with the goal of leading a revival meeting for one church per day
1965	Preached last sermon at the joint General Assembly of the Holiness Church on 23rd July
1965	Death on 2nd August
1965	Funeral service was conducted at *Sinchon* Church on 4th August

Source

Seong-bong Lee, *Malo Mothamyeon Jukeumeuro* [If You Cannot Preach in Words, Preach by Death] (Seoul: Word of Life, 1993): 249-50.

Appendix 3

Summary of Biography (Yong-gi Cho)

1936 Birth on 14th February
1954 Received medical training
1955 Contracted TB after falling from a chin-bar and started reading the Bible
1955 Conversion, Bible study under missionaries Ken Tice and L.P. Richards, and helped the missionaries with interpretation
1956 Started theological education at Full Gospel Bible School
1957 Received calling to be a pastor at a revival meeting led by H. Herman in October
1958 Graduated from the Bible School in the 4th batch in March
1958 First service at Ja-shil Choe's house with four members
1958 First healing ministry in June for a woman who was paralysed for 7 years.
1959 Built a tent church at Daejo-dong in April with about 50 church members
1961 Started military service for 7 months from January to August
1961 Started a new church in *Seodaemun* with missionary J.W. Hurston in October
1962 Completion and dedication of Full Gospel Central Revival Centre in February (about 3,000 people gathered)
1962 Was ordained and changed the church name to Full Gospel Central Church
1964 Took over the church from Hurston (about 2,400 church members)
1965 Married Seong-hye Kim in March
1965 The Home Cell Groups started
1966 Elected as the general superintendent of the KAG in May
1967 Published monthly magazine *Weol-Gan-Shin-Ang-Gyei*
1973 Completion and dedication of a new church building to accommodate 12,556 and established Full Gospel *Osanri* Prayer Centre
1976 Established Youngsan Publisher and Full Gospel Central Bible College
1976 Established Church Growth International
1978 Established Full Gospel Research Centre
1979 Record of 100,000 membership
1980 Embarked on social welfare such as a blood donation campaign of love and call of love
1981 Record of 200,000 membership
1983 Accused of being pseudo-Christian by the Presbytery of *Tonghab*

1984	Changed the church name to Yoido Full Gospel Church with 40,000 membership and started supporting free medical operations for cardiac patients
1985	Retirement of Ja-shil Choe, completion of extension work for the main sanctuary, and 500,000 membership
1988	Established a Christian newspaper, called *Kookminilbo*
1992	Elected as the chairman of the Pentecostal World Fellowship
1993	Set a record as the world's largest church in the Guinness World Book of Records with 700,000
1996	Awarded the Order of Civil Merit, *Mugunghwa* Medal
1999	Honoured with the Korean Church Leadership Award
2004	Established a Christian party called *Gi-Dok-Jeong-Dang*
2005	Awarded the Family of Man Medallion and the *Yujib* Award
2008	Stepped down from pastoral works as pastor emeritus, and established a charity foundation to help those in need

Source

Yong-gi Cho, *Widaehan Somyeong: Huimang Mokhoe 50 Nyeon* [Great Call: 50 Years of Hope Ministry] (Seoul: Yoido Full Gospel Church, 2008): 72-117; 432-35.